ISBN 978-0-259-45313-0
PIBN 10817682

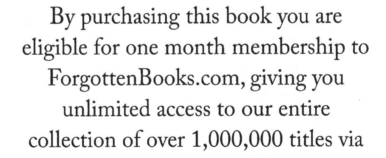

THE TEN TRIBES OF ISRAEL

HISTORICALLY IDENTIFIED

WITH THE

ABORIGINES

OF

THE WESTERN HEMISPHERE.

By Mrs. Simon.

Behold! I was left alone:—these, where had they been?—
ISAIAH XLIX. 21.

He that scattereth Israel will gather him, and keep him, as a shepherd doth his flock.—
JEREMIAH XXXI. 10.

PUBLISHED BY R. B. SEELEY AND W. BURNSIDE;
AND SOLD BY L. AND G. SEELEY,
FLEET STREET, LONDON.
MDCCCXXXVI.

CONTENTS.

To " THE ANTIQUITIES OF MEXICO," the following pages are indebted for the most valuable portion of the testimony by which they are enriched.

This rare and costly compilation, which was a few years ago published by the Right Honorable Lord Viscount Kingsborough, has hitherto been little known beyond the libraries of Universities, and those of a few Noblemen.

" The ANTIQUITIES OF MEXICO " at the present time consist of seven folio volumes, which, with the exception of the sixth, contain fac-similes and drawings from such historical remains, as had escaped the destruction to which all the primitive records and other memorials of the tribes of the New Continent had been condemned by the policy of their invaders in the fifteenth century.

Literary and antiquarian travellers having from time to time transmitted these precious relics to their respective governments, they have been preserved in the Royal Libraries of Paris, Berlin, Dresden—the Imperial Library of Vienna—the Vatican Library, in the Museum at Rome, in the Library of the Institute of Bologna, and in the Bodleian Library, Oxford.

As a specimen of the genius of a primitive race, over whose origin has long brooded a mysterious obscurity ; and as a successful attainment in antiquarian research, the publication of Viscount Kingsborough is highly interesting and curious: but rising as it does to the sublime character of an *illustration* and *confirmation* of Scripture testimony, in disclosing the *Hebrew* origin, history, experience, and genius of that grand division of the Hebrew nation, which, although cut off for a series of ages from their own, and the nations of the earth, have nevertheless occupied a prominent place in the prophetic pages ; the importance of such a testimony (at such an ominous crisis in the history of Christendom,)—so miraculously preserved,—so long withheld,—so unexpectedly reclaimed ;—(whether in its internal or relative character) like the *Bow* of *peace* and *promise*, speaks of a PLACE and state of REST beyond the impending cloud of retributive storm.

PRELIMINARY OBSERVATIONS.

TERRITORIAL empire was immediately after that purification which the earth received from the Deluge, assigned to the three surviving representatives of the present inhabitants of the globe : and the *boundary* of each was soon after specifically determined and defined. The appointment was one of unerring wisdom and universal goodness; but alienation of heart and mind from the divine supremacy soon manifested itself in that self-will which suggests covetous desires, and enforces these by arbitrary violence.

The LORD blessed *all* the sons of Noah on their coming forth from the ark to inherit the baptised earth : it was by coveting the possession of territories beyond their rightful empire, that the sons of Ham forfeited that blessing in which they were originally included, and by this demonstration of *rebellion* against the appointments of the Most High, and *usurpation* of the rights of others, they incurred that curse by which they have been distinguished. ' Covetousness,' by withdrawing the mind and heart from the will of God, and by constituting some *substituted* object supreme in our regard, ' is,' in *essence and effect* ' idolatry.' Hence the incalculable evils of this early infringement of HIS authority who " *appointed* to all nations the *bounds* of their habitations."

b

Self-will and licentious desires prepared the ungodly Ham for that malediction, which a specific provocation at length called forth. It was *prophetically* addressed to him as *the father of Canaan*, whose lawless and impious acts would justify the curse of degradation then pronounced by the patriarch.

An isolated act of provocation would have called for a personal rebuke; but in that prophetic curse, Canaan, the son of the immediate delinquent, is specially implicated, and that most justly.

That the malediction should have been given in the spirit of prophecy—in a *fore-knowledge* of the character which would justify it, was in Israel a common occurrence. Children of eight days old were in this spirit so characteristically named, that not alone their own circumstances, but the history of their tribe was frequently involved in the *prophetic appellation* then given. The descriptive blessings of Jacob and of Moses to the heads of the twelve tribes, fully illustrate this truth.

But why did Noah select Canaan as the worst branch of the family of Ham? did he not foresee that Cush also, and his sons, would invade a great portion of that territory allotted to one of the branches of the family of Shem? and that having thus rebelled against the divine appointment, they, on the warrant of the same *self-will,* would, in renouncing the authority of the Creator, constitute the "host of Heaven" the objects of their supreme regard and homage, together with those 'graven images' which should represent their famous leaders.

Assuredly Noah had a premonition of *their* departure from the Most High, since he foresaw that Canaan would be guilty of a still *more* aggravated enormity.

By sovereign right and choice, the Creator of all had

selected a peculiar territorial domain as the seat of HIS government and administration.

From its geographical position, JERUSALEM, the metropolitan city of this empire, is to the earth at large what the heart is to the human body—the central seat of that life and energy which is diffused from thence to the most remote parts of the frame which it animates.

The heinousness of Canaan's guilt was in having *usurped this* consecrated portion, knowing that it was claimed by the Creator as HIS inheritance, and delegated by HIM to the posterity of Shem, of whose line was to be born in due time, the Messiah. That this knowledge of the purpose of GOD was perfectly understood by Noah, and, doubtless, by him communicated to his sons, Ham and Japhet, there can be no doubt, since his manner of addressing Shem is demonstrative of that expectation. He does not say, Blessed art *thou ;* or, blessed shalt thou be *of* the LORD ; but, Blessed be the LORD God *of* Shem.''[1]

In sacreligiously usurping *that* LAND which in His wisdom the LORD had set apart for the occupancy of that peculiar People whom he had constituted the *depository* of His revealed mind and will—which therefore they were appointed to *minister* to the nations of the earth, Canaan was not alone chargeable with disobedience, covetousness, and injustice, but thus became the means of introducing those detestable and demoralizing idol rites, which not alone would eventually cause the Land to cast them forth of it, but which would necessarily become snares to entrap, and lures to seduce from their allegiance, the rightful occupants who should sojourn amongst them.

In the division of the earth it was inculcated upon Israel:

[1] Eusebius states, " that Noah explained to his sons the will of God, and allotted to each their particular territory, having received his instructions from Heaven."—See Bryant's Myth.

"The LORD'S portion is His people; *Israel is the lot* of
of HIS INHERITANCE;" accordingly it is testified—"Unto
thee will I give the land of Canaan, the lot of your inheritance." Because it was His, it became *also* theirs; the
LORD'S portion being His people. David elsewhere describes
"Judah as His sanctuary." Israel as His dominion.

The Hebrews therefore held the LORD'S Land at will;
and were subject to Him as Supreme Proprietor:—"The
Land shall not be sold for ever; for THE *Land* IS MINE."

It was this Holy portion which was *invaded* and *appropriated* by the race of Canaan; and not alone invaded
and appropriated, but *polluted* by their detestable idol rites.

Cush, or Cutha and his sons, under their lawless and self-
intitled leader Nimrod, invaded the province of Shinar, in
which rightfully dwelt Asshur,[1] a branch of Shem's family.
"Nimrod," it is written, "was a mighty *hunter* "before the
LORD." A term which is scripturally indicative of the
violence, crime, and disorder, of a reckless one. This self-
willed ruler assumed the title of Alorus of Orion,[2] and subsequently as Belus, became an object of idolatrous worship
after his decease.

He was the first who assumed the establishment of an
independent kingdom and government:—"The beginning
of his kingdom was BABEL."   *   *   *   *   *

His *independent* beginning, commenced in rebellion, and
established in *transgression*, was carried on in *opposition*;

---

[1] It appears that the Assyrian Empire in its original grant to Ashur extended
to the extreme eastern coast of Asia, which nearly unites, and probably was
then, united to the westernmost coast of the New World.

[2] Bryant observes, "It is remarkable that the first tyrant upon earth masked
his villainy *under the meek title of Shepherd*—if we may credit Gentile writers,
it was under this pretext that Nimrod framed his *opposition*, and gained an
undue sovereignty over his brethren, having taken to himself the name of Orion,
and giving out that he was born to be a protector and guardian; or, as it is
related by Besorus, "He spread a report abroad that God had marked him out
for a Shepherd of His people."

until that lawless combination of self-wills and self-interests which enmity to His will confederated for a time in one impious design, became by a just retribution so confounded by the *confusion* of their *own* speech and ideas, and consequently so estranged and divided in their efforts and purposes, that each party for itself spread abroad over the face of the country.

"The Tower of Babel," observes Bryant, "was probably designed for an observatory for ' the Host of Heaven;' as well as for a land-mark and strong-hold against the power of the elements. The Ethnic writers describe whirlwinds as the cause of the overthrow of the Tower itself; from which Nimrod not being willing to depart, he was involved in its fall."

The sons of Peleg, in whose days the division of the earth had taken place, were occupants of the territory assigned to their ancestor.

From Ur of the Chaldees was Abraham called, as the federal head of that people, in whom all the families of the earth should be blessed. At Haran, a border part of the Land, he sojourned for several years, but at the command of the LORD, pitched his tent with that of Lot, on a mountain in, or near Jerusalem, where " he built an altar to the LORD."

The lawless occupants certainly knew that the Land should ultimately be possessed by the children of Abraham, for whom from the beginning it had been destined. This is to be inferred from that treaty which the king, attended by his chief captain Phicol, requested at the hand of Abraham in token of amity *hereafter*. " Now, therefore, swear unto me by God, that thou wilt not deal falsely with me, nor my son, nor my son's son," &c. The same thing happened to Isaac many years afterwards. The herdsmen of the king had assumed the right of compelling those of the patriarch to depart from the place

where they were; which led the king, together with his
chief captain, to solicit personally a reconciliation. "And
Isaac said unto them, Wherefore are ye come unto me,
seeing ye hate me?" they said "We saw certainly that the
LORD was with thee, and we said, let there be an oath be-
twixt us and thee; and let us make a covenant with thee
that thou do us no hurt."

Abraham having sojourned so long in the empire of the
Chaldees, as to have given occasion to be considered a Chaldean by *race*, as well as by birth; we are pointedly informed
that "SHEM was the *father of all the children of Heber*,"
the head of the Hebrew nation, whose name they inherit.

Although as a Sovereign the LORD would not have acted
arbitrarily in expelling the usurpers, he mercifully granted
time and opportunity for their amendment, leaving the sins
of an ungodly race to their own *fatal* reaction.

To Abraham it was intimated that he should be gathered
to his fathers in peace—be buried in the Land, and that
his children should be for a season in Egypt, from whence
they should be *delivered* in the fourth generation, when
"*the iniquity of the Amorites*" should be "*full*."

When at length the LORD did conduct His people into the
Land, He thus addressed them, "According to the doings
of *Egypt* wherein ye dwelt; shall ye not do: and according
to the doings of the Land of *Canaan* whither I bring you;
ye shall not do. Ye shall observe MY statutes to keep MY
ordinances, to walk therein: I AM the Lord *your* GOD."

After an enumeration of the *evils* which were to be
shunned, it is added, "*For all these abominations* have the
men of the Land done, who were before you; and their Land
is defiled, and the Land being defiled, *therefore* do I visit the
iniquity thereof upon it; and the Land itself vomiteth out
her inhabitants."

Having contemplated the division of the earth into three shares, these having been appointed for the occupancy of the three sons of Noah throughout their generations, it may be asked, Had the Creator and disposer who is yet to be acknowledged as *"the* GOD *of the whole earth,"* no ulterior design in *reserving* for some *special* purpose present to His foreknowledge, that vast *transatlantic Hemisphere* with which Christendom has but recently become acquainted ?

Although not included in his *design* of appropriation, when the division to which allusion has been made took place, surely it was as a *consequence* reserved for some extraordinary emergency illustrative of the character and government of the Holy One of Israel.

Let us briefly glance at the history of the Hebrew people, after their admission to Palestine under Joshua, the successor of Moses. During the life of this faithful leader, they were loyal-hearted and blessed : but after his decease and that of the generation which had been the eye-witness of so many noble manifestations of Almighty Power in their behalf — their successors through the seducing wiles by which they were beset, fell into a toleration of, and compliance with the idolatrous worship and licentious manners of the surrounding nations.

This withdrawment from their National Head, who, in delivering them from the tyranny of Egypt, claimed at once their homage as their Creator, Redeemer, Guardian, and Governor, rendered the alienated people at once powerless and defenceless. Again and again, when under oppressive tribute, the spirit of their Judges was stirred up to call upon the LORD for help—but time obliterated these impressions, and new provocations called forth fresh calamities.

The rending of the Ten Tribes from the House of David, about seven hundred and forty years before the birth of the

Messiah, forms a marked epoch in the History of the Hebrews, and ought to be scrupulously attended to in all its aspects and bearings, in order that a correct estimate may be formed of subsequent and yet future events and promises which include " *the outcasts of Israel,*" as well as " *the dispersed of Judah.*"

The act of rending themselves in a spirit of atheistical democracy from the House of David—also separated them from the enjoined and indispensable statutes and ordinances which were part and parcel of the Theocratic Law of the Land.

The next step, for which this disloyalty to their King prepared them, was the *substituting of representative* objects of worship in direct violation of one of the great commands in the Law. This aggravated departure from the Fountain of Wisdom and Goodness necessarily resulted in demoralization which, in its re-action rendered them an easy conquest to the victorious Assyrian, who " plucked them up" out of the soil, transplanted them to the remote provinces of his dominion, and substituted in their stead a mingled colony from various parts of the Assyrian Empire.

Hosea, a prophet of Samaria, and belonging to the Ten Tribes, had been commissioned to warn and admonish the transgressors before their expatriation ;—fearlessly did he declare the consequences which their disloyalty was preparing for them—faithfully did he reproach their ingratitude to Him who had " been an Husband unto them" — whose constant love and manifold gifts they had repaid with the basest wanderings of their heart and mind after the dumb vanities of the heathen. He is commanded to reprove and warn them by *types* and *signs*, religion having become in their minds confounded with *visible* representations and mediums.

An adulteress is summoned as the meet representative of their unfaithfulness. The prophet is instructed to call her first child *Lo-Ruhama,* signifying ' *I will no longer have mercy.*' The next was to be named *Lo-Ammi,*—' *Ye are not my people.*' But, as if three millenaries were a parenthesis—"a little moment," it is added:—" Yet shall the children of Israel be as the sand on the sea-shore which cannot be numbered nor measured ; and it shall come to pass, that in the place where it was said " *Ye are not my people,*" it shall be said unto them " *Ye are the sons of the living God,*"—then shall the children of Judah and the children " of Israel appoint themselves one Head, and they shall come up out of the land, for great shall be the Day of Jezreel."

Their guilt is declared, their punishment is determined ; but lest they should *despair* during that long season of banishment—and lest the nations (whose term of probation it should become) might, in the apparent success and maturity of *their* schemes, be induced to *presume,* the entail of the covenant closely follows the sentence of temporary banishment. " She was unconscious that I gave her corn, and wine, and oil, and multiplied the silver and gold wherewith she fabricated *Baal.* I will destroy her vines and fig-trees, whereof she hath said, these are my rewards which my lovers hath given me." Yet, (centuries being anticipated) it is added, " Behold, I will allure her, bring her into the wilderness, and speak comfortingly unto her, and will give her from thence her vineyards, and the valley of *trouble* for a door of *hope*—and she shall be disciplined there as in the days of her youth; and *as in the day when she came up out of the land of Egypt.* And in that day thou shalt call ME *my Husband,* and shalt no more call ME my Lord, for I will take away the name of Balaam (Lord's) out of her mouth, and they shall no more be remembered by their names : and I will betroth thee unto ME in faithfulness, and thou shalt know I am the LORD.   And I will sow her unto ME in the Land, and I will have mercy upon her that had not received mercy, and I will say to those who were "*not My people:*"—"*My people,*"—and they shall say " MY GOD."

To the prophet it was again said, " Go still love a woman who is beloved of her friend yet an adulteress, according to the love of the LORD toward the children of Israel, who look to other gods, and love their grape offerings." While to her it was said, "Thou shalt abide *for me* many days * * thou shalt not be for another— so shall I also be for thee." For the children of Israel shall continue many days without King, without Ruler, without sacrifice, and without an image, and without Ephod, and without Teraphim : afterward shall the children of Israel return and seek the LORD God, and David their King, and shall fear the LORD and His goodness in the latter days."

Notwithstanding that in rending themselves from the House of David, they might be said virtually to have disclaimed and renounced the Messiah to be born from thence : they are graciously assured of their being included in the beneficent *result* of that atonement which (in being rejected as a Prophet,) He should make as their *substitute* and *surety,* and in the mediation which He should effect as their *Advocate* and *Intercessor :*—To which promise the prophet Isaiah thus responds, " All we like sheep *have gone astray,* and the LORD hath *laid upon Him the iniquity of us all.*"

In harmony with this testimony, the Good Shepherd declares, " Them also I must *bring,* and they shall hear My voice, and there shall be one FOLD and one SHEPHERD."

The adversary of the Messiah, having succeeded in tempting His degenerate people to forsake the Fountain of

Eternal goodness, in leading them to false objects of worship, and in bringing upon them all the evils which their defence-less condition involved, at length claimed them as the prey *of death* and the *grave*. But his dominion is invaded by *their* Champion, the power with which *their transgression* had armed him, is contested by that which the *personal* obedience of the Redeemer wields in their behalf; the armour wherein the enemy trusted is overcome, his plea is silenced, his claim is cancelled, his prey is released, himself is judged and con-demned—yet a little while, and his sentence shall be *executed*.

The adversary contended with, and overcame those whom, as the deceiver his temptations had first seduced, and of whom he afterwards became the accuser ; but now *their* Re-deemer contends with *that* enemy ;—*his* power yields to the higher authority of their RIGHTEOUS representative, who in view of His *incarnation* and its glorious *results*, thus testifies ; Shall the prey be wrested from the powerful, or the lawful captive delivered ? Thus saith the LORD God, even the captives of the powerful shall be released, even the prey of the terrible shall be delivered : I will contend with him that contendeth with thee : I will *redeem* thy children—I will *ransom* them from the power of death--I will *reclaim* them from the grave. O death, I will be thy visitation ! O grave, I will be thy destruction !

Thus also are His redeemed taught to identify themselves in the *personal* death and resurrection of the Messiah. "Come, let us return unto the LORD, He hath rent and will restore us ; He hath smitten, and He will bind our wounds ; after two days He will reanimate us, on the *third* day He will *raise us up*, and we shall live in His Presence. Then shall we know, in following on to know the LORD, that His going forth is prepared as the day-spring, and unto us shall He come *as* the *latter*, and as the former rain unto the Land."

Thus were those who were *afar off*, by a NEW and LIVING
way brought nigh—even into the presence of their reconciled
Father *in the person of their risen Advocate and Intercessor,* whose resurrection became the earnest and pledge
of theirs. The miseries of exile,—the powerless degradation of a scarcely tolerated existence among the adverse interests of hostile nations, had taught the outcasts
of Israel a bitter but salutary lesson:—that the ' vain de-
vices,' on whom they had bestowed those affections of the
heart which were *due* to their Creator and Saviour, could
not help them in time of need. They now felt and acknowledged, that regard to these false objects had been the cause
of all that calamity in which they were steeped:—for
now, they who had once been the freemen of no mean
city, were cast forth dishonoured and powerless amongst the
nations who treated with mockery and derision their forfeited preeminence.

Under such circumstances, it were not wonderful to find
them so cured of *artificial substitutes,* as to loathe the very
sight of those idol rites to which their dwelling among
the Assyrian idolaters subjected them; and that desirous of
shunning all intercourse themselves, and anxious that their
posterity should be out of the influence of this seducing and
mortal sin which had brought upon them the fierce indignation of their constant Benefactor, that they should form the
resolution of withdrawing from the neighbourhood of the
Assyrian empire, to some seclusion to which they might be
graciously directed in the prosecution of their penitent enterprise,—for in their darkest season, *hope* still spake of
future *Promise.* This is not supposititious; a valuable
fragment of sacred history, and the last notice on record
of the Ten Tribes after their expatriation is at once graphic
and explicit.—2 Esdras xiii. 14.

The Assyrian empire is involved in an obscurity to which the change of the names of places has chiefly contributed. In the absence of intermediate historical lights, it becomes especially needful in the investigation of so grave a subject as that under review, to recur to those enduring land-marks and characteristics which have been preserved in *that* History, which amid the fluctuating experience of the kingdoms of this world remains unalterably the same.

Two circumstances are to be noted as a key to succeeding events. The first is, that in the original division of territory, the whole of that through which the expatriated tribes passed on their migration to the New Continent, had been appointed to Asshur, the son of the patriarch Shem ; although it had been subsequently invaded and usurped by Nimrod, the son of Cush. Hence the Assyrian empire, from having originally received the name of Asshur, retained that name ; although it is also made mention of as Cush, which is generally translated Ethiopia.

It appears that the Assyrian empire was of short duration after the reign of Esar-haddon ; and that a great portion of the Hebrews continued to sojourn in the provinces of Media Persia, and Tartary. The first invasion of the Assyrian monarch Tiglath-pileser, was B. C. 740 ; by him the inhabitants of Gallilee—the tribes of Reuben, Naphtali, Gad, and the half tribe of Manassah were made captive, and carried to the provinces of Media. The second invasion by Shalmanezer, was nineteen years afterwards, and this captivity, like the former, was placed in Halah and Habor, by the river Gozan. The third conquest, that of Samaria, was by Esar-haddon, B. C. 678, in which the remainder of the Ten Tribes, with the exception, according to Josephus, of about 600, were carried into the land of Assyria, and it is probable that these last exiles smarting under recent infliction,

and not as those who had preceded them in any respect,
attached by domestic ties to the soil, formed that body which
came to the determination of " leaving the multitude of the
heathen to go into a *remote* country wherein *never* had mankind dwelt that they might there keep their *statutes* which
they had never observed in their own Land, and there was
a great way to go, namely a year and a half, and that region
is called Arsareth" (Armenia.)

Doctor Elias Boudinot thus writes. " The country into
which the Ten Tribes were thus transplanted, was very thinly
inhabited and extended farther north than we have any idea
of. Those captive Israelites must have greatly increased in
numbers before their migration more northward and westward; this is confirmed by the names of cities which to this
day bear the names of their founders. *Samarcand* is plainly
derived from Samaria; they have a city on a hill called
Mount *Tabor*. A city built on the river Ardon, is named
Jericho, which river runs near the Caspian sea upon the
north east. There are two cities called *Chorazin*, the great
and the less. The Tartar chiefs are called *Morsoyes* which
closely resembles Moses.

The Tartars boast their descent from the Israelites, and
the famous Tamerlane,[1] (or Timur,) took a pride in declaring
that he descended from the tribe of Dan. Vide note in p.
162, Star of the West.

The author of Historical Researches has traced many
remarkable analogies between the Mogul and Tartar tribes,
and those of the Western hemisphere; with respect to the
conquests of the Mogul, he observes, ' All the continent of

---

[1] The author of Hist. Resear. p. 12, gives from Timour's Institutes, the following characteristic sentiment: ' If the canopy of heaven were a bow, and the
earth the cord thereof; and if calamities were the arrows, and if Almighty God,—
the tremendous and the glorious, were the unerring archer, to whom would the
sons of Adam flee for protection? The sons of Adam must flee unto the LORD.',

Asia, except Hindostan and Arabia, was subdued in 1280, (Hindostan was invaded by Timour, but not possessed by the Moguls till 1525); he adds, we must fully acquiesce in the truth of the remark of the eloquent Gibbon, that the rapid conquests of the Moguls and Tartars, may be compared with the primitive convulsions of nature, which have agitated and altered the surface of the globe.'

Josephus, the Historian, makes mention of the Ten Tribes as then being 'somewhere beyond the Euphrates;' and calls them Adiabaniens.[1] Other Jewish historians relate that they were carried, not only into Media and Persia, but into the northern countries beyond the Bosphorus.' Ortelius speaks of them as being in Tartary. Herodotus affirms that the Scythians, (whom Bryant supposed derived their name from Cush or Cutha,) conquered the Empire of Media, in Upper Asia, soon after the expulsion of the last portion of the Ten Tribes from Palestine. Herodotus, lib. i. c. 157. Prideaux, i. 25—356.

Scythia was the ancient name given to Tartary, which extended from the mouth of the Obey in Russia, to the Dnipier, from thence to the Euxine sea—thence along the foot of Mount Caucasus, by the rivers Kur and Aras, to the Caspian Sea—thence by the White mountains, including part of Russia, with the districts that lie between the frozen and Japan seas.[2] Sir William Jones, Disser. vol. i. p. 142, &c.

---

[1] The river Lyens, which runs a little west of Hala, was anciently called Zeba, or Diava, by Ammianus, which signifies a wolf; whence this portion of Assyria was called Adiabane, and the river Lyens was called sometime Ahavah, (love) or Adiabane. It may cast some light on this subject to know that Josephus, in his Antiquities, book xx. chap. v. says, that Helena, queen of Adiabane, who had embraced the Jewish religion, sent some of her servants to Alexandria, to buy a great quantity of corn ; and others of them to Cyprus, to buy a cargo of dried figs, which she distributed to the Jews that were in want. This was in the time of the famine, mentioned by Agabus, Acts xi. 28, and took place in A. D. 47, or thereabouts. This shows that there were many Jews in that country.

[2] From the mouth of the Danube, to the sea of Japan, the whole longitude of Scythia is about one hundred and ten degrees, which in that parallel are equal to

" The Caspian or Circasian Straits, through the mountain of Caucasus, lies about midway between the Euxine sea to the west, and the Caspian sea to the east, through Iberia. After passing through the Strait on the north, keeping a little westward, you pass on in the neighbourhood of the Euxine Sea through Armenia Minor, into Syria Proper, and by the head of the Mediterranean Sea to Palestine, without crossing the Euphrates.   But all who are in Persia, in Armenia Major, and in the eastward of Mesopotamia and beyond Babylon, must pass the Euphrates to get there."— Star in the West, page 167.

Giles Fletcher, LL.D. in his treatise, printed in 1667, observes :—" as for two of these Colonies of the Samaritan Israelites, carried off by Salmanassar, which were placed in Harak [1] and Harbor, they bordered both on the Medians (where the others were ordered on the north and north-east of the Caspian Sea, a barren country.) So that those tribes might easily meet and join together when opportunity served their turn, which happened unto them not long after, when all the provinces of Media, Chaldaran, and Meso-potamia with their rulers, *Merodach*, and *Baladan*, and *Dejoces*, called in Scripture Arphaxad, by desertion fell away from the Assyrians in the tenth year of Esar-haddon, and that these tribes did not long after re-unite themselves and join in one nation."   Doctor Boudinot observes, "They

five thousand miles. The latitude reaches from the fortieth degree, which touches the wall of China above one thousand miles northward to the frozen regions of Siberia.—Robertson's View of the Progress of Society in Europe, p. 335.

[1] " Harrah, or as it is called by some, Hara, which in Hebrew signifies bitter, is the root from whence it is used to signify a mountainous tract, and thus gave that name to the country north of Assyria, near to Media, which perhaps ran through it. On the north of this tract runs the river Araxis, now called Aras. Obarius, 296. Oharius, on whom much dependence may be placed, describes the source of the river Araxis to be in the mountains of Ararat, of Armenia, so that Harah is no other than the province of Iran, situate between the rivers Charboras or Araxis, as it is called in the Anabasis of Xenophon and Cyrus, now called Aras and Kur."   Star in the West.

must have known the success of the Scythians, then the
Medes, and then the Persians under Cyrus, which was
followed by the easy conquest of the whole of Media
and Persia, as Herodotus has shewn in his history, and by
which they must have been encouraged in so important a
business. The power of the kingdom was also comparatively weak, at so great a distance from the capital, and
distracted with political cabals and insurrections against
Astigages, who reigned over both Media and Persia, and
who was conquered by his grandson Cyrus. And it is not
improbable but that a removal more north, by which such
restless subjects would leave their improvements and real
property to the other inhabitants, and extend the territory
of their governors, would not have been disagreeable
either to the princes or people of that country. Again,
" the usual route from the Euxine sea to the northward of
the Caspian sea, through Tartary and Scythia, to Serica
and the northern parts of China, by which the merchants
carried on a great trade, might enable the tribes to travel
northward and eastward, towards Kamschatka. At least
this is the assertion of that able geographer D'Anville, in
his ancient geography, written before the late discoveries
of Cook and others."—Vol. ii. p. 521—523.

" But the most minute and last account we have of
them, is in the thirteenth chapter of the second book of
Esdras."

" These Israelites, then, accordingly executed their purpose, and left their place of banishment in a body, although
it is hardly to be doubted but some, comparatively few, from
various motives, as before observed, remained behind ;
although their places may have been filled up by many
natives, who might prefer taking their chance with them
in their emigrations, which were common to the people

of that region, especially the old inhabitants of Damascus removed to the river Ker by Tiglath Pilezer, some time before the taking of Samaria, and the removal of the ten tribes. They proceeded till they came to a great water or river, which stopped their progress, as they had no artificial means of passing it, and reduced them to great distress and almost despair. How long they remained here, cannot now be known; but finally, God again appeared for them, as he had done for their fathers of old at the Red Sea, by giving them some token of His presence, and encouraging them to go on; thus countenancing them in their project of forsaking the heathen." Star in the West.

The Historical Records of the transatlantic people are to *authenticate this migration through Asia,* as well as the *expectation* of a Redeemer, and that *redemption of their bodies,* from the power of the grave, which the prophets ascribe to Him, and which was the Hope of Israel.

The events which are to fulfil this expectation being represented as simultaneous, and at the *close* of ' the times of the gentiles,'—or end of the existing world or age, the following extracts from *this page of future history,* come home with all the weight and power of that Truth to which all must sooner or later—willingly or unwillingly bow.

The deliverance from Egypt was altogether prefigurative of that ultimate redemption, which at His second coming, shall crown the travail of the Messiah's soul; hence it is said, " Behold the days come when it shall no more be said, the LORD liveth who brought up the children of Israel from the land of Egypt; but the LORD liveth that brought up the children of Israel from the Land of the *north;* and from all the lands whither he had driven them; and I will bring them unto their own Land, that I *gave* to their fathers. Behold, I will send for many fishers, and they shall fish them; and for many hunters, and they shall hunt them ; * * Therefore I will make them to know at *that* time—I will cause them to *know* Mine hand and My power, and they shall know that My Name is JEHOVAH." " Remember not the former doings, neither revolve the acts of old times, Behold, I will do a new thing ; now shall it begin —and shall *ye* not know it? I will even make a way in the wilderness, and give rivers in the desert. The wild beasts shall reverence Me, the ostrich, and the daughters of the owl, because I give water-springs in the wilderness, and streams in the desert to refresh My people, My chosen. This people I have formed for Myself, *they shall manifest* My glory."

The prophet Ezekiel thus characterises the same place and people. " As I live, saith the Lord God, assuredly with a strong hand and an *extended* arm, and with ardent zeal will I govern you, and I will bring you out from the peoples, and will gather you out from the countries wherein ye are scattered, and I will bring you unto the wilderness of the people, and *there will I plead with you face to face, like* as I pleaded with your ancestors *in the wilderness of the land of Egypt ;* thus will I admonish you, saith the Lord God, and I will cause you to pass under the rod, and will bring you under the obligation (fetter) of the covenant ; and I will purge out from among you the rebellious, and those who transgress against Me. I will bring them forth out of the countries where they sojourn ; and they shall not enter into the Land of Israel : and ye shall know that I am YEHOVAH."

The prophet Hosea testifies to the same prospective experience. " Therefore, behold, I will allure her, and bring her into the wilderness, and speak comfortingly unto her, and will give her vineyards from thence, and the valley of tribulation for a door of Hope ; and she shall be taught there, as in the days of her youth, as in the days when I brought her up out of the land of Egypt. And it shall be in that Day, saith the Lord, thou shalt call Me my Husband, and shalt no more call me my Lord. And I will betroth *thee* unto *Me* in righteousness, and in justice, and in loving-kindness, and in mercies. I will even betroth thee unto Me in faithfulness; and thou shalt know the LORD." " And it shall come to pass in that day, that the LORD shall smite off from the channel of the river unto the stream of Egypt, and ye shall be gathered one by one, O ye children of Israel. And that day the great trumpet shall be blown, and they shall come who were ready to perish in the land of Assyria, and the outcasts in the land of Egypt, and shall worship YEHOVAH in the holy mountain at Jerusalem." On this passage much additional light is reflected by the words of the Divine prophet. " And He shall send His angels with a great sound of a trumpet, and they shall gather together His chosen from the four winds, from one extreme under Heaven to the other." The generation which should live to see the *first* symptoms of returning life in the long dormant vine of Israel, and fig-tree of Judah, shall also see its fruition. " This generation," (said He of those who shall see these things *begin* to come to pass,) " shall not pass away till *all* be accomplished."

" And God said unto Jacob, arise and go to Bethel, and sojourn there; and build there an altar unto God, who appeared unto thee when thou didst flee from the face of thy brother." " The Land which I gave to Abraham and Isaac, to *thee* will I give it, and to thy seed after thee will I give the Land." In blessing the two sons of Joseph, Israel thus testified of their prospective inheritance. " God Almighty, who appeared unto me in Luz, in the land of Canaan, blessed me, and said unto me, Behold, I will make thee fruitful, and multiply thee, and will make of thee a *multitude of nations,* and will give *this Land* unto thy seed after thee, for an *everlasting* possession; and now thy two sons Ephraim and Manasseh, who were born unto thee in Egypt before I came thither unto thee, shall be mine—as Reuben [1] and Simeon shall they be to me." " And he blessed Joseph and said, God, before whom my fathers Abraham and Isaac did walk—the God who sustained me all my life unto this day—the angel who redeemed me from all evil, bless the youths, and let my name be named upon them, and the names of my fathers Abraham and Isaac, and let them increase into a multitude in the midst of the earth. Moreover I have given to thee one portion above thy brethren, which I won out of the hand of the Amorite with my sword and with my Bow."

The portion to which allusion is here made, was prospec-tive, even as the weapons are emblematical of that faith by which Israel laid hold of the Word of God, and that prayer by which he appropriated His promises. In the blessing which the dying patriarch gave to Joseph, the same Bow is alluded to in the hand of Joseph. " Joseph is a fruitful branch, a fruitful branch to look upon, whose off-shoots extend over the wall; with bitter pride they (the adversaries) shot at him, but his Bow abode in strength; and the power of his hands continued strong by the hands (oversight) of the Omnipotent of Israel, from whom is the Shepherd, the Gem of Israel—even by the God of thy fathers, who shall help thee; and by the Almighty who shall bless thee with the blessings of Heaven above,—the blessings of the abyss that lieth under—the blessing of the fields and of the womb. The blessings of thy father have prevailed unto the utmost

---

[1] The portion of the first born (a double portion) having been forfeited by Reuben, was given to the tribe of Ephraim.

bounds of the enduring mountains, they shall continue on the head of Joseph, *and on the crown of the separated* from his brethren."

Moses prospectively characterizes the tribe of Ephraim in his blessing upon Joseph, in language almost identical; "And of Joseph, he said, Blessed of the LORD be his land for the precious gifts of Heaven, for the dew and for the void place (abyss) that coucheth beneath. For the precious gifts brought forth by the sun, and for the precious things put forth by the moon ; and for the chief things of the enduring mountains and for the precious things of the eternal high places ; for the precious things of the earth in its fulness,—His favour that dwelt in the thorn-bush continues on the head of Joseph : and on the *crown* of the separated from his brethren."

This language is peculiarly significant, when it is recollected that *Ephraim* was the *crowned* head, to whom, in its *extension*, the blessing was directed.

The secluded tribes are by the prophet Isaiah thus graphically characterized : Ho! to the land of quivering wings, which is beyond the river of Cush, that sendeth messengers by sea, in light vessels upon the face of the waters, saying, Go ye swift messengers to an extended nation, whose land has been meted out and trodden under foot—to a people terrible before and since—a people of strength, meted out and trodden down, whose land the rivers[1] have invaded :[2] All the dwellers upon earth, and the inhabitants of the land when He lifteth up a signal upon the mountains ' *behold*,' and *when* He bloweth the trumpet ' *listen*,' for thus the LORD said to me. I will remain quiet (be inactive.) I will observe in My dwelling place in still warmth, (serene heat)

---

[1] נהרים used metaphorically of the confluence and inundation of nations.
[2] The root is booty, or prey.

as the Light at a threshold,[1] and as the dew upon the harvest field ; for before the harvest when the blossom is full, and the embryo grape is ripening in the flower, he shall both cut off the twigs with knives, and lop off the branches. They shall be left together, unto the fowls of the mountain, and to the ravening beasts of the earth ; the fowls shall harvest upon them, and the beast of the earth shall winter upon them. At *that* time shall be brought to the LORD of hosts as a costly present ; a people terrible and far removed—a nation meted out and trampled under foot, whose land the rivers have spoiled, to the appointed Place, to the Land of the dwelling Place of the Name of the LORD of hosts, the Mount Zion.' Isaiah xviii. The image of quivering or fluttering wings, seems to be descriptive of the *expecting* attitude of the people to whom the allusion is made; as doves plume and put in motion their pinions preparatory to an expected flight ; in this beautiful attitude they are also characterized by David. ' Although ye have been hid in the stalls (places in the suburbs where sacrificial victims were penned) as the wings of a dove, radient as silver, and gleaming as gold, shall ye come forth.' This applies to the identical period and event, of which Mount Zion shall be the scene. ' Wherefore do ye contend, ye high mountains ? This is the Mountain in which God desireth to dwell, yea, Yehovah shall dwell there for ever.' ' The LORD said, I will bring *again* My people from Bashan, I will bring also from the seclusion beyond sea.' ' Princes shall come forth from Egypt, Cush shall speedily stretch forth her hands unto God.' Psalm lxviii. 13, 22, 31.

The prophet Isaiah adopts the same imagery, " Who are these that fly as a cloud, and as doves to their win-

---

[1] עב an architectural expression—the colonnade or entrance to a Temple.

dows? Surely the islands shall attend upon Me, and the ships of Tarshish first, to bring thy sons from afar, their silver and their gold with them, unto the Name of YEHOVAH thy God, and unto the Holy Israelite, for He hath glorified thee," Isaiah lx. 8, 9. "In that Day there shall be a Branch from the Root of Jesse, to Him shall the nations seek, and His Rest shall be glorious. And it shall be in that Day, that the LORD shall put to His Hand a second time to Redeem the remnant of His people which shall remain, from Assyria, and from Egypt, from Pathros, from Cush, from Elam, from Shinar, from Hamath, and from the islands of the sea. And He shall set up a standard *for the nations*, and He shall assemble the banished of Israel, and gather the dispersed of Judah from the four extremes (wings) of the earth." " And the Lord shall utterly cut off the tongue of the Egyptian sea, and with a mighty wind shall He shake His Hand over the river, and shall smite it in the seven streams, and men shall walk over in their shoes, and there shall be an high-way for the remnant of His people which shall be left from Assyria, like as there was to Israel in the day that they came up out of the land of Egypt." Isaiah xi.

It is to be noted that during his natural life, Abraham possessed only one field which he purchased of the sons of Heth:—and yet it was said to Abraham, I will give unto *thee*, and to thy seed after thee, the Land wherein thou art a *stranger*—all the Land of Canaan for an *everlasting* possession, and I will be their God." Gen. xvii. 8.

Accordingly, when Sarah died, Abraham stood up from before his dead, and thus spake to the sons of Heth. " I am a *stranger* and sojourner with you, give me possession of a burying-place with you that I may bury my dead out of my sight."

The martyr Stephen is peculiarly explicit respecting the

prospective inheritance : " He gave him (Abraham) none inheritance in it—no, not so much as to set his foot on ; yet He promised that He *would give it to him* for an *inheritance* and to bis seed after him, when as yet he had no child." Acts vii. 5.

Jacob had also only one field in the Land wherein he was a *stranger,* which he purchased from the sons of Hamor, and which is thus recognized in after times. " Then cometh he to a city of Samaria (Sychar) near to the parcel of ground that Jacob gave to his son Joseph—now Jacob's well was there."

In like manner, as a memorial or pledge of *future* possession at the very time when Jerusalem was beseiged by the king of Babylon, and when Jeremiah the prophet was shut up in the court of the king's prison, because of the faithfulness of his testimony—even then, although he should never return from that captivity, he was commanded to *purchase a field.* The prophet was amazed at the command : until Hanameel offered to sell him the field, the right of redemption being his. " Then I knew that it was the Word of the LORD, and I bought the field of Hanameel that was in Anathoth, and weighed him the money, seventeen shekels of silver ; and I subscribed the *evidence,* and took witnesses, and weighed the money in the balances ; and I took the evidence of the purchase, as well that which was sealed as that which was open."

" Thus saith the LORD of hosts, the God of Israel, Take these evidences of the purchase, as well that which is sealed, as that which is open, and put them in an *earthen vessel,* that they may *continue* many days. For thus saith the LORD of hosts, Houses, and fields, and vineyards shall be repossessed in *this* Land."

Jeremiah thus despondingly pleads : " Behold the engines

are brought unto the city, and the city is given into the hands of the Chaldeans, who fight against it in the midst of sword and famine and pestilence, and what thou hast said has come to pass, and Thou beholdest!—yet, O LORD God, thou hast said to me, Buy thee a field for money, and take witnesses, although the city is given into the hands of the Chaldeans. Then came the Word of the LORD to Jeremiah, saying, Behold I am the LORD, the God of all flesh: Is there anything too hard for Me?   *   *   *   *
" Behold I will gather them out of all countries whither I have driven them in mine anger and in mine indignation: and I will bring them again unto THIS PLACE, and will cause them to dwell securely; and they shall be My people, and I will be their God; and I will give them one heart and one WAY, that they may reverence ME constantly for the good of them, and of their children after them, and I will make an everlasting covenant with them in stability, to endure for their good; and I will put My fear in their hearts that they shall not depart from Me; yea, I will rejoice over them to do them good, and I will plant them in *this* LAND of a truth with My whole heart and with My whole soul. For thus saith the LORD, Even as I have brought all this great evil upon this people, so will I bring upon them all the good that I have promised them; and fields shall be bought in this LAND (whereof ye say it is desolate without man and beast, it is given unto the hands of the Chaldeans) men shall buy fields for money and subscribe evidences, and seal them, and take witness in all the places around Jerusalem, for I will cause their captivity to return, saith the LORD." Jeremiah xxii.

In like manner it was said to Daniel, ' Go thy way and repose till the end, for thou shalt *stand up in thy lot at the end* of the days. The call again is to the land of wings. Ho!

Ho! fly from the land of the *north*, for, saith the LORD, I have spread you abroad as the four winds of Heaven, saith the LORD. Save yourselves from the daughter of Babel, for thus saith the LORD of Hosts, after the glory, He sendeth me to the nations which spoiled you, for they that injure you, touch the apple of His eyes. For behold, I will shake Mine hand upon them, and they shall be for a spoil to their servants, and ye shall know that the LORD of hosts hath *sent* Me. Sing and rejoice, O daughter of Zion : for behold I come, and I will dwell in the midst of thee, saith the LORD, and many nations shall become united to YEHOVAH in that day, and shall be My people ; and I will dwell in the midst of *thee*, and thou shalt know that the LORD of hosts hath *sent* Me unto thee. And the LORD shall inherit JUDAH *His portion in the Holy Land*, and shall *again* choose JERUSALEM. Be *still*, O all flesh before the LORD, for He is roused from His Habitation of Holiness.

" Rejoice greatly, O daughter of Zion, shout O daughter of Jerusalem, behold thy King cometh unto thee, just and gracious, humbly carried upon an ass, and upon a colt the foal of an ass. And I will take away the war chariot from Ephraim, and the war-horse from Jerusalem, and the battle-bow shall be unstrung, and he shall speak peace to the nations, and His dominion shall be from sea to sea, from the river (Euphrates) to the ends of the earth :—as for thee also, whose covenant is by blood, I have released thy prisoners from the abyss wherein is no water. Turn you to the strong hold, ye captives of Hope, even in this day do I declare that I will render precious gifts double unto thee. When I have bent Judah for Me, and filled My Bow with Ephraim, and raised up thy sons, O Zion, against thy sons, O Greece, and made thee as the warriors' sword, and the LORD shall be seen over them, and His arrow shall go forth as lightning, and the LORD God shall sound the trumpet (of Jubilee,) and shall go amid whirlwinds of the south. And the LORD God shall save thee in that Day, even the flock of His people, for they shall be as the gems of a crown, lifted up as an ensign upon His Land. I will strengthen the House of Judah, and I will redeem the House of Joseph, and I will bring them to establish them, for I have mercy upon them, and they shall be as though I had not banished them ; for I am the LORD their God, and will hear them. And they of Ephraim shall be conquerors, their heart shall rejoice as with wine; yea, their children shall see it and be glad ; their heart shall rejoice in the LORD. I will hiss to them and gather them, for I have redeemed them, and they shall increase as they have increased, and I will sow them in peoples, and they shall remember me in *far countries*, and they shall live, and with their children, return again. And I will bring them a second time out of the land of Egypt, and gather them from Assyria, and I will bring them unto the country of Gilead and Lebanon, and place shall not be found for them. And he shall pass through the waters with affliction, and shall smite the waves in the sea, and all the deeps of the river (Euphrates) shall be dried up ; and the pride of Assyria shall be humbled, and the dominion of Egypt shall cease, and I will strengthen them in the LORD, they shall walk hither and thither in His Name, saith Yehovah."

The preceding considerations teach us to expect that the sons of Joseph have become in their seclusion as the countless stars, ' a multitude of nations,' not only on the earth, but expecting (in the place of separate spirits,) the voice which shall restore to them at once their *redeemed* bodies and inheritance. They who are alive and remain at the coming of the LORD, (whose voice shall call forth the prisoners of hope from their concealment,) shall not prevent those who are *asleep*. Such as (like the Sadducees of old,) have explained away to a shadowy abstraction the resurrection of the body can form a very inadequate idea of the substance and locality which this most heart-cheering truth afforded to Abraham, and the heirs of those promises which in their redeemed bodies should be fulfilled to them. They did not view the age or world to come, as invisible in the sense of being immaterial and impalpable; to their mind it was invisible only in the manner that the celestial luminaries are so, when for a season hid by the *intervention of dense clouds and smoke*. Their faith supplied the place of vision, for they knew that in *reality* and *substance*, a KINGDOM and KING were in *reserve*, and should *visibly* appear when the Roman Empire (the last of the four interposing Monarchies) shall have, like those which it supplanted, in turn become the subject of that *dissolution* to which all that is in *opposition* to the Law of God is destined.

Again, to Jacob the promised Land was confirmed, when the LORD appeared as the Head of that mystic ladder, which resting upon earth should, (as a type of the Messiah,) become the medium of restored communion between Heaven and earth, "I am the LORD God of Abraham thy father, and of Isaac—the Land whereon thou liest, to thee will I give it, and to thy seed, and thine offspring shall be as the dust of the ground, and thou *shalt spread abroad to* the west, and to the east, and to the north, and to the south; and in thee, and in thy seed shall all the families of the earth be blessed. And behold I am with thee, and will preserve thee *in all places* whither thou goest, and will bring thee again to this Land, for I will not forsake thee until I have accomplished that which I have declared." A series of ages having elapsed, the house of Israel is described as tacitly saying,

" behold, *our* bones are dead, and our hope is gone, for we are *cut off* from our parts." "Thus saith the LORD God, Behold, O My people, I will open your graves, and bring you unto the LAND of Israel; and ye shall know that I am YEHOVAH, When I have opened your graves, O My people, and have *redeemed* you out of your graves; and shall put My Spirit within you, and ye shall live, and I shall restore you to your own Land: *then* ye shall know that I the LORD have spoken and *performed*, saith the LORD."

David beautifully compares this resurrection-Day to the dew of the morning: " From the womb of the morning shall appear the dew of thy bringing-forth."

It should be determined what is the nature of redeemed existence—of incorruptible and glorious bodies, before it is asked how the limits of the promised Land can contain the myriads who shall make good the promises *there* for a Thousand years, before a still progressive state is entered upon. Upon Mount Zion alone were prospectively seen, 144,000 of the Twelve Tribes, and with them a great multitude of those from among the Gentiles who had chosen the better portion—thus having been made meet for the inheritance of the holy ones in Light. Revelation vii.

The Prophet Isaiah testifies to this comforting Truth which the Apostle characterizes as " The Hope" of Israel. Acts xxvi. 6. " Thou hast increased the nation O LORD, thou art glorified! LORD, in trouble they have besought thee, they poured out a secret prayer when Thy chastening was upon them." Thy dead shall *revive*—with My dead body shall they arise. Awake, rejoicing, ye that dwell in the dust; for as the dew to the light, so is thy dew, for the earth shall yield up the preserved (praying). And it shall come to pass in that Day, the LORD shall smite off from the channel of the river (Euphrates) unto the river of Egypt, and ye shall be gathered one by one, O ye children of Israel, and in that Day the *great* (Jubilee) trumpet shall be sounded, and they shall come who were ready to perish in the land of Assyria, and the outcasts in the land of Egypt and shall worship the LORD in the holy Mountain at Jerusalem.

Of this grand ultimate convocation, the Apostle Paul thus speaks: "Now we entreat you, brethren, by the coming of our LORD Jesus Christ, and by our *gathering* together unto Him." * * "The LORD Himself shall descend from Heaven with a shout, with the voice of the archangel and with the trumpet of God, and the dead in Christ shall rise first."

It was by His bodily restoration to renewed life that the promises to the fathers became confirmed, His reanimated body being the earnest and pledge of those of His redeemed. Hence His *rejection* in His office of Prophet by that *remnant* of the two tribes (which remained after the building of the second Temple,) constituted Him the atonement for the whole—whether present or absent, as also in design for the whole world.

It was of the *result* which His atonement should accomplish, that the Great Shepherd of the flock thus spake: "Other sheep I have which are not of *this* fold, them also I must *bring* (again) and they shall hear My voice" (as Lazarus had heard it) "and there shall be one Fold and one Shepherd." The prophet Ezekiel gives this piece of future history in detail: "Thus saith the LORD God, Behold I will take the children of Israel from among the nations, whither they are gone and will *gather* them on all sides, and bring them into their own LAND; and I will make them one nation in the LAND upon the mountains of Israel; and one King shall be King to them all; they shall no more be two nations, neither shall they be divided into two kingdoms any more for ever;

neither shall they defile themselves any more with their idols, nor with their detestable things, nor with any of their transgressions; for I will *redeem* them out of their dwelling-places wherein they have sinned, and will purify them; so shall they be My people, and I will be their God, and David My servant shall be King over them, and they shall all have one Shepherd; they shall also walk in My judgments and observe My statutes and do them; and they shall dwell in the Land that I have given unto Jacob My servant, wherein your fathers have sojourned, and they dwell therein they and their children's children for ever; and My servant David shall be their Prince for evermore. My Tabernacle also shall be with them; yea, I will be their God, and they shall be My people; and the nations shall know that I, JEHOVAH, do sanctify Israel, when MY SANCTUARY shall be in the midst of them for ever."

PRELIMINARY NOTICES OF SPANISH HISTORIANS.

IN order to form a just estimate of the value of testimony, it is necessary to obtain some knowledge of those who record it, since respectability and authentic sources of information constitute their claim to the attention and regard of the reader. The duration of their sojourn, their perfect knowledge of the language, records, and antiquities of the people, whose manners and customs they narrate, as well as the relative circumstances in which themselves were placed, and the interests with which they were connected, are all to be taken into consideration. The Spanish Historians, whose names frequently occur in this work, were all members of the Romish communion, the greater part ecclesiastics, and, as their names indicate, chiefly of Hebrew descent.

Those early Spanish writers, unanimously recognized and acknowledged the manifold analogies which demonstrate the transference of the Levitical economy to the New Continent; but while some of them discerned in this circumstance an indisputable proof of the Hebrew origin of the newly-discovered People; others accounted for this almost *fac simile* resemblance by asserting that Satan had counterfeited in this People, (whom he had chosen for himself,) the history, manners, customs, traditions, and expectations of the Hebrews, in order that their

B

minds might thus be rendered inaccessible to the faith which he foresaw the church would in due time introduce amongst them !

The Historians who ranked themselves as the advocates of the former of these alternatives, were LAS CASAS, SAHAGUN, BOTURINI, GARCIA, GUMILLA, BENAVENTA, and MARTYR. Those who maintained the latter hypothesis were TORQUEMEDA, HERRERA, GOMARA, D'ACOSTA, CORTEZ, D'OLMES, DIAZ. The circumstances in which Herrera and Gomara were placed, (the former having been Royal Historiographer, and the latter Chaplain to Cortez,) admitted of their taking only the orthodox view of the subject. The " *secret correspondence*" of Cortez with Charles v. together with the rigorous censorship which was exercised by 'the holy tribunal,' sufficiently prove that even this least offensive view of the subject was to be expressed with reserve.[1]

The testimony of writers who rejected the evidence of those *facts* which they nevertheless admitted and recorded, is peculiarly valuable, since the reader of the eighteenth century is more likely to draw conclusions from these *admitted facts*, than to assume that hypothesis which left *them* at liberty to acknowledge them as such.

---

[1] " The secret correspondence of Cortez with the Spanish court, which probably still exists, either in the archives of Simancha, or the Escurial, would, if ever published, throw great light on a mystery which religious and state policy kept concealed. Peter Martyr does not refer to two or three letters of that conqueror, but to " a *huge volume*," which was laid before the council of the Indies, of which Garcia de Loisa (the Emperor's confessor) was president, and both he and Gomara (who was Chaplain to Cortez,) confess that they have imposed reserve upon themselves, in treating of the Mexican superstitions."—Antiq. Mex. fol. vi. page 329.

DON BARTHOLOMEW LAS CASAS.

" That [1] Las Casas was firmly persuaded that the Indians were descended from the Hebrews, is evident from his own words, [2] " *Loquela tua manifestum te ʃecit,* your speech betrays you," as recorded by Torquemeda. If the work of that illustrious prelate, (who was intimately acquainted with Columbus, whose life he wrote, and who was one of the first Spaniards who proceeded to the continent of America, where he must have had an opportunity of becoming acquainted with the traditions, &c.) had ever been published, we should have known his reasons for coming to that conclusion : that bishop was too rational to adopt the hypothesis embraced by Acosta and Torquemeda, that the Devil had actually counterfeited the history, laws, rites, ceremonies, and customs of the Jews in the New World, but he believed that the Hebrews had colonized America."

[1] *Bartolome Las Casas,* a famous Dominican Spaniard, first bishop of Chiapa, and highly worthy of memorial among the Indians. The bitter memorials presented by this excellent prelate to King Charles V., and Philip II., in favour of the Indians against the Spaniards, printed in Seville, and afterwards translated and reprinted in odium to the Spaniards, into several European languages, contains some particulars of the ancient history of the Mexicans. He wrote other works, one a General History of America, in 3 vols. folio. Two volumes are in the celebrated Archives Simancas, which have been the sepulchre of many precious Manuscripts on America. Clavegero Disser. The remonstrance of Las Casas, see Appendix.

[2] " The words " *Loquela tua manifestum te fecit,*" in reference to the Mexicans and other Indian tribes, whom he took to be real Hebrews, deserve the most serious attention, because we have here the opinion of a person who was well acquainted with the Mexicans and Peruvians, and who proceeded to America immediately after its discovery by the Spaniards, spent there the greater part of a long life, and *solemnly recorded in a testamentary document,* his conviction of a fact which he might have had many reasons for not choosing to divulge." Antiq. Mex. p. 331. (" Las Casas even goes so far as to say that the language of the Island of St. Domingo was corrupt Hebrew." Ibid.) " At the same time that great credit must be attached to so solemnly recorded an opinion, it cannot be said that the learned prelate was guilty of any indiscretion in promulgating it ; but the contrary is proved by the proviso which he made respecting the publication of his history—that it should not be printed till fifty years after his death ; *this work was never* published, and Don M. F. Navarette says, that when it was referred some years ago to the Academy of History at Madrid, to take their decision respecting its publication, they did not think it *convenient.*"—Ibid.

"The observation which we have made above, that the ecclesiastics were not encouraged to communicate what they knew from intercourse with the natives and the perfect knowledge which they had acquired of the Mexican language, and of the religion and antiquities of the American natives is as strange as that the American Chronicle of Las Casas and the Universal History of New Spain by Sahagun, should never have been published. The former of these works must have been of enormous magnitude, if we may judge of the size of the whole, from only having seen that part of it which is preserved in the British Museum, which includes the preface to the first books. Las Casas explains in the preface, which is very long, the reasons which induced him to undertake the work, which were primarily of a religious nature, although it would appear that he was also desirous of opposing a true history to the many false relations and misrepresentations which he complains that writers on the affairs of America had unblushingly published. It is extraordinary, considering the ability of the Author, and the many years which he devoted to the composition of his History, and the consequently well-known fact of the existence of such a work, that it should have been carefully preserved from every eye."

"Nicholas Antonio and Pinelo both name it; but it does not appear that the former saw any of it, or the latter more than a part. That portion of the work, containing an account of the religion, manners, and customs of the new world, was termed apologetical, because he must have endeavoured to palliate in it some manners and customs which were used as a plea, by the greedy proprietors of *encomiendas*, to press the crown to deprive the Indians of all civil rights, and to reduce them to the condition of absolute slavery. And how could that learned prelate have set up a stronger defence for the Indians, than by shewing that their institutions were derived from the Hebrews; however, time, through the perversion of traditions, might have corrupted them?"

"That the Apologetical History treated of the *religion* of the Indians is evident, since Torquemeda says that Las Casas asserted in his Apology, in M.S. that " *Quetzalcoatl* went from Tula to Yutican," &c. A Spanish writer, giving a sketch of the life of Las Casas, says, speaking of his history, "Las Casas himself, in the year 1556, added a note to it, with his own hand, saying that he bequeathed *his History* [1] in confidence, to the College of the order of Friars, Preachers of St. Gregory, in Valladolid, requesting the prelates not to allow any layman, nor the collegiates to read it during the period of forty years; at the expiration of which it might be printed, if it was for the advantage of the Indians."

BERNARD DE SAHAGUN.

"*Bernard de Sahagun*,[2] one of the first preachers in New Spain, says that he found it to be a universally received

[1] "This work consisted of six decades, each of which comprised the history of ten years, except the first, which, beginning with the events of 1492, ended in 1500. The learned prelate declared that he had employed thirty-two years in the composition of this work, which comprised the History of the W. I. Islands and Continent, the American Chronicle of Peru and Yutican, as well as of Nicaragua, Chiapa, Guatamala, Mexico, and the other kingdoms of New Spain; we need not feel surprised that it should have extended to six folio volumes; but that no portion of a work so interesting should ever have been published, either by the Order to which he bequeathed it, or by public authority, or by private individuals, cannot be ascribed to accidental causes. Torquemeda remarks, "Las Casas had many powerful enemies because he spoke *great truths*."— p. 265.

[2] *Bernard de Sahagun*, a laborious Franciscan Spaniard, having been sixty years among the Indians, made great proficiency in the knowledge of their language and history. Besides other works, he composed, in twelve large vols. a Universal Dictionary of the Mexican Language, containing what related to the geography, religion, political and natural history of the Mexicans. This work

tradition amongst the nations, confirmed by the testimony of their historical paintings, that a colony had arrived long before the Christian era, on the coast of America, from a region situated to the north-east, called Chicomoztoc, first touching on the shores of Florida. The Archbishop of Mexico, Cardinal Lorenzana, afterwards Archbishop of Toledo, who published an edition of Cortez' Letters in Mexico, in the year 1770, would have derived some instruction from the perusal of the History of Sahagun, and certainly would not have assumed it as an undeniable fact, that America had never been colonized from the north-west ; neither would he have put a different construction on that passage of the speech of Montezuma to Cortez, where he declares that his ancestors were from the *east*, than the words of that Monarch fairly admit. The Archbishop says, in a note subjoined to Montezuma's speech. " Los Mexicanos por tradicione viniron por el Norte de la Provecha de Quevera y se Luben ciertamente sus mansiones." This information he perhaps obtained from the examination of some of the *confiscated* papers of *Boturini*, which remained in Mexico, in the vice-regal archives, some of which he says were submitted to his inspection."

"*Sahagun*, in the prologue to the Universal History of New Spain, expressly says that he was impeded in the progress of his work, by the great discouragement he met with from those who ought to have forwarded it. He states in his second book, that amidst the commendation bestowed upon it, in the Chapter of his Order, which was held in 1569, it appeared to some of the *Definitors*, that it was contrary to their vow of poverty to expend money on writing such

of immense erudition and labour was sent to the royal historiographer of America, resident at Madrid, by the Marquis Villamanrique, viceroy of Mexico. He wrote also the General History of New Spain, in four vols.--*Clavegero Disser.*

histories; and that they therefore obliged the author to discharge his amanuensis, (as *he* was more than seventy years old, he could not, on account of the trembling of his hand, write at all) and his writings remained for more than five years, without any thing further being done to them. In the mean time, the Provincial deprived the said author of them all, and scattered them over the province. After the lapse of some years, brother Miguel Navarro, came as commissioner to those parts, and recovered, by ecclesiastical censures, the said works at the request of the author. Grateful for the assistance which he had received from the commissioner, Rodrigo de Segura, he dedicated it to him, overwhelming him with eulogies for having redeemed it!— " rescuing it" as he declares, " from beneath the earth, and even from under the ashes." (265) Sahagun further complains, that he was forcibly deprived of a very valuable painting, representing the great Temple, with the court by which it was surrounded, which he says was sent to Spain. It is very evident that every thing in Mexico, calculated to draw attention to the ancient history of the country, more especially if connected with *religious* recollections, was carefully removed from notice, immediately after the conquest. Pieces of sculpture were mutilated or buried,— paintings were burned,—temples and edifices, which, from their size, it was impossible to destroy, were suffered to fall into oblivion ; and magnificent monuments of ancient art, such as the temples of Pelenque,. and the palaces of Mitlan, were passed unnoticed by Spanish authors."

" Sahagun, when engaged in the compilation of his history, after it had been taken away from him and again restored, received three cautions :—First, to write nothing to prove that the Hebrews had colonized the new world ; Secondly, to be guarded in what he said of the Devil's having imitated

God, in taking to himself a chosen people in the new world, and counterfeiting the rites and ceremonies of the Jews; and, Thirdly, not to advance the hypothesis that Christianity had ever been proclaimed to the Indians, or to treat too largely on the history of *Quetzalcoatl.*"

" The Bibliotheca of Pinelo, a work, the express object of which was to *illustrate* the History of America, by *extracts from, and references to, valuable and unpublished* M.S. preserved in the most famous libraries of Spain and the public archives, especially those of Simancos, to which the author, through the interest of the Duke of Medina de las Torres, obtained access, exists only in an epitome; and of the larger work, a learned writer has observed, *" not a leaf has been found."*—Garcia's History of the Peruvian Monarchy is also *unknown.*—Siguenza's Mexican Cyclography is stated to have been *lost* through the negligence of his heirs, and many other interesting works are said to have *perished, or been lost in a similar manner.* It has been remarked before, that the office of royal historiographer of the Indies does not appear to have been instituted solely for the purpose of promoting the cause of truth, and the increase of knowledge: and it may be further observed that the council of the Indies, which took cognizance of all writers treating of America, requiring that they should be, previously to publication, submitted to a strict censorship, with the power of recalling or prohibiting, even *after* the publication, any work they thought fit, proceeded in a diametrically opposite spirit."—Mex. Antiq. vol. vi.

BOTURINI.

The Cavalier Boturini, an Italian by birth, visited the New Continent with a view to literary and antiquarian research.

"This Milanese traveller," observes Humboldt, "had crossed the seas with no other view than to study on the spot the history of the native tribes of America; but in traversing the country to examine its monuments, and make researches into its antiquities, he had the misfortune to fall under the *suspicion* of the Spanish government. After having been *deprived* of the fruit of his labours, he was sent in 1736, as a state prisoner to Madrid. The king of Spain declared him innocent, but this did not restore to him his property; and this collection, the catalogue of which Boturini published at the end of his Essay on the American History of New Spain, printed at Madrid, lay *buried* in the Archives of the University at Mexico; those valuable relics of the culture of the Aztecs were preserved with so little care, that there scarcely exists at present an eighth part of the hieroglyphic records taken from the Italian traveller."—Mex. Antiq. vol. vi. p. 136-7.

"Boturini's small work, entitled 'Idea de una nueva Hist. Gen.' &c. published in Madrid, in 1746, notwithstanding his dedication of it to the king, and his preliminary protest which has *six different licences* for publication prefixed to it, remains unpublished. The preliminary protest is as follows, "Although the occasion of writing this *Historical Idea* has obliged me to *meditate* upon the *secrets* and scientific paintings of the Indians; nevertheless, so far am I from separating myself in the slightest degree from the purity of the Catholic religion in which I was born, that I would rather readily die in its defence; and whatever I say here I submit, with the most humble obedience to the judgment, &c. of our holy Roman Catholic and mother church."

"At this distance of time when the state of the world is so different from what it was in the sixteenth century, it may not be readily conceived how easy it was for the council of the Indies, through the power vested in it, of permitting or prohibiting the general circulation of all writings relative to America, *to keep the rest of Europe in a state of darkness respecting the history of the New Continent*. For three centuries those who successively composed that council, exercised their function as *censors* with the greatest vigilance. If powerful patronage or inadvertence on their part suffered in the first instance any *obnoxious* work to appear in print, it was sure soon to be recalled. Thus the history of the Indies, by Gomara, dedicated to Charles v. and the Conquest of Mexico, by the same author, dedicated to Don Martin Cortez, son of the celebrated conqueror, became prohibited books soon after their publication ; but there were *other* works against which a silent war was waged in Spain. —ibid. 269—70.

" We shall only further remark, that the history of Peru is enveloped in much greater obscurity than that of Mexico. The real cause of less being known of the history of the Peruvians in Europe, &c. (notwithstanding Garcillassa de Vega, himself of the race of the Incas, wrote in the latter end of the sixteenth century, a history of Peru,) is probably that Peru was discovered many years after the discovery. and conquest of Mexico, and Europe was not to be surprised a second time by a sudden appearance of fresh Ocean Decades and Mythological Paintings."—p. 270.

" A part of the paintings collected by Boturini was sent

to Europe in a Spanish vessel, which was taken by an English privateer. It was never known whether these paintings reached England, or whether they were thrown into the sea as of no value."

"The greater part of the MS. of Boturini, those which were confiscated in New Spain, were torn, pillaged, and dispersed by persons who were ignorant of the value of these objects. What exists at present in the palace of the Viceroy, composes only three packets, each seven hands square, by five in height. They remained in one of the damp apartments of the ground floor of the Archives of government, which the Viceroy, Count Revillagagedo removed, because of the humidity mouldering the papyrus with alarming rapidity. We feel a sentiment of indignation on seeing the extreme negligence with which these valuable remains were abandoned, which had cost much care and labour, and which the unfortunate Boturini, fired with the enthusiasm which is peculiar to enterprising men, calls in his historal essay, ' the only property which he possessed in the Indies, and which he would not change against all the gold and silver of the New World."

"The library of the University of Mexico is no longer in possession of any original hieroglyphics. The richest and finest collection of this capital, is that of Jose Antonio Richardo, member of the congregation of San Felipe Neri. The house of this enlightened person, adds Humboldt, was to me what the house of Seguenza was to the traveller Gumilli. Richardo has sacrificed his little fortune in collecting Aztec paintings, and in copying those he was unable to purchase. His friend Gama, author of several astronomical memoirs, bequeathed him all the most valuable hieroglyphics and manuscripts which he possessed. In the new Continent, as well as in the other country, *private individuals,* and those not the most opulent, become the *collectors and preservers* of objects which are worthy the protection of governments."—Humboldt, pp. 188-9.

GARCIA.

" Garcia, in his famous treatise on the Origin of the Indians, says in the 232nd page, introduction to the third book, Many have supposed, and the Spaniards generally who reside in the Indies believe, that the Indians proceed from the Ten Tribes who were lost in the time of Salmanassar, king of Assyria, of whom Rabbi Schimon Sugati, who is named Sincha by Bartolocia, says, "nothing is certain, *nor is it known where they dwell.*" This opinion is grounded on the disposition, nature, and customs of the Indians, which they found very similar to those of the Hebrews; and although some learned men are uninclined to assent to such a belief, I nevertheless have bestowed great diligence upon the verification of this Truth. *I can affirm that I have laboured in this more than in any other part of my work, and from what I have found thereto relating, I shall lay such foundations for the edifice and structure of this hypothesis, as will be able to contain its weight.* The entire of Garcia's third book of the Origin of the Indians, treats accordingly of the likeness which in their laws, their customs, their moral qualities and habits, their ceremonies, sacrifices, and inclinations to idolatry, and even in their early History, the two nations bore to each other. In the first chapter he criticises the passage of the Apocryphal book of Esdras, which induced the Jews themselves to think that they had colonized America, and others to treat with grave attention that singular history. The manner in which they had crossed from one continent to another was also a subject of discussion. In the sixth chapter, which is the most curious of all, he institutes a comparison between the Jewish moral and ceremonial laws, and those of the Mexicans, and shows how nearly they agreed.[1] In the seventh he compares the Hebrew language with that of the Indian idioms, and in the eighth he replies to some objections of Acosta."[2]

GENERAL NOTICES OF THE OPINIONS OF TORQUEMEDA, HERRERA, D'ACOSTA, GOMARA, CORTEZ, D'OLMES, TORIBIO, BENAVENTE, MARTYR, AND GUMELLA.

" When we read in *Gomara*, and other early Spanish historians, of the prodigies which preceded the overthrow of Mexico, so nearly resembling those which Josephus records to have happened shortly before the final destruction of Jerusalem, it is impossible not to perceive the spirit in which these relations were composed, and the feelings which were latent behind the comparison." p. 329. Half revealed truth becomes generally persuasive, as soon as recognized, because those who do not even purpose to bestow information, must certainly be exempt from the charge of deliberately intending to deceive."

The Peruvians, when first discovered by the Spaniards, had attained a high degree of civilization, and it would

---

[1] It must be recollected that the Spaniards intentionally consigned the arts, history, religion, and ancient monuments of America to oblivion, and that they denied to the Mexicans and Peruvians the knowledge of many arts which were arrived at even a flourishing state of perfection among them. " *Garcia* declares that in Paraguay, iron money resembling in shape the shell of a tortoise, was used, which animal is represented on the oldest Greek coins, those of Thebes."— P. 68.

[2] A curious parallel of the Hebrews' and Indians' Moral Law may be found in the third book of Garcia's Origin of the Indians, which he has entitled ' *Como los Indios guardaron los Preceptos del Decalago.*' How the Indians obeyed the Ten Commands in the Decalogue."—*Antiq. Mex. vol.* vi. *p.* 381.

appear from a passage of Gomara's History of the Indies, that the Spaniards were struck with the resemblance of some of the tribes of India to the Jews. " They are all very like Jews, in appearance and voice, for they have large noses and speak through the throat."

" *Torquemeda*, who does not allow that the Mexicans borrowed any of their analogous customs from the Jews, nevertheless, in treating in the thirty-seventh chapter of the tenth book of his Indian Monarchy, of their art of divination, expresses himself thus, " *Segun doctrina falso de estos diabolicus Rabbinas*," by which he clearly shews the channel of his thoughts."

" Such was the reserve the Spanish historians imposed upon themselves in treating of *Quetzalcoatl* (the Mexican Messiah) that his *name* in fact would scarcely have been handed down to us but for the preservation of a chance copy of the first edition of the Indian Monarchy, by *Torquemeda*." " Again, it is evident that in Mexico, great pains were taken by the monks and clergy to root out the remembrance of him, and legendary tales relating to his life, were not allowed to be inserted in books published either in that city or in Spain. The temple of Cholula was dedicated to Quetzalcoatl; *Bernal Diaz* in his history, declares that he had forgot the name of the *idol*, to whom it was dedicated, although he remembers the number of steps which led up to the temple ! This was either out of compliance with the wishes, or in obedience to the command of others."—p. 169.

" It is singular that *Torquemeda*, who was so well acquainted with the Mexican Mythology, should say so little of Totoc,[1] occupying as he does, the next place to Quetzal-

---

[1] *c* and *z* sound soft in the Mexican language as *s* in the English.

coatl, in the Mexican calendar. This silence on the part of Torquemeda, must either be attributed to the oblivion in which half a century had involved many of the religious traditions of the Mexicans, or to the MS. copy of the Indian Monarchy having been *mutilated*, previously to licence being granted to publish it. Two writers have declared this to be the case. The editor of the second edition complains, that the first chapter of the second book, ' *Clave de la de esto obra*,' has been entirely omitted; nor did he think it expedient, as he himself says, to request licence to print it, although he adds, " Reasons for secrecy seemed no longer to exist."—p. 179.

" The early Spanish writers believed that the Mexican and Peruvian government, laws, and commonwealth, were modelled after the manner of the Jews, though the reason they assign for this is absurd; they say that Satan was jealous of the institutions which God had given to His chosen people, and therefore determined to imitate them in the new world. They have not failed either to point out some curious traits of resemblance to Hebrew usages, in certain acts performed by the Kings and Incas, and in the external marks of reverence these monarchs received from their subjects."

" Unfortunately, ecclesiastics received no encouragement to write histories of that nation; nor, does it appear that they were allowed to publish them :—since the works of Mendieta, of Toribio de Benavente, or Motolina, (a copy of whose valuable history Dr. Robertson seems to have procured from Spain; but of which he evidently made no use,) and of *D'Olmas* and *Sahagun*, have never been printed; and, strange to say, the royal historiographer of the Indies, *Herrera*, attempts to discredit the relations of Torquemeda, which may account for the relation of the latter author having become so excessively rare, not more than a century after its publication, that the editor of the second edition says, that he despaired for a long time of being able to procure a copy of it in all Spain ; but reasons too long to be here recited, perfectly convince us that the office of royal historiographer of the Indies was instituted quite as much for the purpose of *veiling* as of developing truth. And certainly in a country and in an age where the authority with which a person wrote, was so nicely scrutinized, as the criterion of his merits, Herrera, who really possessed the talents, if he had not the candor of an historian, had it in his power, if he had felt disposed, to deprecate by animadversion, and to consign to oblivion by criticism, the works of contemporary historians, who did not write with the same authority," p. 282, 283. Without stating his reasons for dissenting from Las Casas, he assumes it as an undoubted fact, that the Devil had taken unto himself a chosen people in the new world, and counterfeited in them the history of the children of Israel, and their pilgrimage from Egypt. He assumes this fact, but is very *reserved* in stating the reasons which induced him to do so, and very *concise* in his account of the Mexican *migration ;* the same reserve actuating other Spanish historians who possessed equal means of obtaining information with Herrera, has nearly robbed the world of a secret which it is hoped may yet be brought *to light.*"— Antiq. Mex. vol. vi. p. 263.

The Mexican paintings seem to have become objects of suspicion and mistrust, even in Europe. The first that were sent to Spain, came to Charles v. in 1519. Peter Martyr mentions them.—His description corresponds more exactly with the painting which is preserved in the royal library at Dresden ; some of the symbols contained in it are not unlike Hebrew letters. Peter Martyr gives the following description of these paintings, in an epistle addressed to Leo x. "We have sayde before that these nations have bookes whereon they write, and the messengers, who were procurators for the new colony, Coluahana, brought many of them into Spayne."—Peter Martyr again says, "I have heretofore sayde that they have bookes, whereof they brought many to Spayne, but this *Ribera* saith, they are not made for their use of readinge : I suppose them to bee bookes, and that those characters and images signified some other thinges, seeing I have seen the like thinges in the obeliskes and pillars at Rome, which were accounted letters, consideringe also that we reade that the *Caldeis* used to write after that manner."

" It does not appear that Peter Martyr had the opportunity of seeing any more of " these *bookes*," or that any further presents of that kind were sent to the king of Spain, &c. *Ribera*, from whom Peter Martyr received the information that the Mexican paintings were merely patterns for clothes and jewels, was the intimate friend and companion of Cortez ; he had been four years in Spain and had acquired a knowledge of the Mexican language ; he must therefore have known the real use of those paintings, and what his motive could be, in saying that they had no signification nor meaning, it would be difficult to explain." " Rigid orders were given, shortly afterwards, to the Bishop and clergy of New Spain to cause them all to be burnt." " Spain passed some extraordinary laws, prohibiting lawyers, surgeons, literati, Jews, heretics and the descendants to the third generation, of persons, *suspected by the Inquisition,* and foreigners of all sorts, who had not received a licence at Seville, from passing over to America."

" Father *Joseph Gumilla* says, in page 59 of the Oronoco Illustrada, " I affirm, in the second place, that the nations of Oronoco and its streams, observed many Hebrew cere-

monies, during the time of the paganism which they followed blindly and rudely, without knowing wherefore,
(ceremonies) that had been transmitted by traditions, handed
down from father to son, without their being able to assign
any reason for the practice of them."—p. 272. Torquemeda,
acknowledging that the religious rites, ceremonies, and even
moral laws of the Indians closely resembled those of the
Jews, thought it more probable that the devil had instructed
the Indians in them, than that the Hebrews had carried
them over to America. Learned men of the present age
will not consider themselves bound by the example of those
of the sixteenth century; and that learning is most useful,
the object of which is the attainment of truth, with a regard
for the best interests of mankind."

"All that Peter Martyr says of Huitzilopoctli, the
tutelary deity of Mexico, whose temple he briefly describes
in his eight decades, is comprised in a single line, in the
fourth chapter of his fifth decade, where he writes to Adrian
VI. 'It is a fearful thing to be spoken, what they declare
and report concerning their idols;' and he does not so much
as mention Quetzalcoatl." p. 329.

"On the supposition that Cortez discovered the Jewish
religion, established in Mexico, it is easy to assign a reason
for the three years' delay, in sending over regular clergy
from Spain, notwithstanding the pressing solicitations which
Cortez, *publicly at least*, made to the Emperor, to that
effect: since the real cause might have been to *avoid
scandal*, and to have time to *root out*, by the *secular arm*,
the traces of Judaism, which could not fail to strike a clerical
order of men, however they might have been overlooked
by the military followers of Cortez. It is proper however to
observe that this delay, which seems very extraordinary,
considering the age, the zeal of the Spanish nation, and

above all, the state of the *new vineyard*, is ascribed, in the second chapter of the fifteenth book of Torquemeda's history, to other causes, amongst which are enumerated the death of Pope Leo x, and the Emperor's doubts whether he could conscientiously annex to the crown of Spain, the newly discovered kingdom. The analogy between many of the Mexican and Jewish superstitions afford convincing proof that they were derived from a common source, and it is a curious fact that many obscure passages of Scripture may be elucidated by referring to the works of Torquemeda, Gomara, and Acosta."

" Herrera, almost in the very words of Acosta, notices, in the seventeenth chapter of the second book of his third Decade, that custom (viz. circumcision) as prevalent amongst the Mexicans ; and *Bernal Diaz* is quite explicit on the subject, in the following passage of the 207th chapter of his history of the continent of New Spain. "In some provinces they were circumcised, and they had flint knives with which they performed the ceremony." p. 334. Since no testimony can be more positive as to a matter of fact than that of Bernal Diaz, respecting the existence of this rite amongst the Indians, his means of information can alone be called in question ; but that point he has himself settled by premising to his account of these sacrifices, this remark—' The sacrifices which I have seen and known, I write down here from memory.' Of the history of Bernal Diaz, but one opinion has been formed, that its style is rude, and the narrative perfectly authentic. Dr. Robertson thus characterizes it—' It contains a prolix, minute, and confused narration of all Cortez' operations, in such a rude vulgar style as might be expected from an illiterate soldier. But as he relates transactions of which he was a witness, and in which he performed a considerable part, his account bears all the marks of authenticity, and is accompanied with such a pleasing naïvetè, with such interesting details, and with such amusing variety, and yet so pardonable in an old soldier, who had been, as he boasts, in 119 battles, as renders his book one of the most singular that is to be found in any language.' ' *The earliest Spanish writers*, who wrote on the affairs of America, such as Peter Martyr, (who scarcely would have ventured to have stated a deliberate falsehood to the Pope, and one which he, sooner than any other person, would have been capable of detecting,) and Gomara, who was chaplain to Cortez, and dedicated his History of the Conquest of Mexico to Don Martin Cortez, his son, and therefore had the best means of information ; and Bernal Diaz, and other Spanish writers also, who are acknowledged to be men of the greatest learning and research, such as were Garcia and Torquemeda, who had themselves visited America, have all declared that various Indian nations used circumcision. On the other hand, many European literati, and scholars who wrote in the *succeeding* age, who were not Spaniards, who had never[1] visited America, who were little conversant with Spanish authors, whose studies were chiefly confined to classical literature, and *whose ƒears* were excited by the progress of the Reformation, and by every thing calculated *to provoke ƒresh topics* of religious controversy, vehemently denied that such was the fact. They argued as if they thought it derogatory to the honour of God to make the admission ; for not being able to derive the American circumcision, like the Colchian, the Egyptian, and the Phœnician, from the

---

[1] " Some persons have written histories and published them *without having been in the places concerned*, or having been near them when the actions were done ; but those men put a few things together by *hearing*, and insolently abuse the world, and call *those writings* by the name of Histories."—Josephus, book i. p. 265, to Appion.

Jews, without conceding that the Indians might have borrowed other superstitions from them, and that they had colonized the western hemisphere,—their only resource was to attempt to throw discredit upon the testimony of the most respectable Spanish authors: since the other alternative of maintaining that the Devil had imitated, amongst the Indians, this venerable sign of the ancient covenant God had made with Abraham, might have appeared to them of dangerous adoption, and likely to entail inconvenient consequences.—There is an old remark, than which none has been more frequently perverted to sophistical purposes, merely from not considering the nature of the truths alluded to, and distinguishing great moral truths from historical truths, and time taken for an indefinite period, from time only amounting to a few centuries, which is, *" Tempus probat veritatem."* This, like the other *" Vox populi, vox Dei,"* is only true in part, and especially in religious matters, ought to be received with caution; for how is it possible that what was doubtful two hundred years ago, should be certain now.—Shakspeare somewhere observes that " uncertainties do crown themselves assured."—But still it is to be recollected that false religious creeds are, in the beginning, like despised weeds which are blown about, and inclined by every wind of doctrine; but that in time, they become trees of stately growth, under which nations repose, and the shade of which often casts a deadly influence around. Neither are the opinions of learned men, or of any particular age, any test of truth—since the erroneous opinions which the learned men of the sixteenth century, (emphatically called the enlightened age of the revival of letters) adopted with regard to contemporaneous historians, (for so the history of the state in which religion, civilization, and the arts, were found amongst the Indians, by the first

Spaniards who visited the continent of America, may be designated) afford a striking proof. If, however, the errors of past times cannot serve the useful purpose of beacons, to light on the way to truth those who follow, they will, at least forcibly admonish the too credulous, who are inclined to take every thing for granted, which they believe former ages to have believed ; to reflect upon the possibility of a former age having been itself deceived, and thus transmitting its delusions to posterity."—p. 334. note.

" It is surprising that Acosta, who has traced no less strong a resemblance between the ritual observance of the Jews and Mexicans, than Garcia has discovered in their moral code, and who even ventures to express himself as follows in the eleventh chapter of the fifth book of his history of the Indians—" *Sic quicquid dicant alii a Domino et Servatore nostro Jesu Christo, prope nihil uspiam in evangelio suo constitutum et ordinatum est, quod Sathanas variis modis æmulari et in superstitiones Gentiles convertere, non annisus sit : id quod ex dienceps dicendorum attentione clarius et manifestius elucebit,*" should still reject the rational conclusion of Las Casas that the Jews had colonized America."

" Was it, we may ask, in consequence of Acosta's having been so much *later* an historian than Las Casas ; and having visited America nearly fifty years later than that illustrious prelate, when the active exertions of the early missionaries and Spanish clergy, had *already rooted out* many of the primitive superstitions of the Indians, that he did not become sensible of what had so *forcibly struck Las Casas?* Or was it that he dared not avow an opinion, which would not have been tolerated in the age in which he lived, and was consequently compelled to advance an absurd hypothesis ? Or finally, had Las Casas access to any means of information of which Acosta was deprived, such as original Hebrew documents—a copy of the *Teo-moxtli* or Divine Book of the Toltecas: the history of Votan, or books in any other language which might have been discovered, among the Indians? for where all has been misrepresentation or concealment, proof cannot be said to exist of alphabetic writing having been wholly unknown in America, or that it might not have been a secret like the ιερα γραμματα, or sacred characters of the Egyptians, which were only known to the priests, who might have thought with that famous nation of antiquity, that exoteric doctrines were best calculated to keep them ignorant and superstitious."—p. 332.

" The time has perhaps arrived, when authentic monuments, affording matter upon which to found reasonable discussion, will enable men of information to decide upon the certainty of the prospect of the Jews having, in early ages, colonized America. The notion prevailed that conviction was probably felt in Europe, at the beginning of the sixteenth century that this was the case; but those who entertained these sentiments, although furnished with the necessary proofs, would have been compelled to *keep the secret locked up in their breasts*, lest they should have cast a scandal upon a received religious notion, *that the dispersion of the Jews was the fulfilment of prophecy*; since now, if it could have been shewn that the riches of Peru, or the throne of Mexico, or *political ascendancy* in any part of the New World, had become the lot of the dispersed[1] Hebrews, would

---

[1] " *The dispersed of Judah*" have only enjoyed for eighteen centuries, a *tolerated* existence amongst the hostile and adverse interests of the kingdoms of the world. The representatives of these kingdoms exercised the same dominion, as soon as " *the outcasts of Israel*" were discovered. But even admitting the summit of splendour to which the Mexican and Peruvian empires had attained in the later period of their history, especially under Montezuma and Huayna Capac; they never forgot that they were in that kind of adversity and disgrace which is incident on *banishment* under any circumstances, therefore the Scripture verity of their being in that state of exile, " a proverb and byeword of reproach," the receiver and *not the giver*, the ruled and *not the ruler*, is not in the least impugned by the discovery of the seclusion of the Lord's banished.

the prophecy seem to be accomplished respecting them, where it says that they should borrow and not lend, should be the tail and not the head. We cannot refrain from inserting in this place, a passage from the 42 page of the 5th volume of the present work, because the expression *outcasts*, (desechados) as applied by the Mexicans to themselves, is there so singularly introduced, and savours so strongly of the tone of complaint, in which the Hebrews, wherever residing, and however well off in their temporal concerns, have been accustomed to indulge ever since the fall of their empire. " Remember the words which I now address to thee, my son ; let them be a thorn in thy heart, and a cold blast to afflict thee, that thou mayst humble thyself, and betake thee to inward meditation. Consider, my son, that it has been thy lot to be born in a time of trouble and sorrow, and that God has sent thee into the world at a period of extreme destitution. Behold me, who am thy father: see what a life I and thy mother lead, and how we are accounted as nothing, and the memorial of us has passed away. *Although our ancestors were powerful and great,* have they bequeathed unto us their power and greatness? No truly, cast thine eyes upon *thy relations and kindred who are outcasts.*[1] Wherefore, although thou

---

[1] The Jews themselves, as has been elsewhere observed, have entertained a strong belief that America has been colonized by their race ; grounding their belief on what is said in certain chapters of the Old Testament, of the people of the Isles, to which Isles, a Hebrew appellative word, *signifying the west,* has been given, (evidently shewing that they could not have been Ceylon, or the Isles of the Indian Archipelago,) as also on many analogies in the laws, rites, customs, and ceremonies of the Indians; but more especially in the following passages of the 13th chapter of the 2nd book of Esdras, "And whereas thou sawest that he gathered another peaceable multitude unto him : those are the ten tribes which were carried away prisoners out of their own land, in the time of Osea the king, whom Salmanasar the king of Assyria led away captive, and he carried them over the waters, and so came they into another land. But they took this counsel among themselves, that they would leave the multitude of the heathen, and go forth into a further country, *where never mankind dwell,* that they might there keep their statutes which they never kept in their own land. And they entered into Euphrates by the narrow passages of the river. For the

thyself art noble and illustrious, and of famous *lineage;* it becomes thee to have ever present before thine eyes how thou oughtest to live."—p. 385.

The commentator on the Mexican Antiquities observes,—-" the 1st reason for concluding the Indian tribes to be of Hebrew descent, is in their belief in the symbolical purification of water : the inhabitants of Utican gave to water, with which they baptised their children, the title of the water of *regeneration.* The Indians of Utican invoked HIM, whom they believed to be the living and true God, of whom they made no graven image. The 2nd reason for believing that the religion of the Indians was Judaism, is that *they used circumcision.* 3rd. That *they expected a Messiah.* The 4th, that many words connected with the celebration of their religious rites, were *obviously of Hebrew* extraction. 5th. That Las Casas, the bishop of Chiapa, who had *the best means of verifying the* fact was of this opinion. 6th. That the Jews themselves, including some of the most eminent Rabbis, such as Menasse Ben Israel, and Montesinos, maintained it both by verbal statement and *in writing.* 7th. The dilemma in which most of the Spanish writers, such as Acosta and Torquemeda, have placed their readers, by leaving them *no alternative,* than to come to the decision, whether the Hebrews colonized America, and established their rites amongst the Indians ; or whether the Devil had counterfeited in the New World the rites and ceremonies which God gave to his chosen people. The 8th is the resemblance which *many* ceremonies and rites of the Indians bear to those of the Jews. The 9th is

Most High then shewed signs for them, and held still the flood, till they were passed over. For through that country there was a great way to go ; namely, of a year and a half: and same region is called Arsareth. Then dwelt they there until the latter time ; and now when they shall begin to come, the Highest shall stay the springs of the stream again, that they may go through."

the similitude which existed between the Indian and Hebrew *moral laws*. The 10th is the knowledge which the Mexican and Peruvian traditions supplied, that the Indians possessed the history *contained in the Pentateuch*. The 11th is the Mexican tradition of the *Teo-moxtli*, or Divine Book of the Toltics. 12th. Is the famous *migration from Azltan*, or (Asia). 13th. The traces of *Jewish history, traditions, laws, customs, manners*, which are found in the Mexican paintings. 14th. The frequency of *sacrifice* amongst the Indians, and the *religious consecration of the blood and fat* of the victims. 15th. The style of the *architecture* of their Temples. 16th. The *fringes* which the Mexicans wore fastened to their garments. 17th. A similarity of the manners and customs of the Indian tribes *far removed* from the central monarchies of Mexico and Peru, to those of the Jews, which writers who were not Spaniards, have noticed, such as Sir William Penn,[1] &c." pp. 115, 116.

---

[1] " Their eyes are black like the Jews—they reckon by moons—they offer the first-fruits—they have a feast of Tabernacles—their altar stands on *twelve* stones —their mourning lasts a year.—Their customs of women are like those of the Jews,—their language is concise, masculine, full of energy, resembling the Hebrew ; one word serves for three, and the rest is supplied by the understanding of the hearers. Lastly, they *were to go into a country which was neither planted nor sown ;* and he that imposed that condition upon them, was well able to level their passage thither, for we may go from the Eastern extremity of it, to the West of America.—Penn's Letter on the present state of the lands in America," p. 156.

MIGRATION.

'AMERICA had been discovered nearly two hundred years before reflecting minds had begun to inquire into the peculiarities of its first inhabitants, and as they, instead of collecting evidence from corresponding facts, gave at once their own speculations as the end of inquiry, we have only a mass of contradictory theories. To their amazement they discovered no negroes, although every temperature of other parts of the globe are to be found in America, and although the powerful operation of heat produces a striking variety in the human race. The colour of the natives of the Torrid Zone in America is slightly darker than that of the people of the more temperate parts of the continent. Accurate observers who have viewed the Aborigines in very different climates, and provinces far removed from each other, have been struck with the amazing similarity of their figure and aspect. Pedro de Cicca de Leon, who had an extensive acquaintance with the tribes, observes, 'The people, men and women, although they are such a vast multitude of tribes or nations, in such diverse climates, appear nevertheless *like the children of one family.'*

The Abbe Clavegero says of the (Aztecs or) Mexicans— 'They were the last people who settled in Anahuic—they formerly dwelt in *Aztlan,* a country north of the gulph of California; judging by the rout of their emigration, according to Boturini, *a province of Asia.*[1]

Montezuma evidently refers to the remote tradition of their landing when he informed Cortez that they had arrived on the continent with a mighty lord. 'We have,' said he, 'ruled these tribes only as *viceroys* of *Quetzalcoatl* our God and lawful Sovereign.'

The Abbe Clavegero observes—'Their ancestors came into Anahuic from the countries of the north and north west.' 'This tradition is *confirmed by the many ancient edifices built by these people in their migration.*' Torquemeda and Betancourt mention having seen these most ancient edifices.'

Boturini says " that in the ancient paintings of the Toltics were represented the *migration of their ancestors through Asia, and the northern countries of America, until they settled in the country of Tullan,* and even endeavours in his General history to *ascertain the rout they pursued in their journey.*"[1] " The countries in which the ancestors of those nations established themselves being where the most westerly coast of America approaches the most easterly part of Asia,[2] it is probable that they passed either in canoes or on ice, if the continents were then not united by land. *The traces which these nations have left lead us to that very strait.* This latter is the opinion of Acosta, Grotius, Buffon, and others. We have examples of the same kind of revolutions in the past century. Sicily was united to the continent of Naples as Eubia, now to the Black Sea, and to

---

[1] In the ancient paintings of this migration, Torquemeda says, " *There is an arm of the sea represented* which I believe to represent *the deluge! !* Accordingly we find its fac simile in the migration, in the work of Clavegero, bearing the title of " *The Deluge.*"

[2] Clavegero says, the conclusion (viz. that the ancestors passed from the most eastern parts of Asia to the most westerly of America) is founded on the constant and general tradition of those tribes, &c.

Bœotia. Diodorus, Strabo, and other ancient writers say the same thing of Spain and Africa, and affirm that by a violent irruption of the ocean upon the land between the mountains Abyla and Calpe, that communication was broken and the Mediterranean Sea was formed. The people of Ceylon had such a tradition that an irruption of the sea separated their island from the peninsula of India.'

' It is certain,' says the Count de Buffon,[1] ' that in Ceylon the earth has lost forty leagues which the sea has taken from it.' Pliny, Seneca, Diodorus, and Strabo, report innumerable instances of similar revolutions, which are related in the theory of the earth of the Count de Buffon. We suppose that the sinking of the land at Kamschatka has been occasioned by those great and extraordinary earthquakes mentioned in the records of the Americans *which formed an era almost as remarkable as that of the deluge.* Clavegero continues ' the Bishop of Mexico[2] issued an edict to commit all records of their ancient history to the flames. The successors of the first monks regretted this fanatical zeal, as nothing remained of the history of the Empire but tradition, and some fragments of their paintings which had escaped the barbarous research of Zumeraga. There, in a square of the market, a mass like a little mountain was reduced to ashes, to the inexpressible affliction of the Indians. From this time forward, they who possessed any were so jealous, that it was impossible for the Spaniards to make them part with one of them.' vol. i. p. 407.

' Cav. Boturini upon the faith of the ancient history of the Toltics says, ' that observing in their own country, *Hue-*

---

[1] Buffon accounts for the introduction of the various animals into the new continent in the same manner. For opinions of various writers, see Appendix.

[2] Baron Humboldt observes " it is remarkable enough, that a Franciscan monk, Torquemeda, should have branded as a barbarian, Bishop Zumeraga, too notorious for the destruction of the History of the Aztecs.'

huetlapallan,[1] how the solar year exceeded the civil one,
by which they reckoned about six hours, they regulated it
by interposing the intercalary day once in the four years;
which they did more than one hundred years before the
Christian era.' He says that ' in the year 660 under the
reign of *Ixlalalcuechahuatli*, in Tula, a celebrated astronomer, called *Huematzin*, assembled by the king's consent,
all the wise men of the nation; and with them painted that
celebrated book called TEo*moxtli*, or " *Divine Book*," in
which were represented in very plain figures, the origin of
the Indians, their dispersion after the confusion of tongues,
their subsequent *journeying in Asia*, their first settlements
upon the Continent of America, the founding of the kingdom of Tula, and their progress till that time.

Robertson in his History observes, " The possibility of a
communication between the two continents in this quarter
rests no longer upon mere conjecture, but is established by
undoubted evidence. The distance between the Marion or
Ladrone islands and the nearest land in Asia is greater than
that between the part of America, which the Russians discovered, and the coast of Kamschatka, and yet the inhabitants
of these islands are manifestly of Asiatic extract. If notwithstanding their remote situation we admit that the Marion
islands were peopled from the continent, distance alone is no
reason why we should hesitate in admitting that the Aborigines of America may derive their original from the same
source. It is probable that navigators may in steering
further to the north, find that the continents are still nearer.
According to the information of the barbarous people who
inhabit the country about the north east promontary of Asia,
there lies off the coast a small island to which they can sail

---

[1] The repetition of *Hue* is to signify the *ancient* place, Hue-Tlapallan having
been named after it in the New Continent.

in less than a day, and from that they can descry a large
continent covered with forests, and possessed by a people
whose language they did not understand. By them they are
supplied with the skins of martins," &c. " It is remarkable
that in every peculiarity, whether in their persons or dispo-
sitions, which characterize the Aborigines, they have some
resemblance to the inhabitants scattered over the north of
Asia, but almost none to the nations settled in the extremities of Europe. We may therefore refer them to the
former origin, and conclude that their Asiatic progenitors
having settled in those parts of America where the Russians
have discovered the proximity of the two continents, spread
gradually over its various regions. *The Mexicans point out
their various stations as they advanced from the interior
provinces, and it is precisely the same rout which they must
have taken if they had been emigrants from Asia.*"

Doctor Williams in his history of Vermont remarks,
" These straits are but eighteen miles wide, and they
are full of *islands,* the Indian tradition says, ' *the sea
is eating them up.'*

Monsieur de Quignes, an ancient writer, in one of his
memoirs, speaking of discoveries before the time of
Columbus, says, " These researches, which of themselves
give us great insight into the origin of the Aborigi-
nals, lead to the determination of the rout of the colony
sent to the continent." He thinks *the greater part of
them passed hither by the eastern extremities of Asia,
where the two continents are separated by a narrow strait
easy to cross.* He reports instances of women, who from
Canada and Florida have travelled into Tartary without
seeing the ocean. In this case they must have passed the
straits on the " ice."

" As for the civilized states of the two Americas," writes

(the author of a critical work [1] in the Hebrew language) the period of their discovery does not exceed 300 years; and with respect to their uncultivated populations, as they could not have sprung from the ground like mushrooms, they must infallibly have emigrated one way or other, &c. or they must have emerged from Asia, by way of *Behring's Straits* on the north-east of that continent; and the period of their migration, accordingly was unknown until recently."

He adds, "I would here recommend to notice a book written by Ethan Smith, pastor of a church in Poultney in the United States of America, entitled a 'View of the Hebrews,' and comprehending accounts of various English, French, Spanish, and Portuguese tourists who diligently inquired into the nature of, and all the particulars relative to the natives of that hemisphere. They all coincide in their account relative to the primitive settlers of America (who were ignorantly styled American savages,) that they were all of one stock, namely of " the *ten tribes* who were carried away by the Assyrian kings to Halah and Habbor, the river Gozen or Ganges, and the cities of Media," who in a short time made their way towards the east of Asia, *crossed the ice at Behring's Straits,* north-east of Asia; and in process of time multiplied and spread themselves all over America, from north to south, &c."—p. 9.

The author of 'Historical Researches in Mexico, &c.' finds in the Indian tribes an extraordinary resemblance to the Mogul and Tartar nations; [2] and this is easily accounted for, if, as the Mexicans affirm *one tribe remained in these countries.*

---

[1] A Theological and Critical Treatise, &c. on the Primogeniture and Integrity of the Holy Language. By SOLOMON BENNET.

[2] Historical Researches. By JOHN RANKING.

Constantine Beltrami, a literary traveller and discoverer, in a series of letters addressed to the Countess
Compagnoni, in Italy, observes, " The facility of passing
to this country from the *Asiatic* territories, by the narrow
straits of Behring, while immense oceans roll between it and
the other quarters of the globe ; all these circumstances, it
must be allowed, speak for their *Asiatic* origin, and a new
discovery of the highest interest must be considered as
yielding evidence almost amounting to conviction. The
skeletons of Mammoths which have been found in America,
have been ascertained exactly to resemble those found in
Siberia and the eastern parts of Asia. It is universally
admitted that these Mammoths are of Asiatic origin. You
perceive, therefore, that *this very interesting discovery in
the animal kingdom has also been eminently valuable by
throwing light on the origin of the tribes of America.'*—
' Discovery of the source of the Mississippi.'

Doctor Boudinot states, that another " missionary passing
on his return from China, by the way of Nantz, related the
like story of a woman whom he had seen from Florida, in
America ; she informed him that she had been taken by
certain Indians, and given to those of a distant country ;
had travelled regions exceedingly cold, and at length found
herself in Tartary ; had there married a Tartar, who had
passed with the conquerors into China, and there settled."—
See Star in the West.

In connexion with the fact that the Emperor of Russia
holds at this day *the sources of the Euphrates*, and that
that *arm of the sea*, which the tribes had crossed on their
migration, is bordered by his empire ; the following passage
of scripture history—the last notice which we have of the
ten tribes after their expatriation, is curiously illustrative.
" They took counsel among themselves that they would

leave the multitude of the nations and *go forth into a further country, where never mankind dwelt : that they might there keep their statutes*, which they never kept in their own land. And they entered into *Euphrates by the narrow passages of the river ;* and the " Most High " then *shewed signs for them* and *held still* the flood till they were passed over ; for through that country there was a great way to go, namely of a year and a half, &c." 2 Esdras xiii. 41, 42.

The Mexican tradition is in perfect accord with the preceding testimony—they affirm that they travelled through *Aztlan*, or Asia, and had *an hundred and four domiciles during their migration*.

Describing an extraordinary medallion, Du Paix says, " If I may venture to express an opinion, it would be that the principal side of this medal records *the migration of a colony*, which, after encountering many difficulties, at last arrives at the land of its destination : whilst the reverse signifies the flourishing and prosperous state which the same colony should afterwards attain." He then describes " a historical device, composed of a mysterious hieroglyphic group, of which the principal figure is that of a man kneeling in the attitude of a suppliant. The beard denotes the sex

[1] Of the discoveries which they made of the art of moulding in stucco, he says, " the subject at which we now arrive is so mysterious, that its elucidation would require the art of a diviner."

" Surrounded as I am with all that amazes and perplexes me, I shall begin by describing the large *historical alto-relievos* which still exist in perfect preservation, although the greater part of those that once ornamented and illustrated these temples, have mouldered beneath the hand of time. The stucco employed in the composition of them, was admirable in quality. I term it natural stucco, for it does not appear to contain either sand, powdered marble, or any sort of adulteration ; it is hard in the extreme, besides being beautifully white. With this substance all the relievos which enriched the walls of these buildings, and splendid monuments were executed." p. 478-9. " I feel persuaded," he adds, " that these *alto-relievos were historical representations*. Each figure is in the act of presenting a *Branch as well as a child at the Temple*. Considerable variety is displayed in their dress. It would appear that this nation had two methods of expressing its ideas, one by *letters and alphabetical signs*, the other by *obscure and mysterious symbols*." Monuments of New Spain, in Antiq. Mex. Vol. vi. p. 481.

of the figure. Placed between the ferocious and menacing heads of two monsters, nearly resembling the Egyptian crocodile, he seems not without imminent peril to have gained admission to this romantic, luxuriant, and fruitful portion of the globe."

"The reverse of this medallion represents the same mountainous, yet luxuriant scenery, but the effigy of a lofty Tree in the centre, covered with fruit and spreading foliage, is that which chiefly attracts attention, &c. We perceive at the root of the tree, a scaly serpent entwining itself round the trunk. The Eagle perched on the summit of an adjoining mountain." Monuments of New Spain, in Antiq. Mex. p. 470.

' Don Antonio del Rio, was commissioned by Charles the Third, to examine and take drawings from the antiquities, as well of sculpture as of painting among the Mexicans. This intelligent artist discovered two figures in painting, representing *Votan with the*[1] *emigrants on both continents as an historical event, the memory of which he was desirous of transmitting to future ages.*" By comparing *Votan's*[1] narrative with the duplicate effigies of him which are found sculptured on stones in one of the temples of *the sacred city*, we shall have a very conclusive proof of its truth, and this will be corroborated by so many others, that we shall be forced to acknowledge the history of the Aborigines excels those of the Greeks and Romans, and the most celebrated nations of the world, and is *even worthy of being compared with the Hebrews themselves.*' Cabrara in Clavegero.—Vol. i. p. 112.

' It is to be regretted, that the place is unknown where these precious documents of history were deposited ; but still more it is to be lamented, that the great treasure should have

---

[1] *Votan* signifies in the Chiapanese dialect, the HEART *of the people ;* and is the same individual as the Mexican *Quetzalcoatl.*

been destroyed. This treasure,[1] according to Indian tradition, was placed by Votan himself as a proof of his origin,
and as a memorial for future ages in the *Casa lobrego*
" *house of secrecy,*" that he had built in a breath, (a metapho-
rical term to imply the very short space of time employed in
its construction.) He committed this deposit to the care of a
distinguished female, and a certain number of Indians
appointed annually for the purpose of its safe custody. His
mandate was scrupulously observed for many ages by the
people of *Tacoaloga*, in the province of *Socanusco*, where it
was guarded with extraordinary care ; until being discovered
by the prelate before mentioned, he obtained and destroyed
it.' They were publicly burnt in the year 1691.

" It is possible that *Votan's* History was the tract alluded
to by Nunez de la Vega, or another similar to it, may be
the one which is now in the possession of Don Ramon de
Ordoney y Aguir, a native of Cuidad Rial. He is a man
of extraordinary genius, and engaged in composing a work,
the title of which I have seen, being as follows, *Historia
del Cielo y de la Tierra*, which will not only embrace the
original population of America, *but trace its progress from
Chaldea*, &c. its *mystical and moral Theology, its mythology, and most important events.* His literary acquirements,
his application, and study of the subject for more than thirty
years, and his skill in the Tzendal language, is an evident
proof of its having been copied from the original in hieroglyphics, immediately after the conquest."

---

[1] "This treasure " (writes Zumerago) " consisted of some large earthern
vasses of one piece, and closèd with covers of the same material, in which
were represented in *basso relievo* the figures of the Indian *pagans* whose names[*]
are in the calendar, with some *precious stones*, and other superstitious figures;
these were publicly burnt in the square." The same *Votan* makes mention
of having visited that LAND where the HOUSE of GOD was.' See Clavegero.

---

[*] " The Chiapanese placed in their calendar twenty of their most illustrious ancestors to
signify the months of their *lunisolar* year; these were *Mox, Igh*, VOTAN, *Ghanan, Abagh,
Tox, Moxic ;* LAMBAT, *Molu, Elah, Batz, Enoch,* BEN, *Hix, Tziquin, Chabin, Chix,* CHINAX,
Cabegh, Aghnal."

" At the top of the leaf, containing the History of Votan, the two Continents are painted in different colours, and two small squares placed parallel to each other in angles: the one (representing Europe, Asia, and Africa,) is marked with two large *SS* upon the upper arms of two bars, drawn from the opposite angles of each square, forming the points of union in the centre."

"That which indicates America, has two 𝕊 placed horizontally on bars, but I am not certain whether on the upper or lower,—I believe however upon the latter. When speaking of places, he had visited on *the old continent :* he marks them on the margin of each chapter with an *upright* S, and those of America with a *horizontal* ꙅ. Between these squares stands the title of his history: " Proof that I *am Coatl*,[1] because HE is *Chivim*." He states that " he had conducted seven families from VALUM VOTAN to this continent, and assigned lands to them ; that he is the third of the VOTANS ; that having determined to journey until he arrived at the ROOT OF HEAVEN, in order to discover his kindred the Coatlans, and make himself known to them ; he

---

[1] It is proper to state, that the Mexican *Coatl*, has been substituted for *Culebra*, the Spanish term for serpent ; since it seems equally incongruous when put into the mouth of *Votan*, as into an *English* translation of his record.

The ancients were as much accustomed to consider the *serpent* as the symbol of that *subtlety* which is an attribute of *wisdom*, (as a moral essence) as moderns are in the habit of restricting the term to that deterioration of intellect, which evinces its evil origin in whatever is false, deceptive, cunning ; these being only the means for the attainment of that end, which the intense selfishness of those whom it characterises have constantly in view. Dr. Cabrara, with perfect composure, appropriates to *Rome*, the title " ROOT OF HEAVEN," which *Votan* gives to that Land where he had visited, *the* " *House of God.*" Once assuming that *Rome* is the supplanter of Jerusalem, and that the mother church of Christendom is the supplanter of " THE EARTH'S ONE SANCTUARY," it is easy for the advocates of things *as they are*, to make all the other camels go through the same needle's eye.

The commentator on the Antiq. Mex. observes: " Since wise as a serpent was a Hebrew proverb, the Jews might in some critical posture of their affairs, such as would have been their discovery of the West Indian Islands, or Continent of America, when the exercise of prudence and circumspection would have appeared necessary to keep the secret, have assumed this epithet as a kind of motto for caution." Vol. vi. p. 52.

made four journeys to *Chivim*, and when he arrived, that *he went to Rome*, and saw the Great HOUSE OF GOD, &c.; that he went by the road which his brethren the Coatlans had penetrated, that he *marked* it, and that he passed by the houses of the thirteen *Coatlans*. He relates that in returning from one of his voyages, he found seven other families of the *Tzequil* nation who had joined the first inhabitants, and recognized in them the same origin as his own,—that is, of the Coatlans." So far Doctor Cabrara, from whose treatise, entitled " *Teatro Critico Americanos*," this paragraph has been taken." Ibid.

EXPLANATION OF THE HIEROGLYPHIC DRAWING OF GUMELLI CARERRI.

The bird[1] placed on the hieroglyphic of *atl* (water) denotes *Aztlan* (Asia.) The pyramidal mountain with steps is a TEO-*calli*, (house of GOD.) I am astonished[2] at finding

[1] Huitziton was a person of great authority among the Aztecs, (in Asia) who for some reason, not remembered, persuaded his countrymen to change their country. Whilst he was thus meditating, a bird was heard singing on a bush, *ti hui, ti hui,* (which is in their language "*let us go.*") "Do you hear that," said Zacpaltzin, " it is the warning voice of the secret deity, to leave this Continent and to find another." These influential persons drew the body of their people, viz. six other tribes, over to their party; this relates to the Aztecs, who arrived with six other tribes by land."—See Clavegero.

[2] 'M. D'Humboldt,' writes the commentator on the Antiq. Mex. ' who has given with his interesting observations, a plate of Gumelli Carerri, the subject of which is the famous Mexican Migration, observes " that a *palm-tree grows near the altar*, and that this tree does *not* grow in northern climates, from which the Mexicans have been generally supposed to have originated, but in southern climes, *such* as Egypt, and Palestine, and Judea, in which latter country they were famous for stately beauty. On the supposition of the Colonies having proceeded from these northern countries to America, the following names of places on the New Continent, which the Mexicans are said to have called after the names of places in the country which their ancestors had formerly inhabited, might seem to have correspondence with that of some city or province in Asia. *Tulan Chorula (Tlapalan,* country of the Red Sea.) *Chicomoztoc,* (the seven caves.) *Colhuacan,* TEO-*colhuacan,* (hill of God) or the hill upon which the temple of Churula was founded. It may be here observed that the particle TEO in the Mexican language, prefixed to names of persons, places, and nations, and meaning Divine, is prefixed to Hebrew words."—Vol. vi. p. 126.'

' I durst not speak of Gumelli Carerri,' says the celebrated author of the History of America, ' because it seems to be a received opinion that the traveller was never out of Italy, and that his famous *Giro del Mondo* is an account of a fictitious voyage.' ' It is true,' observes the Commentator on the Mex. Antiq. ' that Robertson does not seem to adopt the opinion he advances, for he judiciously adds, ' that this imputation of fraud does not appear to him founded on any good evidence.' ' I can,' says Humboldt, ' affirm it to be no less certain that Gumelli was in Mexico, &c. than that Pallas has been in the Crimea, and Mr. Salt in Abyssinia.'

' Gumelli's descriptions have that local tint which is the principal charm of narratives of travels. A respectable author, the Abbe Clavegero, who traversed

a *palm-tree* near the TEO-*calli*. This plant certainly does
not indicate a northern region, nevertheless it is almost
certain that we must look for the first country of the
Mexican nations, Aztlan *Hue-hue-Tlapallan* and *Amequima-*
can at least forty-two degrees of latitude. The fifteen
chiefs have the simple hieroglyphics of their names above
their heads. From the TEO-*calli* erected in Aztlan to
Chapaltepec, the figures placed along the road, indicate the
places where the Aztecs made some abode and the towns
they built, *Zocholco* and *Oztotlan*, humiliation, and the place
of tents. *Mizquihuala*, denoted the mimosa, (wild vine) bearing fruit, placed near the TEO-*calli*. *Teotzapotlan*, place
of holy fruits. *Ilhuicatepec Papantla*, herb with broad
leaves. *Tzompango*, place of human bones. *Apazo*, vessel of
clay. *Atlicalaquian*, a crevice, in which a rivulet disappears.
Quachtitlan, a thicket, inhabited by the eagle. *Atzcapozalio*,
an ant's nest. *Chalco*, place of precious stones. *Pantitlan*,
place of spinning. *Tolpellic*, mat of rushes. *Quachtepec*,
the eagle's mountain. *Tetepanco*, a wall, composed of small
stones. *Chicomoztoc*, the seven tents or grottos. *Huitz-*
quilocan, place of thistles. *Xaltepozanhcan*, places from
which sand is extracted. *Cozcaquivuco*, name of a vulture.

Mexico, almost half a century before me, had already undertaken the defence of
the *Giro del Mondo*,"—The same tone of veracity, (and we must insist on this
point,) does not appear in *the notions* which the author professes to have borrowed from the recitals of his friends, and if we compare all that is symbolical
and chronological in the paintings of the Migration with the hieroglyphic contained in the MS. of Rome and Veletri, &c., the collection of Mendoza and of
Gama, no one certainly would give credit to the hypothesis that the drawing
of Gumelli is the fiction of some Spanish monk, *who has attempted to prove by*
apocryphal documents, that the traditions of the Hebrews are found amongst the
indigenous natives of America. All that we know of the history, the worship,
the astronomy, and the *Cosmogonical fables* of the Mexicans, forms *a system, the*
parts of which are closely connected with each other.'—Humboldt's Researches,
vol. ii. p. 61.

It appears that the notions which are here referred to, are the general belief
of the early writers, that the Aborigines were of Hebrew race. The Baron
does not admit that conclusion, although his literary and antiquarian researches
in America do their part in constituting that manifold mass of evidence the
" *parts of which* " he has well observed, " *are closely connected* " as a whole.

Qechcatitlan, place of mirrors. *Axoxochuitl,* flower of the ant. *Zepetlapan,* place were is found the feldspar. *Apan,* place of waters. Teo-*zomoco,* place of the divine animal. *Choltepec,* mountain of the locusts. *Coxcox,* king of Acolhuan. *Mixuahan,* place of child-birth, the city of *Temazcatitlan,* or *Tonacatitlan,* on which reposed the Eagle which had been pointed out by the *oracle* to mark the place where the Aztecs were to build the city and finish their journeyings." [1]—Antiq. Mex. vol. vi.

" Gumelli asserts that the bundles of rushes tied represent periods of one hundred and four years. [2] We first distinguish the *ten* chiefs of the colony that founded the empire, &c. They meet with the objects which form the arena of the City of Mexico, near the stone surmounted by an Indian *fig-tree,* on which is an Eagle. Ibid. p. 178. Humboldt adds, *this genealogy of nations reminds us of the ethneogra-phical table of Moses,* and it is so much the more remarkable as the Toltics and Aztecs, among whom this tradition

---

[1] ' Almost all the names and places of the Mexican Empire,' observes Clave-gero, ' are compounds, and signify the situation and properties of the places with whatever memorable circumstances they are associated.'
  Of the many historical paintings of which this celebrated migration made the subject, none appears to have escaped the barbarous zeal of Zumerago, except one at Rome, another at Veletri, and a third which originally formed part of the museum of Boturini, and that of Gumelli. Besides the concentration of evidence which has been produced on this part of the subject, the Abbe Clavegero, enu-merating the native and Spanish historians, thus makes mention of two native writers. " Christoval del Castillo, a Mexican Mestee. *He wrote a History of the Journeyings of the Aztecs, or Mexicans, to the country of Anahuic,* which MS. was preserved in the library of the Convent of Jesuits at *Tepozotlan.* Thus also he writes of Siguenza, who, " having a collection of ancient paintings and manu-scripts, applied himself with assiduity to illustrate the antiquity of the kingdom ; besides many mathematical, critical, historical and poetical works composed by him, he wrote in Spanish the Mexican Cyclography, a work of great labour, also the History of the *Chechemecan Empire, in which he explains what he found in Mexican manuscripts and paintings concerning the first colonies which passed from Asia to America,* and the events of the most ancient nations established in Anahuic, &c.'
  [2] The Americans of Chili have three hundred and sixty days, twelve months, and days of twelve hours ; it is possible that the Aztecs may have derived this division of time from eastern Asia, vol. ii. p. 245.

is found *considered themselves as belonging to a privileged race very different from that of the Otomites and Olenecks,"* ibid. p. 248.

"Torquemeda's account is *singularly confirmed by an original Mexican painting which once formed a portion of the historical museum of Boturini, &c.* ; this painting consists of twenty-three pages folded in the usual manner of the Mexican paintings. The first page contains a picture of AZTLAN, and *the passage of the Mexicans across an arm of the sea,* and likewise their arrival at *Huey-Colhuacan* in the first year of one of their lesser cycles : as also the representation of their god *Huitzilopochtli* speaking to them *through the mouth of the bird.* If more detailed paintings of this migration had been saved from the overwhelming[1] destruction in which the annals of the New World were involved (for in Tezcuco alone, according to Clavegero, Zumerago, first Bishop of Mexico, caused a little mountain of paintings to be collected in the square of the market-place and burnt) we should have been acquainted with the history of this pretended migration in its minutest circumstances, since," adds the commentator, " the national vanity of the Mexicans must have been highly flattered at believing themselves to be the chosen people of God," &c.

" It is sufficient in this place," observes the commentator on the Mex. Antiq. in order more fully to corroborate

---

[1] Zumerago seems to have reasoned in the same style as a Mahomedan bigot of old, who when Philoponus wrote entreating the Caliph to preserve the historieal manuscripts of the famous library of Alexandria, returned this answer,— ' If the books agree in all points with the *Alcoran,* this last would be perfect without them, and *consequently they would be superfluous :* but if they contain any thing *repugnant* to the doctrines and tenets of *that* book, they ought to be *destroyed as being* pernicious.'

'The books were accordingly dispersed through the city to heat the baths, of which there were 4000, but the number of books was so immense, that they were not entirely consumed in less than six months.' "Thus," says Astle, "perished by fanatical madness the *inestimable Alexandrian library,*" &c.— " Origin and Progress of Writing." See Preface.

the opinion of the *interpreter* of the Vatican Manuscript
Codex, to notice some few analogies which Garcia has pointed
out, to which we shall add some others mentioned by other
writers. And first, with respect to the *famous migration*
of the Mexicans from *Atzlan* to the country of *Anahuac*,
which, he says, was like the journeying of the children
of Israel from Egypt, there were not wanting those who
affirmed that the Indians feigned the one when they heard
of the other. For they say the Mexican nation which was
that which arrived from the seventh cave of lineage, departed
from the province of *Aztlan Teo-colhuacan*, by command
of their idol, named *Vitziliputzli*, (or rather of the devil,
who was in the idol whom they adored as God.) He therefore commanded them to *leave their country*, promising that
he would make them princes and lords of the provinces
which the other six nations whose departure had preceded
theirs, had peopled ; that he would give them a very abundant land, with gold, silver, precious stones, feathers, &c.
They accordingly set out, carrying their idol with them in
an ark made of rushes, which was borne by four priests,
with whom he communicated privately : informing them of
the events of the journey, advising them of what was to
happen, giving them laws, and teaching them rites, ceremonies, &c. causing the heaven to *rain bread, and drawing
from the rock water to quench their thirst*, with other
marvels resembling those which God wrought in favour of
the children of Israel. They never proceeded a step without the approbation and command of their idol, as to when
they should journey on, and where they should halt ; and
what he told them they punctually obeyed. The first thing
that they did wheresoever they stopped, was to procure a
habitation for their false god. And they always placed
him in the middle of a *tabernacle* which they pitched, the

ark being always placed upon an *altar.* This having been done, they sowed the ground with corn and other leguminous plants in use amongst them : but so implicitly did they obey their god, that if it seemed good to him that they should gather it, they gathered it; if not, on his commanding them to raise their camp they left all behind, wheresoever they had settled, pretending that thus the whole land would remain peopled by their nation. Who will not own that this departure and migration of the Mexicans resembles the departure and pilgrimage of the children of Israel from Egypt, since these, like those, were admonished to go forth, and to seek a land of promise, and both the one and the other took with them their God as their guide, and consulted him in an *ark*, and built him a *tabernacle*, and accordingly he advised them, and gave them *laws* and ceremonies, and they each in the same manner spent many years before they arrived at the promised land."—*Origen los Indios*, lib. iii. cap. iii. sec. 5.

" Acosta gives a similar account of the *migration* and pilgrimage of the ancestors of the Mexicans. Torquemeda gives a more detailed account in his Indian Monarchy, ending thus, ' although they were all of the same race and lineage, still they did not all compose a single family, but were divided into four tribes: the first was called the *Mexican;* the second the *Tlachochealas;* the third the *Chalemacas;* the fourth the *Calpilcas;* others say these tribes were *nine*, namely, the *Chaliese, Matlanquicas, Zepanacas, Malinese, Xochmilcas, Cuitlahuas, Chichunnas, Mizquis*, and *Mexican.*' The *Azticas*, therefore, quitted their country under the guidance of *Zacpaltzin* and *Huitzon*, in the first of the first cycle; for they commenced the computation of their years from that period; and proceeded some stages on their journey, in which they employed the space of a year, at the end of which they arrived at a place called *Hueycolhuacan*, where they remained three years. In this place (they say) the *devil* appeared to them in the form of an idol, declaring to them that it was *he who brought them out of the land of Aztlan*, and that He should accompany them, being their God, to favour them in every thing, and that they should know that his name was *Huitzilo-pochtli*,[1] who is he whom the Greeks named Mars, the god of battle. He desired them to make him a seat in which they might carry him, which they formed out of rushes, and ordered that four should be chosen to be his attendants : for which office *Quachuatl*, *Apennatl*, *Zeycahohuatl*, and *Chuniahunan* were named, and the supreme chiefs who directed the troops were *Huitziton* and *Zacpaltzin*, who were the heads of these families. All these arrangements afforded great satisfaction to the *Azticas*, who perceived that now they should not pursue their journey blindfold, but should carry with them their god, who would guide them, whose servants they were thus named, TEO-*lamacotzin*, and the seat on which he sate TEO*zpalli*, and the act of carrying him on their shoulders TEO*mama*. This being the beginning of the *Devil's* proceedings among this people, they marched from that place to another, where there was a large and thick tree where he caused them to stop, at the trunk of which they made a small altar, upon which they placed the idol, for so the *Devil* commanded, and they sat down under its shade to eat, but whilst eating, a loud sound proceeded from the tree, and it rent in the middle. The *Azticas*, terrified at this sudden accident, considered it a bad omen, and surrendering themselves up to affliction termi-nated the repast. The chiefs of the families, doubtful as to

---

[1] The great and terrible God.

the event, consulted their god, who taking aside those whom
they now named Mexicans, said to them, Dismiss the eight
families, and tell them that they may proceed on their
journey, for that you are to remain here and proceed no
further at present. The Mexicans did so; and although they
felt regret at forsaking the others, inasmuch as they were all
brothers and friends, and at rejecting their entreaties, praying that they might all proceed together, they left them and
prosecuted their journey. The one party being now separated from the other; the Mexicans, with whom the idol
god, *Huitzilopochtli*, had remained, went to him and asked
what he intended to do with them. On this the *Devil* replied, You are now apart and separated from the rest, and
accordingly I desire that as my chosen people, you should
no longer call yourselves *Azticas*, but *Mexicans*. And at
the same time that he changed their name, he put as a sign
on their foreheads, &c. He likewise presented them with a
bow and arrows, and a *chillali*, which is a net, into which
they put *Tecomatas* and *Zicaras*, telling them that these
were the instruments which should prevail among them,—
(which, adds the commentator, was the case, for a *bow* and
arrows are emblematical of wars.)"

" And hence it remains proved that the Mexicans and all
the other nations and families who came to people New Spain,
do not derive their origin from these seven caves, since we
have seen that it was merely a place in which they dwelt in
huts for the space of nine years. *Many traces exist in all
these countries toward the north, of this migration, of which
I have seen edifices and ruins of ancient habitations, the
greatest and most superb that can be imagined.*'—p. 242.

" As the authority of Herrera, Royal Historiographer
of the Indians, will have weight with those who consider
that his office must have given him access to a variety of

curious documents relative to Aztlan, it may be proper to add what he says in the tenth and eleventh chapters of the second volume of his third Decade of *the same migration.*" " Never did the *Devil* hold such familiar converse with men as He, *(Vitziliputzli,)* and accordingly he thought proper in *all* things to copy the departure from Egypt, and the pilgrimage performed by the children of Israel. The name of the chief who conducted the people was Meçi, from whence the proper name of *Mexican* is derived." "The account of the Mexican migration by Herrera corresponds with the former in all the essential circumstances. It is much to be regretted that an important chapter in Torquemeda's Indian Monarchy, which would have thrown much light on this subject, should never have been allowed to be printed. This chapter, forming the first of the second book of the Indian Monarchy, the place of which is supplied by the second chapter was inscribed, ' *De como el Demonis* &c.' ' How it has been the wish of the *Devil* to substitute himself in the place of GOD by taking a chosen people which he constituted in the Mexicans.' The editor of the second edition calls this chapter ' the foundation and key-stone to the work,' and says in his preface that he extremely regretted being obliged to omit it, but that he did not think it *expedient to request license to publish it.* But he afterwards adds that his regret has diminished on finding the same conception delineated with great brevity and clearness by the learned Garcia, and he cites the authority of so learned a man, not only to supply the deficient chapter, but that his work may be more easily understood which treats of this subject as a matter of discussion, and that no one may judge that to be neglect which was *obedience.*"—Antiq. Mex. Vol. vi. p. 242.

" Miracles performed by God on their quitting Aztlan;

Himself forsaking heaven to be present in their camp as their
legislator and the guide of their way, and assuming the titles
of YAO-TEO*tle Tetzante*TEO*tl,* (the God of war, the terrible God,) to strike fear and dismay into the breasts of their
enemies, it is probable that they would have made the
subject of their finest paintings. It cannot be doubted
from what Boturini says of the Mexicans singing in the
Court of their Temple the great exploits of *Huitzilopoctli,*
that they like the Jews *recorded in hymns the miraculous
events of their own History ; and that they represented likewise in painting the famous migration from Atzlan, and the
signs and wonders wrought in their favour by their tutelary
Deity,* is asserted by Torquemeda in the following passage
wherein he describes the ceremony of adoring and carrying
the image of *Huitzilopoctli* in the Mexican month *Toxcatl.*
"They carried before this litter a kind of painted roll of
papyrus, *ninety feet in length,* one in breadth, and as thick
as a finger. A number of young men carried this roll,
supporting it very carefully with arrows, that it might not
be injured on its surface, being entirely covered with
paintings in which *all the mighty acts* which He *(Huitzilopoctli)* was believed to have performed in their favour ;
and all his titles and the epithets which they had bestowed
upon him, in return for the victories which *He had* granted
them were recorded. They walked in procession before
their *false god,* singing his proverbs and glorious deeds, (an
act which was due to God alone) before whom those his
chosen people sung, saying, "God of vengeance who freely
acted, &c." and again, "Let us sing unto the Lord who has
gloriously manifested himself;" assuming the character of
the divine GOD of battles, and of the punisher of iniquities
who swallowed up king Pharaoh in the waves." "But this,"
adds the dutiful son of the church, "need cause no surprize,

since we prove in the whole course of this work that that *cursed deceiver seeks to substitute himself for God in every thing* wherein he can liken himself to Him, which God Himself has permitted and overlooked by His own secret counsels and decrees and for reasons which His divine majesty Himself knows. The procession and dance terminated at sun set, at which hour precisely they made an offering of *Tomales* a kind of *bread offering* which the Mexicans, *like the Jews*, presented at their Temple, and which was *only lawful for the priests to eat.*" [1]

" It is probable that Torquemeda, in comparing the songs of the Mexicans in honour of *Huitzilopoctli*, with those which the children of Israel sung in commemoration of their escape from Egypt, wished the readers of his Indian Monarchy to revert to that omitted chapter in his work, in which he likens the *migration of the Mexicans from Aztlan* to that of the children of Israel from Egypt: *all* the circumstances attending which were, it is to be presumed, recorded in the painted roll which was carried in procession, and afterwards laid at the feet of *Huitzilopoctli*. How much it is to be regretted that not a single Mexican painting of this description has been preserved, which would have thrown so much light on a mysterious page of history, &c."—Antiq. Mex. Vol. vi. p. 145.

The fac simile of the painting of Carerri is thus introduced in the Antiq. of Mexico:—" *Copia d'una antica dipintura conservata da Don D'Carlo Signenza nella qualle stasegnata e descritta la strada che tennero gli antichi Mexicani quando da monte vennero ad abitare nella lacunna du oggedi si dice di Mexico co geroglyphice significante i nomi de luoghi et altro.*"

---

[1] Levit. xxiv. 8, 9.

NAMES AND TITLES OF THE CREATOR.

THE character of the Holy One of Israel, being a manifold unity of moral glory, the distinctive *manifestation* of which originated those Names and Titles which served to express His Powers, it may be useful as a subject of intellectual contemplation, as well as illustrative of that portion of the subject under review, to trace to their Hebrew [1] source, those surprising analogies which are demonstrative of the origin of the Peruvian and Mexican theology.

Tonacateuctli, (Lord of our bodies, or life,) was He who resided in the garden of *Tonaquatitlan. Ometecuitli,* (Most High) is another title. He is represented crowned as Supreme, and is the Father of *Quetzalcoatl. Tezcatlipoca,* (God of Heaven) is another title, and is, under this character, assigned the *first* and *last* place in the calendar. He is emphatically styled ' the God of Fire,' and is described as holding forth a *mirror,* surrounded by thick darkness, or density, on a *Mountain,* and is said to have the wind as a messenger. *Xiuleticeutli,* derived from etherial blue, is another title for the God of Heaven, who is also said to be " the God of Ages," (or years); the Eternal YOA and TEO. *Huitzilipoctli,* and *Vitziliputzli,* are other titles for the Supreme, as the great and terrible One, who they affirm, time immemorial had, as their Leader and Protector, done marvellous things.

---

[1] See Appendix.

Tlalocateutli, (Master of Paradise) is another title; and Quetzalcoatl, whom they believe to have partaken of the Divine and human natures for the purpose of Redeeming whatever had become the prey of transgression and death, through the first introduction of evil, is precisely character-ized as the Messiah of Moses and the Prophets. Not only did the Mexicans believe in the incarnation of the Eternal Word, and that Redemption which should be the result of His obedience unto death as the second Adam, but they, like David, contemplated, as a part of future history, His burial and descent into hades; fully entering, as their paint-ings testify, into the meaning of these words—" Thou wilt not leave my soul in hades, nor wilt thou suffer Thy Holy One to see corruption." Again they testify of His ascent to the Father, and of His receiving gifts, precious and manifold, for His people, of whose redemption from the power of death and the grave, His resurrection was the earnest and pledge. " Thou hast ascended up on high; thou hast led captivity captive; and thou hast received gifts for men—even for the rebellious." Again, they represent the risen LORD (and son) of David, as for a season sitting and waiting at the right hand of Power. " The LORD said unto my lord, sit thou at My right hand until I make thine enemies thy footstool." "Yehovah hath sworn and wilt not repent: thou art a Priest for ever after the order of Melchizedec." But what is still more demonstrative of the minute-ness of detail in their knowledge of the order of these future events is, that they recognize a time when His foes having *been made* His footstool, the same יה ישע whom David celebrates by His name, Yah, as the Ruler of His redeemed people, is subsequently represented on his

---

[1] Psalm cx. 5.

E 2

Throne of Mount Zion, where, in honor of His inauguration, יהוהי (the LORD) acts at His right hand.[1] It was the opinion of some Spanish writers, that Queltzalcoatl received the title of Huitzilopoctli, from the belief that He ascended into Heaven. They also thought, that because Tonacateuctli is compounded of a word signifying precious, and left hand, that therefore it was at the left hand of Tonacateuctli, that He was seated ; but this is drawing inferences from an arbitrary analogy, in contradiction to established national usage; for the *right* hand of the Incas, and kings of Peru and Mexico was esteemed the place of honor. Baron Humboldt observes, with reference to this circumstance. ' The *right* hand of Montezuma, it is to be observed, was the place of honour ;' &c. " That it was so amongst the Jews may be inferred from the expression in the Psalm—" On His right hand did stand the queen," &c. Hence it is more probable that *Quetzalcoatl* was seated on the right hand of *Tezcatlipoca*, than on the left, as Boturini affirms in the following curious passage of his Idea of a New General History of America, ' This divinity was called, as well in the first as in the second age, *Huitzilopoctli*, from their ancestors believing that he was seated on the *left* hand of Tezcatlipoca, as they now believe in the second age, that He is on that of *Quetzalcoatl*, and being uncertain on which hand paid more respect to a seeming analogy in the language than to Mexican usages, and so confounded the right hand with the left."—Humboldt in Antiq. Mex.

[1] Psalm cx. 5.

NAMES AND ATTRIBUTES OF THE CREATOR.

Extracted from Antiquities of Mexico, vol. vi.

" *Xiuletl,* in the Mexican language, signifies *blue,* and hence was a name which the Mexicans gave to Heaven, from which *Xiuleticutli* is derived, an epithet signifying " *the God of heaven,*" which they bestowed upon *Tezcatlipoca,* or *Tonacateuctli,* who was painted with a crown as LORD of all; as the interpreter of the Codex Tellereano-Remensis affirms in the 107 page of the translation, to whom they assigned the FIRST and LAST place in the Calendar, emphatically styling him the GOD *of Fire.* Xiuleticutli may bear the other interpretation of the " GOD OF AGES," the "EVERLASTING ONE;" which, connected with the Mexican notion of fire being the element more peculiarly sacred to Him, recalls to our recollection the 9th and 10th verses of the 7th chapter of Daniel's description of the vision of the ANCIENT OF DAYS, from " before whom issued a fiery stream, and whose Throne was like the fiery flame."—p. 392.

" Daniel says, " I beheld till the thrones were cast down." Daniel's description of his vision resembles in its imagery the passage in the 9th chapter of the 6th book of Sahagun's History of New Spain, in which the newly elected king of Mexico returns thanks to *Tezcatlipoca,* who was *Xiuleticutli* the " GOD OF HEAVEN," or " the GOD OF YEARS." The Deity worshipped by the Peruvians under the name of *Pachacamac,* and of *Verachoca,* (the former of which signifies the Creator,) was the same as *Tezcal.* The FATHER, *the* Great Light, the SON *of* the Great Light, and the BROTHER *of* the Great Light, to the last of whom the moon might have been dedicated, as the sun seems to have been to the first."

Humboldt observes, that " the TEO-*calli* of Mexico was dedicated to *Tezcatlipoca,* the first of the *Aztec,* Divinities after TEO-*tl,* who is the supreme and invisible Being, and to *Huitzilopoctli,* the god of war."

" *Tezcatlipoca* is He who appeared to that nation on the mountain of the mirror, and they say it is He who tried *Quetzalcoatl,* the doer of penance."—Antiq. Mex. p. 100.

" How truly surprising it is to find that the Mexicans who seem to have been unacquainted with the doctrine of the migration of the soul and the Metempsychosis *should have believed in the incarnation of the only Son of their supreme God, Tonacateuctli.* For Mexican mythology speaking of no other Son of God, except *Quetzalcoatl,* who was born of *Chimelman,* the virgin of Tula, (without man,) by His *breath* alone, by which may by signified his WORD or WILL, when it was announced to *Chimelman,* by the celestial messenger whom He dispatched to inform her that she should conceive a son,) it must be presumed this was *Quetzalcoatl,* who was the only son. Other authors might be adduced to shew that the Mexicans believe that this *Quetzalcoatl* was both God and man; that He had previously to His incarnation existed from eternity, and that He had been the Creator of both the world and man; that He had descended to reform the world by endurance, and being King of Tula, was crucified for the sins of mankind, &c. as is plainly declared in the tradition of Yutican, and mysteriously represented in the Mexican paintings."—Humboldt in Antiq. Mex. p. 507, *notes.*

" TONACATEUCTLI was believed by the Mexicans to reside in the garden of *Tonaquatatitlan :* He was the Father of Quetzalcoatl, and was named OMETECUTLI, which signifies the MOST HIGH; that word being compounded of one, twice, which particle, when prefixed to an adjective, has an intrusive force, like the Latin *ter.* The meaning of the proper name of *Tonacateuctli,* is ' the Lord of our bodies, or life,' and it is to be remarked, that the Hebrews styled Jehovah, the Lord of all flesh, or of all living things, the expressions being synonimous, because animal life cannot exist without flesh ; hence it is apparent that the Tree of Life was called, with the greatest propriety by the Mexicans, *Tonaquaiutl.* This tree must have been celebrated in the Mexican Mythology, since it has a distinct place assigned to it in the *Tonalamatl,* or Mexican Calendar."—p. 517, 18 (notes.)

YAO-ALLI-*tiecatl,* which proper name signifies obscurity and wind ;[1] that epithet having been applied by them to the Deity, for the reason contained in the ejaculation with which the first prayer in the 6th book of Sahagun, commences, " O valliant Lord, beneath whose wings we shelter and defend ourselves, and find our protection ; thou art invisible and impalpable, just in the manner of obscurity and density." " And here we shall take occasion to observe, that *Acosta,* not knowing that *Yaoall-iecatl,* compounded of *Yo-alli,* night, and *ehecatl,* wind, was an epithet belonging to *Tezlcatlipoca,* led him into the error of asserting that the Mexicans *adored night, wind, and darkness,* on the festival of *Tezcatlipoca,* imploring *their* succors and protection ; and he has fallen in almost the next sentence into the graver error of maintaining, that the religion of the

---

[1] The same word *Ruach,* characterises *Spirit* and *wind* in the Hebrew language.

Mexicans did not hold out threats to the wicked of any punishment in a future state."—p. 523.

" *Acosta*, in the twelfth chapter of his Natural History of the Indians mentions the resemblance which he perceived between the Temple of the Sun at Cozco and the Pantheon at Rome. The commentator on the Mexican Antiquities observes, that this resemblance was "not pointed out by Acosta in reference to the style of its architecture, but to the images, &c. which were placed in it. And this remark, whatever might have been the association of ideas which led to it, could scarcely have been expected from *Acosta*, who evidently not caring how many gods the Peruvians owned, provided they had more than one, says in the thirteenth chapter of the fifty-sixth of his Natural History of the Indians, *Si universa Indicæ linguæ nomina evolvamus ex omnibus tamen ne unicum inveniemus quod Deo genuinum sit æqué ac apud Hebræos El, apud Arabes, Ala : idque tam in Cusco, quam in Mexico. Ideoque hodie Hispanicum vocabulam Dios imitantur, illud definiunt ac explicant per proprietates Indicorum idiomatum, quorum frequentia et veriá sunt.*" In venturing to use a tone of levity in speaking of an author whose wilful errors on some material points do not entitle him to unqualified praise, it is by no means our intention to disparage the merits of so justly celebrated an historian, who still it should be recollected had a theory to support, and became later in life rector in the College of Salamancha, a proof that his writings were not disagreeable to the age in which he lived. A concession however in the very passage in which he intended to demonstrate that the Indians had no idea of one supreme God, and that the Peruvians did not adore him under the name of *Pacha-camac* and *Verachoca*, paves the way to the important question, whether if the Saracens worshipped Jehovah under

the name of Alohim, or Allah, the Mexicans might not equally
have adored him under that of *Yoa*. And if the former
epithet, &c. which was in the earliest ages revealed to the
Jews, and believed by the more ancient patriarchs, became
the war cry of the Mahometan hosts, why may not the latter
have been equally profaned in the new world in hymns?"
&c. p. 528, notes.

" Sahagun no where says that they attributed divinity to
the elementary portions of nature : fire and water were in no
manner considered sacred by them, but as the *symbols* of
XIULETICUTLI and of CHALCHIUITLICUE. p. 530, notes.

" Garcia says of the Chiapanese, " the chiefs and men of
rank in Chiapa, &c. call the FATHER *Icona*, the SON *Vacah*,
and the Holy SPIRIT *Es-Ruach*,[1] and certainly these names
resemble the Hebrew, especially the last, for *Ruach* is
Spirit."—Garcios Origin los Indios, in Mex. Antiq. p. 122.

" Herrera remarks of the martial and tutelary God whom
the Mexicans represented as seated upon an azure globe.
" The Mexicans notwithstanding confessed a supreme God,
the Lord and framer of the universe, and He was the principal object whom they adored, looking up to heaven and
calling him the CREATOR of heaven and of earth, and the
' WONDERFUL,' with other epithets of great excellence."—
p. 64.

With reference to one of the Mexican paintings, the
commentator thus writes—" The plate represents Him
who when it appeared good to Him *breathed* and divided
the waters of the heaven and the earth, &c. He had no
temple, nor did they offer sacrifice to Him, so that here we
see the pride of those who despised God long ago from the
beginning has displayed itself, since the *Devil* has chosen to

---

[1] אתררוה Isaiah lxiii. 10. From the want of *r* the Es-Ruach of the Chiapanese was pronounced by the Mexicans Eh-Euach.

apply to himself what St. John says of God, that on account of His Greatness no Temple which our gratitude could erect would content him."—p. 198.

They speak of the Supreme Deity QUETZALCOATL, or more properly speaking *Demon* TONACATEUCTLI, who was also called CITINATONTLI, who, when it appeared good to Him *breathed* forth or begot QUETZALCOATL, &c. when He sent His ambassador they say to the virgin of Tula. They believed Him to be the God of the wind, and He was the first to whom they built temples perfectly round. They say it was He who should *effect the reformation of the world* by penance, since according to their account His Father had created the world, and men had given themselves up to evil, on which account it had been so repeatedly destroyed. *Citinatonatli* sent his Son into the world to reform it. We certainly must deplore the blindness of these miserable people, against whom St. Paul says, *the wrath of God has been revealed,* [1] inasmuch as his eternal truth *was so long kept back* by the injustice of attributing to this DEMON what belonged to God; for He being the sole Creator of the universe, and He who made the division of the waters which these poor people have attributed to the *Devil*, when it appeared good to Him, despatched the heavenly ambassador to announce to the virgin that she should be the mother of the eternal word, who when he found the world corrupt, *reformed it,* [2] by doing penance, &c. for our sins and not the wretched *Quetzalcoatl*, to whom this miserable people attributed this work. They celebrated a grand festival on the arrival of His sign, as we see in the sign of the four earthquakes, because they apprehended that the world would be destroyed on

---

[1] It would be difficult to show in what other sense than in that of their *invaders* this can be applied to the tribes of the New Continent.

[2] The *evidence of our senses* demand that this term should be put in the *future* tense.

that sign, as He had foretold to them when He disappeared in the Red Sea, which event occurred on the same sign. As they considered him *their Advocate,* they celebrated a solemn festival and fasted." p. 208.

"Jerusalem and her King, compared to a hen ready to protect her brood under her wings, as well as the analogous metaphor of shadowing like a tree of spreading foliage; was familiar to the ancient Mexicans, and was frequently employed by them in their prayers to the gods: *Quetzalcoatl* is emphatically styled Maker and Creator, as in the following passage of the 25th chapter of the 6th book of Sahagun, into which brief space many Jewish notions are crowded."[1]

[1] "My dear daughter, precious as a jem and as sapphire, who art good and noble, it is now certain that our LORD, *who is every where,* and shews kindness to whom He will, has remembered you, &c. Perhaps your sighs, and tears, and the lifting up of your hands before the Lord God—and the prayers and supplications which you have offered in the presence of our Lord, whose Name is *obscurity* and *density,* in watches at midnight, have merited his favour; perhaps you have watched, perhaps you have employed yourself in weeping and in offering incense in His presence; perhaps for the sake of these things, our Lord hath dealt mercifully with you; perhaps on this very account, it was determined before the beginning of the world, in heaven and in hell, that His kindness should be shown to you; perhaps it is true that our lord *Quetzalcoatl,* who is the *maker* and *former,** has shown you this grace. Perhaps it had been decreed by the man and woman divinely named *Ometicutli,* and *Ometicoatl,*† &c. Take care, O my daughter, not to allow yourself to feel proud on account of the favour which has been shown to you: take care that you say not within yourself, *I* have conceived. Take care that you attribute not this favour to your own *deserts,* for should you do so, *you* will not be able to hide your *inward* thoughts from our LORD, for nothing is hidden from Him, be it even within either *rock* or *tree:* and thus you would excite His displeasure against you, and He would send some chastisement upon you, slaying your child in the womb, or causing it to be born an idiot, or to die in tender infancy; or perhaps our Lord would visit you with some disease, of which you would die; for the fulfilment of our wish to have children, depends upon the sole mercy of God, and if our *thoughts are at variance with this truth,* we defraud ourselves of the boon which He vouchsafed us. Perhaps daughter, pride will render you unworthy of letting the light behold that infant which is about to come forth to this world." "A tone of Jewish sentiment, it must be confessed, pervades the entire of this address. While Christian ethics, Scriptural allusions, and Hebrew customs, are all wonderfully mixed up." —Notes, p. 516.

* A Scripture expression signifying creating and regenerating power, "*who created thee O Jacob, and formed thee O Israel.*"
† This may apply to the *feminine* הַחכמה (WISDOM) and this is the more probable, as we find in the term Ometi *coatl* the symbol of wisdom, viz. *serpent.*

" It was customary for the priests to dress themselves in
the same costume as that accorded to the Deity, whose
feast they celebrated ; hence it may be inferred from the
stone which M. Humboldt describes, as dedicated to *Tezcatlipoca*, which supposition will serve to explain the nature
of the ancient symbol worn on the advanced foot of the
principal figure ; since the Mexicans, in allusion to their
belief that God had appeared to them in fire and smoke on
Mount *Tezca*, (the Mount of the Mirror,) when the proper
name which they bestowed upon Him of *Tezcatlipoca*, (compounded of *Teza*, the name of the mountain, *til* dark, and
poca smoke, in reference to the manner of his manifestation,)
always represented Him with the symbol of the smoking
mirror which was placed on His head, or His foot, and sometimes on both, as in the 18th and 22nd pages of the Borgian
MS. this God was named by the Mexicans, Yoa ; and the
smoking mirror on His foot reminds us of the prophet's
description of the presence of Jehovah. " Before Him went
the pestilence, and burning coals went forth at His feet,
&c." [1] whilst the proper name of *Tezcatlipoca*, recalls to our
recollection the 18th verse of the 19th chapter of Exodus,
descriptive of the descent of God upon Mount Sinai. So
important an event in the Hebrew history as the promulgation of the Mosaic code of laws, might it readily be conceived, have disposed the Jews, who are fond of bestowing
many names upon God, either to use at first, or invent in
later ages, an epithet commemorative of the times when He
conversed with Moses in the mountain. They likewise
emphatically styled the Laws that were given to them " *The
Mirror of God*," declaring that they beheld in them, as in a
mirror, His will clearly revealed, and hence they argue that

---

[1] Habakkuk iii. 5.

the Law has [1] never been repealed, because the will of God must needs be immutable." Supp. Notes, p. 1.

"The Mexicans styled *Tezcatlipoca*, "Valiant Lord," because they considered him the God of battles, by which title He is expressly designated in the prayer which the Mexicans addressed to Him, beseeching of Him victory over their enemies, which prayer will be found entire in the third chapter of the sixty-sixth of Sahagun. A short extract is here inserted, not only because it contains the above mentioned title, but on account of the Jewish tone and sentiment which pervades it, and its *scriptural phraseology*,[2] and likewise it serves to illustrate an observation of Torquemeda, in the note to page 245 of the volume: "And inasmuch as your Majesty is Lord of battles, on whose will depends victory, who *forsakest* when thou wilt, and standest in need of no counsel from any one; since thus it is, I supplicate your Majesty to deprive our enemies of reason—*to make them as drunkards*, in order that they may throw themselves into our hands, and without harm to us, may all fall into the hands of our men of war, who endure poverty and hardship. O may it please thy Majesty, since thou art God, and canst do all things, and ordainest all things, and art ever employed in directing the affairs of the universe, and in ordering and providing for the prosperity, and glory, and honor, and fame of *this thy commonwealth, &c.*"—p. 523.

"The notion of *Tezcatlipoca protecting the people beneath His wings:* which metaphor was employed by the ancient Mexicans, who emphatically styled themselves "His People,"

---

[1] "Think not that I am come to abrogate the Law." "Sooner shall heaven earth pass, than one jot or tittle of the law fail." Matt. v. 17. Malachi iv. 4.

[2] The Mexican oath was as follows:—" I swear by the sun, and by the existance of our sovereign mother the earth, that nothing which I affirm is false, and in confirmation of my oath I partake of this earth. The adjuration of Moses is analogous. " I call heaven and earth to witness against you this day, &c."

and their kingdoms, and the throne of their kings, *God's throne and His seat of judgment*, strongly assimilates itself to the language of David in the fourth verse of the ninety-first Psalm. They likewise considered the supreme God their *shield* and *buckler*, the proper name of *Chimalman*, [1] which is derived from the Mexican name for shield, and being compounded of that term by the elision of the final syllable *li* and *man* (devoid of signification) as is most probably here the case, and which would perhaps have been *Mar*, but that the Mexican language [2] wants the letter *r*, may not unreasonably be supposed to have been the virgin of Tula, the mother of *Quetzalcoatl*."—p. 523.

Du Pratz, who had a special intimacy with one of the guardians of a Temple in a tribe near the Mississippi, was informed that " By their word expressive of the Deity, they mean a SPIRIT surpassing other spirits as much as the sun surpasses a taper." " The guardian said in comparison of this GREAT ONE, all else were as nothing. He made all that we see—and all that we cannot see! His is perfect goodness! He made all things by His word, or will; that subordinate spirits are his servants. The superior order of these they call ' HIS *Free Servants*'—those being the spirits always in the presence of the MASTER OF LIFE—and ready to execute His will with an extreme diligence. That the air is the region of many good and evil spirits—that the latter have a chief who is more mighty in *evil* power than all the rest—who had become so daring, that the GREAT SPIRIT had bound him, so that he could do the *less* harm."

Adair, who lived long among the Northern Indians, says,

---

[1] A curious feature of identity in the Hebrew and *Aztec* Migration, is with reference to Miriam, who under the name of *Chimalman*, " was *shut out several days from the Aztlan camp* in consequence of her quarrel with *her brothers, the leaders* of the Aztecs, or Mexicans," Numb. xii. 15.—Antiq. Mex. vol. vi. p. 367.
[2] The Mexican language wants the B, D, F, G, R, and s.

" These tribes believe the higher regions to be inhabited by good spirits, whom they call Holy Ones, or relatives of the GREAT SPIRIT, or HOLY ONE. They say accursed beings possess a dark region—the former attend to favour the virtuous and just amongst men—the latter accompany and instigate by their malice, the vicious. Several warriors have told me that the concomitant holy spirits have forewarned them by intimation, of danger of which they were not aware at the time, but which afterwards they have found to have been inevitable.

" *Pachacamac* is represented as sitting upon an animal not unlike a cherubim, the figures of bird, beasts, &c. may allude to *Pachacama* (or Creator), under which the Peruvians adored their Supreme God;[1] for although they believed, as did also the Mexicans, that the supreme Deity was incorporeal, they still, like the Hebrews, acknowledged Him in the human form."

" God's promise to Jeremiah, " thou shalt be as My mouth," was known to the Mexicans, since the newly-elected King of Mexico, in a prayer of thanksgiving to *Tezcatlipoca*, there emphatically says of kings in general " they are thine instruments and thine images to govern Thy kingdom, Thou being in them and speaking from their mouth, and they declaring Thy words."

Kircher says, that none of their *symbols were without secret meaning*. The mirror in the hand of *Tezcatlipoca* denoted His prescience, which beheld every thing as in a mirror; and the skull and heart, according to Torquemeda, signified that He possessed equal power over life and death.—p. 419.

---

[1] The Peruvians regarded Pachacama as the Supreme Creator and preserver of all things here below: they adored him in their hearts as the invisible God. —Vega.

" HUITZILOPOCTLI was called YA-O.   It is singular that he should have been called the *ineffable*."—p. 145.

" *Huitzilopoctli* is a compound name.   Boturini derives it from *Houitziton*, the Lord of the tribes during their peregrination, and supposes that their Leader represented the *Creator whom they have worshipped time immemorial before they commenced their wandering life under Honitziton*. Some say this divinity is a pure Spirit : others represent Him embodied as a man : this God, having been the Protector of the tribes *led them* (according to their account) *during many years* of their wandering life, and at last settled them in the place where they built the city of Mexico."

' On his head was a beautiful plumage shaped like a bird ; on his neck a *breast-plate* composed of *ten figures of human hearts :* in his right hand a rod[1] in the form of a *serpent,* &c. This description, the human hearts, the compound name, the Divine leader, &c. and the story of His incarnation, compared with the medal which represents a Tree with the seven tribes, or houses springing from its *root*, are in the main, however, obscure and blended, just such fragments of tradition as might have been expected from the descendants of the Ten Tribes, without letters, for so many ages.'

---

[1] Torquemeda observes in the forty-eighth chap. of the thirteenth book of his Ind. Mon. " that a *wand* was placed in their hands, which they believed would *sprout* on their arrival in Paradise."

Doctor Boudinot, in his ' *Star in the West*,' observes of the same traditionary rod or branch :—" The Indians have an old tradition, that when they left their own native land, they brought with them a *sanctified rod*, by order of an oracle, which they fixed every evening in the ground, and were to remove from place to place on the continent, till it blossomed in one night's time."—See Clavegero.

QUETZALCOATL.

' WHILST,' observes Humboldt, ' the Mexicans offer analogies sufficiently remarkable in their ecclesiastical hierarchy, in the number of the religious assemblies, in the severe austerity of their penitentiary rites, and in the order of their processions; it is impossible not to be struck with this resemblance, in reading with attention the recital which Cortez made to the Emperor, Charles V. of his solemn entrance into Cholula, which he[1] calls *the holy city of the Mexicans.*' * * ' A people who regulated its festivals according to the order of the stars, and who engraved its festivals on its public monuments, had no doubt reached a degree of civilization superior to that which has been allowed by De Pauw, Raynal, or Robertson. These writers considered every state of society barbarous that did not bear the type of civilization, which they, according to their systematic ideas had formed ; these abrupt distinctions into barbarous and civilized, cannot be with truth admitted.'—Vol. i. pp. 408-9.

' Men with beards and with clearer complexions than the nations of Anahuac, make their appearance without any

---

[1] " The motto taken by Cortez," observes the Commentator of the Mex. Antiq. " *Judicium Domini apprehendit eos,*" seems obliquely to refer to the Mexican tradition of the destruction of Tulan, &c. In referring the motto of Cortez to the destruction of Jerusalem, which happened so many centuries before his day, we must suppose, entering into the feeling of the Spanish General, that he recognized in Mexico a *second Jerusalem*, and in his own conquests a triumph over the Hebrews of the *New World*, as Titus had before vanquished those of the old."

indication of the place of their birth ; and bearing the title of priests and legislators, of the friends of peace and the arts which flourished under its auspices, operate a sudden change in the policy of the nations who hail their arrival with veneration. *Quetzalcoatl, Bachica, and Manco Capac,* are the sacred names of these mysterious beings. *Quetzalcoatl,* clothed in a dark sacerdotal robe, comes from Pannes, from the shores of the Gulph of Mexico. *Bachica* presents himself on the high places of Botoga, where he arrives from the Savannahs, which stretch along the east of the Cordilleras. The history of these legislators is intermixed with miracles, religious functions, and with *those characters which imply an allegorical meaning.* A slight reflection on the period of Toltec migration, the monastic institutions, the symbols of worship, the calendars, and the form of the monuments of Cholula and Sogomazo, and of Cuzco, leads us to conclude that it was *not* in the north of Europe that *Quetzalcoatl, Bachica,* and *Manco Capac,* framed their code of laws ; every consideration leads us rather toward Eastern Asia,' &c.—p. 30.

Extracts from the Antiq. of Mex. vol. vi.

"The Mexican Deity, *Quetzalcoatl,* was, to their belief, *born of a virgin,* a native of the city of *Tulan,* who, being a devout person, and engaged in sweeping the altar in the Temple, perceived a ball of feathers falling through the air, which having taken up and placed in her girdle, she became pregnant. *Quetzalcoatl* was called on earth [1]   *   *   * and in heaven, *Chalchiluclyth,* (the Precious Stone of

---

[1] In the original Spanish MS., this appellative was obliterated.

suffering and of sacrifice,") &c. " The *destruction* of Tulan, constitutes an epoch in the Mexican chronology, and is the fourth in order, of the catastrophes which had befallen the world. They kept every four years another fast of eight days, in memory of three destructions which the world had undergone; and accordingly when this period had arrived, they exclaimed four times, " *Lord, how is it, that the world having been so often destroyed, has never been destroyed?* " They named it the festival of *Renovation:* to represent the festival of renovation, they led children by the hands through the dance.'—p. 103.

" The sign of *Nahui Ollin,* or four earthquakes, was dedicated to *Quetzalcoatl,* whose *second* advent, together with the *end* of the world, the Mexicans expected would be on the same sign."—p. 107.

" His feast is called the feast of the Lords, viz. ancients— it lasted four days from the first of *Ocelotl,* (the sign of the earth) to the fourth earthquakes, or destructions. In the seventy-second plate of the Borgian MS., *Yztapal Nanazcaya,* or the fourth age of the Mexicans, that of *flints* and *canes,* memorable for the birth of *Quetzalcoatl,* and the *destruction* of the province of Tulan, seems to be represented. *Quetzalcoatl* is there painted in the attitude of a person crucified, with the impression of nails in his hands and feet, but not actually upon a cross, and with the image of death beneath his feet, which an angry serpent seems threatening to devour. The skulls above signify that the place is *Tzonpantli,* a word which exactly corresponds with the Hebrew name, *Golgotha.* The body of *Quetzalcoatl* seems to be formed out of a resplendent sun, and two female figures with children on their backs, are very copiously presenting an offering at his feet. The Mexicans sometimes added the epithet of *Tlatzatli* to *Tzonpantli,* when the signification of both

names became *the place of precious death, or martyrdom;*
Tlatzatli in the Mexican language, meaning precious, or desired. " The seventy-third plate of the Borgian MS. is the
most remarkable of all, for *Quetzalcoatl* is not only represented
there as crucified upon a cross of Greek form, but his burial
and descent into hell are also depicted in a very curious
manner. His grave, &c. is strewed with bones and skulls,
symbolical of death; the head of the devouring monster on
the left signifies the descent into hell, and that he had been
swallowed up in death, which could only dismember, but
could not cause his body to corrupt or decay, since he
resumes his perfect form in hell, and seems to compel[1]
Metlantecutli the lord of the *dead to do him homage.*
Metlantecutli was a different personage from *Tontemoque,*
the former presiding over hell, the region of the *dead,* and
the latter over *hell* the place of punishment." p. 167.

" The Mexicans expect that *Quetzalcoatl* shall prepare the
way for *Tlaloc,* as of an adamant that shall fall from heaven,
and produce[2] a new race of heroes." " The Mexican paintings
afford some representation of this flint called by Acosta
" *Thunderbolt,*" giving *as it were birth to children.* The
Mexicans, says Boturini, believe that *Tlaloc* was secretary
of God, who in His name wrote His laws amid lightnings, and
published them in thunders. *Quetzalcoatl* was also represented by the figure of *Halocatcoatl,* which signifies the
Lion of the human kind : other analogies extending to all
the symbols mentioned above might be pointed out between
the types referring in the Old Testament to Christ, and the
epithets bestowed by the Mexicans on *Quetzalcoatl.* From
the little that has been preserved of the life of *Quetzalcoatl*

---

[1] Hosea xiii. 14.   Isaiah xxvi. 19.
[2] They addressed God in these words—" Lord whose servants we are, grant
this."

it would appear," adds the commentator, "that he was very anxious to verify in his own person some of the ancient prophecies relating to the Messiah, and that for this purpose he went about studiously performing certain actions, by which they might appear to be fulfilled."—p. 109.

" *Quetzalcoatl* they say is He who *created* the world, and they bestowed on him the title of the Lord of the *wind*, because they said that when it seemed good to *Tonecatuctli* He *breathed* and begot or produced *Quetzalcoatl*. They created round temples to him without any corners. They said that it was He who was the Lord of the three signs which are here represented, and who formed the first man." That a *Messiah* is promised to the Jews all agree, therefore in their prayers they beseech God that he may come quickly; but who he is, or when he shall come, is much controverted. A very remarkable painting occurs in the Codex Borgian, in which *Quetzalcoatl* is represented in a sumptuous Temple seated on *a Throne*, a *sword*[1] *proceeds out of his mouth*, and an eagle is hastening *to prey on the dead bodies slain by them* under the throne. Above is the symbol of the sun which half conceals the body of a *lamb*. *Quetzalcoatl* is again represented on the same page, in the act of sacrificing a demon whom death seems ready to devour."

" They the Indians were descended from the race of *Quetzalcoatl*; for this reason they held lineage in great account, and wherever they chanced to be, they said, ' *I am of such. a lineage.*' Before the image of their first founder whom they call *Votan*, wood and incense were always burning. Holding up of roses and flint-knives, partly covered with branches of rose trees, denote the commencement of the suffering of *Quetzalcoatl*. The subject of this plate is the

---

[1] Daniel ii. 45. Isaiah xlix. 2. Rev. xix. 21.

announcement to *Chemelham* that she should be the mother of *Quetzalcoatl.* It is singular that this season of suffering and affliction, from which, according to the belief of the Mexicans, they were to be relieved by the coming again of *Quetzalcoatl,* should have nearly corresponded in its duration with the period which intervened between Adam and the coming of Christ. *Quetzalcoatl,* according to the opinion of some authors, received the appellation of *Huitzilopochtli* from the belief which the Mexicans entertained, that he had ascended into heaven, and was seated on the left hand of *Tonecatuctli.''* " Rosales in his edited History of Chili declares, that the inhabitants of this extreme southern portion of America, situated at the distance of so many thousand miles from New Spain, and who did not employ paintings to record events, accounted for their knowledge of some doctrines of Christianity by saying, that in former times, *they had heard their fathers say, a wonderful man had come to that country, wearing a long beard, with shoes, and a mantle such as the Mexicans carry on their shoulders, who performed many miracles, cured the sick with water, caused it to rain, that their crops of grain might grow, kindled fire at a breath, healing the sick, and giving sight to the blind: and that he spoke with as much propriety and elegance in the language of their country, as if he had always resided in it, addressing them in words very sweet and new to them, telling them that the Creator of the universe resided in the highest place of heaven, and that many men and women resplendent as the sun dwelt with Him.* They say that shortly after, he went to Peru, and that many in imitation of the habit and shoes which that man used, introduced amongst themselves the fashion of wearing shoes, and the loose mantle over the shoulders, either fastened with a clasp at the breast, or knotted at the corners, whence it may be inferred that this man was some apostle whose name they do not know. This is the account given by Rosales of that wonderful man, and it deserves to be remarked as quite in accordance with the gloomy and misanthropic character with which the Incas loved to invest religion, that they converted an object of reverence into one of horror, by assigning to him the attribute of breathing fire from his nostrils. The Indians, adds the worthy son of the church, availing themselves of the lofty metaphors of their language, have bestowed the name of *Quetzalcoatl* upon the glorious apostle,[1] which signifies the serpent bird, intimating by the last the swiftness with which he had passed from a distant country to theirs, and by the serpent the wise circumspection of the law which he had to preach, the value of which was further denoted by the feathers of the bird, which they called *Quetzalli*, and infinitely esteemed, since they wore them, not only as an ornament in war, but likewise at their public dances and solemn *festivals.*"—Catalogo del Museo Indiano, p. 51, in Antiq. Mex.

" The Mexicans bestowed the appellation of *Toplitzin* on *Quetzalcoatl*, the literal signification of which is, *our son*,[2] or our *child;* that proper name being compounded of, *To,* our, and *piltzin,* boy or child, and as so called by the cognate terms of *piltozitli*, and *pilzintin*, and it may not unreasonably be assumed, since analogies which are numerous, and not isolated, as their number increases, increase also in the ratio of the probability, not only that the Mexicans were acquainted with Isaiah's famous prophecy, but to

---

[1] The Catholics, it is curious to observe, fixed on ' Thomas.' As an illustration of the kind of miracles which characterized the church, it is well to observe, that under the modern title of " the glorious apostle Thomas," *Quetzalcoatl* ceased to be thought a *demon*, and had even, it was affirmed, taught *Christianity!*

[2] Isaiah ix. 6.

mark their belief of the accomplishment of that prophecy in the person of *Quetzalcoatl,* that they named him *Toplitzin,* no less on account of his having been *born of a virgin* of the daughters of men, than because another equally celebrated prediction of the same prophet, declared that he should receive a name *from that very circumstance.* Therefore the Lord himself shall give you a *sign.* " Behold a virgin shall conceive and bear a son, and shall call his name Immanuel."[1] And the proper name *Toplizin* does indeed bear a signification corresponding to " *God with us,*" which means " *God domesticated amongst men,*" and the full force of the expression is preserved in the term *Toplitzin,* which might be interpreted, " *the son of Man;*" for the Mexicans believe that *Quetzalcoatl* took human nature upon him, partaking of all the infirmities of man, and was not exempt from sorrow, pain, or death, which he suffered *voluntarily to atone* for the sins of man. They also believed that he alone had a human ·body, and was of corporeal substance ; a notion which we can only wonder whence it could be derived."—Antiq. Mex.

" Both these authors (*Las Casas* and *Torquemeda*) assert that *Quetzalcoatl* had been in Yutican, and there can ·be little doubt, when we reflect on the mysterious history of *Bachab,* that the cross discovered by M. Du Paix in the ancient Temple of Palenque, was connected with the tradition of his crucifixion.[2] The four female figures each holding in her

---

[1] Isaiah vii. 14.

[2] "—If such testimony as Las Casas, Remesal, De Salchar, and Torquemeda, may still, from the importance of the subject, stand in need of further corroboration before belief can be yielded to the tradition of Yutican, which even went so far as to affirm that *Bachab* had been crucified by *Eupuco,* it is afforded by this discovery. M. Du Paix also discovered in the province of *Tlascala,* which bordered on Cholula, a bust which so entirely corresponded with the description given by Herrera of *Quetzalcoatl,* which was adored in that city, that we cannot refrain from referring to the fifty-third plate of the second part of his monuments, which contains a representation of it under the No. 23, the *bird's face* was perhaps only

arms an infant, which adorn the walls of another temple in the vicinity of that just mentioned, probably represent *Chibreries,* or *Chemelham,* and the infant Quetzalcoatl."— p. 507.

It is singular that the Mexicans should have viewed *Quetzalcoatl* in the light of " God and of man,"—of a *Father* and of a *Son*—of the Creator of the world, and of him by whom the world was finally doomed to be destroyed, since it is hard to reconcile such conflicting notions with each other. That they did so, will appear from passages extracted from the sixth book of Sahagun's history of New Spain, which contains the prayers addressed by the ancient Mexicans to their gods, as well as from what already has been said of the belief which the Mexicans entertained that the world would be destroyed when the sun was in the sign of the four earthquakes. *Quetzalcoatl* is emphatically called *Father*, in the exhortation which the Mexican priest addresses to the penitent, who had come to make confession to him of his sins, whose entire speech will be found, p. 359 of vol. v, of the Antiquities of Mexico.

In this painting *Quetzalcoatl* is represented as borne on

a sign symbolical of his *absence,* or it might have been the bill of *Huitzlan,* from the proper name *Huitzilopochtli,* and to the bird which invited the Mexicans *out of the bush to set out on their pilgrimage from Aztlan.* It deserves to be remarked that both the hands of the figure seem to be *pierced,* the marks of the nails are visible. The tradition current in *Yutican,* that *Eupuco crowned Bachab with thorns,* appears also to be preserved in the head-dress. A *crown of thorns* of another fashion may be recognized on the head of another piece of sculpture discovered by M. Du Paix. This figure in relievo, is represented in the ninth plate of his monuments, part third, No. 13, and the crown seems to be formed out of the thorns of the aloe."

" Although in anticipation of the objection which some persons may be inclined to make that the finding a cross on the confines of Yutican, was no proof that the people of that province believed as a matter of faith in the crucifixion of an individual, we shall insert a passage from Cozollados' history of *Yutican,* which is very remarkable, as the cross there mentioned had the image of *a person crucified, sculptured on it.* The Spanish ecclesiastics and laity, in order not to affirm any thing which was not entirely certain, an inscription was placed on the back of it which says, *This cross was found in Cozumal without tradition."*—p. 171.

Eagles' wings, as in Exod. xix. " All faces shall gather blackness," may explain why the figures with such faces often occur in the Mexican paintings; and as regards the deformity of features which the Mexicans attributed to *Quetzalcoatl*, the words of Isaiah liii. which the Jews understood in an *exaggerated* sense, as belonging to the Messiah, may be reconciled with " *His visage was so marred more than any man*," and again, " *He hath no form nor comeliness.*"

" Another painting," observes the interpreter of the painted records, " represents the ambassador or angel announcing to Eve, or the woman whose seed was to *bruise the serpent's head*, alluded to in p. 74 of the Vatican MS. Another immediately follows representing *Quetzalcoatl* slaying the beast whose power was in its tail." " It is singular that Eve should be receiving a rose from the ambassador. This was called the age of the roses."—p. 176.

" If," adds the commentator, " the Jews had perverted another expression of Scripture, viz. " I am Alpha and Omega, the first and the last, the beginning and the ending," they have painted the signs dedicated to *Quetzalcoatl*, before and after the symbols allotted to the twelve tribes, as seems to be the case in the 74th page of the Borgian MS., where the skull or symbol of death placed over the signs, signify that *He had redeemed them from it*. The two signs dedicated to *Quetzalcoatl*, are the *wind*, and the green-plumaged *serpent* which occupy the *first* and *last* place amongst these signs. In the 39th page of the Mexican paintings in the possession of M. Fejervary, at Pest in Hungary, a curious representation of *Quetzalcoatl*, as it would appear, occurs in the shape of " *a serpent fixed upon a pole.*"—p. 313.

Kircher says, " that none of those symbols were without secret meaning. The mirror in the hands of *Tezcatlipocha*, denoted His presence, which beheld every thing as in a mirror, and the skull and heart according to Torquemeda, signify that He possessed equal power over life and death."— p. 419.

" It is a very remarkable, and no less mysterious fact, that the representation of a *sheep* or *lamb, crowned as it were for sacrifice, and pierced with a spear,* should sometimes occur in the Mexican paintings. Fabrega calls it a crowned or sacred rabbit, but Baron Humboldt says, that according to *traditions,* which have been preserved to our days, it is a *symbol of suffering innocence.* The Baron describes it in the following passage, which is extracted from his American Monuments. " *Un animal inconnu orné d'un collier et d'un espèce de harnois, mais percé de dards : Fabrega le nomme lapin couronné, lapin sacré! On trouve cette figure dans plusieurs rituels des anciens Mexicains. D'apres les traditions que se sont conservées jusqu'à nos jours, c'est une symbole de l'innocence souffrante; sans ce rapport cette representation allégorique rapelle l'* AGNEAU *des Hebrews, on l'ideé mystique d'une sacrifice expiatoire destinée à calmer la colére de la Divinité. Les dents incicives, la forme de la tête et de la queue paroissent indiquer que le peintre à voulu representer un animal de la famille de rongeurs,"* &c."
"M. Humboldt's description applies to a representation of this animal in the Codex Borgiana. It is also twice painted in the 20th page of the lesser Vatican Manuscripts, in the lower compartments of which it is alive, and adorned for *sacrifice ;* in the upper dead, with its " *side pierced with a spear.*" If the rabbit had been an animal known only to the Mexicans by tradition or indistinct recollection, which had been preserved by means of their ancient paintings, it would not be difficult to suppose that the figures under considera- tion, were intended to represent it ; but as there was no

animal with which the Mexicans were better acquainted, this cannot be the case. In Natural History likewise, the *teeth* and the *feet* are very decisive of the species of animals, while the shape of the ears and tail are scarcely considered ; and it will here be observed, that the configuration of the head of the upper figure is much less like a rabbit than that of the lower, whilst the shape of the nose in both is decidedly different. The same animal is also variously painted in different Mexican pictures ; but the characteristic mark of a *divided* hoof, is decidedly preserved." " In the 2nd part of the picture preserved in the Royal Library at Dresden, the style of which differs from that of the Mexican picture, it seems to be four times represented ; the upper figure appears to be *descending from above*, and the lower is *recumbent*, emblematical perhaps like the *Lamb of the Hebrews, of innocence suffering under temporary persecution*. The heads of the other three figures which are themselves a combination of real and imaginary forms, can be referred to no particular species ; but nature preponderates in the shape of the body, legs, and feet of the animals intended to be represented, and plainly indicates the class to which they belong. It deserves also to be remarked, that the same figure of a *lamb, with its body formed of the sun's disk*, is painted on the pyramidical roof of a Temple, in the 6th page of the Borgian MS. and in a curious representation of *Quetzalcoatl*, as it is to be supposed, seated on a dragon or leviathan, whish occurs in the 14th page of the Mexican paintings that formerly belonged to Archbishop Laud, and which is at present in the Bodleian Library at Oxford. It is probable, that the hieroglyphic by which the Mexicans represented suffering innocence, was originally a *lamb*, imperfect representations of which are found, but in process of time was designated a rabbit, an animal with which they were better acquainted; *traces of the former still continuing to exist in the Mexican paintings,* and to be accounted for on the same principle as Baron Humboldt explains the presence of the words " *Tulian Hallulaz,*" in the song which the people of *Cholula* were accustomed to sing in dancing round their TEO*calli,* and which he says belonged *to no language now in existence in Mexico.*"—p. 308.

Of a tradition respecting *Quetzalcoatl,* Humboldt observes, ' the great spirit, *Tezcatlipoca,* offered *Quetzalcoatl,* a beverage, which in rendering him immortal, inspired him with a taste for travelling, particularly with an irresistible desire of visiting a distant country, called by tradition *Tlapallan.*[1] The resemblance of this name to that of *Hue-hue-Tlapalan,* the country of the Toltics, appears not to be accidental. But how can we conceive that this white man, priest of Tula, should have taken his direction, as we shall presently find, to the south-east toward the plains of *Cholula,* and then to the eastern coasts of Mexico, in order to visit this northern country, whence his ancestors had issued," &c. " *Quetzalcoatl,* in crossing the territory of *Cholula,* yielded to the entreaties of the inhabitants, who offered him the crown. He dwelt twenty years amongst them, taught them to cast metals, ordered feasts of eight days, and regulated the intercalations of the *Toltic* year. *He preached peace to man, and would permit no offering to the divinity than the first fruits of the harvest.* From *Cholula, Quetzalcoatl* passed on to the mouth of the river *Goasacoalu,* where he disappeared, after having declared to the *Cholulans,* &c. that he would return in a short time, *to govern them again in renewed happiness.* It was the posterity of this saint whom the unhappy Montezuma

---

[1] " *Country of the Red Sea.*"

thought he recognized in the soldiers of Cortez. "We know by our books," said he, in his first interview with the Spanish general, " that myself, and those who inhabit this country, are not natives, but strangers who came from a great distance. We know also that the Chief, who led our ancestors hither, returned for a certain time to his primitive country, and then came back to seek those who were here established. He found them married to the women of this land, having a numerous posterity, and living in cities which they built. Our ancestors hearkened not to their ancient Master, and he returned alone. We always believed, that his descendants would one day come to this country. Since you arrive from that country where the sun rises, and as you assure me you have known us, I cannot doubt but that the king who sends you is our natural Master.'—First Letter of Cortez.

" Another very remarkable tradition still exists among the Indians of Cholula, according to which the great pyramid was not originally destined to serve for the worship of *Quetzalcoatl*. ' After my return to Europe, on examining at Rome, the manuscripts in the Vatican library, I found that this same tradition was already recorded in a manuscript of Pedro de los Rios, a Dominican monk, who, in 1560, copied on the very spot all the hieroglyphics he could procure. He adds " this history reminds us of those *ancient traditions of the east, which the Hebrews have recorded in their sacred books.*"

" To prove further the high antiquity of the tradition, Rios observes that it was contained in a hymn which the *Cholulans* sung at their festivals, dancing around the TEO-*calli ;* and that this hymn began with the words *Tulian hululaey,* which are words belonging to no dialect at present known in Mexico. In every part of the globe on the side of the

Cordilleras, as well as the isle of Samothrace, in the Ægean sea, fragments of primitive languages are preserved in religious rites. The size of the platform of the pyramid of Cholula, on which I made a great number of astronomical observations, is 4,000,200 square metres. From it the eye ranges over a magnificent prospect, &c. We view at the same time three mountains higher than Mount Blanc, two of which are still burning volcanoes. A small chapel, surrounded with cypress and dedicated to the Virgin de los Remedios, has succeeded to the temple of the god of the wind, &c. An ecclesiastic of the Indian race celebrates mass every day on the top of this antique monument. In the time of Cortez, *Cholula* was considered as a *holy city*. Nowhere existed a greater number of *Teocallis*, of priests and religious orders (*Tlamalazque,*) no spot displayed greater magnificence in the celebration of public worship, or more austerity in its penances and fasts."—Humboldt's Res. pp. 97, 98.

"They call the *morning star* after *Quetzalcoatl ;* they say he took this name on occasion of his disappearance."—p. 123.

"With respect to the appellation *Mexi,* or *Mezetli,* (the other name by which *Quetzalcoatl* was known among the Mexicans) ; it is very remarkable that it is precisely the same as the Hebrew word which signifies *the anointed.*"—p. 82.

"The virgin was represented in the Indian paintings, of whom the great Prophet should be born, and that his own people would reject and meditate evil against him, and would put him to death : accordingly he is represented in the paintings with his hands and feet tied to the tree. The manner in which he had returned to life again, and ascended to heaven, was likewise painted. The Dominican fathers said they had found these things among some Indians, who inhabited the coasts of the South Seas, who stated they had received the traditions from their ancestors."— Monarquia Indiana, lib. 15, c. 49.

Baron Humboldt notices the same in the following curious passage extracted from his work, entitled American Monuments in Acosta's Natural History of the Indies, twenty-eighth chapter especially. —p. 163.

' *Cozas* was chief of the twenty men who commanded fasting and confession, affirming that *Bachab* had been put to death,' p. 165. Torquemeda informs us that *Quelzalcoatl* had been in Yutican, and was there adored. The interpreter of the Vatican Codex says, in the following curious passage, " that the Mexicans had a tradition that he, *(Bachab)* died upon the tree*, and he adds, *according to their belief, for the sins of mankind.*" p. 168. " If more history, paintings and monuments of *Yutican* had been preserved, we should have been enabled to determine whether *Bachab* and *Quetzalcoatl* were two different names for the same Lord, who was worshipped alike by Yutican and Mexico." The *Chiapanese* called the same Lord *Votan,* which signifies the HEART of *the people.* Of *Quetzalcoatl,* they relate that he proceeded on his journey toward the Red Sea (which is represented); when about to part from them, he desired them to restrain their grief and to expect his return, which would take place at the appointed time ; accordingly they expect him even to the present time—and when the Spaniards came to their country they believed that it was He; and even in the year 1550, when the Capotecas revolted, they alleged as the cause of their insurrection the report that their God, who was to *Redeem* them, had already come. Cortez and Gomara, in relating the horrors which the Mexicans sustained during the last days of the siege, both mention that they consoled themselves in their last sufferings with the hopes of going to

Quetzalcoatl, that even the enemies of the city of *Chollula* bound themselves to make pilgrimages to it. And *this was on account of the great love which they felt towards him, for in truth the dominion of Quetzalcoatl was sweet, and he exacted no service from them but easy and light things, instructing them in such as were virtuous, and prohibiting such as were wicked, evil, and injurious, teaching them likewise to abhor them.* Hence it appears' continues Torquemeda, ' that the Indians who celebrated human sacrifices, did not so voluntarily, but from the great fear which they entertained of the Devil, on account of the threats which he held out to them, that he would destroy them, and sending bad seasons and many misfortunes upon them, except they duly performed the worship and service which they owed to him as a tribute and mark of vassalage from the right which he pretended to have acquired over them many years before. They declare that he remained with them during the entire period of twenty years, at the expiration of which he departed, prosecuting his journey to the kingdom of *Tlapallan*, taking along with him four virtuous and principal youths of the same city. Amongst the other doctrines which he delivered to them, he charged them to tell the inhabitants of the city of Chollula that they might be certain of the arrival by sea, at some future time, from a region situated towards the rising sun, of white men, like him, and that they were his brethren. The Indians accordingly always expected that prophecy would be fulfilled ; and when they beheld the Christians, they immediately called them gods, the sons and brothers of *Quetzalcoatl,* although *after they knew them, and had experienced their works,* they no longer believed them to be divine, for in that city a signal massacre was perpetrated by the Spaniards unequalled till that time in the Indies, or perhaps in

G

most other parts of the globe.   Others say that the people
of *Chollula* always believed that he would return to console
and govern them, and when they saw the ships of the
Spaniards coming, they said that their god, *Quetzalcoatl*,
was now returned, and that he was bringing the temples
over the sea in which he intended to dwell; but that when
the disembarkation took place, they remarked, "*these gods
are many—it is not our god, Quetzalcoatl.*" p. 260.   They
say that *Quetzalcoatl*, whilst in this mortal life, wore long
robes, reaching to the feet, from a sense of decency, with a
mantle above interspersed with red marks.   They preserved
certain *green* gems which belonged to him with great veneration.   " His image had a very ugly face, a large head, and a
thick beard—*they placed it in a recumbent posture, covered up
with mantles, and they say that they did so as a token that
he had again to return, and to reign over them, and that
out of respect to his great majesty it was proper that his
image should be covered up, and that they placed it in a
recumbent posture to denote his absence ; like one who re-
poses, who lays himself down on his side to sleep, and that
awakening from the sleep of absence, he would rouse himself
up to reign.*"   The inhabitants of *Yutecan* venerated and
revered this God, *Quetzalcoatl*, and named him *Kukulcam*.
They heard moreover that the kings of *Yutecan* descended
from him whom they call *Cocomem*, which signifies judges."

   " St. Chrysostom (adds the commentator) commenting upon
the passage, " There shall come a star out of Jacob," cites the
authority of some who " said that those gentiles, believing in
the future appearance of that star, appointed twelve sentinels
who, at stated seasons of the year, ascended to the top of a
high mountain, (named Victorial,) and remained there three
days praying to God, and *beseeching Him that He would
manifest to them the star of which Balaam had prophecied,*

who having beheld it, the kings came to adore *the new-born infant Saviour.* I know not whether the *Devil,* jealous of this prophecy, and desirous of keeping *another people in a continual state of watching and anxiety,* instituted this piece of fraud amongst the Indians of New Spain, to understand which it is proper that I should premise that in ancient times there was a man of the kingdom of Tula who was named *Quetzalcoatl, who was a famous magician and necromancer,* whom they afterwards worshipped as a God, and who was accounted a king of that country. He was conquered by another *more powerful magician,* such another as we may suppose Zoroaster of Babylon to have been, who deprived him of his kingdom. From thence he went to the city of *Chollula,* whither the other pursued him; when forsaking his kingdom he fled to the sea, pretending that the God who was the GREAT LIGHT called him to the side of the sea, to the borders of the east, but he promised that he would again return to avenge himself of his enemies, and to *redeem his people from their afflictions* and the yoke of tyranny under which they groaned, for they said of him that he was very *compassionate and merciful,* that he was preserved in the recollection of those who lived in that age, and acquired much greater credit in all the ages which afterwards succeeded, and the Mexicans so *fully believed his return, that their kings, when mounting the throne, took possession of the kingdom upon the express condition of being viceroys of their lord Quetzalcoatl, and of abdicating it on His arrival and obeying him as vassals.*"[1]

" Mankind perceiving that through Quetzalcoatl, so fortunate an era had commenced, began to imitate him, and following his example, to practise self-denial, and to make

---

[1] This is a curious caricature or distortion of the tradition which it gives, but is valuable as a confirmation of facts.

offerings of their temporal possessions. In the due performance of these rites, *Quetzalcoatl* invented temples, or quis, as common places of *prayer* among the people; he founded the four here represented; in the first of which the princes and nobles *fasted,* and in the second the lower classes of the people; the third was denominated, the house of the *serpent,* in which it was unlawful for those who entered, to lift up their eyes from the ground; the fourth was the temple of *shame,* where they sent all sinners and men of immoral lives. When using reproachful language, they used to say—" Go to *Tlazapuliateo!* "

" Of *Quetzalcoatl* they say, here he had remained some time, but he was called from thence. They entertained so lively a recollection of him, that they adored him as a god, first, because he taught them the art of working in gold and silver, which they had not till then seen or known in the country. Secondly, because he *never wished nor permitted sacrifices of blood, of slaughtered men or of animals, but only of bread, roses, spices, flowers, incense, and other sweet perfumes : and thirdly, because he forbad and prohibited with much success, wars, robbery and murder, and other injuries which are done by men to each other. They say that whenever they named in his presence bloodshed, war, or other evils calculated to afflict humanity, he turned aside his head and stopped his ears, in order not to see or hear them. They likewise praise him for his great purity and uprightness, and his exceeding temperance.* This god was held in veneration and reverence throughout all those kingdoms on account of his peculiar attributes."

" Las Casas, bishop of Chiapa, relates in his apology, which is in MS. in the convent of St. Dominic, that when he passed through the kingdom of Yutican, he found there a respectable ecclesiastic, of mature age; he charged him to proceed into the interior of their country, giving him a certain plan of instruction, in order to preach to them : at the end of a year, thus he wrote to the bishop—he had met with a principal lord, who informed him that they believed in God, who resided in heaven, even the Father, the Son, and the Holy Spirit. That the Father was named YEO*na*,[1] the Son *Bah-ab*,[2] who was *born of a virgin,* named Chibirias, and that the Holy Spirit was called *Euach.*[3] *Bah-ab,* the Son, they said was put to death by Eupuco, who scourged him, and put on his head a crown of thorns, and placed him with his arms stretched upon a beam of wood, and that on the third day he came to life, and ascended into heaven, where he is with the Father; that immediately after the *Euach* came in his place as a merchant, bringing precious merchandize, filling those who would with gifts and graces, abundant and divine."—Antiq. Mex. p. 162.

---

[1] Yehovah.   [2] Son (of) Father.   [3] Spirit.

THEOCRATIC GOVERNMENT.

BARON Humboldt discoursing on the *Theocratic* form of government of the Zac, Bolga, and Peruvians, remarks, that 'by the tradition of the former, their government was founded by a "mysterious personage," who lived in the temple of the SUPREME LIGHT, *two thousand years ago.*' Of *Quetzalcoatl* (which signifies the serpent with green feathers) they say ' he introduced the " boring" of the ear, that he walked " *barefoot,*" himself seeking as a *chosen place of retirement* the volcano Cetceptl, or mountain of speech, &c. He held the reins of government, taught them to cast metals, ordered fasts, and regulated the intercalations of the Toltic year. Though their ancient legislator is called by a name importing a serpent with green feathers, yet " He was an *ancient man and white bearded"*—called by Montezuma a " holy man, who led and taught them many things."

Don Alonza Ercilla says in his History of Chili, " The religious belief of the Auricanians is sublime. They acknowledge a supreme Being, whom they denominate by a word expressive of Supreme Essence. They also call him The SPIRIT of Heaven—the GREAT LIFE—The Thunderer—the Omnipotent—the Eternal—the Infinite. The government of this glorious CREATOR is the prototype of *their* polity. They are *all* agreed in the immortality of the soul, this animating and consolatory truth is deeply rooted and *innate* with them. They hold, that man is formed of two substances essentially different—the corruptible body and the incorruptible and eternal spirit. They have a tradition that the earth was covered with water, yet *not destroyed*—and that the same earth shall be covered with fire but *not destroyed.* There shall be great *signs before the end,* &c."

Locke, one of the ablest men Great Britain ever produced, observes, " that the commonwealth of the Jews, differed from all others, being an absolute Theocracy. The laws established there, concerning the *worship* of the one invisible Deity, were the *civil* laws of that people, and a part of their *political* government, in which God Himself was the Legislator."

" In this," observes Doctor Boudinot, " the Indians profess the same thing precisely. This is the exact form of their government, which seems unaccountable, were it not derived from the same original source, and is the only reason that can be assigned for so extraordinary a fact."

" It may be said, that the Jews were long governed by judges and kings. But these were not of their appointment, but of the appointment of God under Him, as his *substitutes* or *vicegerents.* " Blessed be the LORD thy God, who delighted in thee, to set thee on HIS Throne to be king *for* the Lord thy God." [1] Again, " They have not rejected thee ; but they have rejected Me, that I should not reign over them." [2] Again, " And now ye think to withstand the KINGDOM of the LORD, *in the* hands of the sons of David." [3]

" Agreeably to the Theocracy or divine government of Israel, the Indians think the Deity to be the *immediate* Head of their state. All the nations of the Indians have an inexpressible contempt of the white people. They used to call us, in their war orations, *the accursed people :* but they flatter themselves with the name of *the beloved people,*

[1] 2 Chron. ix. 8.   [2] 1 Samuel viii. 7.   [3] 2 Chron. xiii. 8.

because their supposed ancestors, as they affirm, were under the *immediate* Government of the Deity, who was present with them in a very peculiar manner, and directed them by prophets, while the rest of the world were aliens and out-laws to the covenant. When the old archimagus, or any one of their magi, is persuading the people at their religious solemnities to a strict observance of the old beloved or divine speech, he always calls them the *beloved* or *holy people*, agreeably to the Hebrew epithet *ammi*, (my people) during the Theocracy of Israel. It is their opinion of their Theocracy, that God chose them out of all the rest of man-kind, as his peculiar people.

" When any of their beloved people die, they soften the thoughts of death, by saying, *he is only gone to sleep with the beloved* '*forefathers*, and usually mention a common proverb among them, "*neitak intahah*," the days appointed, or allowed him, were finished. And this is their firm belief, for they affirm that there is a fixed time and place, when and where every one must die, without any possibility of averting it. They frequently say, " Such a one was weighed on the path, and made to be light." They always ascribe life and death to God's unerring and particular providence." [1]

[1] Adair in the Star in the West.

RELIGIOUS OBSERVANCES.

" IN every thing relating to the treatment of the Mexican children, even in the mode of punishing them, the Mexicans resembled the Jews. *Torquemeda* has also observed that festivals took place at the *naming* of the Infant, and afterwards on its being *weaned;* omitting further mention of *baptismal ceremonies and the use of circumcision,* both which it may be presumed, on the authority of very ancient writers, *were in use amongst the Mexicans.*"

" In nothing did the civil policy of the Mexicans more closely resemble that of the Hebrews, than in *their dedicating their children to the Temple,*[1] and afterwards sending them to be instructed by the master or superior Rabbi in the doctrines of their religion and moral and ceremonial laws. *Torquemeda* says that the ceremony of

[1] *Torquemeda* says "The same time in which this offering or purification was made, one of the old men held the child in his arms, whence it is plain that *either these people descend from the Hebrews, or that the devil gave them these rites and ceremonies to emulate those with which God honoured his people. Certain however it is that greater would have been this triumph of the accursed Demon if he had,*" &c. &c.

Baron Humboldt remarks, with reference to this passage of the interpretation of the collection of Mendoza, "*that the Mexican custom of naming children in the presence of three other children who were parties to the ceremony was analogous to the Jewish rite of baptising the proselytes before three witnesses.* The remaining rites of baptizing the children, and after presenting them with an offering at the Temple, seem to be a confusion of Christian ceremonies with Jewish customs and traditions, which however distant the period, or intricate the manner in which it was effected, the longer we meditate on the religious rites of the Mexicans and the Peruvians, the more we are inclined to believe did actually take place, (viz. the colonization of the new continent by the Hebrews.) The custom of offering their children at the Temple was peculiar to the Jews, and no other nations imitated them in this except the Mexicans."—p. 45.

dedicating their children to the military profession, was also a religious one."

He continues, " I likewise wish it to be noticed, that the Devil commanded amongst this vain Indian people, that the first thing a father bid his children do, should be to love and honor their gods." [1] Of the *excellent* nature however of the *moral precepts* which the Mexican parents inculcated on the minds of their children, the same author is a witness; where, adducing the authority of the book of Ecclesiasticus, in favour of the early education of children, quoting the seventh chapter, page 230, he says, the Indians strictly fulfilled this doctrine. " This doctrine" adds Torquemeda, " we shall find wonderfully approved amongst the Indians of the territory of New Spain, who not only took care to nourish their children with food and bodily aliments, for the sake of strengthening their bodies, but also with *admirable moral doctrines in order to render them rational and proper members of a civil community; and that they might live the life which had been allotted to them as befitted those who possessed minds capable of reason and order: since the doctrines of those Indians are characterized with much prudence and counsel. I will not omit to record their conversations and exhortations to their children, since from them it will be apparent that neither natural law, nor that of grace, nor human policy could demand more, as far as moral policy is concerned, setting aside the knowledge of the true God."*

These exhortations were translated from the Mexican language into the Spanish by the venerable Father Andrew

---

[1] It is certainly doing the Mexicans injustice to suppose that their embodiments of the attributes of God were considered by them as distinct gods. It would therefore be more in character with the rest of their peculiarities to introduce the Hebrew term אלהים which implies a concentration and manifestation of *powers* in one essence. It is impossible for our translated term to express this, for either it is simply *God* in the sense of a *unit*, or else in *combination of persons* it is *gods*.

D'Olmes, a brother of the order of the glorious Father St. Francis; (who laboured in this vineyard and new plantation of the Holy Gospel with the greatest diligence, undergoing great and numerous hardships in laying the foundation of this new church,) which exhortations in the Mexican language I have in my possession; and I can venture to affirm that neither the said Father D'Olmes, nor the Lord Bishop of Chiapa, Don Bartholomew Las Casas, who obtained them from him, nor I, who now own them, and have bestowed pains on understanding them, and thoroughly comprehending their metaphors; have known how to translate them into the same softness and sweetness as the natives uttered them in their own language. They impressed upon them the duty of serving the Gods, carrying the children with them to the Temples on appointed days, and hours, in order that they might acquire a liking for the same teaching when they should live separate from them, and become fathers of families."—p. 57.

" The early Spanish writers have not failed to point out some curious traits of resemblance to Hebrew usages, in certain acts performed by the Kings and Incas, and in the external marks of reverence these monarchs received from their subjects: these consisted in *their Kings presiding at sacrifices, dancing on great religious festivals; in being consecrated to the regal dignity by the hands of the high priests, with a pretended holy unction; in being invested with a crown and bracelets as the insignia of majesty. In his wearing a signet on his arm; in his rending his garments on receiving intelligence of any national calamity; in his saluting with a kiss,* the general who brought him tidings of a victory; in his employing regular couriers for the despatch of public matters; in the ceremonies with which his subjects were accustomed to enter the palace—(taking*

off their sandals, as in the temples of the gods,) as not
looking the king in the face, but *addressing him with their
eyes on the ground,* and finally, *in burning incense and
precious perfumes at his funeral.*"

Herrera remarks " that the priests of *Vitzliputzli,* were
entitled to *succeed to their office, by being born of families
resident in certain suburbs of the city, especially marked
out for the purpose.*" Numbers i. 53. The dress was a
crimson vest, resembling a robe, with open sleeves, to which
were fastened *fringes* as a border."—p. 69.

Amongst the Jews, all wars, not excepting their civil
ones, bore a religious character, &c. and in the twelfth
chapter of **Deuteronomy,** directions are given to the priests[1]
to accompany and exhort the soldiers to battle. The interpreter of the collection of Mendoza says, that priests
likewise followed the Mexican armies, not only for the
purpose of joining the combatants, but also to *perform
certain religious ceremonies,* in which some analogy is discovered between the customs of the two nations."

" It has already been observed, that many analogies
might be pointed out, in the usages of the Mexicans and
Jews, in reference to their treatment of their kings. But
omitting, in this place, to notice the oath which was admin-
istered to the kings of Mexico, at their coronation, by the
high priest, (which is described by *Gomara,* p. 122, of his
History of the Conquest of Mexico, in which the kings
made a *covenant with the people to protect the established
religion, to preserve the laws, and to maintain justice,*

---

[1] The Hebrews in going to war were accompanied by a Priest to serve some
of their special occasions in it ; and after a sacred unction bestowed upon him,
(we are told by Maimonides) he was called מלחמה משח (Priest of the war.)
" *That Incas waged war for the express purpose of compelling other nations to
lay aside what they deemed their idolatry, and embrace the knowledge of the
true God,* we have the authority of *Acosta,* and other eminent historians for
asserting."—p. 49.

reminding us of what David did, on a similar occasion, as recorded by Samuel—" So all the elders of Israel came to the king to Hebron, &c." and the great burning of spices and other odoriferous substances, which took place at the funerals of the kings of Mexico, which was also customary at the funerals of the Jewish kings, we shall remark that the regalia, worn by the kings of both nations, were nearly the same. Amongst the Jews, they consisted of a *crown* and *bracelets,* as is evident from 2 Sam. i. 18, where the Amalekite announces to David the death of Saul, bringing him, not his sword and armour, but what he thought would be a more agreeable present to an aspirant to the throne, the royal insignia. A *sceptre* was also part of the Jewish regalia, and a *mantle.* The *crown* of the Jewish king more nearly resembled a *mitre* than the crown worn by emperors and monarchs. A *crown* and *bracelets, sceptre* and *mantle* constituted, though not the entire, the principal part of the royal costume of the Mexican kings. The crown was named TEO*catli,* and the bracelets *Cozcatl,* and they are both represented in the 57th plate, in the collection of Mendoza, as forming a specimen of the dress worn by the Mexican kings, since the regal apparel of Montezuma differed but slightly from that of Moquihuix. It is true as a general remark, that both nations, in their costume [1] and the external decoration of their persons and buildings, nearly resembled each other. " *Set me as a seal upon thine heart, as a seal upon thine arm,*" and it is very singular since there was

---

[1] " Montezuma wore *sandals* embroidered with gold. The Mexican paintings shew that the use of shoes amongst the Mexicans was very general; their heroes, &c. are always represented with them. p. 230. They call themselves," says *Gumilla,* " to the third degree of kindred, brothers and sisters, this was a Hebrew custom in the time of Abraham. What *Gumilla* affirms of the frequency of *ablution,* and *anointing* themselves with oil, corresponds with the account of *Torquemeda* and *Clavegero. Oil was used likewise at the consecration of the high priests and the kings.*"

something peculiar in the Hebrew fashion, that this should have been a Mexican custom likewise, as we learn from *Cortez, Torquemeda, and Bernal Diaz.*"

" *Torquemeda* says, in the 20th chapter of the 8th book of his " Indian Monarchy," that the priests and ministers who lived in the great Temple of Mexico, were more than five thousand, who resided by day and by night within its walls, occupied in the service of the Temple. *These priests are constantly named Levites by Acosta,* and certainly that learned author may be excused for giving them that appellation, as the Temple service of the Mexicans was in reality very like that of the Jews."—p. 281.

" The offerings of the Mexicans consisted, like those of the Jews, *in the lives of animals, (or blood,) incense, and the first fruits, which, like the Jews, they presented three times a year, which Torquemeda undertakes, in the following manner to explain.* " It is certainly a thing calculated to create astonishment to see, in their offerings of the *first fruits,* the two republics resemble each other, but we need not feel so much surprise at it, since it was the *Devil* who persuaded and instigated them ; who, as we have proved in the whole course of this history, wished to *substitute himself* for God, *(remèdar a Dios),* whenever it was possible ; and this being the case, the task was more easy, inasmuch as these Indians are extremely addicted to *religious worship,* he found little trouble in inducing them to tender to him this kind of offering and sacrifice, which, as we have observed, *all paid very generally and regularly, without being either remiss in the offering, or inexact in its proper quantity.*"— Monarquia Indiana, cap. 21, lib. 8. in Antiquities of Mexico.

"The interpreter of the larger Vatican MS. says that *the light was obliged to be always kept burning in the Mexican Temples ; and instancing this and other traits of resemblance between the Mexicans and the Jews, he shortly afterwards adds, from all these circumstances, the fact is plain and probable, that this nation descends from the Hebrews, since all the ceremonies of this chapter are as it were, according to the text in Leviticus, such as, that the people shall not touch the holy things; and again as in Exodus, that light should be always in the temple, and incense, and trumpets, and sacred vestments."*—p. 66.

" *Cinna*-TEO-*Calli* was the proper name of a Mexican Temple, and which may be recognized as forming part of a compound name. The word *Cinna,* which corresponds exactly with the word Sinai, the mountain from which God delivered the laws and tables of stone to Moses. Its accompanying symbol is two rows of arrow-headed characters engraved upon a single table of stone. Similar rows of characters occur in the 65th and 73d pages of the larger Vatican MS., and in the 3d page of the first part of the Codex. The expression, arrow-headed characters, and table of stone, is applied here rather improperly to these symbols, in order to point out the possibility of the inclosed square, representing a table of stone, and of the lines which it contains, alluding to alphabetical writing."

" A respectable writer says, that the inhabitants of Florida made use in their religious songs of the exclamation, " *Hosannah,*" and their priests were named *Yohewas.*"—Collection of Mendoza, p. 71·

" It is certainly curious, that the Mexican mode of fortification seems chiefly to have consisted in their Temples, which were also like that of Jerusalem arsenals, and in the thick walls which surrounded their cities, protected on the outside by a fosse, with ramparts above."

" The Incas of Peru wore a *tassel* on the forehead,[1] as

---

[1] Some writers have thought that the Indians of Haiti or St. Domingo, named

the insignia of royalty, which, considering that they ac-counted thamselves the representatives of *Verachocha*, might have served to remind them *to keep his laws*, and like the rose worn by the *Muscas*, have been in imitation of the dress of *Bachiha*. The mitre upon the head of *Suga-moxti*, the founder of the empire of Botoga, and those upon the heads of the 10th and 11th Incas of Peru, are very deserving of notice, and remind us that the Incas of Peru, and the Zippas of Botoga, considered a priest the founder of their respective dynasties. The mitre does indeed seem to have usurped the place of the crown in the New World, for the *Copilli* worn by the Mexican monarch was a half mitre, and the coincidence is curious, that all the native Indian Monarchs, at the period of the discovery of America by the Spaniards, should have worn *mitres as the insignia of royalty.*"—P. 518—19.

" Acosta says, that the Inca, after confession, *walked into an adjoining river, bidding its waters receive his sins, and carry them into the sea, that he might be rid of their power.*" * * " In the 212th page of the 1st vol. of the Religious Customs of all Nations, the following passage occurs; " The ancient Hebrews formerly laid all their sins upon a he-goat, which they afterwards drove into the desert; but the modern Jews, instead of a goat, now throw them on the water." After dinner they repair to the brink of a pond, and then shake their clothes over it with all their might ; this practice is taken from the 19th verse of the 7th chapter of Micah. The Jews, as well as the Peruvians, entertained a

the phylacteries, which they bound to their hair *Zemes*. Piedrahuta in the 3rd chapter 1st book of his History of the Conquest of New Grenada, describes the stranger who preached to the *Mozcas* or Indians of Botoga,—whom some named *Nem-que-che-ba*, others *Bachicha*, and others *Inke*, as wearing a kind of phylae-tary on his forehead, in imitation of which the Indians of that province continued to wear roses of feathers hanging over their eye-brows, until the conquest of the territory by the Spaniards."

notion, that the sins of the fathers were visited upon the children."—p. 301.

" The Incas[1] went to war *for the express purpose of bringing the other tribes over to their faith.* Accordingly, we find that from New Mexico, to the extreme province of Chili, which resisted successfully the invasion of the Incas, the same religion with different[1] modifications of rites and ceremonies prevailed; and circumcision, although not universally practised, was one of its characteristics."—p. 306.

" Sahagun says in the fourteenth chapter of his first book, in mentioning the festival of *Xuhilhuitl, that the Mexicans ate on one of their fasts unleavened bread.*"—Ibid.

" It deserves to be remarked, that as amongst the Jews certain cities were appointed as cities of refuge, to which criminals might fly, and escape the punishment of the laws; *so amongst the Mexicans and other Indian states, there were appointed places of refuge to which culprits might fly and claim the rights of sanctuary.*"

Dr. Boudinot observes—" in almost every Indian nation there are several peaceable towns, called old beloved, ancient, holy, or white towns. They seem to have been formerly towns of refuge : for it is not in the memory of their oldest people that ever human blood was shed in them, although they often force persons from thence, and put them to death elsewhere."—Star in the West.

The places of refuge amongst the Southern Indians, were the palaces of their kings, called by the Mexicans *Tecpan*—wherever there was a palace, there was a city of refuge

---

[1] Of the Inca Nezahualcojotl, the Abbe Clavegero observes, " To his sons he said that although in conformity with the usages of the people, he permitted religious homage to *images* they should in their hearts detest their worship, which was only deserving of contempt, as it was *directed to lifeless forms;* that he acknowledged no other God than the Creator of heaven. He did not forbid image worship in his kingdom, though he inclined to do so, that he might not be deemed by the people sacrilegious."

likewise. But it may also be infered, although it is not
stated by the Indian writers, that the Mexican TEO*calli*,
especially the greater Temple of Mexico, were places of
refuge, and that the city of *Cholula was a city of refuge*."

" It is unnecessary to quote Scripture to shew, that to
offer incense in their Temple was a Jewish custom; since no
nation ever came so near the Jews in their prodigality in
making this offering to the Deity: but it deserves to be
remarked, that the Jews were *expressly commanded* in the
fortieth verse of the twenty-third chapter of Leviticus, to
*carry boughs and branches of trees in their hands as a reli-
gious ceremony;* " And ye shall take to you on the first day
boughs and branches of goodly trees; and of palm trees,
and the boughs of thick trees: and ye shall rejoice before
the Lord your God seven days."

" The Mexicans were accustomed to decorate their temples
profusely with boughs of trees and flowers; and to *carry them
in their hands in certain festive processions.* It is said in the
thirty-fifth chapter of Exodus of the Israelites, " And they
came both men and women, as many as were willing-hearted,
and brought bracelets, and ear-rings, and tablets, all jewels
of gold: and every man offered of an offering of gold
unto the LORD." The Mexican paintings shew, that the
Mexicans were accustomed to present at the shrine of their
gods jewels of gold, bracelets, and necklaces; and it would
also appear, that they placed *loaves of bread* in the sanctuary of their temples before their idols, which must
remind us of the Jewish shew-bread. *Acosta,* describing in
the ninth chapter of the fifth volume of his Natural and
Moral History of the Indies, the adoration which the Mexicans paid to their three principal Deities, of *Vitziliputzli* and
Tlaloc says, Præter haec etiam, &c." See Antiq. Mex. vol.
vi. p. 292.

Torquemeda says, " that in one of the Mexican months, the Mexicans celebrated a festival by going up to a neighbouring mountain, and building a kind of *tabernacle with boughs* for one of their principal idols. In the forty-second plate of the first part of the Monuments of M. Du Paix, under number ninety-seven, a stone table occurs in relievo containing four figures seated, &c. having a very *Jewish cast of countenance*, with *long beards;* one of whom holds what appears to be a *branch of palm or willow* in his hand. Between them in the centre is the *place of a Temple.* Exultation is evidently depicted in their countenances while there is something votive in their attitude."—page 292.

The purple veil said to have been spread before the shrine of *Tezcatlipoca*, and to have been painted with skulls and bones, recalls to our recollection the 35th verse of the 36th chapter of Exodus, in which mention is made of the veil of the tabernacle. *Torquemeda* says " that the skulls and bones which occupied the place of the Cherubims in the temple of *Tezcatlipoca*, signified that God possessed equal power over life and death." " In the same way as amongst the Jews, none were permitted except the Levites to enter the place of the Sanctuary, so the Mexican ritual forbade any but the priests to enter the Sanctuary of *Tezcatlipoca*." Acosta, describing the temple of that god in the 13th of the 5th book, says :—

" As the Temple in Jerusalem contained great store of gold and silver vessels which the king of Babylon pillaged, so the Peruvian temples were excessively rich in precious vases, especially that of Pachacamac, near Lima, from which *Acosta* observes Francis Pizarro and his soldiers obtained immense quantities of gold and silver vases."

It was customary among the Jews to summon the people to worship by the sounding of horns ; and to *blow trumpets,* was a religious ceremony which Moses declared in the 23d chapter of Leviticus, that God himself appointed. " And the LORD spake unto Moses, saying, speak unto the children of Israel, saying, in the seventh month, in the first day of the month, shall ye have a sabbath, a memorial of blowing of trumpets, an holy convocation : " and again in the 29th chapter of Numbers, " In the seventh month, in the first day of the month, shall ye have a sabbath, a memorial of blowing of the trumpets unto you.'' It is not a little curious that according to *Torquemeda,* the Mexicans should have been summoned to prayer at stated hours by the blowing of horns, in the same way as the Jews, although they were acquainted with bells ; and that according to *Garcia,* they should have approached the temple with the same reverential custom of *pulling off their sandals* when within a certain number of paces distant from it. See Exodus iii. They have likewise imitated the Jews in their *sacerdotal* costume, and *Garcia,* in the 2nd chapter of the 36th of the account of the Indians, treating of the resemblance [1] of the Indian dress to that of the Jews, says, " *Father Augustin Davila, Arcopisco de St. Domingo, ressere on su Historia*

---

[1] The natives of Peru in ancient times allowed their hair to grow long like the Nazarites, with the exception of that class called Orezonis ; and those who are yet unconquered, wear at the present day the hair in this fashion. That this was the dress and costume of the Hebrews, is evident, as well from their histories, as from their ancient paintings, which represent them habited in this apparel : and this kind of dress and sandals was worn by the apostles. The two articles of apparel, the mantle and tunic which are worn by the Indians of Peru, were what Samson laid a wager on, and which are named in Scripture the tunic talis, and syndon, which are the same as what the Indians of Peru call cusma and paca, and the Spaniards, camiseta, and mantan. It would appear from what *Garcia* here asserts, who speaks from *observation, having himself been many years in Peru,* that the dress of the Peruvians was more like that of the Jews, than was the Mexicans ; whilst the sandals of the people of New Spain, *were strictly in the Hebrew fashion.* If that learned author, as well as *Acosta,* had sought out the Hebrew analogies, in the customs and manners of the Indians of New Spain and Peru, before *Spanish* intercourse had rendered many of those customs obsolete, and had put their books in the beginning of the sixteenth century, instead of the beginning of the seventeenth : perhaps they would have found that *no Hebrew fashion* was wanting in the New World."—Ibid.

*Dominicana del Nuevo Mondo, como en un pueblo, Ila-
mado Tamaculapa que es en la Misteca de Nallaron
unas vestiduras sagrádas de al que ellos teieen por escon-
didas los Indios.*" The Arcopisco of St. Domingo, relates
in his Historia Dominicana of the New World, that some
sacred vestments were discovered in a town called *Tecpan*,
in Mexico, which had belonged to the person whom they
considered the High Priest, which nearly resembled those
worn by the High Priest of the Mexican nation, which vestments the Indians kept concealed.—P. 293.

" In the twelfth part of that manuscript in the Bodleian
Library, which seems to represent the *migration* of the
Mexicans, or some other subject connected with a descent
into hell, and which is unfortunately only a fragment of a
large painting, from which a part has evidently been torn
off; the figure of a Mexican priest occurs in a dress very
like that of the high priests of the Jews ; *the linen ephod, the
breast plate, and the border of pomegranates* described in
Exodus, *are there represented.* The golden bells are wanting, but those ornaments will be found in the valuable
paintings preserved in the Royal Library at Dresden,
attached to the dress of several of the figures, as was
ordained in the 28th chapter of Exodus, in the use of the
dress of the Jewish high priest." *Gomara* has observed,
" that a *girdle* sometimes formed part of the Mexican
costume."

" The head of the above-mentioned priest seems to be
ornamented with ribbons interwoven with the hair ; but the
Mexican TEocatli, or crown, which bore a much closer
resemblance to the head-dress of Aaron, than the episcopal
mitre, is represented in the same page of the Oxford manuscript, on the head of another figure ; it also frequently
occurs amongst the paintings of the college of Mendoza, and

is there always painted *blue*. This crown or mitre was worn by the Mexican kings, and likewise by the judges; the former had it richly adorned with *plates of gold*. Those kings, it is supposed, united pontifical with regal dignity ; although the ostensible head of the Mexican religion was the high priest, who at his consecration to the office, was *anointed with oil.*" Exodus xxix. p. 296.

" Thou shalt make a plate of pure gold, and grave upon it like the engravings of a signet, HOLINESS UNTO THE LORD : and thou shalt put it on a *blue* lace, that it may be upon the *mitre,* upon the *fore-head* of the mitre shall it be." These things deserve to be noticed in the Mexican *mitre.*   It frequently consisted of a *plate of gold* on a *blue* ground.   It was tied to the hair by a *lace* or ribbon, and was perpetually worn on the *fore-head* of the kings *or the priest.*   The breastplate of the high priest is described in Exodus xxviii."

" The *breast-plates* of the Mexicans appear to have been of different shapes and sizes, and *to have been set with precious stones.*   In the 13th page of the original Mexican paintings preserved in the library of the Vatican, the figure of a priest occurs with a round breast-plate attached by a chain to his neck, and near him appears to be two other breast-plates, one square, and the other of a round form."

" It is to be supposed, that so solemn an injunction to the Jews to wear *fringes* on the borders of their garments, would be scrupulously obeyed throughout their generations. Reference to the 8th page of the Oxford MS. will shew that it was a Mexican custom to wear *fringes* and borders fastened to their apparel, and an examination of any of the Mexican paintings contained in this volume, will establish the fact."—p. 299. Antiq. Mex.

" Acosta, in the 25th chap. of the 5th book of his Natural

and Moral History of the Indies, says, Daniel's description in his vision, resembles a passage in the 9th chap. of the 6th book of Sahagun's History of New Spain, in which the newly-elected King of Mexico returns thanks to the God of heaven,—the God of years : the following is the passage alluded to. " Who am I, O LORD ! and of what account, that thou shouldest place me in the rank of those whom thou regardest, and knowest, and numberest among thine allies and elect, whom thou dost esteem as persons sustaining the highest honour, and such as are born and educated for dignity and royal thrones : and accordingly hast endowed them with talents and wisdom, selecting for that purpose those who are *descended from noble and illustrious lineage*, who have been brought up with those expectations, and who have been baptized in the signs and constellations which preside at the birth of kings, that they might become *thy instruments, thy images* to govern kingdoms, Thou being in them, and speaking by their mouth, and they declaring Thy words, that thus they might, *in conformity to the will of their ancient God, and Father of God,—even the God of Fire, whose habitation is in the waters which battlements and encompasses where He dwells—surrounded with works—as it were of roses, whose name is Xuileticeutli, who determines, examines, and brings to an issue, the controversy of the multitudes, cleansing Thy people as it were with water, before whom are ever present in attendance, the noble ones, &c.*"—p. 364.

" Both nations (viz. Hebrews and Mexicans) were most punctual in the payment of their religious offerings, and first fruits, &c. The Mexicans, as Montezuma informed Cortez, feared if they failed in this part of their religious duties that they would incur the severest vengeance, &c. And the prophet Malachi, or rather God speaking through the mouth

of that prophet, assures the Jews that they were under a
peculiar blessing promised in the third chapter of the book
of Malachi."   *   *   *

"The paintings of the
Mexicans shew that censers were used in profusion in the
ceremonies of their *religion*. *The priests lodged round the
temples in chambers built for the express purpose*, and it
appears from the twenty-seventh verse of the ninth chapter
of Chronicles, that a certain portion of the Levites lodged
round the Temple built by Solomon. *The Mexican temples
contained fountains in the courts, in which the priests performed their ablutions*, and Solomon is said to have made
a molten-sea which contained two thousand baths, which
served the same purpose, and stood in the court of the Temple. Every thing relating to *preserving unextinguished the
sacred fire which burnt in the Temple, was considered by the
Mexicans as a matter of the utmost consequence.* The manner
in which they kindled the sacred fire is not precisely known :
that it was a religious rite accompanied with certain ceremonies, cannot be doubted ; and we may even be permitted
to believe from an expression in the fourteenth verse of the
nineteenth chapter of Ezekiel : "And fire has gone forth
from a rod of her branches, which hath devoured her fruits,"
that they were acquainted with the Mexican method of
kindling fire by wood."

"Many passages of scripture lead us to imagine that the
ground-plan of the great Temple of Mexico resembled that
of Jerusalem."[1]—p. 378.

"Reasons for supposing that the Mexicans were acquainted
with the book of Job, will be found at page 382 of this vol.

---

[1] It deserves to be remarked, observes the commentator, that the name of
the HOLY HOUSE, which Josephus always bestows upon the temple of Jerusalem, is the literal signification of the Mexican TEO-CALLI.

(Mex. Antiq.) and their custom of shaving their hair, *sitting upon the ground, and sprinkling dust upon their heads as a sign of humiliation,* closely resembles what is said in the first chapter of that book, of the mourning of Job and his friends."—p. 523-5, notes.

" According to Rabbinical doctrine, the accusations of Satan were confounded by the noise of the trumpets which Moses commanded the priests to blow on their solemn festivals, and which the Mexicans, (as it were, in compliance with the precept contained in the eighth verse of the tenth chapter of Numbers. " And the priests, the *sons of Aaron*, shall blow with the trumpets, and they shall be to you an ordinance throughout your generations ")—continually sounded in the courts of their temples; a custom which the interpreter of the Vatican Codex, believed they had borrowed from the Hebrews, as he unequivocally declares p. 224 of the present volume," (viz. Antiq. of Mexico.)

In connection with this *typical silencing* of the enemy and avenger, a striking passage occurs with respect to the perfection of praise from *guileless lips.*

" The Mexicans believed that the intercession of children in behalf of men are efficacious with God ; we shall quote a remarkable passage from the twenty-first chapter of *Sahagun's* History, in confirmation of this curious fact. " They say that it is for their sake that God preserves the world, and that they are our intercessors with God ;" which passage, adds Aglio, deserves to be considered in connection with what is said of children in the eighth Psalm, " *Out of the mouths of babes and sucklings hast thou ordained strength because of the enemy and the avenger.*"—p. 517-18. notes.—Ibid.

Of the same peculiarity of belief, the interpreter goes on to observe, " They believed that they were dear to God,

and that they interceded with Him for men : that at their
death they went to heaven, and were nourished by *the Tree
distilling milk which grew in the garden of Tonacateuctli*
where they ever abided in the presence of *Tonacateuctli;* the
name of the tree was *Chichiualquanitl,* and a representation
of it will be found in the fifth page of the lesser Vatican MS.
When we recollect what is said in the New Testament, of
little children, and the mysterious words, " Take heed that
ye offend not one of these little ones *who believe in me.* For
in heaven their angels do always behold the face of my
Father who is in heaven," &c. " Considering at the same
time, that the signification of *Tonaquatitlan,* is, *the Place
where grows the Tree of our bodies or life,* that word being
compounded of *tonacaqu,* the human body, and *quanitl,*
which signifies a tree or piece of wood ; to which is added
a particle of local reference :—Can a doubt remain in our
minds that the Mexicans borrowed some of their notions
about children from the scriptures, and had heard of the Tree
of Life which grew in the garden of Eden, the fruit of which
is said in the twenty-second verse of the third chapter of
Genesis, to confer *immortality on the taster,*" &c.

One of the curious and characteristic notices which we have
from the Abbe Clavegero, is as follows : " At the foot of the
hill is *now* the most famous church in the new world, dedicated to the true God ; where people from the most remote
corners assemble to *worship* the celebrated and truly *miraculous image* of the most *Holy Lady* of Guadaloupe ; *thus*
converting a place of abomination into a mercy-seat, where
religion has distributed its favours," &c.

Speaking of these " abominations," he says, " The divinity
of these false gods was acknowledged by prayers, kneeling,
prostrations, with vows and fasts, and other austerities, sacrifices, and offerings." * * " They prayed upon their knees,

with their faces turned toward the east, and therefore made
their sacrifices with the door to the west." " There was a
Temple, or as the Mexicans called it ' *House of God*'
where," continues Clavegero, "the king of Mexico retired
at certain times for the purpose of *fasting* and *prayer*. The
high priest had also a place of retirement within its pre-
cincts. There were also within its enclosure a house of
entertainment for the reception and accommodation of those
strangers who came on devout visits to the Temple. There
were ponds in which the priests *bathed*, and a fountain of
whose waters they *drank*." " In the pond called Tezcapan,
many bathed in obedience to a particular vow made to their
gods. The water of *one* of the fountains was esteemed *holy*;
it was drank only at the most solemn feasts." " There were
places allotted to the rearing of birds for the *sacrifices*, and
gardens in which odoriferous herbs and flowers were used
for the *altar*." " All the old historians speak with wonder
of the multitude of places of worship." " Cortez wrote to
king Charles V. that from the top of one Temple he had
counted more than four hundred towers of others."[1] Of
the most ancient, the worthy Abbe observes, " The lofty
pyramid raised by the Toltics, remains to this day in that
place where there was formerly a temple consecrated to the
false deity, and now a holy sanctuary[2] *for the mother* of the
true God ; and the pyramid, from its great antiquity, is so
covered with earth and bushes, that it seems more like a
natural eminence than an edifice." " We are ignorant indeed
of its dimensions, but its circumference at the lower part is
more than half a mile." " We have reason to believe that

---

[1] " Certifico a vuestra Alteza que yo contè desder una mosqueta, quatro cientas
y tantas torres en la dicha cuidad (de Cholula) y todas son de mosquetas."—
Letter to Charles V. Oct. 30, 1520.

[2] Thus Cortez addressed the Lord of Champoella, after ordering his soldiers to
throw down and destroy *their* images. " That as they could never more adore
those detestable images of the *Demon* their *enemy*, he would place in their stead

that tract of country called TEO*totlalpan*, ' Land of God,'
was so named for being the possession of the Temples."
" There were besides, daily great numbers of *free offerings*,
from the devout, of all kinds of provisions, and ' *first fruits*,'
which were presented on returning thanks for seasonable
rains, and other blessings of heaven," " The surplus of the
provision contributed for the maintenance of the *priests*, was
distributed amongst *the poor*, for whom also there were
hospitals in all the larger towns." " The high priests were
the oracles whom the king *consulted* in all the more important affairs of the state, and no war was ever undertaken
without their approbation. It belonged to them to *anoint*
the king after his election," &c. " For *incense* they made
use of an aromatic gum, but on certain festivals they employed *chapopotli*, or bitumen of Judea; the censers were
of clay or gold." " The priests [1] observed many fasts and
great austerity of life, they seldom even *tasted* wine; all
the time of their ministrations in the temples they were
living in *separation* from their wives. Incontinence was
punished with death by bastinado. Those who failed to perform the nocturnal duties of the temple (*repairing the fire*
which was *never suffered to go out*, &c.) had boiling water
poured on their heads."

" Many of the Mexican paintings would seem to imply
that the Mexicans were acquainted with various books of
the Old Testament, and had even attempted to express in
brilliant colours and hieroglyphics, the very same metaphors

---

an *image* of the *true Mother* of God, that they might *worship* and implore *her
protection* in all their necessities." " He caused an altar to be made after the
model of the *Christians*, and placed the image of the *Most Holy Mary* there ! " &c.

[1] " The prophet Jeremiah in verse 21 of the eighth chapter of his prophecy thus
figuratively describes the grief which he felt for the afflicted state of his land, &c.
which passage might have induced the Mexican priests to paint their faces black
as a symbol that they mourned and were afflicted for the sins of their people.
" For the hurt of the daughter of my people am I wounded, I am black," &c.—
Ibid. p. 364.

as had been employed by the prophets whose frequent denunciations of vengeance against the Jews and other nations on account of their sins, might have laid the foundation of a school for painting among the Mexicans, which would convey the same ideas of religious terror to the imagination, but through the medium of another sense. *How, it may be demanded, could so many scriptural images and allegories have presented themselves to the minds of the Mexicans, if they had not had some acquaintance with the forcible language of the prophets; and from what source could they have been derived?"*

" Mexican paintings contain allusion to the restoration of the dispersed tribes of Israel; and we may remark that it is not improbable that the three principal figures in the pages 89, 90, of the lesser Vatican MS. represented each of them as a sucking infant—no doubt introduced with some mysterious design, may refer to the famous prophecy of the *return* of the Jews to *their own land, &c."* " *Rejoice ye with Jerusalem, and be glad with her, all ye that love her: rejoice for joy with her, all ye that mourn for her: that ye may suck and be satisfied with the breasts of her consolations; that ye may draw forth with delight, of the abundance of her glory.* For thus saith the LORD, I will extend *peace* to her like a river, and the influx of the Gentiles like a flowing stream; then shall ye *suck,* ye shall be *borne upon her arms* and *dandled upon her knees.* As one whom his mother comforteth so will I comfort you; and ye shall be comforted IN JERUSALEM."

" The supposition that the three female figures with infants at their breast, refer to the above prophecy, is chiefly founded on the situation which they occupy in the Mexican paintings which precede and follow them; since the *Branch* is found in the same page as one of the figures, and that

Quetzalcoatl slaying the Leviathan or Dragon, occurs in the next page, which appears to be a *consummation* of the shadows, types, and symbols with which that and the other Mexican paintings abound."[1] Zech. iii. 8. vi. 12. Psalm lxxx. 15. Isaiah iv. 2.

" In the Bodleian Library is a symbol very much resembling a jaw-bone, from the side of which water seems to issue forth, which might allude to the story of Samson slaying a thousand Philistines with such a jaw-bone which remained miraculously unbroken in his hand, and from which he quenched his thirst. In the first page of the Borgian MS. a remarkable representation of *Quetzalcoatl*, cast forth from the jaws of some amphibious animal occurs, in reference to which curious painting it would be interesting to know whether the Hebrews had any tradition that their Messiah would be devoured by a monster who would afterwards be compelled to yield up his prey ; like the *serpent* in the seventy-fifth page of the lesser Vatican MS. which a fierce *Eagle* compels to disgorge a *lamb*—the symbol of suffering innocence amongst the Mexicans, according to Humboldt, which corresponded to the *lamb* of the Hebrews, and which afterwards was a type substituted for the latter by the Hebrews of Mexico, and refered by them to *Quetzalcoatl* in the same manner as their brethren of Peru appeared to have replaced the sacrifice of sheep in the old world, by those of *llamas* in the new : the *former species of animal being unknown to the Indians before the arrival of the Spaniards among them.*"—p. 6 1.

" In Exodus xix. 6, God commands Moses to address the following language to the Hebrews, " Ye shall be unto Me a kingdom of priests, an holy nation." The Mexicans

---

[1] The paintings more particularly referred to are in the seventy-seventh and seventy-ninth pages of the lesser Vatican MS.

resembled the Hebrews in being a nation of priests, &c. Jeremiah's apostrophe, " I am called by Thy Name, O LORD God of Hosts." This text may receive some illustration from the following curious passage of *Sahagun's* History, in which that learned author gives some account of the ancient *Toltecas,* " *they were very religious and much addicted to prayer, they worship one God only whom they name Quetzalcoatl,* whose priests bore likewise the same appellation." Of a particular person with whom the author had conversation, he goes on to say, " He was frequently accustomed to declare that there was one God only, and Lord, whose name was *Quetzalcoatl,* and that he requires no other sacrifices than *snakes* and *butterflies.*" [1] We here only wish to refer to the thirty-sixth page of the present work, viz. (Antiq. of Mex.) in order to point out the probability that God's promise to Jeremiah, "Thou shalt be as my mouth," was known to the Mexicans since the newly-elected king of Mexico in a prayer of thanksgiving to *Tezcatlipoca,* there emphatically says of kings, &c. " They are thine instruments, and thine images to govern thy kingdoms, Thou being in them, and speaking through their mouth, and they declaring Thy words," &c.

The Abbe Clavegero institutes an interesting comparison between the religion of the Mexicans and that of the ancient Greeks, Romans, and other famous nations. He observes, "The Romans, like the Greeks, shewed the *opinion* they entertained of their gods [2] by the *vices* which they ascribed

---

[1] From a people abounding in allegory might these not be *symbolic of evil desires and vain thoughts?*

[2] " *Jove* that licentious omnipotence, that " Father," that " king" as the poets style him, sometimes as a *satyr,* as in the case of Antiope, or as a *swan,* as in that of Leda, or as a *bull,* in that of Europa, or as *gold,* to corrupt Danae, accomplished his guilty purposes. Of the same stamp were the subaltern train, especially the *dei majores,* or *select* gods, as they were called. "Select," says St. Augustine, "for the superiority of their *vices.*" "What good example could those nations imitate in their gods who had nothing consecrated but their

to them.   Their whole mythology is a long series of *crimes;* the whole life of their gods was made up of *enmities, revenge, incest, adultery,* and other *base passions,* capable of defaming the most degenerate of men."

"The Mexicans entertained very different ideas of their deities. We do not find, in all their mythology, traces of the least of that depravity which characterized the idols of these nations.   The Mexicans honoured the *virtues,* not the vices, of their divinities. The Mexicans believed they had a strong aversion to every species of vice, therefore their worship was calculated to appease that displeasure which the guilt of man provoked, and to procure their favour and protection by repentance and religious respect."

"There is not to be found in the rites of the Mexicans the least trace of those abominable customs which were so commonly blended with those of the Romans and other nations of antiquity.   But how could they celebrate the feasts of *Venus, Bacchus, Priapus,* &c. without such depraved practices.   How was it possible for them to have been ashamed of those vices which they saw *sanctioned* by their own divinities? "   "We confess that their sacrifices were cruel, and the Mexican austerities beyond measure barbarous.   The Romans, while under the kings, sacrificed young children to the goddess Mania.   Authors cited by Suetonius, affirm that Augustus, in honor of his uncle, Julius Cæsar, who was by this time *deified* by the Romans, sacrificed three hundred Romans, partly senators and partly knights, upon an altar erected to the *new deity.*   Nor were the Spaniards free from this practice."   "If those Spaniards who wrote the history of

crimes. What merits obtained deification for *Leena* among the Greeks, and to *Lupa Fuula* among the Romans?   But what shall we say of the Egyptians who were amongst the first authors of superstition? They not only paid worship to the most loathsome animals, but leeks, onions, and garlic."—Clavegero Disser.

Mexico, had not forgotten this, they would not have wondered at such sacrifices among the Mexicans." "What numbers of men must have been consumed in those hecatombs of the ancient Spaniards!" "*The Mexican sacrifices have been greatly exaggerated by those whose interest it was to defame them.*" "In their inhumanity to their prisoners the Mexicans voluntarily partook in their own case, as the dreadful austerities [1] of the priests, &c. demonstrate." —Clavegero Dissertation.

"Emanuel Mores and Acosta affirm that the Brazilians marry in their own tribe or family. Charlevoix writes of the Hurons and Iroquois, that the wife is obliged to marry her husband's nearest kinsman."—Star in the West.

Beltrami, a literary traveller describing a marriage ceremony amongst the Sieux, adds, "The father grants his request on condition of his remaining with him, and hunting

---

[1] By Father Ovales' account, the Indian priestly austerities were not mitigated by that kind of gospel which the church had introduced. He observes of a solemn festival and procession. "This procession is divided into three troops; the first of which carries La Veronica to the cathedral, where it stays for the second, in which comes the Redeemer with his cross, *so heavy that he is forced* to kneel often; in sight of a vast multitude the Veronica comes, and kneeling down to the *image* of Christ, which is a very large one, *seemingly wipes his face, and then shews the people the representation of it remaining* in the handkerchief; then appears the third procession; in which comes St. John, shewing the Virgin Mary, that dolorous spectacle," &c. "There are to be seen some people whipping themselves with divers sorts of penance, each one according to his own devotion; yet the processions which are called *by excellence* "the bloody processions," are performed this night. This is from the Chapel of the *true* cross." He who carries the cross is obliged (besides the collation, which he provides for the preacher, &c) to provide men to attend the procession and relieve the *whippers* who often draw so much blood as to faint away ; and others take care to cut off some of the *spurs* of the disciplines, for they used to have so many on that *they almost kill themselves*, nay, I have seen some of so indiscreet a zeal, that they used certain buttons with points, so sharp, that if they were let alone, it is a dispute whether they would not die before the end of the procession. Before this, go also two others, both of them *bloody processions*—one of the Indians, and it is this which has most whippers." "There is another ;" "a great *cross* is set up, and when the *image* of the Virgin comes to it, it *lifts up its eyes*, as one who misses the sovereign good which hung upon it, and drawing out a white handkerchief, applies it to the eyes, as if crying, and then opening the arms, embraces the cross, and kneeling, kisses the foot of it once or twice, all this is done *so dexterously* that one would swear it were a living creature."— See Ovale Hist. in Pinkerton Coll.

for him a year longer : such are the wages of the Sieux.
Among the Chippeways he is not at liberty to remove till he
has obtained offspring of his marriage.   Here we find is
the case of Jacob and Laban.—See letters to Countess
Campagnoni.

Charlevoix, speaking of the northern Indians, observes,
that " the greater part of their feasts, their songs, and their
dances, appeared to him to have had *their rise from religion ;*
and yet preserve some traces of it.   I have met with some
persons," says he, " who could not help thinking that our
Indians were descended from the *Hebrews,* and found in
every thing some affinity between them and that people.
There is indeed a resemblance—as not to use knives at certain meals, and not to break the bones of the beast that they
ate at those times (and we may add that they never eat
the lower part of the thigh, but always reject it.)   The separation of their women after the manner of the Jewish," &c.

Bertram observes, that " In every town or tribe there is
a resident high priest usually nicknamed by the whites, the
powow, the juggler, the conjurer, &c. besides several of
inferior rank.   But that the oldest high priest or seer always
presides over spiritual affairs, and is a person of great consequence.   He maintains and exercises great influence in
the state, particularly over the military affairs, their council
never determining on an expedition without his sanction and
assistance.   These people believe most firmly that their
priest or seer has communion with powerful invisible spirits,
who they suppose have some delegated share in human
affairs."   He further adds, that " these Indians are no
idolators, unless their puffing their tobacco fume towards
heaven, and *rejoicing at the appearance of the new moon*
may be termed such."   " It is evident," observes a writer
conversant with their customs, that " they use the smoke of

their calmut in a *sacred* manner, as the Jews did their *incense*—and as to the new moon, as they reckon their time by
it, they are as careful observers of it as the Jews are."—See
Star in the West.

Smith in his history, observes of the Indians in the year
1681, that " their religious solemnity of singing and dancing
was performed rather as something handed down from their
ancestors than from any knowledge of its origin. They said
their Great King also created them, and that He dwelt in a
glorious land where the spirits of the just should go and live.
Their most solemn worship was the sacrifice of their first fruits,
in which they burnt the fattest buck and feasted together on
what else they had collected. But in *this sacrifice they
broke no bones of the animal.* When done, they gathered
them very carefully," &c.—p. 140. The same writer assures
us that " twelve men take each a stone which they make
hot in the fire, and place them together after the manner of
an altar within the tent, and thereon burn the fat of the
insides of the sacrifice. At the same time they cry to the
worshippers outside ' We pray—or praise l' They without,
answer, ' We hear !' Those in the tent then cry aloud
Yoh-hah ! After the fat was offered, some tribes burned
tobacco finely cut, in imitation of incense. Other tribes
chose only ten men and ten stones."

Doctor Beatty visited the Delaware nation, of whom Sir
William Penn bears a similar testimony. The occasion of a
great council was a proposition whether they should go to
war. " At this time," says he, " they killed a buck and
roasted it, as a kind of sacrifice on twelve stones, which
they would *not suffer any tool of iron to touch.* They did
not eat of the middle joint of the thigh.' " In short," he
adds, " I was astonished to find so many of the Jewish
customs prevailing among them, and began to con-

clude there must be some affinity between them and the Jews."

" The Muscoghea tribe," says Dr. Boudinot, " sacrifice a piece of every deer they kill at their hunting camps or near home. If the latter, they dip the middle finger in the broath, and sprinkled it over the domestic tombs of their dead," &c. Charlevoix informs us, " That to be esteemed a good hunter, a man must fast three days without the least nourishment, having his face covered all the time. When the fast is over, the candidate sacrifices to the GREAT SPIRIT a piece of each of the animals he intends to hunt. His family and relations do not touch these devoted gifts ; they would as soon die with hunger as eat any of them."

" A people who have lived so long separated from the nations of the earth, are not to be wondered at in having forgotten the meaning and end of their sacrifices."—Boudinot's Star in the West.

Boturini informs us that he discovered one of those knotted cords called by the Peruvians *quipos,* and by the Mexicans *Nepohuali-zitzin,*[1] in the possession of a powerful lord of the province of *Tluxcallan.* It was so consumed by age, that it served only to convince me that they had been used, (although sparingly) ; it would appear equally probable that paintings resembling those of the Mexicans had formerly existed in Peru, although consigned to perpetual oblivion by the prudence of those who thought that such documents had better never be brought to light. The same reason may be assigned for Europe after the lapse of three centuries, being before the publication of the American monuments of

---

[1] Doctor Robertson observes of the Peruvians : " Every officer intrusted with the Inca's commands might proceed alone throughout the empire without opposition, for on producing a *fringe* from the royal Borla, &c. the lives and fortunes of the people are at his disposal."—Hist. Amer. vol. ii. p. 308.

Baron Humboldt, ignorant whether the soil of the new world possessed any marks of antiquity ! "

" We come," says the commentator on the Antiquities of Mexico, " to another precept by which we find from the indubitable testimony of their own paintings, that the Mexicans followed more· scrupulously the Jews of the middle ages : viz. " Thou shalt make thee fringes," &c. From the " four corners of thy vesture," (which could not apply to the girdle) it may be inferred, that the *square*[1] mantle which covered their body is understood, and that was precisely the part of the dress to which the Mexicans fastened *fringes*." " Further arguments," he adds, " may appear unnecessary, to establish the fact that, in military matters as well as in their civil institutions, the Mexicans resembled the Jews. It is a remarkable fact which admits of no doubt (the proof of it being found in their paintings) that the Mexicans evinced a predilection for exactly the same numbers as the Jews."—p. 77·

The attachment of the wandering tribes of the north, for their dogs, is as proverbial as is their traditional contempt for the term " *dog*." The following notices are illustrative of this peculiarity :

The French accompanied by their Indian allies, came to the state of New York, in order to attack the Onondagoes, one of the confederate tribes of that territory, which had espoused, or rather which had been allured into the British interest. On entering the Indian village, they found only a very aged man, the others having fled during the darkness of the night. One of the allies of the French stabbed the

---

[1] This is the well known tallis which the Jews all over the world use in their synagogues. In eastern countries it was the common daily covering, as is evident from the circumstance related by the evangelists where the woman touched the fringe of the tallis, or square mantle, improperly translated " hem of his garment." For the origin of the tzitzis, or fringe, see Deuter. xxii. 12.

old man; who thus indignantly addressed him, "You ought rather to make me die by fire, that these French *dogs* may learn how to suffer like *men*—you their Indian allies--you *dogs of dogs,* think of me when you come to suffer through them."—See Hoyt's Indian Wars, p. 159.

Mr. M'Kenny, an agent of the United States government, writes, " there is hardly any thing on which an Indian sets so much value as his dog—this is proverbial; but yet he is constantly referred to as an object of *contempt.*" [1] He illustrates this by an interesting incident of which he was an eye witness.

It was customary to call the nations because of their *lawless excesses, dogs.* There is a remarkable instance of this in the prophetic appeal of David; who seeing by faith that the *Romans* would be the executioners of the sentence which the religious world of Jerusalem pronounced against the Messiah, thus characterises that event: " Deliver my darling from the power of the dogs; " in the same manner we find apostate professors designated 2 Peter ii. 22. Isaiah characterises false teachers as such, lvi. 11. Philip. iii. 2. Matt. vii. 6. the term is applied to unregenerate characters, as also xv. 27. Rev. xxii. 15.

" Father Joseph Gumilla says in the 59th of the Oronoco Illustrade : " I affirm in the second place, that the nations of the Oronoco and its streams, observed many Hebrew cere·monies during the time of their paganism, which they followed blindly without knowing wherefore ; they had been trans-

---

"[1] It appears that an Indian had been falsely accused of murder. We told him if he had been guilty, we would have tried him by our laws, and if on proof it had turned out that he had been found guilty, he would have been hanged. During this examination his brother came up to the table greatly agitated. He said he knew the murderers had upbraided him because he would not join them. Another Indian declared he was *innocent.* The governor said, Will you put your hand on your breast and swear *that,* in the presence of the GREAT SPIRIT? The moment the interpreter put this question, he looked him full in the face and answered, " *Am I a dog,* that I should *lie?* " 2 Samuel iii. 8.

mitted by tradition—handed down from father to son, without their being able to assign any reason for the practice of them." " There is not that Jew in existence," he adds, " who holds the flesh of the pig, &c. in such abhorrence, as these said Gentiles," &c. Lafitau and Rochfort, of the Caribs observe, " They reject with abhorrence some of the richest bounties of nature ; refusing to eat the hog, the sea-cow, the turtle, and the eel, with which their rivers are stored ; this motive," it is added, " has been supposed to arise from religious motives like the Jews." &c.[1]

Acosta says, " the garments of the southern Indians are shaped like those of the ancient Hebrews, being a square or (tallis) over a loose coat."—See Clavegero.

Beltrami observes of the *ephod,* which he found amongst the Indians beyond the Mississippi. " It passed from *Asia*

---

[1] Adair, who was for forty years amongst the northern tribes, thus writes " They reckon all birds of *prey,* and *night* birds, to be *unclean* and *unlawful* to be eaten. Not long ago, when they were making their winter hunt, and the old women at home were without meat, I shot a fat hawk and desired one of them to cook it; but though I strongly importuned her by way of trial, she decidedly refused it for fear of contracting pollution, which she called the ' *accursed* sickness.' It must be acknowledged," he adds, " they are all degenerating, insomuch that the Chocktaws, on account of their great scarcity began to eat horseflesh, frogs, &c. which are accounted in the highest begree impure by the neighbouring tribes ; who in ridicule of the Chocktaws for their canabal apostacy, call them ' the *evil* Chocktaw.' When *swine* were first bronght among them, they deemed it such a horrid abomination in any of their people to eat the flesh of that *filthy* creature, that they *excluded* the criminal from all *religious* communion in their circular house, or quadrangular square of sacred ground—as if he had eaten unsanctified fruit. I once invited the Archimagus to partake of my dinner; but he excused himself saying, ' In a few days he had a holy duty to perform, and that if he should eat evil or accursed food, it would spoil him. Shukapa (*swine-eater)* is the most opprobrious epithet with which they brand us. When the English traders were making sausages of *blood,* I have observed the Indians cast their eyes upon them with the horror of their forefathers when they viewed the defilement of the sanctuary. An instance lately occurred which sufficiently proves their aversion to *blood.* A Chickasaw woman became ill with a complication of disorders. The Indian physician could not cure her, after having tried all his remedies, he at last ascribed it to eating *swine's* flesh, or *blood,* and said that such an accursed sickness *overcame* the power of all his beloved things and medicine,' &c. I asked her sometime afterwards from what cause her illness proceeded? She said, ' *The accursed sickness,*'—having eaten after the manner of the white people with the *issih ookproo* (the accursed blood) *in them.*"—See Adair in Star of the West.

into Greece, thence to Rome, and lastly to these countries ; for this specimen of the short tunic with wide sleeves, which come down to the girdle, &c. is precisely the ephod. That the women should wear necklaces, &c. is not extraordinary, but what does surprise one, is, that like the women of antiquity, they offer them to the spirits of their departed relations, of which I have been an eye-witness."—Discov. of the Sources of the Mississippi.

Edwards observes, " they call their uncles and aunts *fathers* and *mothers,* which is a Hebrew custom ; and wear their clothes in the fashion of the Hebrews."—Hist. West Ind.

" It is not a little singular, that the Mexicans should have made use of a *cup,* in order that by this mode of divination, which Torquemeda describes in the following passage of the 48th chap. of the 6th book of his Indian Monarchy, they might discover stolen goods, and who the thief was, and where they were concealed, since it will argue some acquaintance with the History of Joseph."—Antiq. Mex. p. 105.

The mode of twisting[1] or *wringing off* the head from the body of birds to prevent death by strangulation, is similar to that practised by the Mexicans in their *daily sacrifice,* not of young pigeons, but of quails, as we learn from Sahagun,[2] where the phrase is *arrancardolas la cabeza,* wrenching off their heads."

Gumilla says, " *anointing with oil and perfumes,* (which was so peculiarly a Jewish custom, that even Christ himself

---

[1] " There is a curious painting in the Borgian ᴍs, (the 44th), in which thirteen squares surrounding the person of *Quetzalcoatl,* seem to contain twelve birds and one dragon-fly, which was held in abomination by the Jews, and for which the figure of an animal, &c. is perhaps making atonement by the sacrifice of some clean bird, the head of which he has *twisted off the body, so as not to cause death by strangulation."*—Antiq. Mex. vol. vi. p. 274.

[2] Appendix to the 2nd book of his History of New Spain.—Antiquities of Mexico, vol. vi. p. 100.

reproaches the pharisee for being wanting in that mark of courtesy, in which Mary Magdalene excelled,) *was a usage which continued in such full form on the Oronocos*, that it would require a chapter by itself to explain it ; besides which, if we consider the indispensable obligation which they were under, to *bathe themselves three times a day, at least twice, who will not confess that the Indians resemble the Jews. I shall note down other marks of Judaism.*"— Antiq. Mexico.

*   *   *   *   *   *

" With reference to the cherubimic figures borne on the four chief standards[1] among the Hebrews—" the head of a *lion*,"—" of a *man*,"—" of a *bullock*,"—" of an *eagle ;*" Adair writes—" At *present indeed*, the most numerous tribe generally bears the highest command ; but their old warriors assure us it was not so, even in their remembrance. The title of the " old beloved man," or archi-magi, is still hereditary in the panther family. As no lions are found in North America, the panther is the nearest representation of it. The Indians give a name *compounded* of *celestial* and *terrestrial* to each cherub, which reflects great light on the subject. They call the Buffalo—the Indian Bull, YAnasa, (sacred bull); the panther, *   * (cat of God) ; the human figure— YA-*we*, (holy man), and the eagle—*Ovola*, a word compounded of divine power and fire."—Star in the West.

" The Hebrews had various ablutions and anointings. The Indians observe the same practice from *religious* motives. " When," writes Adair, " the ground is covered with snow, they turn out of their warm lodges, men, women, and children, at the dawn of day, adoring YOHEWAH at the gladsome light of morn, and thus they skip along,

---

[1] The standard of the Peruvian Incas was an eagle gazing upon the sun.

singing his praise till they get to the river, when they plunge
in. If the water is frozen, they break the ice with religious
zeal. The neglect of this has been deemed so heinous, that
they have scraped the arms and limbs of the delinquent with
snakes'-teeth, not allowing warm water to relax the stiffened
joints. The criminals scorn to move themselves in the least
degree, be the pain ever so intolerable ; if they did, they
would be laughed at by their relatives, first for being *vicious*,
and next for being *timorous*."—Adair, in Star in the West.

" The Indian priests and prophets " [1] he adds, " are
initiated [2] by *anointing*. They first undergo a medicated
vapour bath for three successive evenings in a small green
hut constructed for the purpose. During that time they
drink only a dilution of snake-root to cleanse their bodies, and
prepare them for their *holy beloved offices before the Divine
Being* whom they invoke solemnly by his *essential Name*.
After this, their priestly garments and ornaments are put
on, bear's *oil being poured on their heads*. If they could
procure olive or palm oil, they would *prefer* it. The other
is the *only* substitute."—See " Hope of Israel," and Adair.

" According to the Mosaic law, women after child-birth [2]
absented themselves from *all* society, forty days for a male,
and double that period for a female child. The Muskohge
mothers are separated for three moons after their delivery,
exclusive of that in which the event took place."

Baron La Hontan writes, " the Indian mothers purify
themselves after travail, thirty days for a male child, and
forty for a female."

" The Hebrews became *polluted* by touching a *dead* body.

---

[1] For an account of an initiation into the priest's or prophet's office in one of
the Northern tribes, by the Jesuit Lafitau,—See Appendix.

[2] " The ceremonies of ablution practised among the Indian mothers, &c. led
the Spanish priests to the belief, that at some distant epoch, Christianity had
been preached among them."—Antiq. Mex.

The Indians, in order to *prevent* pollution, when the sick is past hope of recovery, prepare a grave and tomb, anoint his head, and paint his face : when his breath ceases, they soon inter the corpse. One of a different family *will not pollute himself for a stranger* ; though, when living, he would have hazarded his life for his safety. The relations who become unclean by performing the funeral duties, must live *apart* from the clean several days, and be cleansed by one of the *religious* order. See " Hope of Israel."—Adair.

Wailing for the dead was customary among the Hebrews, the antiquity, as well as the sacredness of it, are manifest. Thus saith the LORD, ' Did not thy father do judgment and justice, and *then* it was well with him ? He judged the cause of the poor and needy, and then it was well with him.—Was not *this to know Me* saith the LORD ? But thine eyes and thine heart are not but for thy covetousness, and for to shed innocent blood, and for oppression, and for violence to do it ; *therefore* thus saith the LORD, of Jehoiakim, the son of Josiah king of Judah, they shall *not wail* [1] *for him*, saying, ' ah my

---

[1] " In his letters to the Countess Campagnoni, (Beltrami writes thus of the newly-deceased Indian,) " All his relations are seated round him, and for some time observe a profound silence, exhibiting countenances at once indicative of serious-ness and grief. Each person then addresses him, some in pathetic tones, but without tears ;—others more emphatically, but still calmly. Where are you my beloved husband ? you are present indeed, but you do not speak to me ; you are now entirely in the society of spirits, and can no longer interest yourself about your wife, but your wife will never cease to interest herself about you; your eyes are employed in looking upon something more amiable and engaging than your wife. Perhaps you even have it not in your power to remember me. Your wife will nevertheless remember you. The sun, moon, and stars, shall witness me deploring your loss, and I will make no delay in rejoining you. Catalani could not sing *Ombra adorata aspettami*, with more expression than the Indian widow uttered this address."

Another said, " Why is there silence now on those lips, which lately spoke a language so energetic and expressive ? You are gone to the place where you existed, before coming to these countries, but your glory will remain with us for ever." A third said, " Alas! Alas ! Alas ! that form which was viewed with such admiration, is now become as inanimate as it was three hundred win-ters ago. But you will not be for ever lost to us, we will rejoin you in the supreme region of spirit, &c. Meanwhile, full of respect for your virtues and your valour, we come to offer you a tribute of kindness ; *your body shall not be*

brother,' they shall *not lament* for him, saying,[1] ' *ah!*
Lord!' or ' *ah his glory!'* he shall be buried with the
burial of an ass, drawn and cast forth beyond the gates of
Jerusalem."

Boudinot writes, " They often sleep over these tombs,
which, by the loud wailing of the women at dusk of eve, and
dawn of day, on benches close to the tombs, must awaken
the memory of their relatives very often."—Star in the
West.

It was customary[2] for the Hebrews to bury with the illustrious dead, many valuables. Josephus notices this ancient
custom, when by the treachery of an apostate of the As-
monean family, the Syrian invader robbed the sepulchre of
David of three thousand talents of gold, which had for one
thousand three hundred years been entombed with his body.

" On the death of the husband the squaws shew the sincerity of their grief by giving away to their neighbours
every thing they possess. They go out from the village and
build for themselves a small shelter of grass or bark, and
mortify themselves by cutting off their hair, scarifying their
skin, and in their insulated hut they lament incessantly.
If the deceased has left a brother, he takes the widow to his
lodge, after a proper interval, and considers her as his wife
without any preparatory formality."—Hope of Israel, p. 208.

exposed in the fields to beasts of prey, but we will take care that *it*, like *yourself*,
shall be *gathered to your forefathers.*" He adds, " the face of the corpse is turned
to the *east.*"—Discovery of the Source Mississippi.

[1] The Chocktaws employ mourners for the dead, as the Hebrews, and both they
and the Chickasaws term a person who does so, *Yah-ah, (Ah Lord.)*

[2] It was invariably the custom of the Indians to bury with the dead his effects,
no enemy ever molests those bodies which had once been the dwelling-
places of the immortal part of their being. The grave, with them, proves a
place inviolably sacred.

" On the Talapoose river were found two brazen tablets, and five of copper.
They esteemed them so sacred as to keep them secreted in their holy of holies,
without touching them except at their festivals, some had writing on them, and
had been buried with their beloved prophets." This is attested by William
Bolsover, Esq. 1759.

" I have noticed, (writes Mr. Makenny, in his late Tour,) several women here carrying with them rolls of clothing. On inquiring what it imported, I learn that they are widows who carry them, and that they are the badges of mourning. It is indispensable, when a woman of the Chippaway tribe loses her husband, for her to take off her best apparel, and roll it up, confining it by means of her husband's sashes : and if he had ornaments, these are put on the top of the roll, &c. This she calls her husband, and it is expected that she is never to be seen without it. If she walks, she takes it with her; if she sits down in her lodge, she places it by her side. This badge of widowhood she is to carry, *until some of her husband's family shall call and claim it*, &c. She is then, but not before, released from her mourning, and at liberty to marry again. Sometimes a *brother of the deceased takes her for his wife at the grave of her husband*, which is done by the ceremony of walking over it. And *this he has a right* to do. I was told by the interpreter, that he had known a woman left to mourn after this manner for years, none of her husband's family having called for the token of her grief. At length it was told her that one of her husband's family was to pass, and she was advised to speak to him on the subject. She told him she had mourned long, and was poor, having no means to buy clothes—those she had being all in the mourning badge, and thus *too sacred* to be touched. She expressed a hope that her request might not be interpreted into a wish to marry ; it was only made that she might be placed in a situation to get some clothes. He answered, that he was then going to Mackinack, and would think of it. In this state of uncertainty she was left, but on his return, finding her *still faithful*, he took her " husband," and presented her with clothing of various kinds. Thus was she rewarded for her constancy."

This custom is so evidently, (however modified,) of *Hebrew* origin, that it is not a little surprising Makenny should say he " found *nothing* Jewish among them, *except their houses of purification.*"

CIRCUMCISION.

THE testimony of Herrera, Garcia, Diaz, Torquemeda, Gomara, and Martyr, are unanimous in establishing the practice of circumcision among the tribes of the New Continent. " Herrera," (observes the commentator on the Antiq. Mex.) " almost in the very words of Acosta, notices in the seventeenth chapter of the second book of the third Decade, that this custom was prevalent among the Mexicans; and Bernal Diaz is quite explicit on the subject in the following passage of the twentieth chapter of his Hist. of the Conq. of Mex. " In some provinces they were circumcised, and they had *flint* knives with which they performed the ceremony."—Ibid. p. 334.

With respect to circumcision, *Martyr* and *Gomara*, whose veracity as historians was never doubted, both affirm

---

[1] " The Indians to the eastward say, that previous to the white people coming into the country, their ancestors were in the habit of using circumcision, but latterly, not being able to assign any reason for so strange a practice, their young people insisted on its being abolished."—Star in the West.

M'Kenzie says the same of the Indians whom he saw on his route. History, p. 34. Speaking of the nations of the Slave and Dog-rib Indians, very far to the north-west, he says, " Whether circumcision be practised among them, I cannot pretend to say, but the appearance of it was general among those I saw."

" The Dog-rib Indians live about two or three hundred miles from the straits of Kamschatka."

Dr. Beatty says, in his journal of a visit paid to the Indians on the Ohio, about fifty years ago, that an aged Indian informed him, that an old uncle of his, who died about the year 1728, related to him several customs and traditions of former times; and among others, " that circumcision was practised among the Indians long ago, but their young men making a mock at it, brought it into disrepute, and so it came to be disused."—Journal, p. 89.

that *the Indians were circumcised.* The former, addressing Leo X. in the tenth chapter of the third *Ocean Decade,* says, speaking of the Indian fugitive who came to the Spanish settlements of Darien. " He sayde further, that in his country there were cities fortified with walls, and governed by laws; that the people used apparel, but of what religion they were I did not learne, yet hadde our Manne knowledge both by words and signs of the fugitive, that they were *circumcised.* What think ye now hereby most holy Father, or what doe you divine may come hereof when time shall have subdued all these under your throne?" And in the first chapter of his fourth Decade, inscribed to the same Pontif, he gives the following description of the people of *Yutican.* "This nation is not appareled with woole, because they have no sheep, but with cotton, after a thousand fashions and diversely colored. Their women are clad from their waiste to their ancles, and cover their heads and brests with vayles." " This people frequent their temples often. They are great idolaters, and are *circumcised, but not all.*"

" In the third chapter of the same Decade, he says, that the inhabitants of the Island of Cozumilla, situated on the coast of *Yutican,* were circumcised. *Garcia,* likewise, in the following passage of the first section of the eighth chapter of the third book of his Origin of the Indians, confutes the error of *Acosta* respecting the use of circumcision amongst the Indians."

" It is certainly very extraordinary to find from the " *Oronoco Illustrada*" of *Gumilla,* and Carreat's Voyages to the West Indies, that in nations remote from each other, as those of the Oronoca, and the tribes who lived on the confines of Peru, on the banks of La Plata, as well as the Chalachaques, a people situated between Peru and Tecumion, *all used circumcision, and abstained from the flesh of swine. Captain Cook also discovered that circumcision had extended to the Islands of the South Sea.* " How, to use the words of *Gumilla,* are these moral phenomena to be explained? The Mexicans, besides this rite, marked the breasts and arms of the children on the feast of *Toxcatl,* with another sign which *Torquemeda* compares in the following passage of the sixteenth chapter of the tenth book of his Indian Monarchy, with the analogous ceremony of marking the sign of the cross upon the breast, &c. of the faithful among Christians with the holy oil and chrism." [1]

" Gomara and Gumelli say, that the Silivas circumcise their children the *eighth* day after their birth. Sahagun says, in the twenty-fourth chapter of the second book of his History, describing the attire of the Deity Huitzilopoctli. " If they believed that *that* god had commanded *circumcision,* it is probable that their *symbol,* the '*flint knife,*' upon that part of his dress was a *memorial of that* ordinance." —Ibid. p. 271.

" The earliest Spanish writers, &c. such as *Martyr,* (who scarely would have ventured to state a deliberate falsehood to the Pope; (and one which he sooner than any other person would have been capable of detecting,) and *Gomara,* who was chaplain to *Cortez,* and dedicated his History to *Don Martin Cortez,* his son, and therefore had the best

---

[1] " It is no light thing to note, that on this day the priests make a scar on the breasts and stomachs of the male and female children, and on the wrists and fleshy parts of the arms of others, impressing them as it were with the iron and mark of the *devil, to whose service they offered them, in order that they might be known as his:* in the same way that God commands that those of *his fold should be anointed on their breasts with the holy oil, and on their foreheads with the most blessed cross of his passion and death, since this is the sign with which God is accustomed to mark those who are his,* (as circumcision was formerly amongst his ancient people,) which is now the *cross and holy chrism:* hence John bade the persecutors and murders desist from the work of slaughter, until the servants of God were marked on their foreheads, since *this is the kind of sign* by which he distinguishes those who are *his, as the owners of cattle mark their herds with a particular print or sign.*"—p. 394.

means of information ; and *Bernal Diaz*, and other Spanish writers also, who are acknowledged to be men of the greatest learning and research, such as were *Garcia* and *Torquemeda*, who had themselves visited America, have all declared that various Indian nations used circumcision.

" The ceremony of circumcision was performed with a '*flint knife*,' as is evident from the twenty-fifth verse of the fourth chapter of Exodus, &c. which induced *Garcia* to suppose that the reason why the *Tecpatl*, or *flint knife*, was held in such reverence, was on account of its connexion with *circumcision:* and *Torquemeda* says, that the Totomacs, a numerous nation, inhabiting a mountainous country to the east · of Mexico, *circumcised their children*, " *and that the High Priest, or the next in order and rank, performed the ceremony with a flint knife.*" [1]—Monarchia Indiana, cap. 48, in Mex. Antiq. vol. vi.

" That the Mexicans believed the earth and the sun drunk up the blood of the innocent is clearly proved by a lord who in a speech to the king of Mexico, recently elected, takes occasion to caution him not to draw down on himself the anger of God. It may here be remarked that most of the speeches in Sahagun's History of New Spain, have a strong unction of Jewish rhetoric ; " the same complaisant mode of speaking of themselves as God's peculiar people, the same familiar communication with deity beginning frequently as in Abraham's dialogue with God, with the word ' peradventure,' the same unceasing solicitude after dreams, visions, and inspirations, the same manner of addressing each other as brethren, and finally the same choice of metaphors distinguish the compositions of the Jews and Mexicans, which may serve in some measure, to explain the specimens of Mexican eloquence."

[1] The Flint knife is one of the signs in the Mexican Calendar.

K

"The Lord's slaying Leviathan, which the Jews understood to refer to the time of their Messiah, seems to be alluded to in the ninety-sixth page of the lesser Vatican, MS.

"I cannot fail to remark that one of the arguments which persuades me to believe that this nation descends from the Hebrews is to see the knowledge they have of the book of Genesis; for although the Devil has succeeded in mixing up so many errors, his lies are still in such a course of conformity with catholic truth, that there is reason to believe that they have had acquaintance with this book, since this and the other four books which follow, are the Pentateuch, written by Moses, and were only found amongst the Hebrew People. There are very strong grounds for believing that this nation proceeds from them," &c.

"In nothing did the civil policy of the Mexicans more closely resemble that of the Hebrews, than in their dedicating their children to the Temple, and afterwards sending them to be instructed by the Master or Rabbi, in the doctrines of their religion and moral and ceremonial laws. Torquemeda says, "that the ceremony of dedicating children to the military profession, was also a religious one. Amongst the Jews, all wars, not excepting their civil ones, bore a religious character," &c. "And in Deuteronomy, directions are given to the priests [1] to accompany and

---

[1] "When the *war chief* beats up for volunteers, he goes thrice round the dark winter house, *contrary* to the sun's course, whooping the war-song and beating the drum. He then declares the occasion of the war. He strongly urges his kindred and warriors and others, who fear not bullets and swords, to come and join him with manly cheerful hearts, assuring them that as they are all bound in one love-knot, so they are ready to hazard their lives to avenge *the crying blood* of their kindred; that the piety of obeying the old beloved customs had hitherto checked their daring generous hearts, but now those hinderances are no more; he then proceeds to whoop for the warriors to join him, and sanctify themselves for success according to their ancient manner."

The town of refuge, called *Coate*, is on a large stream of the Mississippi. "Here, some years ago," says Doctor Boudinot, "a brave Englishman was protected, after killing an Indian in defence of his property." He informed Mr.

exhort the soldiers to battle. The Interpreter of the Collection of Mendoza says, "that the priests likewise followed the Mexican armies, not only for the purpose of joining the combatants, but also to perform certain religious ceremonies, in which some analogy is discovered between the customs of the two nations. That the Incas waged war for the express purpose of compelling other nations to lay aside their idolatries and embrace the knowledge of the true God, we have the authority of Acosta and of other eminent historians, for asserting."—p. 49.

"Father Joseph Gumelli, in his account of the nations bordering on the Oronoco, relates that they punished adultery like the ancient Hebrews, by stoning the criminals to death before the assembled people."—Edwards's West Indies, vol. i. p. 39, note.

"It is not a little singular, also, (as establishing that to be a fact which few persons would feel inclined to suspect) that the Mexicans and the Jews should have believed that similar divine judgments (even when these were of a very peculiar nature) would follow the commission of similar crimes. The fifth chapter of Numbers records the extraordinary effect produced on a guilty woman whose husband was jealous by her drinking the bitter water in the trial of jealousy. And *Torquemeda* says, that nearly the same kind

---

Adair, "that after some month's stay in this place of refuge, he intended to return to his house in the neighbourhood; but the chiefs assured him it would be fatal to him. So that he was obliged to continue there, until at length he succeeded in pacifying the friends of the deceased," &c.

In another part of the Muskagee was the ancient beloved town called *Coosak*, which implies *a place of safety for those who have slain undesignedly*. "In almost every tribe," he adds, "there are these "peaceable towns," which are called "*sacred beloved towns*." It is not within the recollection of the most aged, that ever blood was shed in them ; although the refugees have often been forced out of them and put to death elsewhere. And this is a sacred duty—the manes of the slain crying to the nearest of kin for redress. This has often seemed a revengeful disposition, when, with more justice, it ought to have been traced to a higher motive, however much obscured and mistaken."—See Boudinot's Star in the West, and Hope of Israel.

of threat was held out by the Mexican priests to induce the virgins to dread the vengeance of God when they violated their vow."—p. 55.

Edwards observes in his History of the West Indies, "The Indians would not eat the Mexican hog or the turtle, but held them in the greatest abhorrence." Gumilla observes, "Neither would they eat the eel, nor many other animals; and birds they deemed impure." Even the Rev. Dr. Mather, one of the spiritual Israel, "who felt " *necessitated*" " unto the *rooting out*" the aboriginal *Canaanites*, and who published a work entitled ' Magnalia, &c. Wars of the Lord,' does admit, amongst other points of resemblance, which he could not but acknowledge, that *these " salvages had a great unkindness for our swine."*

Hearne, who published a work in 1795, entitled a Journey to Prince of Wales's Island, remarks, "that some Indians who had killed an Indian at Copper River, considered themselves in a state of uncleanness, which induced them to practice some very curious ceremonies. In the first place all who were concerned in the murder, were prohibited from cooking any sort of food, either for themselves or others. They refrained also from eating many parts of the deer and other animals, particularly the entrails and blood; and during their pollution their food was never sodden with water, but dried in the sun, eaten quite raw, or broiled when a fire could be procured."—2 Samuel xv.

James Adair, Esq. who spent forty years amongst one of the northern tribes, writes, " They affix very vicious ideas to eating impure things, and all their priests and prophets, and war leaders, before they enter into their religious duties, observe the strictest abstinence on this point. Formerly, if any of them did eat in white-mens' houses, or even of what had been cooked there, while they were sanctifying themselves, it was esteemed a dangerous pollution."

Kelly in his Sketch of the Oregons, observes, " There are many things in the religious faith and observances which bear a strong analogy to the Hebrew ritual. Besides the instances above, they observe a day of fasting and humiliation and prayer. They have also annually, celebration of a solemn nature which lasts seven days, on which occasion they have thanksgiving sacrifices. From these and many other circumstances respecting their dress, ornaments, genius, and customs ; from the great resemblance in complexion, figure, manners, and even language which these people, and those on the islands in the Pacific bear to the inhabitants of the Island of Cratoatoa, lying in the entrance of the Straits of Sundan, the important inference may be drawn, that the Hebrews had effected the settlement of the Western continent," &c.

Major Long, an agent of the United States Government, published a work entitled an " Expedition to the Rocky Mountains," thus he makes mention of the *ark* of the Omawhas : " The Omawha branch is divided into two powerful sections, one of which is interdicted from eating the flesh of male deer and male elk, in consequence of having their great *mystic medicine* (ark) enveloped in the skins of these animals. The shell, which is regarded as an object of the greatest sanctity and superstitious reverence by the whole nation, has been transmitted from the ancestry of this band, and its origin is unknown. A *skin lodge* or *temple*, is appropriated for its preservation, in which a person constantly resides charged with the *care* of it, and appointed its guard. It is placed upon *a stand, and is never suffered to touch the earth*. It is concealed from sight by several envelopes, which are composed of strands of proper skin

plaited together. The whole constitutes a parcel of considerable size, from which various articles are suspended,
such as tobacco and the roots of certain plants. *No person
dares to open the coverings* of the sacred deposit, *in order
to expose the shell to view.* Tradition informs them that
curiosity induced three different persons to examine the
mysterious shell, who were *immediately punished for their
profanation by total blindness.* Previously to undertaking [1]
a national expedition against an enemy, *the sacred shell is
consulted as an oracle.* For this purpose the maji of the
band seat themselves around the great *medicine* lodge; the
lower part of which is hung round and thrown open *like
curtains,* and the extreme envelope is carefully removed
from the mysterious parcel, that the shell may receive the
air. During this ceremony, an individual occasionally inclines his head forwards, and listens attentively *to catch
some sound* which he *expects to issue from the shell,"* this is
considered as a favourable omen, and the nation prepares
for the projected expedition with a confidence of success."

"They are," adds Major Long, " of opinion that the
WAHCONDAH has been more profuse of his gifts, especially
the knowledge of letters to the white people, than to themselves. They consider the *result* of experience thus easily

---

[1] Adair, speaking of Indian "cities" (or places) "of refuge," says, with
reference to the ark which went out to the war, " I observed that if a captive
taken by the reputed power of the holy things of their ark, should be able to
make his escape into one of these beloved towns, or even into the winter house
of the archimagus, he is delivered," &c. "It is also worthy of notice that they
never place the ark on the ground. They rest it on stones, or short logs, where
they also seat themselves. And when we consider in what a surprising manner
the Indians copy after the observances of the *Hebrews* and their *strict purity* in
the war camps; that *opae*, "the leader," obliges all, during the campaign, which
they have made with the beloved *ark*, to stand every day they are not engaged
in warfare from sun-rise to sun-set, and after a fatiguing days march, and scanty
allowance, to drink warm water embittered with the snake-root in order to
purification; that they have also as strong a faith in the power of their ark as
ever the Israelites had of old, ascribing the success of one party to their stricter
adherence to the law than the other. We have strong reason to conclude them
of Hebrew origin.

transmitted, " like the operation of some *mystic medicine.*"
" But they claim a superiority in natural intelligence," &c.

" They esteem themselves more generous, brave, and hospitable to strangers than the white people, and these beneficent virtues with them, mark " the perfect man." If a white man or stranger enters the habitation of an Indian, he is not asked if he has dined, or if he is hungry,—but independently of the time of the day or night, the pot is put on the fire, and if there is a single pound of venison in the possession of the family, that pound is cooked and set before him." * * *

FESTIVALS.

It has been justly remarked that "ancient customs become *modified* by change of situation and circumstance, after a great lapse of time."

The transference of the Levitical economy to the New Continent is a striking comment on this observation; for in reflecting on that disregard of " the statutes and judgments of the LORD, which had caused their expatriation, the tribes seem in their ' outcast' state to have even zealously continued for more than two thousand years in such a modified observance of these, as change of situation and circumstances, and want of the written WORD admitted.

In failing to be governed and instructed by the revealed mind of God in their Land, they were to experience, as an act of retribution, the want of it when " afar off." Hence the prophet foretold, that " not a *famine* of bread and water, but of *hearing the words of the* LORD," should be *their* punishment—a famine which they should deeply feel and deplore, when they should " wander from sea to sea, &c. to seek the Word of the LORD, and *should not find it*."[1]

Hieroglyphic and other painted records, together with oral tradition, became a substitute for the *written* WORD, but these artificial means were comparatively cold and ambiguous, and however they might have traced the outlines of their ritual and historical peculiarities, they could not enter into the minute detail of these, and were moreover subject to more or less of that tincture of *error which necessarily accompanies such mediums of conveyance.*

" Language," observes a late Hebrew critic, " is subject to three qualifications, viz. הגיוני (cogitative), בטוי (organic), and כתבי (writing). There is an *inherent* connection between these three qualifications ; the first terminates *in* the *first* person ; the second is to deliver verbatim *to* the *second* person *present*; but the third is to *communicate* to persons *absent* and to *posterity*. These three qualifications are infallibly absolute and essential objects to man as an intellectual being. A man when deficient of this *triplex* is an *unfinished* being."[2]

" Four times a day," writes Clavegero, "They offered incense—namely, at day-dawn, mid-day, sunset, and at midnight. The last offering was made by the priest whose turn it was to do so, and the most respectable officers of the Temple attended it."

" For incense on certain Festivals they employed the bitumen of Judea, but usually they burned copal or other aromatic gums. The censers were either of clay or of gold. The Hebrews had a rejoicing Festival on the ingathering,

---

[1] There is a self-constituted famine more grievous in its character, and more fatal in its results than that under which the outcasts of Israel have been left to pine for a series of ages:—that which in *explaining away* the *integrity* of the written WORD (in order to *self* or *party monopoly*) *starves* the heart while it *inebriates* the mind. Amos viii. 11, 12.

[2] Theological and Critical Treatise, by Solomon Bennet, p. 35.

called the Feast of Tabernacles. It was commemorated wi:h temporary verdant booths, in which certain prescribed leafy branches were interlaced in remembrance of their having sojourned in temporary lodges in the wilderness. The willow and palm, &c. emblematic of humiliation and triumph, were united in these tabernacles. It has always been a tradition among them that the *triumphant* Messiah would come at the celebration of *the feast of Tabernacles* into HIS BELOVED CITY; and that his herald Elijah, the ancient prophet, would precede that coming six months:—that *he* would come at the feast of passover to announce His triumphant advent to "*restore* all things, and *turn* the hearts of the fathers to the children, and those of the children to the fathers," preparatory to that event.

" It will be recollected that Peter unmindful of *time* and *season,* and not knowing what he said for joy at that demonstration of the *identity* of the Sufferer and the Victor of which he was an eye witness, exclaimed, " let us make three Tabernacles, one for thee, one for Moses, and one for Elias."

"The coming of the Messiah therefore is connected (in the warrant of Scripture expectation, as well as traditionary hope) with the *Feast of tabernacles,* which the Jews believe will then come together with the *Jubilee* period.

We have this festival in an obscure manner in the following extract from the Abbe Clavegero:

" In their twelfth month (October) they celebrated the feast of *the arrival of the gods,* which they express by the word TEO*tlico,* which name they gave to both the month and the festival. On the sixteenth day of this month they covered all the temples and the corners of the streets of the city with *green branches.* On the eighteenth, the gods, according to their accounts, began to arrive. They spread before the door of the sanctuary of the god, a mat, made of the *palm tree,* and sprinkled upon it some powder of maize."

"The High Priest stood on watch all the preceding night, and went frequently to look whether footsteps were observable on the mat. Sometimes a cry was made, "Our great God is now come." When all the priests and crowds of people repaired there to greet Him, and celebrate His arrival with hymns and dances, which were repeated the rest of the night."—See Clavegero.

"The feast of trumpets seems to be discernible in the Abbe's description of the following faded memorial: "The second of the four principal festivals, was that which they made in honour of the great God. Ten days before it, a priest dressed in his most elaborate manner, went into the Temple, with a bunch of flowers and a horn or flute of clay which made a very shrill sound. Turning his face toward the ' *east,*' and afterwards to the other three principal ' winds,' he sounded the horn loudly, and then, taking up a little dust from the earth with his fingers, he put it to his mouth and swallowed it. Upon hearing the sound of the horn, all knelt down; criminals were thrown into the utmost terror and consternation, and with tears implored the God to grant pardon for their offences," &c. "All the people tasting a little particle of earth, after the example of the priest, who supplicated for favor and mercy."

"The day before the festival, all the virgins and youths, as well as the nobles, wore wreaths. Then followed a procession through the lower area of the Temple, where flowers and odorous herbs were scattered, two priests offered incense to the *idol,* while the people were kneeling," &c.

He adds, "The dances were more solemn in *Tlascala, Huetxotzinco,* and *Cholula.* In like manner the festivals at the beginning of every thirteen years were attended with more pomp and gravity. They had a festival called *Tezcalli*, ' *Behold the* HOUSE!'

" We have already noticed that the Mexican jubilee period was every fifty-two years. The following extract seems to point to the ancient jubilee :

" But," continues Clavegero, " the festival which was celebrated every fifty-two years, was by far the most splendid and imposing, not only among the Mexicans, but likewise among all the nations of the Empire, or who were neighbouring to it.

" On the last night of their century they extinguished the fire of all their temples and houses, and broke their vessels, earthen pots, and utensils, preparing, as it were, for the end of the world, which at the termination of each cycle they expected.

" The priests, attended by the people, travelled during the night, six miles out of town, to a certain mountain, on the top of which the new fire was to be kindled.

" All who did not go forth with the priests, stood anxiously upon terraces to wait the result. As soon as the fire was kindled, they all at once exclaimed with joy, and a great fire was made on the mountain that it might be seen from afar. Immediately they took up portions of the sacred new fire, to carry to their respective households. [1] Every place resounded with mirth and mutual congratulations, &c.

---

[1] 'We cannot,' writes Clavegero, 'express too strongly the care which parents and masters took to instruct their children and pupils in the history of their people ; they made them learn speeches and discourses, which they could not express by the pencil ; *they put the events of their ancestors into verse, and taught them to sing them. This tradition dispelled the doubts and undid the ambiguity which paintings alone might have occasioned, and by the assistance of those monuments perpetuated the memory of their heroes, and of virtuous examples, their rites, their laws, and their customs.*'—See Clavegero.

The Feasts of Weeks, or the Hunters' Feast, or Pentecost.—An ancient missionary, who lived a long time with the *Outaowaies*, has written, that among these savages, an old man performs the office of a priest at the feasts. That they begin by giving thanks to the Great Spirit, for the success of the chase, or

"The illuminations during the first nights were extremely magnificent, their ornaments of dress, their entertainments, dances, and public games, were superiorly brilliant."

hunting time. Then another takes a cake, breaks it in two, and casts it in the fire. This was upwards of eighty years ago.

Dr. Beatty says, that once in the year, some of the tribes of Indians beyond the Ohio, choose from among themselves twelve men, who go out and provide twelve deer; and each of them cuts a small saplin, from which they strip the bark, to make a tent, by sticking one end into the ground, bending the tops over one another, and covering the poles with blankets. Then the twelve men choose, each of them, a stone, which they make hot in the fire, and place them together, after the manner of an altar, within the tent, and then burn the fat of the insides of the deer thereon.* At the time they are making this offering, the men within cry to the Indians without, who attend as worshippers, "We pray, or praise." They without answer, "We hear." Then those in the tent cry *ho-hah*, very loud and long, which appeared to be something in sound like halle-lujah. After the fat was thus offered, some tribes burned tobacco, cut fine, upon the same stones, supposed in imitation of incense. Other tribes choose only ten men, who provide but ten deer, ten saplins, or poles, and ten stones.

The southern Indians observe another religious custom of the Hebrews, as Adair asserts, by offering a sacrifice of gratitude, if they have been successful, and have all returned safe home. But if they have lost any in war, they generally decline it, because they imagine, by some neglect of duty, they are impure; then they only mourn their vicious conduct, which defiled the ark, and thereby occasioned the loss.

Like the Israelites, they believe their sins are the procuring cause of all their evils, and that the divinity in the ark will always bless the more religious party with the best success. This is their invariable sentiment, and is the sole reason for mortifying themselves in so severe a manner while they are out at war; living very scantily, even in a buffalo range, under a strict rule, lest by luxury, their hearts should grow evil, and give them occasion to mourn.

From Mr. Adair, the following account, or rather abstract of his account, of the feast and fast of what may be called their Passover, and feast of First Fruits, is made.

"On the day appointed (which was among the Jews, generally in the spring, answering to our March and April, when their barley was ripe, being the first month of their ecclesiastical, and the seventh of their civil year, and among the Indians, as soon as their first spring produce comes in) while the sanctified new fruits are dressing, six old beloved women come to their temple, or sacred wig- wam of worship, and dance the beloved dance with joyful hearts. They observe a solemn procession as they enter the holy ground, or beloved square, carrying in one hand a bundle of small branches of various green trees; when they are joined by the same number of beloved old men, who carry a cane in one hand, adorned with white feathers, having green boughs in the other hand. Their heads are dressed with white plumes, and the women in their finest clothes, and anointed with bears' grease, or oil, having also small tortoise shells and white pebbles fastened to a piece of white dressed deer skin, which is tied to each of their legs. The eldest of the beloved men, leads the sacred dance at the head of the innermost row, which of course is next the holy fire. He begins the dance, after once going round the holy fire, in solemn and religious silence. He then

---

* Thou shalt sprinkle the blood upon the altar, and shall burn their fat for an offering made by fire, for a sweet savour unto the LORD.—Numb. xviii. 17.

HERRERA observes, "The Mexicans celebrated the principal festival of their god *Vitziliputzli*, in the month of May, and two days before the festival, the virgins who were shut up

in the next circle, invokes *yah*, after their usual manner, on a bass key, and with a short accent. In another circle, he sings *ho, ho*, which is repeated by all the religious procession, till they finish that circle. Then in another round, they repeat, *he he*, in like manner, in regular notes, and keeping time in the dance. Another circle is continued in like manner, with repeating the word *wah, wah*, (making in the whole, the divine and holy name of *yah, ho, he, wah*.) A little after this is finished, which takes considerable time, they begin again, going fresh rounds, singing *hal-hal-le-le-lu-lu-yah-yah*, in like manner; and frequently the whole train strike up, *hallelu, hallelu, halleluyah, halleluyah*, with great earnestness, fervour, and joy, while each strikes the ground with right and left feet alternately, very quick, but well timed. Then a kind of hollow sounding drum, joins the sacred choir, which excites the old female singers to chant forth their grateful hymns and praises to the divine Spirit, and to redouble their quick, joyful steps, in imitation of the leader of the beloved men, at their head.

"This appears very similar to the dances of the Hebrews, and may we not reasonably suppose, that they formerly understood the psalms and divine hymns, at least those which begin or end with *hallelujah*; otherwise how comes it to pass, that all the inhabitants of the extensive regions of North and South America, have and retain these very expressive Hebrew words, and repeat them so distinctly, applying them after the manner of the Hebrews, in their religious acclamations.

"On other religious occasions, and at their Feast of Love, they sing *ale yo, ale yo*, which is the divine name by the attribute of omnipotence. They likewise sing *he-wah, he-wah*, which is the immortal soul drawn from the divine essential name, as deriving its faculties from *yo-he-wah*. These words of their religious dances, they never repeat at any other time, which has greatly contributed to the loss of their meaning; for it is believed they have grown so corrupt, as not now to understand either the spiritual or literal meaning of what they sing, any farther than by allusion to the name of the Great Spirit.

"In these circuitous dances, they frequently also sing in a bass key, *aluhe, aluhe, aluwah, aluwah*. Also, *shilu-yo, shilu-yo, shilu-he, shilu-he, shilu-wah, shilu-wah*, and *shilu-hah, shilu-hah*.* They transpose them also several ways, but with the very same notes. The three terminations make up the four lettered divine name. *Hah* is a note of gladness and joy. The word preceding it, *shilu*, seems to express the predicted human and divine Shiloh, who was to be the purifier and peace-maker. They continue their grateful divine hymns for the space of about fifteen minutes, and then break up. As they degenerate, they lengthen their dances, and shorten the time of their fasts and purifications; insomuch, that they have so exceedingly corrupted their primitive rites and customs, within the space of the last thirty years, (now about eighty years) that, at the same rate of declension, there will not long be a possibility of tracing their origin, but by their dialects and war customs. At the end of this notable religious dance, the old beloved women return home to hasten the feast of the new sanctified fruits. In the mean time, every one at the temple drinks plentifully of the *cussena* and other bitter liquids, to cleanse their sinful bodies, as they suppose. After which, they go to some convenient deep water, and there, according to the ceremonial law of the Hebrews, they wash away their sins with water. They then return

---

* Cruden in his Concordance, says,—"Shiloh ought to be understood of the Messiah. Jerome translates it,—He who is to be *sent*, and manifestly reads Shiloach, *sent;* instead of Shiloh."

in the Temple kneaded flour of bledas, and roasted maize
with honey, and formed a large idol of dough, and on the
day of the festival, before the dawn, the virgins came forth
in new white apparel, crowned with ears of roasted maize,
and wearing chains of the same hanging down below their
left arms, &c.   During this day they bore the name of
sisters of *Vitziliputzli, &c. All the people humbled themselves, and taking dust from the ground, strewed it on their
heads,* since this was a ceremony which was usual on their
principal festivals.[1]   Afterwards the people went in quick
procession to the mountain *Chapaltepec,* a league distant
from Mexico, and there made a halt and sacrifice, and then
proceeded with the same haste to a place called *Atacinaviaz,*
which was the second resting place: and passed on a league
further to Cuivican, from whence, without stopping, they
returned to Mexico.   This journey of four leagues was
performed in four hours, and they named the procession
Zpaina Vitziliputzli. " *The quick procession of Vitziliputzli,*"
&c. Exodus xii. 33, 34.   The people likewise assisted with
great reverence in this act, (viz. drawing up the image to the
area of the Temple.")   " Having been drawn up, and placed
in a chamber adorned with flowers, the young men of the

with great joy, in solemn procession, singing their notes of praise, till they again
enter their holy ground, to eat of the new delicious fruits, which are brought to
the outside of the square, by the old beloved women.   They all behave so
modestly, and are possessed of such an extraordinary constancy and equanimity
in pursuit of their religious mysteries, that they do not shew the least outward
emotion of pleasure at the first sight of the sanctified new fruits.'
[1] Mr. Penn was at one himself. "Their entertainment was a great feast in
the spring—under some shady trees.   It consisted of twenty bucks, with hot cakes
made of new corn, with both wheat and beans, which they make up in a square
form, in the leaves of the corn, and then bake them in the ashes—they then fall
to dancing : but all who go to this feast must take a small present in their
hand, it might be but sixpence, which is made of the bone of a fish.   The black
is with them as gold, and the white as silver, they call it *wampum*." Afterwards
speaking of their agreement in the rites with the Hebrews, he says, that " they
reckon by moons—they offer their first fruits—they have a kind of Feast of
Tabernacles—they are said to lay their altars upon twelve stones—they mourn a
year—they have the separation of women ; with many other things that do not
now occur."—Star in the West.

Temple strewed many more around, and the virgins brought a quantity of pieces of dough, &c. The dignitaries of the Temple then came forth in exact order, according to their seniority, attired in dresses corresponding to their offices, with garlands and chains of flowers ; they placed themselves around the pieces of dough, and performed over them a certain ceremony, which consisted in singing and dancing, &c. Afterwards the young men and young women who were educated in the Temple came forth, and placing themselves opposite to each other, danced and sung, in praise of the Festival of the Idol, and all the lords and principal persons replied to the song. The whole city flocked to the spectacle, and the Festival being concluded, the Priests took the idol of dough, and distributed the pieces like the holy communion, and gave it to the people great and small, who received it with great reverence, fear, and shedding of tears, declaring that they ate the flesh of God. This being over, an old man of great authority ascended some elevated place, and preached on the law and ceremonies." [1]— Herrera. Mex. Antiq. p. 418.

[1] A curious comment on this Festival occurs : *—" *This took place at night,* and as soon as it was morning, the ministers and high priests proceeded to consecrate it; (if such an act can be called consecration) all the citizens were present, together with crowds of strangers, &c. The consecration being over, all who could, drew near to touch it, as *if it were to touch a relic, or the body of a saint,* although *that* was the lurking place of the *Devil,* &c." " They made this liberal offering, thinking that they were rendering their god a considerable service, and that on account of it he would pardon their sins, which is what *we* are taught by the *sound catholic* doctrines of the holy Scriptures ; that charity diminisheth sin, and if when done to our neighbour it possesses so much force, it will possess much greater when the offering is made unto God; who accordingly has chosen to declare that it avails those who give and bestow for their Justification, and the cleansing away of their sins : although in this place it possesses no meritorious quality, inasmuch as it was done to the Devil, &c. To speak plainer, was done at his instigation." Antiq. Mex.

* The Mexicans computed the period of a day from the noon of one day to that of another, as we are informed by the interpreter of the Codex Telleranis Remesis, p. 152, and this computation arguing to the night a sort of priority over the day, probably induced them to keep the vigils of festivals as a part of the festivals themselves."—Antiq. of Mex. vol. vi p. 505

" The day of the consecration of *that infernal bread and dough* being past, nobody was allowed to touch it, or enter the chapel where it was, but *the priests only, &c.* They afterwards brought forth the statue of the god *Paynalton,* the god of war, the vicar of the said *Huitzilopoctli,* which was made of wood, and carried in the arms of a priest, who represented *Quetzalcoatl,* who was dressed very richly with curious ornaments and apparel, being preceded by another, holding in his hands a large and thick serpent twisted in many folds, which was carried *before,* and was *lifted up on high* in the manner of the cross in our processions. They then lifted the statue of *Paynalton,* and placed it on the altar, by that of *Huitzilopoctli,* and there left it, together with the banner named *Epaniztli,* which was carried in front: the serpent alone was taken away, and deposited in a place allotted to it."—p. 416.

Of the Festival of the sign of *the rose,* they say, " *There is a mansion from which they fell, and where they plucked the rose.*" In order to shew that this Festival was *not* commemorative of good, and that it was celebrated with fear, they painted *the Tree,* "*distilling blood, and cracked in the midst,* and named it the feast of *toil,* by reason of that transgression."

" The Festival for the dead :—while the priests celebrated this in the temples, the entire population ascended the terraces of their houses, and looking toward the *north,*[1] made earnest supplications to the departed of their own lineage, ejaculating aloud, " *Come quickly, since we expect you.*"

" The Festival of the *raising* of the Banners began in December ; a note says, with reference to this painting, " the famous prophecy of the same prophet relating to the LORD'S

---

[1] A note here says, " *they supposed hades to be the north.*"

slaying Leviathan, which the Jews understood to refer to the time of their Messiah, seems to be alluded to."—p. 96, of the lesser Vatican M.S. " In the Name of our God we raise up our banners." Psalm xx. 5.

" In the tenth chapter of his twelfth book, *Torquemeda* affirms, that the *Devil counterfeited amongst the Indians the Feast of Passover.* This third month of the Mexicans commenced on the fifteenth of March, which like the solemn Passover of the Jews, lasted eight days, when they offered the first fruits. The ripe grain and the ears, it was *unlawful* for them to taste before they had presented the said *first fruits to the priests.* The Indians observed the same custom on this third month, (the Pasqua) which they celebrated in honor of their (ancients or lords.) Before the arrival of the day appointed for carrying these first fruits to the temples and altars, no one dared to touch them, for they were forbidden to do so by an express law, as the Jews were forbidden to taste the ears of corn : and (adds the complacent son of the church,) " It might well *provoke a hearty laugh from Christians, to see that the Devil wished to constitute himself the god of the first fruits,"* &c. —p. 282.

" The Festival of the *New Moons* was another Mexican solemnity so analogous to the *Neomanio* or Jewish Festival of the New Moon, that *Torquemeda* describing the former says, ' If this custom be attentively considered it will be found to have been *stolen* from the Hebrews, of whom Saint Thomas says that it was ordained that the *Neomanio* should be kept at the commencement of every month, in memory of the government and preservation of all things ; which same preservation is that which our Indians pray for in their *Neomanio,* at the commencement of each of their months. ' But my reply to this objection would be, that the *Devil*

taught them, &c. p. 283. ' But,' adds the commentator,
' if our surprize is justly excited at being informed by
Torquemeda that the *Devil* had imitated among the Indians the Jews' feasts of *Passover* and the *New Moon,* what
shall we think of the Fast of *Atamal,* which the Mexicans
kept every eighth year (the flint) as a *Sabbatical* year!
eight was a number highly esteemed by the *Christians,* and
as they have *not scrupled to change* the Sabbath from the
seventh day, (on which day it was kept by the Jews,) to the
eighth day, Sunday, on account of the resurrection of Christ
having occurred on that day, we must not reject a striking
analogy because it is open to an answerable objection, since
the Mexicans also have had their reasons for preferring the
eighth to the seventh."[1]

Torquemeda, taking for granted St. Isadore's " excellen-
cies" to be scriptural, seems to consider them more than
sufficient to transfer the attributes of the seventh to the first
day of the week. " Saint Isadore saith, the eighth day *is
the first,*" &c. " On it were formed the elements! on it
were created the angels! on it God bestowed manna upon
his people !"

" Our BEGINNING and our END," [2] were names characteristic of the Festival of *Tutzen,* "since Eve was the
beginning and termination of man's existence." She is a
Suchequacal represented in the forty-eighth page of the
Vatican painting, with two children who appear to have
been *combating, and one of them to have been killed.*"
" Is it not more probable, since the beginning and ending
signs of the calendar are dedicated as symbols of *Quetzalcoatl,* that this allusion is to Him rather than to Eve, *except*

---

[1] " The faithful of the dark ages," observes Basnage, " were informed that after
his resurrection, Jesus (having *neglected* to institute a new day) sent Elias *to the
church with an express order* from him to effect this change."—See Basnage.

[2] It is probable that this title had a more profound allusion.

as she is the mother of the promised Seed of the Woman?"
It is not unfrequent that the first and the second Adam are
contrasted in the Mexican paintings, the following passage
from the Antiq. of Mex. is in point—" *Opposite* Cantico
they placed *Quetzalcoatl* in a golden House, arrayed in
precious gems, and seated as a Priest, with a bag of incense
in his hand—that *as the former had been punished for his
appetite, so He was honoured for His self-denial and sacrifice.*—p. 213. A note here says, " the Mexicans believed
that *Quetzalcoatl* united in his own person the character
of Prophet, Priest, and King."

" Some authors forgetting that the Mexicans in representing a periodical series of signs wrote from right to
left, have taken the last month for the first." [1]—p. 289.

---

[1] The following are the names of the eighteen months—First, *Titil*, to glean,
Itzcalli (to renew houses) from the ninth to the twenty-eighth of January, in the
first year of the indiction of the cycle *Xeuihmolpili*. Second, *Hochilhuitl,* from
twenty-ninth January to seventeenth of February. Third, *Xilomanaliztli—*
Fourth, *Atalcahualca,* (wants rain.) Fifth, *Quachuitlihua,* (month of trees bud-
ing.) Sixth, *Cihualhuitl,* (woman's Festival,) from the eighteenth of February
to the ninth of March. Seventh, *Iacaxipehualiztli,* (feast of the snake's skin.)
Eighth. *Tozoztontli* (month of watching, because the ministers of the temple
were obliged to watch during the Festival celebrated on this month.) From
thirteenth of March to eighteenth of April. *Huey Tozoztli* (grand watching the grand penitence.) From nineteenth of April to eighteenth of May.
Ninth, *Toxcatl,* (garlands of maize were tied round the necks of the priests.)
Tenth, *Tezopachuiliztli,* a censer,) from ninth to twenty-eighth of May. (It
was in this month *Toxcatl* that the fellow soldier of Cortez Alvarado, that
ferocious warrior, made a horrible slaughter of the Mexican nobility assembled
within the enclosure of the Teo-*calli* (house of God.) This attack was the signal
of the civil dissensions that caused the death of the unfortunate Montezuma.)
From May 29 to June 17. *Tehuil-huitztli* (festival of the young warriors).
From June 18 to July 2. *Maccailhuitzintli,* (festival of the departed or dead).
From July 28 to August 16. *Huey-miccailhuitl,* (Grand festival to the memory of
illustrious dead). From August 28 to September 5. *Ochpanzitli,* (besom renewing month). From September 6 to 25. *Pachtli,* name of a wild clinging
vine which is supported and cherished on the trunk or stock of great trees, which
begins to bud this month. From September 26 to October 15. *Ezoztli* Teotlico,
(come from the gods), and also the maturity or perfection of the plant *pachtli.*
From October 16 to November 4. *Tepechuitl,* (feast of the mountains). From
November 5 to December 14. *Quecholli,* (month in which the *Phoenicoptorus,*
(Flamingo), which, on account of its peculiarities is called by the Mexicans Teo-
quechol, (Divine visitor) arrives on the borders of the lake. From December 15
to January 3. *Atemoztec* the descent of renovating showers." No one acquainted
with the metaphoric genius of the Mexicans, will doubt that all these allusions
are replete with prophetic expectation See Clavegero and Antiq. Mex.

Dr. Beatty thus describes a Festival at which he was present on the Ohio. " Before they use any of 'the first fruits,' *twelve* of their elders meet, when a deer is divided into *twelve* parts, and the corn beaten in a mortar and prepared for use by boiling or baking under the ashes. (Of course *unleavened*.) This is also divided into *twelve* parts. These men *hold up* the venison and bread, and *with their faces toward the East acknowledge the bounty* of God to them. It is then eaten. They have at evening another feast which looks like the Passover. A great quantity of venison is provided with other things dressed in the usual way, and distributed among the guests; that which is *left is thrown into the fire* and burned : *none of it may remain till sunrise, nor must a bone of the venison be broken.* Exod. xii. 46. They also purify themselves with bitter herbs and roots."

Beltrami, a literary traveller, thus writes to the Countess Compagnoni, with reference to the same Feast among a tribe west of the Mississippi—" Women and old men station themselves behind the performers, and join chorus in the Canticle. To give you an idea of the clatter and hubbub of music thus produced, it would be necessary to be either an *Indian* or a *Jew*. Public sacrifices are considered indispensable by the Indians, when they hold their grand assemblies for deliberating on the question of peace or war. Here also we trace the resemblance to antiquity. I have been present at one of their feasts; as there was a mystic solemnity connected with it, every individual was obliged to eat or make some other eat the portion set before him ; *to leave a single morsel* on the bark trencher on which the repast was served, would have been an insufferable insult to the divinity to whom it was consecrated."

MODE OF RECKONING.

"They[1] count time," observes Dr. Boudinot, " after the manner of the Hebrews. They divide the year into spring, summer, autumn and winter. They number their year from any of those four periods, for they have no name for a year ; and they subdivide these, and count the year by *lunar* months, like the Israelites, who counted by *moons* as their name sufficiently testifies. The number and regular periods of the Indians' religious feasts, is a good *historical* proof, that they counted time by, and observed a weekly sabbath, long after their arrival on the American continent. They began the year at the first appearance of the first *new* moon of the vernal equinox, according to the ecclesiastical year of Moses."—Star in the West.

[1] ' The Otahietans count by ten and then turn back as the Hurons and Algonquins do; when they come to twenty, they have a new word. They afterwards proceed by scores, and so on to ten score—and ten times ten score. Dr. Parsons has published the names of several American Indian tribes who do the same, viz. the Mohawks, the Onondagoes, the Wyandots, the Shawnese, Delawares, and Carribees."—See Astle's Origin and Progress of Printing.

This is precisely the manner of counting used by the Israelitish people: having got to ten, they begin ten *one*, ten *two*, ten *three*, ten *four*, and so on to twenty, which has a *new* name, &c.

" The mode of reckoning time," says Hunter, " is very simple. Their year begins at the vernal equinox, their diurnal reckoning is from " *evening* to evening" *beginning at sunset.*"

MEXICAN CALENDAR.

" This plate, (writes the interpreter of the Indian records,) represents the first age of the world, which was destroyed by *water*. The world had been peopled by *two* persons whom the triune God placed there at first.

" The world had been subsequently peopled by *three*, (names not mentioned.) *They* (the tribes) were descended from,[1] or of the *race* of *Quetzalcoatl*, and for this reason they hold lineage in great account, and wherever they chanced to be, they said, ' I am of such a lineage.' Before His image, which they called *the* HEART *of the people*, wood and incense were always burning.

The third age is characterized as " the holding *up of roses and flint knives*, partly covered with branches of *rose* tree, which denote the *suffering* of Quetzalcoatl. From this

---

[1] The learned Arias Montanos was convinced that the primitive people of the Western Hemisphere were of the race of *Shem*.

It is not surprising that Sigunenza, who in knowing *only* the religion of the Spanish ecclesiastics, might have been led to suppose his people of the race of *Cham*. His reason for this opinion, we are informed by Clavegero, was the similarity which he found between their pyramidal monuments, and the appellative *Teotl* which he thought bore a strong affinity to the Egyptian *Teuth*. The commentator on the Antiq. Mex. observes, " The learned Siguenza, conversant with the drawings of his people, believed that they had arrived in the Western continent soon after the dispersion of Babel. But if, as he supposed, they were of the race of *Cham*, why did they not observe the *Egyptian modes of idolatry ?* And how came they to the knowledge of *the Hebrew* ritual ? "

The Egyptian pyramids were places of sepulture; whereas those of the Indians were neither hollow, subterraneous, nor (with the exception of the small ones, dedicated to the *planets*) places of interment.

The word *Teotl* is not more analogous to the *Teuth* of Egypt, than to the *Theos* of Greece. Those who build theories on a solitary and dubious sound, have only contributed to create those clouds by which the fair face of this luminous subject has been obscured." Drake observes of the Rev. Mr. Mortimer, a New England divine :--" That the Indians have a *Latin* origin, he thinks evident, because he fancied he heard among their words *Pasco pan*, and hence thinks without doubt, their ancestors were acquainted with the god *Pan !*—History of North Caro- lina, 1. 216, in Drake's book of the Indians, p. 5.

season of suffering and affliction, according to the belief of the Mexicans, they were to be relieved by the *coming again* of *Quetzalcoatl.*"

" They recount to us the history of the creation, of the deluge, of the confusion of tongues, and the tower of Babel, and other epochs of the world ;—of *their ancestors' long journeying in Asia,* with the years previously distinguished by their corresponding characters, or symbols. They record in the year of seven *tochtli,* the *great eclipse* which happened at the crucifixion," &c.

The two signs dedicated to Quetzalcoatl, are two primitive terms, characterizing his first and second coming, viz. that of *wisdom* in its symbol the serpent, and of the *life* or *breath* of the Most High, in that of its emblem the wind, for they, like the Hebrews, express spirit and wind by one term, *ruach.* The catastrophe which they say befel Tulan :—(of which it is to be noted the virgin mother of Quetzalcoatl was a native, and of which he was the anointed king—) " was that which gave rise to a new epoch. This age was called *Yzapal Nanacaya,* (heaven of roses). The sign of this age was *Yztapal,* (a *flint*). The symbol of this fourth age was characterized by two flint knives, encompassed with branches inserted in a cane, (rod) between which the head of the ruler of hell, (or hades) is placed ; and in the following plate representing the fourth age, those two flint knives are decorated with budding branches, alluding to the atonement of *Quetzalcoatl,*[1] at some remarkable era of his life."

" The Mexican paintings describe four ages of the world, the *present* being of the flint-knives and roses. They entertain

---

[1] A characteristic remark of a dutiful son of the church, is too curious to be neglected. " I cannot omit to point out the cunning of the adversary, who so long devised this falsehood among these poor people, in order that at any time they should obtain the knowledge of the origin of our redemption, which was when the angel Gabriel was sent by God to *our Lady,* that when she displayed

a singular idea of a *fifth* age, the commencement of which was to date from the *re-appearance* of Quetzalcoatl,—or destruction of the world for the fourth time, by earthquakes, &c. which they believe would occur on the sign Nahui-ollin : —it is remarkable that the figure of the sun turned into darkness,[1] and the moon into blood, before the great and terrible Day of the LORD come, frequently occurs in the Mexican paintings."

The Mexicans appear to have given due consideration to a subject very explicitly detailed by the prophet Daniel, in what has been well denominated his ' Kalendar.'

The *gold* which symbolized the ancient Babylonic Empire, was not figuratively, nor spiritually, but literally and positively—not only succeeded, but *superseded* by that of which the symbol was *silver*. The Medio-Persian dominion was in turn *superseded* by that which the *brass* indicated, and in due time the Grecian domination was *superseded* by the Roman, which was characterized by the *iron*. The fifth Universal Empire, that of the Messiah, which is symbolized by the *adamant*, shall, as *really* and *politically*, supersede the last aspect of this Roman Empire. Daniel ii. 44, 45.

the most profound humility, calling herself servant; when the angel called her *Lady*, they might attribute to the father of lies, who falsified and counterfeited in their false god Citematonatli, and his ambassador to that virgin." &c.

[1] Torquemeda observes, "In revolving ages, when the American soil was fated to be polluted with *their accursed* rites, it is strange they should have recorded in paintings the *thick darkness that overspread Egypt*, the sad prelude to *maternal woe*, and "that the mighty Hand and outstretched Arm," should be represented in *their superstitious Calendars*." Boturini remarks, in the 52nd page of his Idea of New Gen. Hist. &c. that the Mexicans were accustomed in the month of *Hueytozoztli, to sprinkle* blood on the door-posts of their houses. And Sahagun makes mention of the same ceremony."—Antiq. Mex.

"Baron Humboldt writes, that the *Mozcas*, a civilized nation of the kingdom of New Granada, celebrated the commencement of each of their indictions by a sacrifice. The human victim was called *Guesa*, the *wanderer* (houseless,) and *Quihiea*, a door. Acosta says of this sacrifice, that it was requisite that he should *be without a spot, wound, or scar.* If the word *Guesa* signified to wander in the sense of to pass by, or not to enter a house, connected as it is with the other word *Quihiea*, a door, this *Mosca* sacrifice seems rather to refer to the *Hebrew lamb*, than to astronomical signs."—Ibid. p. 337.

" The painting preserved in the Institute of Bologna, is a *Chiapanese* Calendar; which seems singularly to confirm what Boturini says of the agreement of the twenty Mexican signs of the days of the year, with those of Chiapa, since the first sign at the bottom of the 1st page, is Mexican, which corresponds with *Cipatli*; the 2nd is *Ygh*, and answers to the *Echatl*, (wind); and the 3rd is *Votan*, agreeing with the Mexican sign *Calli*,[1] (house). The same agreement will likewise be found between the Mexican and Chiapanese symbols, &c. The sign of the lamb following the stag, and *Ocelotl*, (lion;) that of *Acatl* the reed or *arrow*. The figure of a *heart*, in which many of the signs of the Chiapanese Calendar terminate, refer, it must be supposed, to *Votan*, the signification of whose name was *the* 'HEART.' Boturini remarks that the system of the Indian Calendar, as well as the symbols employed in them, varied, and that the inhabitants of some of the provinces of *Oaxaca* divided their year into thirteen months, making use of a *lunar* calculation, while the Indian states of the same diocese counted their days by *winds* and *serpents*." " He observes in the following passage, speaking of the planets, *that the week* of the *Chiapanese, like that of the Tulticas, consisted of seven days*, which is the more remarkable, as the alleged ignorance on the part of the Indians of a week of seven days, has been used as an argument to prove that they could not have been

---

[1] Names of the Mexican Monthly signs, 1. CALLI, (house), 2. CUETZPALLIN, lizard), 3. COHUATL, (serpent), 4, MIQUIZTLI, (death's head), 5. MAZATL, (hart), 6. TOCHTLI, (lamb), improperly rabbit, 7. ATL (water), 8. ITZCUMTLI, (dog), 9. OZAMATLI, (ape,) 10. MALINALLI, (grass), 11. ACATL, (cane), 12. OCELOTL, (lion), 13. QUACHTLI, (eagle), 14. COZCAQUANTLI, (vulture), 15. OLLIN, Annual course of the sun. 16. TECPATL, (flint), 17. TINACITL, (rain), 18. XOCHITL (flowers), 19. CIPATLI, 20. ECHATL, (the wind.)

Fish divinity is one of the names which the Mexican gives to *Coxcos* TEO-*cipactli*. The stone found in Mexico, in 1790, which affords the hieroglyphic of the days, represents the sign of *Acatl*, in a different manner from two reeds tied together; we recognize it in a bundle of reeds, or sheaf of *maize* contained in a vase, p. 349. The tutelary god, Huitzilopoctli, had made His appearance on the day of Tecpatl of the year 2 Acatl, p. 393.

descended from the Hebrews. The Indians of *Chiapa*
reckon the number of the *planets* to be *seven,* corresponding
with the signs of the days of the year, the number following
that of thirteen, so celebrated in the Holy Scriptures on
account of the Blessed Creator having *rested on the seventh
day* of the creation of the world.   The names of the Chiapanese Chiefs, whose heads are found in the Calendar, bear a
considerable resemblance to Hebrew proper names, and
even the signs of the Mexican Calendar, seem to have some
reference to the *emblems* [1] *under which Jacob when dying,
predicted the destinies of his posterity.''*   With respect to
burning incense to the *Ceiba* tree, which superstition of the
Chiapanese Nunez de la Vega, treating of their Calendar,
mentions, *from the Root* of which he *says they believed* they
originally sprung :—it might as well have been considered
by him as the Root of David which was to produce that
Branch which is so much the theme of prophetic hope, as
to assume that it was an act of adulation to *Ninus*—which
name the bishop supposed to have been corrupted into
Yoana, and lastly into *Mox.*

   " Boturini,'' writes the commentator, " observes that
he could find no resemblance between the names of the
other ancient chiefs of the Chiapanese calendar and those of
the descendants of *Ninus.''*   He adds, " proceeding now to
the argument by which Acosta attempts to prove, the Indians
could not have been the Hebrews, and which Spezelius has
employed in a triumphant manner, to throw discredit on the
relation of Montecino,—what shall we say when we find in
the writings of Acosta himself, as well as from the works of
Sahagun and Torquemeda, and the commentary of the
anonymous interpreter of the Vatican MS. that the Indians

---

[1] The *Muyscas* had *Bochica* : of this tribe Gumilla says, " the Calendar corresponds to the *Abib* or *Nisan* of the Calendar of the Hebrews.

did expect a Messiah, whom they even called *Meçi* or *Mexi,* whose advent they expected in the year of *one cane;* which was probably on that account named *Xuihteuchtli* (the year of the Lord.) Nunez de la Vega, bishop of Chiapa, in that part of his Diocesan Constitution, where he speaks of *Votan* and of the treasure discovered by himself in the *Casa lobrego,* confirms the account of the interpreter of the Vatican MS. of the *great respect,* amounting to idolatry, which the Mexicans, and the other nations of New Spain, paid to their ancestors, since he not only mentions the stone images of those *ancient Indian pagans* preserved in the *Casa lobrego,* but adds, that their names are in the calendar, and that Votan who was looked upon (by the Chiapanese) as the HEART *of the people* was the third in the order. *Mox* being the first."

" The calendar to which the Bishop of Chiapa refers, was not the Mexican, but the Chiapanese, which Boturini says in the following passage of his Idea de una Nuova Hist. &c. corresponded with that of the Toltics or Tulians. The authority of Boturini, being a man of great learning, is so often refered to, that some surprise must be felt at Gama's assertion, that Don Mariano Veytia, who was appointed Boturini's executor (and became possessed after his death of whatsoever papers had not been *confiscated,*) declared that that celebrated scholar confessed to him when on his death-bed—" *That he should expire without being able to comprehend* the Mexican calendar."[1]

---

[1] A letter from the astronomer Abbe Don Lorenza Hervas, to Clavegero, will more clearly demonstrate the attainment of the Mexicans in that science. " From the work of your reverence, I learn with infinite pain how much the loss of those documents which assisted the learned Dr. Siguenza, to form his Cyclography ; and the Cavalier Boturini, to publish his idea of the general History of New Spain, is to be regretted. The year and century have been from time immemorial, regulated by the Mexicans with a degree of intelligence which does not at all correspond with the arts and sciences. In them they were inferior to the Greeks ; but the discernment which appears in their Calendar, equals them

Names of the twenty ancient lords which were preserved in the Chiapanese calendar:—*Mox, Ygh,* VOTAN, *Ghanan, Abagh, Tox, Moxic,* LAMBAT, *Molo, (en otros Mulo) Elab, Batz, Enob,* BEEN, *Hix, Tziquin, Chabin, Chic,* CHINAX, *Cahogh, Aghual.*

Names of the symbolic signs of the Mexican calendar in

to the most cultivated nations. Hence we ought to infer that this calendar is not the discovery of the Mexicans, but a communication from a *more remote and enlightened people,* and as the last are not in America, we must look for them in *Asia* or Egypt. This supposition is confirmed by your affirmation; that the Mexicans had their calendar from the Toltics (originating from Asia), whose *year,* according to Boturini was exactly adjusted by the course of the sun; and also from observing that other tribes, namely, the Chiapanese made use of the same calendar with the Mexicans without other difference than that of their *symbols.*

" The Mexican year began upon the 26th of February, a day celebrated in the era of Nabonassar, which was fixed by the Egyptians 747 years before the Christian era; for the beginning of their month *Toth* corresponded with the meridian of the same day. If those priests fixed also upon this day as an *epoch,* we have here the Mexican calendar agreeing with the Egyptian, but independently of this, greatly conforming thereto.

" The Mexicans like the Egyptians, added to every year five days which they called *Nemontemi,* or useless.

" It is true, that unlike the Egyptians, the Mexicans divided their year into eighteen months, but as they called the month *mitzli,* or ' *moon,*' it seems undeniable that their ancient month had been *lunar,* verifying that which the scriptures tell; that the *month* ' owes its name to the *moon.*' The Mexicans, it is probable, received the *lunar* month from *their ancestors,* but for certain purposes also instituted another. You have affirmed in your history that the *Miztecas* formed their year into *thirteen* months, which number was *sacred* in the calendar of the Mexicans.

" The symbols and periods of years, months, and days, in the Mexican Calendar are truly admirable. In their century it is probable that the period of *four years* was *civil,* and that of *thirteen, religious.* From the multiplication of these two periods they had their century, or age of one hundred and four years. In those periods an art is discovered not less admirable than our indictions, cycles," &c. "The period of their civil weeks was contained exactly in their civil and astronomical month; the latter had six and the former four, and the year contained seventy three complete weeks, in which particular our method is excelled by the Mexicans, for our weeks are not contained exactly in the month nor in the year. Their period of religious weeks was contained twice in their religious month, and twenty-eight times in their year : but in the latter remained a day over as there is in our weeks. From the periods of thirteen days, multiplied by the twenty characters of the month, the cycle of two hundred and sixty days was produced of which you make mention; but as there remained a day over the twenty religious weeks of the solar year, there arose another cycle of two hundred and sixty days, in such a manner that the Mexicans could from the first day of every year distinguish *what* the year was. " The period of *civil* months, multiplied by the number of days, (that is eighteen by twenty,) and the period of *lunar* months multiplied by the number of days, (that is twelve by thirty,) give the same product, or the number 360; a number certainly not less

the same order:—*Cipatli, Ehecatl, Calli, Cuetzpallin, Cohuatl, Miquiztli, Mazatl, Tochtli, Atl, Ytzeimtli, Ozomatli, Malinalli, Acatl, Ocelotl, Quachtli, Temetlatl, Ollin, Tecpatl, Quailhiutl, Xochitl.*

memorable and in use among the Mexicans than amongst the *most ancient* nations; and a number which from time immemorial, has ruled in geometry and astronomy, and is of the utmost particularity on account of its relation to the circle which is divided into three hundred and sixty parts or degrees. In no nation of the world do we meet with any thing similar to this clear and distinct method of Calendar."

"From the small period of four years, multiplied by the above-mentioned cycle of 360 years, arose another admirable cycle of 1040 years. The Mexicans combined the small period of four years with the period above-named *week* of thirteen years; thence resulted their noted cycle, or century of 52 years, and thus with the four figures, indicating the period of four years, they had, as we have from the dominical letters, a period, which to say the truth, exceeded ours, which is of twenty-eight years, while the Mexican is of fifty-two; theirs was *perpetual*, and ours in *Georgian* years, *is not so*." "So much variety and simplicity of periods of weeks and months and years and cycles, cannot be unadmired; and the more so, as there is immediately discovered that particular *relation* which these periods have to many different *ends*, which *Boturini* points *out* by saying, "The Mexican *Calendar* was of four species; that is, natural for agriculture, chronological for history, *ritual for festivals*, and astronomical for the course of the stars, and the year was *lunisolar*." Boturini determines in the Mexican paintings the year of confusion of tongues, &c. &c. The Mexican lords, therefore, who still preserve some of the ancient paintings might, by the study of them, adduce many lights to chronology. Leaving apart the evident conformity which the symbols and expressions of spring and winter have, with those of Job, who in my opinion lived a short time after the deluge, (as I state in my eleventh volume) it ought to be noted that these symbols which are excellent for preserving the year invariable, demonstrate the use of the intercalary days of the Mexicans," &c.   *   *   *   *

"Lastly, the symbol which you put for the Mexican century, convinces me that it is the same which the ancient *Chaldeans* and Egyptians had. In the Mexican symbol we see the sun as it were eclipsed by the moon, and surrounded by a serpent, which makes four twists, and embraces the four points of thirteen years. This very idea of the serpent with the sun has, for time immemorial in the world, signified the periodical or annual course of the sun.

"We know that in astronomy, the points where eclipses happen have from time immemorial been called (as Briga Romagnoli has noted) the head and tail of the dragon. The Chinese from false ideas, though conformable to this immemorial usage and allusion, believe that at eclipses, a dragon is in the act of devouring the sun. The Egyptians more particularly agree with the Mexicans; for, to symbolize the sun, they employed a circle with one or two serpents; but still more the ancient Persians; among whom their *Mitras* (which was certainly the sun,) was symbolized by a sun and a serpent, and from P. Montfacon we are given (in his Antiquities) a monument of a serpent surrounding the signs of the Zodiac, which cuts them, by rolling himself in various forms about them. In addition to these incontestible proofs and examples, the following reflection is most convincing. There is no doubt that the symbol of the serpent is a thing totally arbitrary to signify the sun, with which it has no natural or physical relation; how then, I ask, have so many nations dispersed over the globe, and of which some have had *no reciprocal* intercourse, unless in *the early ages after the deluge*, attained to this uniformity, &c."—See Clavegero.

HISTORICAL RECORDS.

" WE are naturally disposed to inquire what was the TEO-
MOX*tli*—the name of the Divine Book which contained the
history,[1] mythology, calendar, and laws of the Tultecas.
This word is compounded of TEO, divine; *amitl*, paperus,
and *Moxtli* or *Mostli*; for in the Mexican language *y* and *x*
frequently supply the place of *s*; *tli* is devoid of meaning,
but is a general termination. Mostli then appears to be
Moses, when the sentence would be—" The Divine Book of
Moses." It is necessary to observe that in the Mexican
language, the compounding of words terminating in *itl*, with
other words, an elision of those final letters frequently takes
place, as in the word *acatl*, which is compounded of *atl*,
water; and *calli*, a house."—p. 104.

" A little historical book was found of an Hebrew-Indian
nation, which may probably be that of Been, mentioned by
Nunez de la Vega, (to which tradition, it should be observed, the Bishop of Chiapa lent his much higher authority.) It is impossible not to remark the resemblance which
many of their proper names bear to the Hebrew. In the
last edition of Garcia's Origin los Indios, we find the

---

[1] 'The Mexican history,' observes Humboldt, ' presents the greatest order,
and an astonishing minuteness in the recital of events.' 229. ' The Aztec priests
as we have already observed, followed the different terms of a series from *right
to left*, and not from left to right as the Hindoos, and almost all the nations that
now inhabit Europe. We shall see at Mexico the copy of a painting formerly in
the Museum of the Cavalier Boturini, in which the sign of the month *quecholli*
is followed by thirteen points placed near a Spanish spearman, whose horse has
under his feet the hieroglyphic of the city of *Zenochtilan*; this painting represents the first entry of the Spaniards into Mexico,' &c.—p. 300.

cause which follows inserted by the editor in the text: but Garcia notices himself other Indian names which resembled Hebrew."

" The rumour of inscriptions existing in *Yutican*, reached the ear of the venerable Las Casas also, who probably only doubted the fact, because he had not the opportunity of going there to verify it. If, however, such inscriptions had been numerous in the New World, it is not likely that they would long have survived the mutilating hands of the Spanish missionaries. We may however remark, that two curvilinear ornaments, shaped like the letter S, occur upon a broken bust. The inscription to which Garcia refers as mentioned by Ciça, is spoken of in the following passage of the 87th chap. of his Chron. of Peru. The River which is named Vinaz, is the largest, on the banks of which are situated some large and most ancient edifices, &c. Having inquired of the neighbouring Indians, who were the founders of these ancient structures, they replied, *bearded men, who they say arrived in this country long before the reign of the Incas, and there established their residence*." *Parte Primera de la Chronica del Peru*, cap. 87, p. 221.

"The Peruvian quipos might have been a kind of syllabic writing like that of the Japannese ; and the Spaniards seem to have consigned them to eternal oblivion. As regards the tradition of letters in Mexico, it may be proper to recollect that Torquemeda says of the book [1] which the Indians de-

---

[1] The following testimony is thus introduced by Torquemeda. " Another ecclesiastic named brother Diego de Merçado, a grave father who has been definitor of this province of the Holy Gospel, and one of the most exemplary of men, and greatest doers of penance of his time; relates and authenticates this relation with his signature.—That some years ago conversing with an aged Indian of the Otomies, respecting matters of our faith, the Indian told him that they had in ancient times been in possession of a book which was handed down from father to son, in the person of the eldest, who was devoted to the safe custody of it, and to instruct others in its doctrines. These doctrines were written in two portions, and between the columns, Christ was painted crucified, with a countenance as of sorrow. They said that God was offended, and out of

clared that they buried under ground on the arrival of the Spaniards, between the columns of which Christ was painted crucified, and the intermediate spaces were filled up with alphabetical characters. Sahagun affirms in the following very singular passage, that the children who were educated in the temple in Mexico, learned *hymns which were written down in books in characters; they instructed them in all the verses which they were accustomed to sing, to which they gave the name of divine songs, all which were written in their books in characters.* This passage, from its singularity, has been marked in the original MS." &c.—p. 333.

Of this barbarous act of monkish zeal, Doctor Cabrara thus speaks: " Among the many historical works which fell into the hands of that illustrious prelate, &c. there was one written by VOTAN, the third Gentile placed on the calendar. He wrote an historical tract in the Indian idiom, wherein he mentions the name of the people with whom, and the places where he had been," &c. " This illustrious prelate could have communicated a much greater portion of information relative to VOTAN,[1] and to many other of the primitive inhabitants, whose historical works he assures us were in his own possession, but feeling some scruples on account of the mischievous use the Indians made of their histories, in the superstition of *Nagualism*,[2] he thought proper to withhold it for the reasons assigned in No. 36, section 32 of his preface. Although," he adds, " in these tracts and papers

reverence did not turn over the leaves with their hands, but with a small bar which they had made for the purpose, and which they kept along with the book. This book was buried in the earth for fear of the Spaniards."

[1] " *Votan*, was a celebrated saint amongst the *Chiapanese* and the *Capotecas*, and it is much to be regretted that Nunez de la Vega, Bishop of Chiapa and Socunosco should have destroyed or consigned to oblivion the historical works which he wrote (*or which were at least written by some other person concerning him*) as it would probably have thrown much light on the ancient history of America."—Ibid.

[2] The same with the *Quetzalcoatl* of Mexico, and the *Verachocha* of Peru.

are many things touching primitive paganism, they are not mentioned in this epitome, lest in being brought to notice, they should be the means of confirming more strongly an idolatrous superstition."—34th sect. p. 30, of the Preface of his Constitution, in Antiq. Mex.

" Rosales, in his history of Chili, gives the following account of a curious inscription discovered in that province: " The *tradition* of some apostle having come to preach the gospel in this kingdom, is further confirmed by a marvellous thing which still exists in the valley of Tarna, where there is a stone of a yard and a-half high, and two in length, on which are imprinted the footsteps of a man wearing shoes, who there left the impression of his feet; having been accustomed to ascend upon it to preach to the Indians of the valley, and so leaving his feet imprinted on the stone; and who also wrote on the front of it three lines in plain letters cut in the rock in characters which no one understands or can explain." Ibid.

" Father Joseph Maria Adams, belonging to the society of Jesus, a missionary in the province of Cuio, caused them to be faithfully copied out, and transcribed, and sent them to three fathers of that company, famous for their skill in languages, but none of them were able to read them, so that their signification is still unknown."—p. 332.

Sahagun says, " that in the reign of *Ytzcoatl,* the lords and principal persons amongst the Mexicans (who were the priests, *the government being a Theocracy)* buried their ancient records that they might not fall into the hands of others. This might refer to the destruction of the TEO-*moxtli* (divine book of the *Toltecas)* in the reign of the above-mentioned king, from which the Mexicans might have borrowed their notions and metaphors."

" *Garcia,* citing *Laet,* and likewise on his own authority,

M

says, "that paintings were used in Peru," &c. We have seen some specimens[1] of a similar nature, painted by the Mexicans after their conversion to Christianity, exceedingly rude, in which hardly a trace of the old style of Mexican painting can be discerned, and the same may have been the case with the later Peruvian paintings, from which it would be wrong to form an estimate of the degree of excellence which the art of painting had attained in the time of the Incas."

[1] " It is not easy to give a complete notice of the hieroglyphic paintings that have escaped the destruction with which they were menaced on the first disco-very of America by monkish fanaticism and the stupid carelessness of the first conquerors."—Vol. vi. p. 145.

LANGUAGE.

THE changes to which Language is subjected during a long series of ages, geographical interposition, and inter-marriage, render the mere sounds, a much less certain criterion in tracing it to its original source, than its *construction*, and those *essential* characteristics which are peculiar to the Hebrew, whom the writer of the " Primogeniture and Integrity of the Holy Language," happily characterizes as *" the mother who lendeth to all but borroweth from none."*

The Jews, who had only been in Babylon seventy years, had so corrupted the Hebrew language, as to render it necessary to affix a determinate pronunciation by the introduction of vowel points.

It is, therefore, in the genius of the transatlantic dialects that we are to expect Hebraism, rather than in the use of Hebrew terms; although in their religious rites these have been wonderfully preserved. For example, the same mysterious personage who was by the antient Chiapanese desig-nated *Votan* (HEART *of the people*): by the Tulians *Bah-ab*, (Son of the Father): and by the Mexicans *Toplitzin* and TEO-*piltzin (our son* and GOD'S-*son)*; was by the Peruvians denominated *Ver-chocha* (son and star). This latter term for *son*, viz. בר is Chaldee, and is only used with reference to the Son of God, as in Psalm ii. 7. This term compound-ed with כוכב *star*, no doubt had allusion to that star which Balaam was constrained to declare, would, at a remote period of the world's history, " come out of Jacob, and smite through or consume the captains of Moab."

The Author of Historical Researches, &c. observes, with regard to the number of languages in America, " There are said to be more than a thousand. If an Englishman of the present day is puzzled to understand the English of the four-teenth century, where *writing* or *printing* has always been used, what stability of language is to be expected among Americans who have never had an alphabet?"—p. 470.

Another striking feature of identity in the genius of the primitive languages of the East and the West, is that the same term serves to express *breath or spirit*, and the *wind*. And this peculiarity is restricted to the Hebrew language.

The term יֵת רוּחַ pronounced eth-ruach — was by the Chiapanese exactly so termed—while by the Mexicans, who supplied the use of the letter *r* with that of *l*, called it Eh-euach; and as elision was also practised by them, the same term stands as the sign of Quetzalcoatl on their calendar as *Echa*-tl.

Las Casas affirms that in Haiti (now St. Domingo) the inhabitants spoke corrupt Hebrew; they styled their judges or councillors, *Chochome*; which is precisely the term by which the Jews all over Europe would designate a wise or learned Rabbi. ' He is a great chocham.'

The northern tribes have preserved in many cases the primitive YA-HO-WAH, and also H*allilu*-YAH : Vega affirms that *Halli* was the Peruvian term for praise or triumph.

" Eight youths," writes Vega,[1] who was a descendant of the Incas, (metiffs born of Spanish and Indian parents,) " my schoolfellows sang the *Halli* in the processions, accom-

---

[1] Vega, Book v. c. 2, in Hist. Research. p. 183.

panied by the whole musical choir. They were dressed after the manner of the country, and each carried a plough-share in his hand, this having been the song of the Incas [1] on *agricultural ceremonies;* the Indians were exceedingly delighted at the Spaniards adopting their song in the worship of their God, [2] whom they called Pachacamac." The reasons why the Peruvians did not like some of the northern tribes compound *Halli* with YAH might have been on account of the extreme veneration which they had for the ineffible Name.

The Abbe Clavegero observes [3] of the copiousness of the Mexican language, ' that it abounds in terms that signify material things, while the highest mysteries of religion can be expressed in Mexican without any necessity for introducing the Spanish term *Dios,* that of TEO-*tl* being equivalent to *Ail, Theos* and *Deus.* There was therefore,' he justly adds ' no reason for introducing the Spanish term Dios, but the excessive scruples of the first missionaries,

---

[1] " In the city of *Cozco,* near the *hill where the citadel stands,* there is a portion of land called Col-*cam*-pata, which none are permitted to cultivate except those of royal blood. The Incas and the Pallas solemnized that day with great rejoicings, especially when they turned up the earth (with a kind of mattock). On this occasion the Incas were dressed in their richest jewels, and sang an anthem at the ceremony, so much were they inspired."—Robertson, Vol. ii. p. 315. in Hist. Researches. p. 197.

[2] It was not in praise of the Sun, as has often been erroneously supposed, but of the Supreme Moral Light of the Universe, of which the Sun was accounted the symbol: the term *Pacha* signifies universe, and *camac* is from the verb *camar*, to animate : *cama* is the soul.

[3] The Abbe annoyed with the erroneous statement of Monsieur Du Pauw, (who, " knowing no more about the Mexicans than the little that Dr. Robertson has furnished, intimates that among many *other extraordinary things,* "*they had no words to express metaphysical terms, or to count above the number three ;*") observes, ' we could here give the numeral terms of this language, by which the Mexicans could count up to forty-eight millions at least,' &c. The Mexican language, like the Hebrew, wants the superlative term ; and, like the Hebrew, the comparative term—which are supplied by certain equivalent particles. It is not less copious in verbs than in nouns, as from every single verb others are derived of different significations. The Mexicans combine with more economy than the Greeks did, often cutting off letters and even syllables.— *Teopixqui* (priest) is composed of TEo*tl* (God), and the verb *pia*, to keep, guard, hold.'

who, as they had burned the *historical records* of the Mexicans, because they suspected them to be full of *superstitious meanings* (of which Acosta himself justly complains) likewise rejected the Mexican word TEOTL, because *they supposed* it served to express the *false God* whom they worshipped. But it would have been *better to have imitated the example* of St. Paul, *who* when he found the Greek *Theos* was used to signify certain false deities, &c. did not compel the Greeks to adopt AIL or ADONOI.'

There is a tribe in the south which designates the Most High *Abamengo-ish-to,* which is a compound of the Hebrew terms יש and אב (Father-man) united by the vernacular term for chief, which was mengo. This mengo is identical with the Peruvian mancha or mango-capah, or capac. The last part of which is Hebrew, and signifies an *anointed branch,* כפה 'a palm-branch,'—a proverbial expression for the *highest,* as *rush* is for the lowest.' This analogy might be greatly extended, but perhaps the identity, as far as language is concerned, is already sufficiently established.

For a curious specimen extracted from the work of James Adair, Esq. on the use of the ineffable name יהוה in adjuration by a northern tribe amongst whom he resided forty years.—see Appendix,

Father Charlevoix says the Algonquin and Huron languages are the parents of ten thousand prevailing dialects; of the latter he says—" it has a copiousness, an energy and sublimity perhaps not to be found in the finest languages we know of; and those whose native tongue it is, though now but an handful of men, have such an elevation of soul, as agrees better with the majesty of their language, than with the state to which they are reduced."

" The Algonquin language has not so much force as the Huron; but has more sweetness and elegance. Both have a richness of expression, a variety of turns, a propriety of terms, a regularity which astonishes—but what is more surprising among these barbarians, who never study to speak well, and who never had the use of writing, there is never introduced a coarse word, an improper term, or a vicious construction. And even their children preserve all the purity of the language in their common discourse. On the other hand, the manner in which they animate all they say, leaves no room to doubt of their comprehending all the worth of their expressions, and all the beauty of their language."

Mr. Colden, who wrote the History of the Wars of the Five Nations, about the year 1750, and was a man of considerable note, speaking of the language of those nations, says, " they are very nice in the turn of their expressions, and not a few of them are so far masters of their language, as never to offend the ears of their Indian auditory by an unpolite expression. They have, it seems, a certain urbanity or atticism in their language, of which the common ear is very sensible, though only their great speakers attain to it. They are so given to speech-making, that their common compliments to any person they respect, at meeting or parting, are made in harangues. They have a few radical words, but they compound them without end. By this their language becomes sufficiently copious, and leaves room for a good deal of art to please a delicate ear. Their language abounds with gutterals and strong aspirations, which make it very energetic and bold. Their speeches abound with metaphors, after the manner of the eastern nations."

" The Indians generally express themselves with great vehemence and short pauses, in their public speeches. Their periods are well turned, and very sonorous and harmonious. Their words are specially chosen and well disposed, with great care and knowledge of their subject or language, in order to show the being, power, and agency of the Great Spirit in *all* that concerns *them*.[1]

To speak in general terms, their language, in the roots, idiom, and particular construction, appears to have the whole genius of the Hebrew, and what is very remarkable, and well worthy of serious observation, has many of the

[1] Father Charlevoix, a famous French writer, who came over to Canada very early, and paid particular attention to the Indian natives, says, " that the only means (which others have neglected) to come at the original of the Indian natives, is the knowledge of their languages, and comparing them with those of the other hemisphere, that are considered as primitives. Manners very soon degenerate by means of commerce with foreigners, and by mixture of several nations uniting in one body—and particularly so, amongst wandering tribes, living without civil government, especially where absolute want of the necessaries of life takes place, and the necessity of doing without, causes their names and uses to perish together. From their dialects, we may ascend to the mother tongues themselves. These are distinguished by being more nervous than those derived from them, because they are formed from nature, and they contain a greater number of words, imitating the things whereof these are the signs. Hence he concludes that if those characteristical marks which are peculiar to any oriental nation are found in the Indian languages, we cannot reasonably doubt of their being truly original, and consequently that the people who speak them, have passed over from that hemisphere."

" For this," observes Doctor Boudinot, " there must be an inquiry into facts, the investigation of which, from the nature of the subject, must be wholly founded on well authenticated accounts recorded by writers of character, who may be consulted on this occasion ; or from the information of such persons who have been long domesticated with particular nations, suspected to have originated from the other hemisphere ; or of persons whose occupation or mode of life has led them to visit parts of the globe, the most likely to afford some light on this abstruse subject. And even here our assistance cannot be expected to be great ; but whatever we are able to discover, we will put together ; in hopes that by pursuing this inquiry, though we should arise no farther than bare rudiments, the curiosity of the more learned and persevering, may produce some further and more adequate discovery, to enlighten mankind. The difficulties attending this attempt must be great."

" The Indian languages, having never been reduced to any certainty by letters, must have been exposed to great changes and misconceptions. They are still a *wandering* people—*oppressed* and *distressed on all hands*—driven from their original residence into a wilderness, and even there not suffered to remain stationary ;—but still driven from place to place, debased and enervated by the habitual use of *intoxicating spirits*, afforded them by traders, for the double purpose of *profit* and *imposition*, vitiated by the *awful example* of white people, we are at this day confined to the few traces of their original language, their religion, rites and customs, and a few common traditions that may yet with labour be collected, to form our opinions upon. The Indian languages in general are very copious and expressive, considering the narrow sphere in which they move ; their ideas being few in comparison with civilized nations. They have neither cases nor declensions. They have few or no prepositions : they remedy this, by affixes and suffixes, and their words are invariably the same in both numbers.

peculiarities of that language, especially those in which it differs from most other languages ; and is " often, both in letters and signification, synonymous with the Hebrew language."

´ " Souard in his Melanges de Literature, speaking of the Indians of *Guiana*, observes on the authority of a learned Jew, *Isaac Nasci*, residing at Surinam, " We are informed

" All this, if the writer's information be correct, is very similar to the Hebrew language. He has been informed from good authority, and the same is confirmed by a writer well-acquainted with the subject, that there is no language known in Europe, except the Hebrew, without prepositions ; that is, in separate and express words. The Indians have all the other parts of speech, except as above. They have no comparative or superlative degrees of comparison more than the Hebrews. They form the last, by some leading vowel of the divine name of the *Great Spirit* added to the word. It is observed, by some Jewish, as well as Christian interpreters, that the several names of God, are often given as epithets by the Hebrews to those things which are the greatest, the strongest, and the best of their kind, as *ruach elohim*, a mighty wind. Both languages are very rhetorical, nervous, and emphatical. Those public speeches of the Indians, that the writer of these memoirs has heard or read, have been oratorical, and adorned with strong metaphors in correct language, and greatly abound in allegory. About the year 1684, the governor of New York, sent an accredited agent to the Onondagos, on a dispute that was likely to arise with the French. The agent (Arnold) behaved himself very haughtily towards the Indians at delivering his commission. One of the chiefs then answered him in a strain of Indian eloquence, in which he said among other things, " I have two arms—I extend the one towards Montreal, there to support the tree of peace ; and the other towards *Corlaer*, (the governor of New York) who has long been my brother. *Ononthis* (the governor of Canada) has been these ten years my father. *Corlaer* has been long my brother, with my own good will, but neither the one nor the other is my master. *He who made the world*, gave me this land I possess. *I am free*. I respect them both ; but no man has a right to command me, and none ought to take amiss, my endeavouring all I can, that this land should not be troubled. To conclude, I can no longer delay repairing to my father, who has taken the pains to come to my very gate, and who has no terms to propose but such as are reasonable." Wynne's History of America, p. 402, 403. Vol. i.

At a meeting held with the President, General Washington, in 1790, to prevail upon him to relax the terms of a treaty of peace made with the commissioners under the old confederation, relative to an *unreasonable* cession of a large part of their country, which they had been rather *persuaded* to make to the United States, for *the sake of peace*, and which afterwards they sincerely repented of, *Cornplant*, who had long been a steady friend to the United States, in the most perilous part of the revolutionary war, delivered a long, persuasive, and able speech, which the writer of this preserved, and has now before him, and from which are extracted the following sentences, as a proof of the above assertion. " Father, when your army entered the country of the six nations, we called you the *town destroyer*, and to this day, when your name is heard, our women look behind them and turn pale ; our children cling close to the necks of their mothers ; counsellors and warriors being men, cannot be afraid ; but their hearts are grieved by the fears of our women and children, and desire that it may be buried so deep, as to be

that the language of *Guiana* is soft and agreeable to the
ear, abounding in vowels and synonyms, and possessing a
syntax as regular as it would have been, if established by
an academy." This Jew says that all the substantives are
Hebrew. The word expressive of the soul in each language,
means *breath*. They have the same word in Hebrew to
denominate God, which means Master, or LORD."

heard of no more. Father, we will not conceal from you, that the Great Spirit and
not man, has preserved *Cornplant* from the hands of his own nation. For they
ask continually, where is the land on which our children and their children are
to lie down upon? You told us, say they, that a line drawn from Pennsylvania
to Lake Ontario, would mark it for ever on the east; and a line running from
Beaver Creek to Pennsylvania, would mark it on the west. But we see that it is
not so. For first one and then another comes and takes it away by order of
those persons, who you told us, promised to secure it to us for ever. *Cornplant* is
silent, for he has nothing to answer. When the sun goes down, *Cornplant* opens
his heart before the Great Spirit; and earlier than the sun appears again upon
the hills, he gives thanks for his protection during the night, for he feels, that
among men, become desperate by the injuries they sustain, it is God only that
can preserve him. *Cornplant* loves peace, *all* he had in store, he has given to
those *who have been robbed by your people*, lest they should plunder the innocent,
to *repay* themselves.

"The whole season which others have employed in providing for their families, *Cornplant* has spent in endeavours to *preserve* peace, and at this moment
his wife and children are lying on the ground, and in want of food. His heart is
in pain for them; but he perceives that the *Great Spirit* will try his firmness, in
doing what is right. Father! innocent men of our nation are killed one after
another, though of our best families; but none *of your people, who have committed these murders, have been punished.* We recollect that you did promise to
punish those who should kill our people; and we ask, was it intended that your
people should kill the Seneca's, and not only remain unpunished, but be *protected from the next of kin?* Father! these to us are great things. *We know
that you are very strong—We have heard that you are wise,* but *we shall wait to
hear your answer to this that we may know if you are* JUST."

A speech made by *Logan*, a famous Indian chief, about the year 1775,
was never exceeded by Demosthenes or Cicero. A party of our people fired on
a canoe loaded with women and children, and one man, all of whom happened
to belong to the family of *Logan*, who had been long the staunch friend of the
Americans, and then at perfect peace with them. A war immediately ensued,
and after much bloodshed on both sides, the Indians were beat, and sued for
peace. A treaty was held, but *Logan* disdainfully refused to be reckoned among
the suppliants; but to prevent any disadvantage from his absence to his nation,
he sent the following talk to be delivered to Lord Dunmore at the Treaty. "I
appeal to any white man to say, if he ever entered Logan's cabin hungry, and he
gave him not meat—if ever he came cold and naked, and Logan clothed him not.
During the course of the last long and bloody war, Logan remained idle in his
cabin, an advocate for peace. Such was his love for the white men, that my
countrymen pointed as they passed, and said, *Logan is the friend of white men.*
I had thought to have lived with you, but for the injuries of one man. Colonel
Cressup the last spring, in cold blood, and unprovoked, murdered all the relations
of *Logan* not sparing even my wife and children. There runs not a drop of my

It is said, there are two parent languages among the northern Indians, extending thence to the Mississippi :—the *Huron* and *Algonquin*, and there is not more difference between these, than between the old Norman and French. Dr. Edwards asserts that the language of the Delawares, in Pennsylvania—of the Penobscots, bordering on Nova-Scotia

blood in the veins of any living creature. This called on me for revenge. I have sought it. I have killed many. I have fully appeased their blood. For my country, I rejoice at the beams of peace. But do not harbour a thought that mine is the joy of fear. *Logan* never felt fear. He will not turn on his heel to save his life. *Who* is there to mourn for *Logan?* No, not one." *

" A writer," Adair, "who has had the best opportunities to know the true idiom of their language, by a residence among them for forty years, has taken great pains to shew the similarity of the Hebrew, with the Indian languages, both in their roots and general construction ; and insists that many of the Indian words, to this day, are purely Hebrew, notwithstanding their exposure to the loss of it to such a degree, as to make the preservation of it so far, little less than miraculous.

" Let any one compare the old original Hebrew, spoken with so much purity by the Jews before the Babylonish captivity, with that spoken by the same people on their return, after the comparatively short space of seventy years, and he will find it had become a barbarous mixture of the Hebrew and Chaldaic languages, so as not to be understood by an ancient Hebrew, and in a great measure has continued so to this day. We say such a consideration will show an almost miraculous intervention of Divine Providence, should a clear trace of the original language be discoverable among the natives of our wilderness at this day." " Their words and sentences are expressive, concise, emphatical, sonorous, and bold." Father Charlevoix, in his history of Canada, paid more attention to the Indian languages than most travellers before him, and indeed he had greater opportunities, and was a man of learning, and considerable abilities. He says, " that the *Algonquin* and *Huron* languages, have, between them, *that* of almost all the nations of Canada we are acquainted with. Whoever should well understand both, might travel without an interpreter, more than fifteen hundred leagues of country."

" Their method of invoking God in a solemn hymn, with that reverential deportment and spending a full breath on each of the two first syllables of the awful divine name, hath a surprising analogy to the Jewish custom, and such as no other nation or people, even with the advantage of written records, have retained. It may be worthy of notice, that they never prostrate themselves, nor bow their bodies to each other, by way of salute or homage, though usual with the eastern nations; except when they are making or renewing peace with strangers, who come in the name of *Yah*." After speaking of their sacred adjuration by the great and awful name of God, he says, " When we consider that the period of the adjurations, according to their idiom, only asks a question, and that the religious waiters say *Yah*, with a profound reverence, in a bowing posture of body, immediately before they invoke *Yo-he-wah* ; the one reflects so much light on the other, as to convince me that the Hebrews both invoked and pronounced the divine tetragrammaton Yo-he-wah, and adjured their witnesses

* " Great allowance must be made for translations into another language, especially by illiterate and ignorant interpreters ; this destroys the force as well as beauty of the original."—Ibid.

—of the Indians of St. Francis, in Canada—of the Shawa-
nese, on the Ohio—of the Chippewas, to the westward of
Lake Huron—of the Ottawas, Nanticokes, Munsees, Mino-
mones, Messinagues, Sausikies, Ottagamies, Killestinoes,
Mipegoes, Algonquins, Winnebagoes, and of the several

to give true evidence on certain occasions, according to the Indian usage : otherwise how could they possibly, without letters, have a custom so nice and strong,
pointing a standard of religious caution? It seems exactly to coincide with the
conduct of the Hebrew witnesses, even now, on the like religious occasions."

" Blind chance could not have directed so great a number of remote
nations to fix on, and unite in so nice a religious standard of speech, and
even grammatical construction of language, where there was no knowledge
of letters or syntax. For instance, A, oo, EA, is a strong religious Indian
emblem, signifying, I *climb, ascend,* or *remove* to another place of residence. It
points to A-no-wah, the first person singular, and O E A, or Yah, He Wah, and
implies putting themselves under the divine patronage. The beginning of that
most sacred symbol, is by studious skill, and a thorough knowledge of the
power of letters, placed twice, to prevent them from being applied to the sacred
name, for vain purposes, or created things.

" Though they have lost the true meaning of their religious emblems, except
what a very few of the more intelligent traders revive in the retentive memories
of the old inquisitive magi, or beloved men ; yet tradition directs them to apply
them properly. They use many plain religious emblems of the divine name, as
Y, O, he, wah—Yah and Ail, and these are the roots of a prodigious number of
words, through their various dialects. It is worthy of remembrance, that two
Indians, who belong to far distant nations, without the knowledge of each
other's language, except from the general idiom, will intelligibly converse together, and contract engagements without any interpreter, in such a surprising
manner, as is scarcely credible. In like manner we read of Abraham, Isaac, and
Jacob, travelling from country to country, from Chaldea into Palestine, when
inhabited by various differing nations—thence into Egypt and back again, making
engagements, and treating with citizens wherever they went. But we never
read of any difficulty of being understood, or their using an interpreter.

" Women set apart, they term *hoolo*,[1] that is, sanctifying themselves to
Ish-to-hoolo. So Netakhoolo signifies a sanctified or holy day. So *Okka hoolo,*
water sanctified. Thus *Ish-to-hoolo,* when applied to God, in its true radical
meaning, imports *the great beloved holy* CAUSE, which is exceedingly comprehen-
sive, and more expressive of the true nature of God, than the Hebrew name,
Adonai, which may be applicable to a human being. When they apply the
epithet compounded, to any of their own religious men, it signifies, *the great,
holy, beloved, sanctified, man of the Holy One.*

" They make the divine Name point yet more strongly to the Supreme author
of nature. For as Abba signifies father, so, to distinguish God, as the King of
kings, by his attributes, from their own *Minggo Ishto,* or great chief, they frequently name God *Minggo Ishto Abba, Ishto Abba, Minggo Abba,* &c. and when
they strive to move the passions, *Ishto Hoolo Abba.* They have another more
sacred appellative, which with them is the mysterious essential name of GOD ;—
the tetragrammaton of the Hebrews, or the great four lettered name already
mentioned, *Y. O. He. Wah.* This they, like the Hebrews, never mention al-

---

[1] The present of the infinitive mood of the active verb, is *a hoola,* from the preter
tense of the passive verb hoolo, " I love," that is sanctified or holy.

tribes in New England, are radically the same, and the variations between them are to be accounted for from their want of letters and of communication. " Much stress, (observes Boudinot), may be laid on Dr. Edwards'[1] opinion."

together in common speech. Of the time and place, when and where they mention it, they are very particular, and always with a solemn air.

" The Indians have among them orders of men answering to prophets and priests. In the Muskohge language, *Hetch Lalage*, signifies cunning men, or persons prescient of futurity, much the same with the Hebrew seer. But the Indians in general call their pretended prophets, *Loa-che*, men resembling the holy fire or Elohim. Their tradition says, that their forefathers were possessed of an extraordinary divine spirit, by which they foretold things future, and controled the common course of nature; and this they transmitted to their offspring, provided they obeyed the sacred laws annexed to it. They believe that by the communication of the same divine fire, working in their *Loa-che*, they can yet effect the like. But they say it is out of the reach of *Nana Ookproo*, or bad people, either to comprehend or perform such things, because the holy spirit of fire will not co-operate with or actuate *Hottuch Ookproo*, an accursed people." " A sachem of the Minggo tribe, being observed to look at the great comet which appeared the 1st of October 1680, was asked, what he thought was the meaning of that prodigious appearance? He answered gravely, " It signifies that[1] we Indians shall be wasted, and this country be inhabited by another people."—Smith's New Jersey, p. 136.

[1] Dr. Edwards had been from a child conversant with the Indian dialects, having been above thirty years among them.

Baron Lahontan observes, " Je dirai de la langue Hurons et des Iroquois une chose assez curieuse, qui est qui'il ne s'y trouve point de lettres labiales; c'est a dire, de b, f, m, p. Cependant, cette langue de Hurons paroit être fort belle et d'un son tout a fait beau : quois qu'ils ne ferment jamais leurs livres en parlant." And " J'ai passe quatre jours à vouloir faire prononcer à des *Hurons* les lettres labiales, mais je n'ai pû y réussir, et je crois qu'en dix ans ils ne pourront dire ces mots, " bons," prononceroient *rils ;* " Monsieur." *caunsieur.* " Pontechartrain" *Conchartrain."*

' Lafitau wrote a history where he maintained that the Caribee language was *radically* Hebrew.'— See Clavegero, Memoires de l' Amerique, 11, 236, 237.

CHARACTERISTICS.

OF the Choctaws, Bertram observes, "They were a hardy, subtle, brave, intrepid, ingenuous, and virtuous race. They erect a scaffold twenty feet high in a grave, upon which they lay their dead, and after a sufficient time the bones are placed in a coffin fabricated of bones and splints and deposited in the bone-house. The relations and a multitude follow with united voices, and alternate Hal-le-lu-yahs and lamentations."—-Bertram's Travels. Page 514   *   *,   *   *   *

The same writer adds, "The women are seldom above five feet; they are well formed, have round features, fine dark eyes, and are modest, subtle, and affectionate. The men are a full size larger than European ; they are warlike, merciful, and haughty. They have had furious wars with the Spaniards."   *   *   *   *   *

"Those of the other confederate tribes are tall, finely formed perfect figures ; their countenance dignified, open, and placid ; the eyes rather small, dark, and full of fire; the nose inclining to aquiline ; the brow and forehead strike you with heroism, and their air and action exhibit magnimity and independence ; their complexion is reddish brown."—ibid. p. 481.   *   *   *   *

Brackenridge says, "the government of Natchez[1] is so strictly civilized, that it seems impossible for them to act out of the common high road of virtue."   *   *   *

[1] This tribe was exterminated by the French.

The Rev. Mr. Cushman, in a discourse preached at Plymouth, New England, in 1620, intended to contradict the slanders which were prevalent against the primitive inhabitants, observes, "The Indians are said to be the most cruel and treacherous people—like lions ; but *to us they have been like lambs,* so kind, and helpful, and trusty, that a man may truly say there be few Christians *so sincere and kind.* When there were not six able persons among us, and the Indians came daily to us by hundreds, with their sachemes or princes, and might in one hour have made despatch of us, *yet they never offered to us the least wrong in word or deed* these many years."   *   *   *

' " The history of the Brazillians, from the first incursions of the Spaniards to the year 1776, furnishes a long list of battles, evincive of a valor which no fatigue could weary, no danger dismay."   *   *   *   *

" The Brazil Indians are very numerous, and divided into clans; the degree of their independence depends on their distance from the Portuguese settlements. They are generally of the middle size, muscular, and active, of a light brown complexion, black uncurling hair, and dark eyes, which discover no mark of imbecility of intellect. Nor does the turn of their countenance convey the least idea of meanness or vulgarity ; on the contrary, their looks and expressions are intelligent. None except the Auracanians, have been so difficult to subdue; none have discovered a more invincible attachment to liberty."   *   *

A literary traveller thus writes of the Chyans on Upper Missouri in 1825: " Most of the Chyans never saw a white man before ; they are the finest and wildest looking Indians we have yet seen ; they are the genuine children of nature ; they have all the virtues nature gave, without the vices of civilization. These must be the men described by

Rousseau, when he gained the medal from the Royal Academy of France. They are artless, fearless, and *live in the constant exercise of moral and Christian* virtues—though they know it not." "Some parts of the country are beautiful in the extreme."   *   *   *   *

M. de Lapoterie, speaking of the Cherokees, and other southern Indians, says, " These Indians look upon the end of life to be *living happily;* and for this purpose their whole customs are calculated to *prevent avarice,* which, they think, *embitters* life. Nothing is a more severe reflection among them than to say that a man *loves his own.* To prevent the existence and propagation of such a vice, they, upon the death of an Indian, *burn all* that belonged to the deceased, that there might be *no temptation* for the parent to hoard up a superfluity of domestic conveniences, &c. for his children." " They cultivate no more land than is necessary for their subsistence and hospitality to strangers. At the Feast of Expiation they burn all that is left of last year's crop, &c."   *   *   *   *   *

Colden says, " History cannot give an instance of a Christian king observing a treaty so strictly, or for so long a period, as these barbarians *(as they are called)* have done." —Vol. I. p. 34.   *   *   *   *   *

Clavegero says, " The Mexicans had, as the other tribes a scrupulous regard for truth."   *   *   *   *

Bertram says of the Creek nation, " Joy, contentment, love, and friendship, without guile or affectation, seem inherent in them or *predominates in their vital principle— for it leaves them but with their breath."* Bertram had lost his way among the woods. He saw an Indian at his door beckoning to him to approach and come in. Of himself and horse the best care was taken. When he wished to go, the Indian led him on the right track. He adds,

" They are just, honest, liberal, hospitable to strangers, affectionate to their wives, their children, and relations ; frugal, persevering, charitable, forbearing." It must be recollected this testimony is given of Indians in their *un-sophisticated* state, *before the corrupting influence of the lower class of European emigrants had reached them."* *

"They are," writes Major Long, "of opinion that the WAHcondAH has been more profuse of his gifts, especially the knowledge of letters, to the white people than to themselves. They consider the *result* of experience, thus easily *transmitted*, like the operation of some *mystic medicine.'* "But they claim a superiority in natural intelligence," &c. * * * * *

"They esteem themselves more generous, brave, and hospitable to strangers than the white people, and these beneficent virtues with them, mark "the perfect man." If a white man or stranger enters the habitation of an Indian, he is not asked if he has dined, or if he is hungry, but independently of the time of the day or night, the pot is put on the fire, and if there is a single pound of venison in the possession of the family, that pound is cooked and set before him." * * * *

" Every Indian warrior holds *his honour* and the *love of his country* in such high esteem as to *prefer it to life,* and they will suffer the most exquisite tortures rather than renounce it. There is no such thing among them as desertion in war, because they do *not* fight for hire, but for wreaths of swan feathers. The *just* awards which they *always* bestow on *merit,* are the great and leading—the only motives that warm their hearts with a strong and permenent *love of their rights;* governed by simple and honest laws founded on right reason ; their whole constitution breathes perfect freedom, by which means there glows such

a cheerful warmth of *courage* and *constancy* in each of
their breasts as cannot be described. They believe that
their readiness to serve their country should not be subservient to their own wishes and knowledge, but always
under divine controul. I have seen a large company set
out for war, return in parties, and be applauded by the
united voice of the chiefs because *they acted in obedience*
to their *Nana Ishtahoola,* (guardian angels) who impressed
them."—Adair.   *   *   *   *   *

"Beltrami thus writes to the Countess Compagnoni, Every
Indian is at liberty to speak to the agent; but as *presumption*
and *gossipping* are vices unknown among the red people, it
rarely happens that the agent has to reply to any but chiefs,
civil and military, the orators, or the prophets. Every
individual may also lay their complaints before him against
the traders; but the privilege is rarely used, for the Indians
will revenge themselves, but will not descend to the office
of accusers. There is great dignity and magnanimity in the
silence they observe with regard to the traders, who are not
ashamed to *cheat them* in every possible way. This is one
powerful cause of their constant and increasing hostility to
the civilized. The red men, who are *most in contact with
the white, are uniformly the worst.*" Of a council which
he attended beyond the Mississippi, he thus writes: "I
heard *morceaux* of eloquence worthy of Athens or of Rome.
Peskawé descended from the throne with Spartan dignity,[1]
and *Koudous-wa* extended his hand to him as he ascended
it, with the noble air of a truly generous spirit. I am
sometimes astonished at finding the grand incidents of

---

[1] "The calm repose of person and feature; the self-possession under all circumstances, the incapability of surprise or *dereglement*, and that decision about
the slightest circumstance, and the apparent certainty that he is acting abso-
lutely *comme il faut*, is equally "gentleman-like and Indian-like."—New York
Mirror in London Weekly Journal, Oct. 3, 1835.

ancient and modern history in these wilds. The grave and dignified air of Wa-manetouka contributed to the majesty of the ceremony ; on this occasion he assumed a sacerdotal kind of air ; he consecrated the Calmut, turning the tube first horizontally to heaven, and to earth, east, and west, invoking the GREAT SPIRIT."

Of a hunting expedition, at which he was present, he thus writes: "The chief who accompanied me with M. Renville, let fly his arrow and shot a buffalo," &c. "Never did I see attitudes so graceful as those of the chief. They alternately reminded me of the equestrian statue of Marcus Aurelius, on the capitol, and that of the great Numidian king. Altogether it was the most astonishing spectacle I ever saw ; I thought I beheld the combatants and games of the ancients. I played nearly the same part as the Indians of former times did in thinking the first Spanish beings of superior order. While the chief with his quiver, his horse, and his victim, formed a group worthy of the pencil of Raphael or the chisel of Canova."—Discovery of the Source of the Mississippi.

TRADITIONS.

THE Commentator on the Antiq. Mexico observes, "They represent Eve as always weeping as she looks at her husband, Adam. She is called, *Yexnextli*, which signifies *eyes blinded by ashes*, and this refers to her condition *after* having plucked the *roses*. These *roses* are elsewhere called, " *Fruta del arbor*," (" fruit of the tree.") They fasted eight days preceding the sign of one *rose;* they say all the days of the Calendar apply to this fall, because on such a day, *transgression* was *first* committed. The sign of one cane was dedicated to heaven as that of one *rose* was to *hell*.

Torquemeda in the thirty-first chapter of his Mex. Mon. gives the following description of the goddess *Cihuacohuatl*,[1] who is named by many writers the *Aztec*, or Mexican Eve. One of the goddesses greatly esteemed by the natives of New Spain, was *Cihuacohuatl*, which name signifies the " *woman serpent*," and they say she always brings forth two children at a birth. This woman, Father *Sahagun* says, was the *first* who existed in the world, and the *mother* of

---

[1] Humboldt says, ' The group No.2, represent the serpent-woman *Cihuacohuatl*, called also *Quelazili*, or *Tonachcitua*, *(woman of our flesh)* she is the companion of *Tona-teutli*. The Mexicans considered her as the mother of human kind, &c. We see her always represented with a green serpent. Other pictures represent the feather-headed snake cut in pieces by the great Spirit *Tezcatlipoca*. These allegories remind us of the *ancient tradition* of Asia. In the *woman-serpent* of the *Aztecs*, we think we perceive the Eve of the Semetic nations, &c. Behind the serpent, who appears to be speaking to the goddess *Cihuacohuatl*, are two naked figures, they are different colours, and are in the attitudes of contending with each other   We might be led to suppose that the vases, one of which they have overturned, is the cause of contention. *The serpent-woman* was considered in Mexico as the mother of twin children. They remind us of the *Cain* and *Abel* of the Hebrew tradition.'—I'p. 196, 197.

the whole human race ; who was *tempted by the serpent* who appeared to her in the terrestrial paradise, and discoursed with her, to persuade her to *transgress* the command of God, and that is likewise true, that after having committed sin, &c. she bore a son, and a daughter at the same birth, and that the son was named *Cain* and the daughter *Calmana ;* and that afterwards she brought forth at a second birth, *Abel,* and his sister, *Delborah,* so that she bore them by twin births. The Mexicans therefore designated her for these two properties, *Cihuacohuatl,* which signifies the *woman serpent,* that is to say, whom the serpent *tempted,* and which also signified the woman who brought forth twins, a boy and a girl ; for they call infants born at the same birth, *Cocohua,* or serpents, born from *the woman serpent.*"

The above account of *Torquemeda,* or rather of *Sahagun,* whose authority he cites, is very curious, and is further confirmed by the representation in the forty-eighth page of the lesser Vatican MS. of *Cihuacohuatl,* or *Suchequecal,* with two infants and a serpent near her. Another painting contained in the seventy-fourth page of the same MS. is more remarkable, since it seems clearly to allude to the threat pronounced in the third chapter of Genesis, against the serpent, " I will put *enmity* between thee and the woman," &c. as in fact *the Seed of the woman appears to be there in the act of bruising the head of the serpent with a staff,* whilst the latter has bitten, and is holding in his jaws, *the foot of his adversary.*"

" The present note," adds the Commentator, " contains some ancient traditions evidently derived from the Old Testament, and tending to prove that the Indians were at least acquainted with that portion of it designated the Pentateuch."

" It is impossible on reading what Mexican Mythology

records of the war in Heaven and the fall of *Zontemoque,*
and the other rebellious spirits ; of the creation of Light by
the WORD of *Tonacatlecutli,* and of the dividing of the
waters ; of the sin of *Yzclacolinhqui,* his blindness and
nakedness ; of the temptation of *Suchequecal,*[1] and her
disobedience in plucking the roses from a tree, and the
consequent misery of herself and all her posterity, not to
recognize scriptural analogies and that the Mexican tradition
of the deluge is that which bears the most unequivocal
marks of having been derived from a Hebrew source.

" This tradition records that a few persons escaped in the
Ahuchueti, or *Ark of fir,* when the earth was swallowed up
by the deluge, the chief of whom was *Palecath,* or *Cipa-
quetona,* that he invented the art of making wine ; that
Xelua, one of his descendants was present at the building
of a high Tower which the succeeding generation constructed
with a view of escaping from the deluge should it again
occur ; that *Tonacatecutli,* incensed at their presumption,
destroyed the Tower with lightning, confounded their language and dispersed them. This age, called by them
Atonatiali, or the age of water, closely bordered upon that
of *Tzocnilliexque,* or age of *giants,* and it will be recollected that the age of the *flood* in scripture, was that of the
giants also."

" The fact of the Mexicans recording both in their paintings and songs, the Deluge, the building the tower of
Babel, the confusion of tongues, and the dispersion, &c. being
generally admitted by the Spanish writers on America, it is
almost unnecessary to the authority of any particular author,
to prove what no one will deny ; since *Gomara,* in his

---

[1] It seems much more according to the genius of the Mexican religion, that
this should allude to Eve, as the representative of that woman whose Seed by
them designated TEO-*piltzin* and *Topiltzin,* (God's son and our son), than as the
' serpent woman,' as the name indicates."

history of the Indians, describing the conference of Nicaragua with *Gil Goncales* and the Calezcasters, introduces this chief as putting a variety of questions to the Spaniards. The first of which was, whether they were acquainted with the deluge, and others no less curious, showing that the Indians were not unaccustomed to abstruse speculation, and that besides the knowledge of many traditions contained in the Old Testament, they possessed some information respecting the New. It may be interesting to insert the entire passage of GOMARA, giving an account of this conference. " *Nicaragua,* who was so acute and skilled in the knowledge of the rites and antiquities of his own countrymen, had a long conference with Gil Goncales, and the ecclesiastic. He inquired if the *Christians* were acquainted with the great deluge which had swallowed up the earth, men and animals, &c.; and whether the earth was to be revolutionized, *(trastornár)* or the firmament to remove? *When* and how the sun, moon, and stars, would be deprived of their light? What was the honour and reverence due to the triune God, &c. where souls go after death, and what would be their occupation, &c. He likewise inquired if *the Holy Father of Rome, the vicar of Christ, who was the* GOD *of the Christians, died, and whether the Emperor of Spain who had the virtue and power* they vaunted so much was *mortal;* and *why* such an handful of men were *anxious to obtain so much gold!*" La Historia de los Indios. vol. viii. In Antiq. Mex. vol. vi.

" A very remarkable representation of the ten plagues which God sent on Egypt, occur in the eleventh and twelfth pages of the Borgian MS. Moses is there painted holding up in his left hand, his rod, which became a serpent; and, with a furious gesture, calling down the plagues upon the Egyptians. These plagues were frogs, locusts, lice, flies,

&c. all of which are represented in the pages referred to; but the last and most dreadful were the thick darkness which overspread Egypt for three days, and the death of the first-born of the Egyptians; the former is represented under the emblem of an eclipse of the sun, and the latter, by Mitlantecutli, (god of the dead) descending in the form of a skeleton, from the rod of Moses."

"The curious symbol of one serpent swallowing up others, likewise occurs in the nineteenth page of the same MS. It is not extraordinary that the Mexicans, who were acquainted with one portion of the Exodus—that relating to the children of Israel journeying from Egypt, should also not have been ignorant of another."—p. 47.

"Whether the Indians of the Islands of St. Domingo and Cuba, whose language is said to have been *half Hebrew*, and who, in many of their customs, nearly resembled the Jews, practised the same rites as those in use among the Indians of the continent, it would be difficult to say, but that they possessed *traditions* in common with them evidently derived from a *Hebrew source*, is plain from the following relation of *Torquemeda*, which we cannot refrain from inserting. "It is true that the Indians of the Isle of Cuba say, that they knew that the heavens and other things had been created, and they affirm by three *powers*,[1] one of whom came from such a part,[2] and the other two from other parts. They were perfectly informed of the deluge, &c. The old men above seventy or eighty years of age reported, that when first their countrymen settled in that island, an old man knowing that the deluge was about to happen, built a large ship, in which he embarked with his household and many animals, and that he despatched

---

[1] אלהים.
[2] Probably to express am, was, and shall be, or יהוה.

from thence a crow, which did not return, but staid to prey
upon the dead carcases, and that he afterwards sent a dove,
which came back cooing, and bringing a leafy branch which
resembled a hop, but was not one, on which he quitted the
ship, and made wine of mountain grapes, and became drunk,
and having two sons, one of them laughed, and said to the
other, "Turn him into jest;" but the other reproved him,
and covered his father, who, having slept off the effects of
the wine, and knowing the impudence of his son, *cursed*
him, and pronounced a *blessing* on the other, and from the
former[1] the Indians of these countries were descended."

McKenzie in his Voyages, remarks, that " the Chippawayian tribes entertained a singular idea of the Creation.
They believed that at the first, the globe was one vast and
entire ocean, inhabited by no living creature, save one
mighty mysterious bird, whose eyes were fire, whose glances
were as lightning, and the clapping of whose wings was
as thunder.   On his descent to the ocean, and touching it,
the earth instantly appeared and remained upon the surface
of the waters.   This omnipotent bird then called forth,
while he hovered over the earth and sea, all the variety of
living creatures and other productions."—p. 74·

"There are many varieties of the calling forth of the
creation, given by the widely-separated tribes, all agreeing
in the circumstance of the earth's emerging out of the
water."—See note to Canto iii. of Yamoyden.

" This curious relation *Torquemeda* judges to be so
well authenticated, that he not only gives it a place in his
History, but allows that it may serve as a basis on which
to reason respecting the origin of the Americans, although
he at the same time professes that he will not be bound by

---

[1] This appears to be an error, since the Indians boasted of having belonged to
the same *race as Quetzalcoatl*, that is derived from the Patriarch *Shem*.

the conclusion which others might be tempted to draw from it."—p. 394.

"The following account in *Gomara's* Conquest of Mexico of a certain *Chichimica*[1] prevailing over *Quetzalcoatl*, and binding him and detaining him amongst men, bears some analogy to what is said of Jacob's wrestling and prevailing with God in the thirty-second chapter of Genesis. "The kings of Mexico who are the most powerful and the greatest, and in fact the kings of kings of that country, pride themselves on being and on calling themselves of *Culhua*, declaring that they descend from a certain *Chichimica*, who was a very strong chief, who bound a leather thong round the arm of *Quetzalcoatl* when He was going and *detained* Him, which they considered a great feat, and said, that the man who could bind a God, could bind all mortals, and accordingly ever afterwards they called him *Acalhimatle*, (shoulder blade or arm bone.)

This *Acalhimatle*, became afterwards very powerful and

---

[1] "To *wrestle* and *prevail* with *Tezcatlipoci*. When phantoms without feet skim along the ground, sighing like persons suffering from illness, appear in the night to any one whom they know, are illusions of *Tezcatlipoci*, those who see them nevertheless draw a bad omen from them, and declare and consider it certain that they will soon die, or some misfortune will speedily befal them ; but when they appear to men of courage, such as veteran soldiers, they are ready and prepared for them, and desirous of seeing them in order that they may obtain some piece of good fortune, or a *present of thorns of the Aloe*, which were the sign of it, and if a phantom of this kind presented itself to him who went in search of them, he immediately began to grapple with it, and holding it tightly, said, "Who art thou ?   Speak to me; there is no use in your being silent, since I now hold you tight, and "*will not let thee go.*"   These words he frequently repeated whilst the struggle continued between them, and when the conflict had lasted for a length of time, on the *approach of morning* the phantom spoke and said, "*let me go, for you weary me*; tell me what you desire, and it shall be granted you."   On which the veteran replied, "What wilt thou give me ?"   When the phantom said, "Here is a *thorn*," to which the veteran answered, "I will not have it, why does your gift consist of a *single* thorn; it is *useless*."   And although two or three, or even four thorns were afterwards offered, the phantom was not released from his grasp, until he had given him *as many as he wished*, which on bestowing he thus addressed him, "I grant you riches of all kinds, bidding you prosper;" upon which the veteran warrior let the phantom go, since he now obtained what he sought and desired."—Ibid. p. 406.

a person of great consideration, and laid such a foundation of future greatness *in his sons,* that his descendants became in course of time, kings of Mexico, enjoying the same authority as Montezuma possessed when Ferdinand made him prisoner."—La Conq. de Mex. folio cxx.

" The genealogical descent of the nations of New Spain from *Ixtac mixcoatli* and his *two* [1] wives, serves also to bring to our recollection Jacob and his two wives and sons, and it deserves to be remarked that the proper name *Ix,* seems peculiarly applicable to Jacob, since he was smooth and fair and this name is compounded of two words *Ixtac,* which signifies smooth, and *mixcoatli* a serpent, which is in more than one place in Scripture called a subtle creature, and is characterised by Christ as *wise* in the injunction which he gave to the Apostles to be *" wise as serpents,"* &c.—p. 405.

Other exceedingly curious notions respecting children, were entertained by the Mexicans ; they believed that they were dear to God, and that they [2] interceded with Him for the world and for men ; that on their deaths they went to the garden of *Tonaquatitlan,* where they were nourished by the tree distilling milk which grew therein. The name of the tree was Chichinacquantitl, and a representation of it will be found in the 5th page of the large Vatican MS. where, adds the commentator, we recollect what is said in the New Testament, of little children, and the mysterious words of Christ in the 18th chapter of Matthew. Take heed, &c. for their angels do always behold the face of my father who is in heaven, coupled with the preceding ones in the verse. " But whosoever shall offend one of *these little ones that believe* in me, &c." Con-

---

[1] The name of the one was Yxchcel.
[2] Psalm viii. 2.

sidering at the same time that the signification of *Tonac-*
quachtitlan, is the place where grows the tree of our bodies
or life, that word being compounded of *tonacazo*, the human
body, and *quanitl*, which signifies a tree, or piece of wood,
to which is added, a particle of local reference. Can a
doubt remain in our minds, that the Mexicans borrowed
some of their notions about children, from the Scriptures,
and had heard of the " Tree of Life," which grew in the
garden of Eden, the fruit of which is said, in Gen. iii. 22, to
confer immortality on the taster, &c. *Tonacateuctli* was
believed by the Mexicans to reside in the garden of
Tonaquatitlan. He was the father of *Quetzalcoatl*, and
was also named *Ometecuilti*, (Most High,)" .ibid. That the
Mexicans and other tribes, considered children as gifts from
God, intrusted to their care and discipline, is more fully
illustrated by the following address on the birth of a child,
probably one of the nobles of the kingdom of Mexico.

With reference to their *hope* in the birth of these blessings, which they considered conferred by Quetzalcoatl as the
Saviour, the following address from Sahagun, is peculiarly
characteristic and interesting.

" O lady, dear to me as a daughter, I am solicitous to be
informed of thy health, thou hast endured a severe trial,
thou hast imitated thy mother, the sainted *Ciocoatl-tiqui-*
lachtli. Many thanks have we now to return to our Lord,
because he has vouchsafed to send this precious gem, this
rich *Quetzal*, the image, hair, and nail, of our Lords who
are dead and have *long since* been no more. *The stock in this*
scion of our Lords, Judges, and Kings, has budded, has
bloomed. The *thorn* of the aloe, and the fragrant *cane*,
which our lords and departed kings, who were valiant and
renowned, *planted deep in the soul has sprung up*, has
appeared from you, lady. Our son *Quetzalcoatl* has re-

ceived a precious gem from you. He has obtained a rich
feather. May our Lord be praised, since he has happily
preserved you from danger, and from the warfare which you
fought with death at the time of your delivery. Perhaps
the days of the babe to which you have just given birth, will
outnumber yours; perhaps it may be the will of the Lord
that he shall live; perhaps He that made him will come and
take him from us unto himself; perhaps He will pass him
momentarily before the eyes of His Kingdom and Majesty,
and deprive us of him, turning us into shame because of our
sins, because we are unworthy of enjoying him.[1] O let the
will of the Lord be done! Let him do what seemeth good
unto him. In Him let us place our hope."

" Here in your presence, the babe of our Lord is born,
which is like unto a precious gem, or rich feather, on whose
face you have already fixed your eyes. The child is indeed
a *plant set by his sires:* he is as it were a *fragment of a
jewel cut by the ancients,* who are long since no more. Our
Lord has given this child to us, but we cannot tell whether
he will live, or be like a vision seen in a dream. Our eyes
now contemplate the infant which has been born; that which
I am at liberty to declare, is, that our Lord *Quetzalcoatl,* who
is the Creator, has placed a precious stone, and one of His
rich feathers in the dust before us, and in this poor cane-
built lodge, and I may likewise add, that He has ornamented

---

[1] " It is evident from the concluding part of this salutation, that the Mexican
religion, enjoined resignation and submission to the divine will and hope in
God, which after all, is not an article in any particular creed, but a consolation
which was poured into the cup of misfortune when first presented to man to
taste, &c. We cannot omit carefully to point out here the phrase ' your mother
the godess *Ciocoatliquilachtli,*' since it is perfectly analogous to that of *our Mother
Eve,* she being the Eve of the New World, who as the Mexicans believed, brought
sin into the world, and *entailed death upon her posterity,* as is distinctly stated in
the 63rd chapter of the 6th vol. of Sahagun. This goddess is more frequently
named simply *Ciocoatli* or *Quilachtli.* She is also named Suchiquecal, or
Xochequecal, and in the same manner as the first seems to refer to her temptation by the serpent, so the last seems to allude to her having plucked the forbidden fruit, or roses in *Xochitlicacan,* or the garden of Eden." Ibid.

your neck and wrists with costly jems and rich feathers, such as are difficult to be obtained even for a price, and further, that He has placed in your hands a handful of rich feathers called *Quetzalli*, of perfect form and colour. In return for so signal an act of grace, it is meet that you should address yourself with tears, and prayers, and vows to *our Lord, whose presence is every where;* sigh and mourn until you know whether it be His will, that this precious stone and rich feather, of which we are speaking like persons in a dream, shall live. We know not whether he will grow and arrive at maturity, or whether his term of life will be a few days or years, or whether he will be the *image,* and *glory,* and *renown of the elders,* (who have already passed away) from whom he descends. We know not whether per-adventure, he will *resuscitate the fortunes, and raise the heads of his forefathers.*"

" The concluding sentence of this passage is very remark-able ; proceeding from the lips of the Mexicans, it is enig-matical and unintelligible ; since, if we reflect for a moment that the Mexican Empire was, according to the testimony of all historians at the *height* of its greatness in the reign of Montezuma, the wish here expressed must appear alike devoid of meaning and application, except Mexican History was *something very different* from what historians have represented it to be ; but in the month of *a Hebrew the allu-sion would be plain,* and would strikingly illustrate the truth of a remark previously made in p. 385, that the Jews, wher-ever residing, and however well off in their temporal con-cerns, have been accustomed to indulge in a tone of com-plaint ever since *the fall of their Kingdom.* It has also a tincture of Hebrew rhetoric, since children are in many

---

[1] " The Mexicans considered the Messiah, as regarded his godhead, the Father of the everlasting age ; and as regarded his human nature, the Son, to be born of their race."

parts of Scripture, named the ornaments of their parents, and Christ is called the image of the Father's glory."

Her restored tribes are moreover called the ornaments with which Jerusalem shall attire herself anew, as a bride doth.

The Honourable Elias Boudinot mentions an Indian[1] tradition, which intimates that *nine parts of their people out of ten went over the river*, but the remainder staid behind.

Sir Alexander M'Kenzie says of the Chippawayian tribe,

---

[1] 'As the Indian nations have not the assistance afforded by the means of writing and reading, they are obliged to have recourse to tradition, as Du Pratz, 2 vol. 169, has justly observed, to preserve the remembrance of remarkable transactions or historical facts ; and this tradition cannot be preserved but by frequent repetitions; consequently many of their young men are often employed in hearkening to the old beloved men, narrating the history of their ancestors, which is thus transmitted from generation to generation. In order to preserve them pure and incorrupt, they are careful not to deliver them indifferently to all their young people, but only to those young men of whom they have the best opinion. They hold it as a certain fact, as delivered down from their ancestors, that their forefathers, in very remote ages, came from a far distant country, by the way of the west, where all the people were of one colour, and that in process of time they moved eastward to their present settlements.

'This tradition is corroborated by a current report among them, related by the old *Chickkasah* Indians to our traders, that now about one hundred years ago, there came from Mexico some of the old *Chickkasah* nation, or as the Spaniards call them, *Chichemicas*, in quest of their brethren, as far north as the *Aquahpah* nation, above one hundred and thirty miles above the Natchez, on the south-east side of the Mississippi river ; but through French policy they were either killed or sent back, so as to prevent their opening a brotherly intercourse with them, as they had proposed. It is also said, that the *Nauatalcas* believe that they dwelt in another region before they settled in Mexico. That their forefathers wandered eighty years in search of it, through a strict obedience to the commands of the Great Spirit; who ordered them to go in quest of new lands, that had such particular marks as were made known to them, and they punctually obeyed the divine mandate, and by that means found out and settled that fertile country of *Mexico*.

'Our southern Indians have also a tradition among them which they firmly believe, that of old time, their ancestors lived beyond a great river. That nine parts of their nation, out of ten, passed over the river, but the remainder refused, and staid behind. That they had a king when they lived far to the west, who left two sons. That one of them, with a number of his people, travelled a great way for many years, till they came to Delaware river, and settled there. That many years the king of the country from which they had emigrated, sent a party in search of them, but they have never been heard of since.

'It is said among their principal or beloved men, that they have it handed down from their ancestors, that the book which the white people have was once theirs. That while they had it they prospered exceedingly ; but that the white people bought it of them, and learnt many things from it ; while the Indians lost their credit, offended the Great Spirit, and suffered exceedingly from the neigh-

far to the north west. " They have a tradition among them, that *they came 'from another country, and had traversed a great water*, which was in one place narrow and full of islands, where they had suffered great misery, it being always winter there, with ice and deep snows. At the copper-mine river, where they first made land, the ground was covered with copper, over which a body of earth has since been collected.'"

bouring nations. That the Great Spirit took pity on them and directed them to this country. That on their way they came to a great river, which they could not pass, when God dried up the waters, and they passed over dry-shod. They also say that their forefathers were possessed of an extraordinary Divine Spirit, by which they foretold future events, and controlled the common course of nature, and this they transmitted to their offspring, on condition of their obeying the sacred laws. That they did by these means, bring down showers of plenty on the beloved people. But that this power, for a long time past, had entirely ceased.

' Can any man read this short account of Indian traditions, drawn from tribes of various nations, from the west to the east, and from the south to the north, wholly separated from each other, written by different authors of the best characters, both for knowledge and integrity, possessing the best means of information, at various and distant times, without any possible communication with each other, and from ocular and sensible demonstration ; written on the spot in several instances, with the relators before them ; and yet suppose that all this is either the effect of chance, accident, or design, from a love of the marvellous or a premeditated intention of deceiving, and thereby ruining their own well established reputations ?

' Charlevoix was a clergyman of character, who was with the Indians some years, and travelled from Canada to the Mississippi, in that early day.

' Adair lived forty years entirely domesticated with the southern Indians, and was a man of learning and great observation. Just before the revolutionary war he brought his manuscript to Elizabeth-Town, in New-Jersey, to William Livingston, Esq. (a neighbour of the writer) to have it examined and corrected, which was prevented by troubles of a political nature, just breaking out. The Rev. Mr. Brainerd was a man of remarkable piety, and a missionary with the Crosweek Indians to his death. Doctor Edwards was eminent for his worth and learning, and was intimately acquainted with the Indians from his youth. Doctor Beatty was a clergymen of note, and established character. Bertram was a man well known to the writer, and travelled the country of the southern Indians as a botanist, and was a man of considerable discernment, and had great means of knowledge; and M'Kenzie, in the employment of the north west company, was an old trader, and the first adventurous explorer of the country, from the lake of the woods to the ocean, &c.

' The Indian tradition says, that their forefathers, in very remote ages, came from a far distant country, where all the people were of one colour, and that in process of time, they moved eastward to their present settlements.

' This tradition is corroborated by a current report of the old Chickkasah Indians to our traders, about forty years since, (this was written in the year 1775).

THE TOLTICS OR TULIANS.

"A NORTHERN, but very polished nation, the Toltics, appears in the mountains of Anahuac, on the east gulph of California; declares itself expelled from a country lying north-west of Rio Gila, and called *Hue-hue-Tlapallan;* and brings with it paintings indicating year by year the events of its migration," &c. * * *

'It is very remarkable moreover, that the names which the Toltics bestowed on the cities they built, were those of the countries which they had been compelled to abandon; from this circumstance, the origin of the *Toltics,* the *Chermecks,* the *Acolhuan,* and the *Aztics,* who spoke the same language, &c. will be known if we ever discover in the North of America, or in Asia, a people acquainted with the names[1] of Hue-hue-Tlapallan,—Aztlan,—Teo-colhuacan,—Amaquemacan,—Tehuago and Cozulla.'—Humboldt, p. 179.

"The *Toltecas,*" who were great artists, and who excelled in working jewellery, probably recollected the words of David—"If I forget thee, O Jerusalem!" and it is a

[1] The Mexicans and several other nations, it is to be recollected, had fallen into the disuse of many alphabetic sounds which distinguish the Hebrew language. The substitution of *l* for *r,* of *c* for *m,* &c. must necessarily disguise the pronunciation of Hebrew terms: to which cause of obscurity may be added the termination of *tzin, atl, can, itli,* and others. Thus we arrive at the knowledge of the identity of the name of the virgin of Tula, not by the sound, but by observing that Miriam, the sister of Moses and Aaron, who was excluded certain days from the camp or congregation for contending with her brother, has the *same* name as that by which they designate the virgin of Tula, viz.* *Chemalman.* Thus also we discover Mox or Moxie is by another nation pronounced *Cozes,* as they substitute *x* for *j,* and sometimes *c* for *m.*

* *Chiribrias* is another appellative—that of the Chiapanese.

fact notorious to all, that wherever Jews exist the recollection of the Temple and of its destruction (to preserve among
them the coming of the Messiah, and their own restoration
to the New Jerusalem, and rebuilding of the Temple) continually occupy their thoughts." " The retrospect, however, of *the city* and *the Holy-hill,* which their ancestors
seem to have founded in the new world and called *Churula,*
after Jerusalem, and *Tlactichualtepetc (or the hill of sacrifice)* after Mount Zion, will not be so agreeable to the Jews
of the present day as the prospect of the sceptre returning
to Judah."—Antiq. Mex. p. 388.

" Sahagun, in the first section of the twenty-ninth chapter
of the tenth book of his History of New Spain,[1] describing
the manners of the ancient *Toltecas,* says, " The said
*Toltecas were good men, who studied virtue in their actions ;
they never uttered a falsehood;* and their style of address
and salutation was—' *Sir, my elder brother ;'* or ' *Sir, my
younger brother.'* In speaking, *they never made use of an
oath,* but said ' *verily, it is so ;'* or ' *yea, yea, and nay, nay.'*
There is something evangelical in the style of salutation
and affirmation which Sahagun in the above passage ascribes
to the *Tulticas.*"—Ibid. p. 389.

" That the *Tulticas* were the founders of many of the most
splendid monuments of the New World, may be inferred
not only from the signification of the proper name *Tultica,*
which means an architect, but likewise the figure of a
feathered serpent is sometimes represented in mosaic on the
walls, which undoubtedly referred to the God *Quetzalcoatl.*
A gigantic serpent of this description ornaments the ruins of
the fortress of *Xochtozcaleo.*" " Since nothing appears more

---

[1] " The Mexicans had a tradition that *Totec* had commanded the Tulians or
Tulticas to bind the image of *transgression* with thick ropes and drag it out of
the city of Tulan."—ibid.

admirable in the architecture of the New World than the beautiful and durable Mosaic ornaments which cover the walls of the palaces of *Mitlan*, it is highly probable that these structures were erected by the *Tulticas*, and they furnish an argument in favour of the belief that the *Tulticas* were originally a little colony, which in remote ages had settled in Anahuac, since we do not read that any other nation of the old continent except the Hebrews, ever introduced that style of architecture, whilst Josephus, it should be remarked, commends in the highest terms the skill which his countrymen displayed in uniting together the stones of which the walls of the Temple were composed,[1] the joints of which were scarcely visible."

Speaking of the departure of *Quetzalcoatl* from the *Toltics*, to the distant country of *Tlapallan*, from whence he came, Humboldt observes, " The resemblance of this name to *Hue-huetlapallan*, the country of the *Toltics*, appears not to be accidental. But how can we conceive that this white man, priest of Tula, should have taken his direction, as we shall presently find, to the south-east, towards the plains of *Cholula*, and then to the eastern coast of Mexico, in order to visit this northern country, whence his ancestors had issued." *Quetzalcoatl* in crossing the territory of *Cholula*, or *Chorula*, yielded to the intreaties of the inhabitants, who offered him the reins of government. He dwelt twenty years amongst them, taught them to cast metals, ordered fasts of eight days, and regulated the intercalations of the

---

[1] Humboldt observes, describing an ancient monument call *Xochmalco (house of flowers)* " travellers who examine attentively this work of the native tribes of America, cannot fail to be greatly struck with the polish and cut of the stones which are parallelopipedes; the care with which they have been arranged without cement between the joints; and the execution of the reliefs with which the stones are decorated. * * * * each figure occupies several stones, and from the outlines not being interrupted by the joints of the stones, we may conjecture that these reliefs were sculptured after the construction of the edifice was finished."—p. 710.

Toltic year. *He preached peace to men and would permit no other offerings to the Divinity than the first fruits of the hearvest.*   *   *   *   *   *

" At the period when the Aztics, or Mexicans, one of the seven (or nine) tribes of the Anahuatlas, took possession of the equinoctial region of New Spain, they already found the pyramidal monuments of TEO-tihuacan of Cholula, or Churula, and of Papantla ; they attributed these great edifices to the Tulians, a powerful and civilized nation, who inhabited Mexico five hundred years earlier, who made use of hieroglyphics, who computed time more precisely, and had a more exact chronology than the greater part of the people of the old continent.   The Aztecs knew not with certainty what tribe inhabited the country of Anahuac before the Toltics, and consequently they believed that the Houses of the Deity of TEO-*tihuacan,* and of Cholula, was the work of the Toltics, and assigned to them the greatest possible antiquity they could conceive."

" The truncated pyramid, called by Cortez the principal Temple, was 79 metres in breadth at its base, and 54 metres high.   This was destroyed by the Spaniards.   We shall describe the ancient ones.   This group of pyramids is eight leagues north-east of Mexico, in a plain called *Micoath,* (path of the dead.)"

" The two greatest, dedicated to the sun and moon, are surrounded by several small pyramids from north to south, and from east to west.   One is 55 and the other 44 metres in perpendicular height.   According to M. Oteyza's measurement (made in 1803,) it is higher than the Mycerenus, the third of the great pyramids of Gaza in Egypt, and the length of its base nearly equal to that of the Cephren.   The small ones are 10 metres high, and are said to be the burying places of the chiefs of the tribes.   The nucleus is composed of clay mixed with small stones, and incased by a thick wall of porous amygdaloid. The construction recalls to mind that one of the Egyptian pyramids Sakhara which has six stories, and which is, according to Pocock, a mass of pebbles and yellow mortar, covered on the outsides with rough stones. The two largest pyramids were covered with plates [1] of gold, which were stripped off by the soldiers of Cortez. When the Bishop of Zumarago, a Franciscan Monk, undertook the *destruction* of *whatever* related to the history, the *worship*, and the *antiquity* of the natives of America, he ordered also the demolition of these. The pyramid Papantla, is on the east of the above group, in the thick forest of Tajin. It was discovered by chance thirty years ago—for the Indians carefully conceal from the Spaniards whatever is an object of veneration. It has seven stories, is more tapering than any other, and is 18 metres high and 25 at the base. It is built entirely of hewn stones of an extraordinary size, and very beautifully and regularly shaped—three stair-cases lead to the top. The covering of its steps is ornamented with hieroglyphical sculpture, and small niches. The greatest and most ancient, and most celebrated, in Anachuac, is the TEO*calli* of Cholula."

" A square house was discovered in the *interior*, built of stone, and supported by cypress beams. The bricks were arranged like step-work, in the manner of some Egyptian edifices. There was an altar at the top dedicated to *Quetzalcoatl*, the most mysterious person in the Mexican mythology. He was *a white-bearded man, High Priest of Tula, and also a legislator*. The Indians of Cholula have a remarkable tradition, that the great pyramid was not originally destined to serve for the worship of *Quetzalcoatl*, which

---

[1] Of the Temple at Jerusalem, Josephus thus speaks, " Its front was entirely covered with *skeets of gold*, which at the first rising of the sun, reflected so great a lustre, that it compelled those who looked at it to turn away their eyes, as they would from the sun itself," &c.—Bell. Ind. 5. v. 6. See Wilkins Des. Jer. p. 54.

tradition is recorded in a manuscript of Pedro de Los Rios, in 1556. Rios, to prove the antiquity of this tradition, observes that it was contained in a sacred song which the Cholulans sang at their festivals, beginning with ' *Tulianyah-Hal-uluay*,' words belonging to no dialect at present known in Mexico.' See Clavegero.

Of the Temple of Palenque, M. Du Paix thus writes : " It is impossible adequately to describe the interior decorations of this sumptuous Temple ; the sculptor and the painter seem to have embodied the most exalted conceptions of their art. The hieroglyphics which adorn this mysterious shrine, are innumerable, &c. They are carved on the surface of marble slabs of a fine grain, and of a deep buff colour, ranged in horizontal rows ; they occupy the centre of the building, as in the sanctuary of the Presentation Temple. Our surprise was great on suddenly beholding a cross ; [1] but

[1] Martyr observes of the Tulians "they live under laws, and trafficke together with great fidelitie, exchanging commodities without money. They sawe crosses, and being demanded by the interpreters whence they had them, some say that *a certain man of excellent beauty passing by that coast, left that notable token to remember him by.* Others report that *a certainne man, brighter than the sun dyed in the toil thereof.* But concerninge the truth there is nothing certaine known."

The *Toltics* had erected on a high mountain, the image of *Tlaloccateutli* : this image rudely carved was made of *white* stone, considered as divine (Te*otitli*) by this people, who, like the ancient orientals, attached superstitious ideas to the *color of certain stones*, &c. The Aztecs followed the same worship till the year 1317, when the war with the inhabitants of *Xochimitli* furnished them with *the first idea* of a human sacrifice, and the first which had been made in that country, p. 207. The continual wars of the Aztecs after they had fixed their residence on the lakes, furnished them with a considerable number of victims which were offered in sacrifice, even to *Quetzalcoatl who had preached against this execrable custom*."—Humboldt.

[2] The discovery of *arches* in the New World, although not so mysterious, is quite as *unexplained* a *fact* as that of *crosses*, neither can their existence be accounted for by recurring to the old solution of all the doubts and difficulties to which the Patriarchal institutions, Mosaic laws, and Hebrew rites among the Mexicans and Peruvians gave rise, which proceeded on the assumption that Satan counterfeited in the New World whatever God had ordained in the New Testament, &c. Since an arch is no where mentioned in Scripture, neither did Moses command his countrymen to build their public or private edifices with arches, as he did battlements with which latter injunction the Mexicans seem to have been well acquainted, since *battlements* on houses, and *fringes* on garments were as common in Mexico as in Jerusalem." Ibid. p. 597, notes.

closer examination of it convinced me that it was not the holy Latin cross which we adore," &c.

" I wish it were in my power to explain the signification of the historical figures which so conspicuously adorn the walls of these Temples, a task less difficult than to decypher the meaning of the hieroglyphics. It would appear that this nation had two methods of expressing its ideas, the one by letters or alphabetical signs, the other by obscure and mysterious symbols. These symbols, infinitely diversified in form, were disposed in parallel rows, both *vertically* and *horizontally* on the same stone, so as frequently to form right, but never acute-angles ; this peculiarity in their arrangement is not unworthy of attention. In each line the same kind of symbols often occur ; and the human heads, which are always in profile, are *uniformly turned to the left : a circumstance which leads me to suppose, that like Hebrew writings, those inscriptions were read from right to left.*" Ibid. d. 481.

" These immense ruins," he adds, " scattered over a vast tract of country, and the greater portion of them buried beneath the soil, awaken in the mind of the spectator, the liveliest feelings of curiosity and interest." Ibid. 483.

The following passage is extracted from Don Antonio Del Rio's narrative of his visit to the ruins of Palenque, in which he takes occasion to mention other ancient Temples in Yutican. "The Reverend Father De Soga, a Franciscan Friar, many years collector of alms destined for the holy house at Jerusalem, who in prosecuting the duties imposed upon him from his situation, repeatedly traversed the province ; fortunately happening to be at Palenque, favoured me with a circumstantial account of that country, of which I now avail myself in his own words : ' At the distance of twenty leagues from Meridas southward, are remains of some stone

edifices ; one very large building has withstood the ravages
of time, &c.   The natives give it the name of *Oxmutl*.   It
stands on an eminence, and measures 200 yards on each
façade. The apartments of the exterior corridor, contain pillars
with figures in *medio-relievo*, and are decorated with serpents,
&c. in stucco, besides which are statues of men *with palms
in their hands* in the act of beating drums, and dancing,
resembling in every respect those observable in the buildings
of Palenque," &c.

PERUVIANS.

THE Peruvian History is enveloped in an obscurity which the destruction of their historical records has greatly augmented. Boturini thus laments in a letter to Charles V. these barbarous ' *acts of the faith.*' " These burnings have been frequent and very fatal in New Spain. The Indians deplore them, and so do the Spaniards; and I lament them because I am convinced that these ancient paintings contained not only particular notices of great literary treasures, but likewise of immense treasures stored up in the times of paganism," &c. " I do not despair of being able to perform some day or other, a notable service to your Majesty." Antiq. Mex. p. 407.

This work does not admit of giving a detailed account of the character and incidents of the 14 successive Incas who reigned in Peru. Those of the mysterious reformer,[1] Mango Capac, of Pacha Cutec the ninth in order, of Tupac Yupanqui, and Huania Capac his son, furnish not a few of those illustrative analogies which it is the object of the present re-

---

[1] This reformation seems by the account of Balboa, and other writers, to have been preceded by the earlier reformation by Verachocha, and his companions. " From the MS. of Balboa, some extracts are given relating to the appearance of *certain holy men in Peru who preached anew the* LAW *to the nations, wore long beards and decent apparel,* &c. as also of the famous council-general convoked at Cuzco, by the Inca *Yupanqui, for the abolition of the undue homage which the people paid to the sun, and the promulgation of the decree that* TICI VERACHOCHA PACHAMAC, *was the supreme God the Creator of the universe* (*cosa notable y de admiracion*) as Balboa terms it, to which all the religious orders in the states were summoned, the Inca himself presiding at the solemn conclave." Ibid. v. p. 522, notes. A lord named Cortice Verachocha, came forth from a lake which is in the province of Callasugo, and brought along with him a certain number of persons."—Ibid. p. 404.

search to concentrate: brief notices therefore of these, may suffice to augment the sum of evidence.

Manco Capac is generally spoken of by historians as having introduced the worship of the sun; this mistake seems to have arisen from the title of the GREAT LIGHT, by which many branches of the Indian people characterised the Creator, and this is perfectly scriptural, as we are taught to consider the sun as a symbol or representation of that Great moral Light and Life, which is emphatically called the " Sun of Righteousness." The sun is illustrative of the Divine power and Godhead, as well as are all the other works of the Creator ; the term Great Light, and its symbol the sun, seem to have been considered by historians a synonyme ; and therefore they have erroneously charged the Incas with the worship of the sun, instead of the Great moral Light by whom as men, and as a community, they were greatly enlightened." " Their kings, the Incas," says Garcillasso, (a descendant of the Incas,) " and the amautas (philosophers) had some idea of our Sovereign LORD the Creator, whom they called *Pachacamac; Pacha*, signifies the world, and *camac* is derived from the verb *camar*, to animate ; *cama* is the soul. The Indians regarded *Pachacamac* as the Sovereign Creator and Preserver of all things here below ; they adored Him in their hearts as the invisible God ; they, however, neither built temples nor offered sacrifice in His Name ;[1] but whenever it was pronounced, or that of the sun, or of the king, it was always with the most reverential awe." Vega, b. 2· ch. 2. in Histor. Researches.

[1] When a Curacu was brought before the Spanish Judge at Cuezco, he was presented with a cross that he might *swear* to the truth. The Indian replied, that he did not imagine that he had been baptized to *swear like the Christians.* The Judge then desired him to swear by his own gods, &c. " You are mistaken," said he "' if you think I will profane *that* sacred NAME ; it is *never to be mentioned but in adoration.* You ought to be contented with *my* word; but if you are not, I will swear by the earth, and wish that it may open and engulph me if I do not tell the truth." Vega in Histor. Research : ch. ii. p. 143.

The Inca Tupac Yupanqui XI. said, " Many believe that the sun is a living body, and that he creates whatever exists. If this were the truth, he would not confine himself to the same eternal path. We must consider him to be like an arrow which performs the duty intended by the Archer who sped it."—Vega, vol. ii. p. 93.

" The respect paid to the sun must have been as the symbol of Divine beneficence ; even as that paid to their kings as the viceroys and representatives of the Creator, whom they likewise acknowledged as their Redeemer and Sovereign. A long series of ages had, it appears, produced the usual effect on a people without the written standard of appeal, and without that communion and interchange of thought which constitutes writing a blessing or a curse—a great benefit or a great evil.

From this retrograde state, the Peruvians were at once recalled by the arrival of a mysterious man and woman who were first seen on the border of the lake Titiaca. " They were still in this state," observes the author of Historical Researches, chap. 2. p. 55. " when, we are told, there appeared on the banks of the Lake Titiaca, a man and woman of majestic form, and clothed in decent garments. They were persons of excellent shape and beauty." The titles which these personages bore, were *Mango Capac*, (chief governor, splendid and rich in virtue) and that of his sister *Mamanchic*, empress and motherly protector of his subjects. See Vega, b. 1. ch. 26, in Hist. Resear. c. 2, p. 56.

" These benefactors first told the people that their Father taking pity of their miserable condition, had sent them to reclaim them from their erring ways, to give them laws, teach them morality, and to worship the Great Light who gave life to *all* creatures," &c. " In fine, that they were expressly sent to govern them for their benefit and happiness, with the same care and goodness with which their Father ruled the world."[1]

" Mango had in his hand a rod of gold, two fingers thick, and an ell in length. He said that his Father, the Great Light, had given it to him, and told him, that when he travelled northward from the lake, whenever he rested he was to strike the rod into the ground ; and where, at the first stroke it should go down to the top, on that spot, he should build a temple to the Great Light, and fix the seat of his government. This happened in the vale of Cozco, where he founded that city as the capital of his kingdom.

" He divided his company into two colonies, and called one High and the other Lower Cuzco ; in each of these were at first a thousand families, which he caused to be registered by *quipos* (party coloured and knotted fringe) which was all that was required in a government where there were neither letters, money, nor disputes. Mango instituted Decurians, one over ten, one over fifty, one over one hundred, one over five hundred, one over one thousand ; the last were called *Curaca*, (Governor.) They were censors, patrons, and judges, in small controversies. Idleness was punished with stripes. Each colony had a supreme judge. Theft, murders, disobedience to the laws, and adultery, were punished chiefly by death, in order not to leave a bad man more incenced or necessitated to commit new crimes. A son's possession were never forfeited for his father's offences. These laws had so good an effect, that sometimes a year passed without one execution." * * * " After a long and revered reign, at the approach of the last period of life, Mango Capac called together all his children and grand-children ; he told them he was going to repose himself

[1] See Garcillasso, b. i. ch. 17. Sir William Temple, vol. iii. Robertson, vol. ii. pp. 164—306. Ranking's Hist. Resear. c. 2. p. 57.

with his Father. To his eldest son he left his empire; and advised and charged them all to *continue in the paths of reason and virtue,* which he had taught them, until they followed him on the same journey, and that this was the only course by which they could *prove* themselves the *children* of the GREAT LIGHT, and *as such* be honoured and respected. He commanded his successor, whose name was Sinchi Roca, to govern his people with justice, mercy, piety, clemency, and care of the poor; and that when he should go to rest, &c. he should give the same instructions and exhortations to his successor."

" The Peruvians attributed all their laws, civil and religious, to Mango Capac, and which they thought had been communicated to him by his Father (the GREAT LIGHT;) but their laws were either new or *reformed 'from ancient times.*" " The Incas pretend," adds the historian, " that *one of their kings was a great legislator;* they say that he was a *sovereign priest;* and further, that he was a *renowned captain* who conquered a number of provinces and kingdoms." Hist. Resear. ch. 2, p. 65.

The following account is replete with internal evidence of the identity of *race.* The son of this emperor in his endeavours to abolish idolatry and introduce the worship of that moral Light, whence all that is good is derived, and to whom therefore, whatever is good ought to be rendered as a tribute of allegiance, made several successful attempts; his troops always by his order acting on the defensive. " At length submitting, the Curacas and others, fearful of being punished for their obstinacy, went to the Inca to demand pardon : the *children* marched first, followed by their *mothers;* then the *aged,* the soldiers and officers and their Curacas with their *hands bound,* and *ropes round their necks,* in acknowledgement that they merited death for presuming

to oppose the descendants of the Great Light. To mark
their extreme humility they approached barefoot. The
Emperor received them seated upon his throne, surrounded
by his officers. The Curacas prostrated themselves before
him, addressing his majesty in terms of veneration and religious respect," &c. " They supplicated most humbly for
pardon; but, if it were his majesty's pleasure that *they*
should suffer death, they should consider their lot not unhappy, if the lives of the soldiers who had acted *under their
authority*, should be granted along with those of the aged,
the women, and the children. The Inca commanded that
their hands should be untied, and the ropes removed from
their necks. ' *I did not come hither,*' said the emperor,
' *to deprive you of your lives or your property;* but rather
to enrich you, and teach you to live according to the laws of
reason and of nature; *to quit your idols,* and adore the
(GREAT LIGHT) as your BENEFACTOR and your GOD; therefore return to your dwelling, and continue in the same power
that you have hitherto enjoyed. There you may remain in
health, and *obey laws* which are for your common *advantage.*'
The Inca then permitted the Curacas, in the name of the
people, to embrace his right knee, in token of his protection." &c. Ibid. ch. 2. pp. 69, 70.

Together with the tradition of their migration, and those
future hopes which the Peruvians held in common with the
other tribes, it may be well to notice a discovery near
Cuzco, which shows that the Peruvians had been preceded
by a more ancient portion of the transatlantic family.

" Near the lake Chuchytu (by Titiaca) there was found a
high hillock made by the hands of man. The foundation
was of immense masses of stone, well cemented, to prevent
the prodigious terraces from falling upon each other. At
some distance there were two stone giants, with garments

that reached the ground, and a cap on the head ; they appeared defaced by time," [1] &c. " In another place there were
many extraordinary buildings, among which were *grandes
portes,* many quite entire ; the four corners of each consisting of a single stone ; almost all of them rested on stones
of incredible magnitude, some being thirty feet long, fifteen
wide, and six thick. It is impossible to conceive by what
means these stones had been cut. There is a hall forty
feet by twenty-two, &c. There are stones with representations of men and women cut upon them ; some sitting, others
with vases in their hands, &c. and some *as if crossing a
rivulet,* and statues of women with children at their breast,
some so well executed as to appear quite natural." " The
Indians knew nothing of their origin." [2]

" Inca Roca erected schools for the education of the
princes ; it was a saying of this Inca, that ' If there be any
thing in this *lower* world which we might adore, it is a *wise
and virtuous man, who surpasses all other objects in dignity ;* but how can we pay DIVINE honours to one who is
born in tears, who is in a daily state of change, who arrived
but as yesterday, and who is not exempt from death—perhaps to-morrow." Ibid. ch. 2. p. 75·

Pacha Cutec (the reformer) had an army of 50,000 men ;
he made conquests of countries extending about 130 degrees
of latitude, &c. He founded schools, and erected several
palaces, temples, and aqueducts, &c. He made many new
laws and regulations ; he was severely *just,* and was
esteemed a wise monarch. The following were some of his
apophthegms :—

" He who envies the wise and good, is like the wasp
which sucks *poison* from the *finest flowers.*"

---

[1] Probably only colossal statues.
[2] Vega, b. lii. ch. 1. Humboldt, vol. i. p. 25 in Hist. Resear. ch. ii. p. 74.

" Drunkenness and anger admit of *reformation*, but *folly is incurable*."

" He who kills another unlawfully condemns himself to death."

" A noble and generous heart is known by the patience with which it supports adversity."

" How ridiculous is he who is not able to count by *quipos*, and yet pretends to number the stars."—Vega in Hist. Research. chap. ii. p. 80.

The Inca Yupanqui was by universal consent surnamed *the charitable!* His son Tupac Yupanqui preserved the conquests of his virtuous predecessors ; he " governed his empire with wisdom and mildness." The emperor at length, feeling the approach of death, gave orders that his children " should come into his presence to hear his last injunctions."

He recommended them, by living in *peace* and in *justice,* to *prove* themselves the true children of the Supreme Light. He commanded his successor to pursue the conquest of the barbarous nations, in the imitation of his predecessors, &c. thus died that excellent monarch : his grateful subjects rewarded his noble actions and benevolent heart with the title of *Tupac Yaya*, or Resplendent Father."—Vega in Hist. Hesearch. chap. ii. p. 91.

" The deceased emperor's body was embalmed with solemn ceremonies, and with so much art, that it appeared as if still alive, when seen by Vega in the year 1556. Among other maxims of this Inca, he said—*Avarice* and *ambition*, like other PASSIONS have *no bounds* of moderation : the first *unfits* a man for the government of his own family, or for any public employment ; the second renders the understanding *not* susceptible of the councils of the wise and virtuous." —Vega, vol. ii. p. 293, in Hist. Research. chap. ii. p. 91.

Huayna Capac, after the year of mourning for his father

had expired, set out to visit his dominions, and was every where received with *triumphal arches* and ways strewed with flowers. He had not proceeded far, when on hearing the joyful tidings of the birth of a son, he instantly returned to Cuzco. After twenty days of every possible demonstration of joy, the emperor wishing to signalise the day on which his first-born son was to receive his name, invented the famous golden chain, seven hundred feet in length, and about as large as a man's wrist. In two years it was finished, and the fête was ordered to take place. The dancers, who consisted of the royal princes and great persons at court, held this chain, instead of taking each other by the hand as was usual. They advanced with gravity in solemn cadence, singing the praises of the Inca, towards the throne where he was seated. (This chain has never been found, having been secreted on the first arrival of the Spaniards.)[1]

"Huayna Capac departed with an army for the conquest of the provinces, but was informed that that of Chachapayas was in revolt, and had killed the commanders and soldiers, the rest having been made slaves. On this the emperor concentrated his troops, and sent an offer of pardon to the rebels if they would return to their obedience. This proposal was received with insolence," &c. "The clement and gallant character of the emperor was well known : and some of these, elders with tears in their eyes, prevailed on a lady of their city, who had been one of the mistresses of Tupac Yupanqui, father to his majesty, to wait on the emperor and claim his compassion. She travelled two leagues, and having prostrated herself before him, accompanied by many women, threw herself at the Inca's feet. "Our sole lord,"

---

[1] Vega, vol. ii. p. 364, in Hist. Research. chap. ii. p. 92.

said she, " is it your intention to destroy a province which
has been subdued by the arms of the emperor, your father,
would you not to-morrow repent? you, who have so just a
claim to your title of *Protector of the Poor!* If pardon
cannot be granted to the rebellious, as they have laid down
their arms, take compassion on them : and the reputation
which the descendants of the sun enjoy for their humanity,
will be crowned by such virtuous forbearance. But if you
resolve on revenge, let me be the first sacrificed, that I may
not witness the ruin of my native land." To this speech,
the rest of the women, bathed in affliction, added—" Great
Huayna Capac l have pity on us, on our fathers, our
husbands, our brothers, and our infant children ! "

" The Inca stood silent ; but being affected by the tears
of the women, he approached *Mamacuna,* and made her rise
from the ground. " That to-morrow I should *regret* an act
of severity is certain ; and it is to your prudence that your
nation will owe their lives and fortunes. Return to them
with these tidings, and if you find that they can be grateful
for my kindness, I empower *you* to grant them *in my name
any other* favor you may think right. As a proof of my
sincerity, you shall be accompanied back to your town by four
Incas who are your own sons and are my brothers, attended
only by a few officers proper to establish order, but not by
any soldiers. The *Chachapoyas* were so sensibly affected at
this unexpected mercy, that they environed the spot where
the Emperor had received his mother-in-law, with a triple
wall ; the inner one was of beautiful stone," &c. " There
are fragments now visible ; and these walls would have
lasted for ages, had not *foreigners,* says Vega,[1] demolished
them in the hopes of finding hidden treasure."

---

[1] Vega, book 9, chap. vi. and vii. in Hist. Research. chap. ii. p. 104.

" While Huayna Capac was reposing himself in one of the most magnificent palaces in all Peru, at Tumipampa, a messenger brought intelligence that some extraordinary men, such as they had never seen before, had landed upon the coast, from a vessel of an uncommon appearance ; and that they were making active inquiries, &c. An ancient oracle having predicted the destruction of the empire by strangers of such description; the emperor was too much alarmed to think of further conquests ; and to add to his uneasiness, three years before this event, during the celebration of the feast of the Great Light at Cuzco, a large eagle had been pursued and harassed by five or six small vultures, and as many water-fowls, till they tore and disabled him to that degree that he fell, as if for succour, in the great square in the midst of the Incas. They endeavoured to nourish and cherish the eagle; but he died in a few days. The augurs declared unanimously, that this was a presage of the ruin of the state and the extinction of their religion. This prodigy was succeeded by earthquakes which threw down high mountains; the sea left its ordinary bounds, and frightful comets appeared. A layaca one day ran to the emperor in tears, and so out of breath that he could scarcely speak, to assure him that his mother the moon was surrounded by three circles, one of which was the colour of blood, the second dark green, and the outer one appeared like smoke ; and to explain to him that Pachacamac, by these signs, indicated the extirpation of the royal family, and the ruin of the whole empire. Although Huayna Capac was not insensible to these omens, he would not show a want of fortitude. " Out of my sight!" said he, " Thou hast dreamed all this nonsense about my mother the moon. I will believe none of your augurs, that the sun will permit the destruction of His children till PACHACAMAC Himself assures me of it. The Inca, to provide for misfortunes, raised a fine army, consisting of the best troops in the garrisons of the empire. He ordered all the soothsayers in the different provinces to consult the oracle of Rimac, and particularly the great PACHACAMAC, regarding the interpretation of these commotions in the elements.[1] Their replies were ambiguous, but nothing extraordinary occurred before the death of the emperor.

" Pizarro, in the year 1526, had landed at Tumbez, and the Spaniards for the first time feasted their eyes with the sumptuous temples, the gold and silver opulence, and civilization of the Peruvians," &c. * * * " Pizarro sailed to Spain with these extraordinary tidings ; and returning, he invaded Peru. In February, 1531, he landed in the bay of St. Matthew, with 144 infantry, and 36 cavalry, and was reinforced with about 120 men under Bencanzar and Soto." * * * * " Pizarro pretended that he was an ambassador from a powerful monarch, and that he came to *enlighten the Peruvians with a knowledge of truth; and to* lead them to happiness :[1] he therefore offered his aid to Atahualpa against those enemies who disputed his title to the throne. The Inca's fears were removed, he professed friendship for these mysterious strangers, and sent them presents of great value. When Pizarro had posted himself securely in the palace of Caxamalca, he dispatched his brother Ferdinand and Soto to the camp of Atahualpa, &c. they were received with cordial friendship. They were astonished at the order of the court, and the reverence paid

---

[1] " The king had been particularly alarmed at the appearance of a comet of a greenish colour; besides which his house had been struck by lightning. The priests, the philosophers, and prophets (from their intercourse with the devil, says Vega, who was an *adopted son of the Romish faith)* were certain that destruction was at hand, but would not alarm the public mind with these direful tidings." They believed comets foretold the death of kings and the destruction of empires. —Vega, vol. i. p. 205, ibid. chap. ii. p. 114.

to the Inca. Their senses were dazzled by the rich ornaments of dress, the vessels of gold and silver, and the
number of other ornaments of every kind during the repast
all made of those precious metals."—ibid. chap. ii. p. 126.

" Pizarro invited the Inca to pay him a visit. Ahatualpa
prepared himself to appear with magnificence on so interesting an occasion. He arrived, sitting on a throne, which was
carried on the shoulders of his principal attendants; his
dress being adorned with precious stones, plates of gold,
and plumes of various colours. He was preceded by 400
guards, was attended by singers, &c. and more than 30,000
men.

" When the Inca was near, Father Vincent Valvarde
advanced with a crucifix and breviary; he explained among
other doctrines the appointment of St. Peter, and *the trans-
mission of his power to the popes, who had made a donation
of the new world* to the King of Castile. He *therefore*
required Ahatualpa to *embrace the Christian faith and
submit to the king.* These mysteries were badly interpreted
and were incomprehensible to the Inca, who was indignant:
He asked *where* these things had been learned? *" In
this book,"* said Valvarde. The Inca approached the
volume, *" it is silent"* said he, *" it tells me nothing,"* and
threw it on the ground. The enraged monk ran to his
companions—" To arms! Christians! to arms! avenge this
insult on those impious dogs."

" The martial music struck up, the cannon and muskets
were fired, the horse sallied out to the charge, and the
infantry rushed on sword in hand. Pizarro dragged the
Inca to the ground; and the carnage did not cease till the
close of day—the Peruvians, confounded and dismayed,
made no resistance. Four thousand were slaughtered, and
no Spaniard was even wounded by them. The plunder was

immense.　Ahatualpa, after being forced to submit to a
mock trial, was condemned to be *burnt,* but on a promise
that this would be mitigated if he would embrace the
Christian faith, he consented; and instead of being consumed in the flames, was *strangled at the stake,* (in 1533.)
Purchase remarks that " none of the perpetrators of this
infamous act died a natural death: this was *after* having
accepted as a ransom for the Inca's liberty, to be paid in
three months, as much gold and silver as would fill a room
twenty-five feet long and fifteen feet wide, and as high as a
line which Soto scratched upon the wall with his sword.　It
was filled in two months and a half, and amounted to four
million six hundred thousand ducats."—Gomara in Purchase,
vol. v. p. 230.

" Garcia, in the seventh chapter of the fifth book of the
Origin of the Indians, says of the Peruvians, " We have
still to state what the Peruvians relate of their origin, which
I shall narrate as Joan Betancos writes it, who was one of
the first who entered that kingdom, who was well acquainted
with the language of the Indians called *Quachua,* (language
of the Incas) and being thus qualified, served as an interpreter and linguist, and was on that account ordered by
Don Mendoza, Viceroy of Peru, to compose a history of
the Origin of the Incas of Peru, procuring the necessary
information from the earliest Indians.　Formerly in ancient
times, the kingdom and provinces were enveloped in obscurity.　A Lord, named Contice Ver-achocha, came forth
from a lake which is in the Province of Collasugo, and
brought along with him a certain number of persons."—
Antiq. of Mex. Vol. VI. p. 404.　　*　　*　　*　　*

" Vega says, " The certainty that the law would be executed, rendered crimes so uncommon, that a year has
passed without capital punishment being inflicted through-

out the whole empire. The poor who were blind, dumb, maimed, aged, or diseased, were fed and clothed out of public magazines, and to enable them to forget their sufferings; they were occasionally permitted to be present at public festivities. Not any of them, nor even children after five years of age, were permitted to be idle; each had employment suited to their powers. The temples and private dwellings were visited by persons appointed to that duty, to see that household arrangements, cleanliness, and the proper education of children were attended to. But these laws and customs are gone by, and it may be said, that the natives are again in a barbarous condition."—Vega, book vi. c. 11.

"The Peruvians had such extraordinary respect and affection for their Incas, that there is no instance of personal treason to their prince. The Incas have the high merit of *never permitting their subjects to be oppressed by the governors*, some of whom were sovereigns, some subalterns. Such was the state of the people, that *drunkenness was scarcely ever known*; and no one durst take a single measure of maize from his neighbour."—Vega, book vi. c. 19.

"The place of *Charichanha*, which means (of *treasure*) is where the Temple of the sun is situated, it is called *Yutipampa*, (place of the sun). The Temple was founded by *Mango Capac*; but its chief glory belongs to Inca *Yupanqui*, who endowed it with riches and splendour surpassing human belief. What we call the *altar*,[1] was on the

---

[1] In the hieroglyphic paintings preserved at Vienna, Rome, and Veletri, on the palace of the Viceroy of Mexico, the divinities, heroes, and even priests, are all drawn with large aquiline noses, often pierced toward the point, and ornamented with the mysterious double-headed serpent. Of one of the temples, he says, "*This part* of the temple must be considered as *the most consecrated place*,"—page 130.

"All Spanish authors describe the Temple, dedicated to the sun at Cuzco, as one of the most magnificent structures that ever man consecrated to religious worship, but while they notice the immense size of the stones of which it was

east side of the temple. The four walls were covered with plates of gold. On the great altar stood a representation of the sun in doubly thick gold, and richly set with jewels. It was so immensely large that it almost reached from one side of the Temple to the other. It was so placed that the sun in rising cast his beams upon it, which were reflected with such refulgence that it seemed another sun. At the side of this image (for "the Indians had no other idol") were the bodies of the deceased emperors ranged according to their antiquity; and so perfectly *embalmed* and pre-served, that they appeared as if alive. They were seated upon thrones of gold, which were placed upon tables of the same metal. The visages of the Incas were as if looking on the floor of the Temple, at a figure of the *moon,* with a female visage as the sister and wife of the sun. All the decorations were of *silver.* The bodies of the departed empresses were ranged like those of the Incas. The mother of *Huayna* Capac being placed opposite to the moon's image. The next pavillion was also decorated with silver, it was dedicated to the evening star, and the pleiades which were represented on the ceiling," &c. "Another pavillion was consecrated to thunder, and lightning, and thunder-bolts, as servants of the sun, and therefore the ornaments were all of gold. The fourth was dedicated to the rainbow, as emanating from the sun. The fifth was lined entirely with gold, and was for the special use of the royal high priest of sacrifices, and in which all the Temple deliberations were held." * * * "Some of the doors led to schools, where the Incas listened to the debates of the philosophers, or themselves explained the laws and ordinances."—See Ranking's Historical Researches, Clavegero.

built, and the incalculable riches of which Pizarro and his soldiers plundered it, they say little of its outward appearance or the style of its architecture," &c. —Antiq. Mex. p. 527, notes.

" It is not too much to suppose," observes the Commentator on Antiq. Mex. &c. " that the Hebrews did, on their arrival in Cuzco, and on their acquiring wealth and power in the country, determine to commemorate their ancient Temple, by building three other Temples of great magnificence in imitation of it. Such as were the Temple of Pachacamac situated at the distance of four miles from the city of Lima, and the great Temple of Mexico. The foundation stones of the former of these Temples, are said by some Spanish writers to have been soldered together with gold and silver, and the interior plated with gold, as was also those of the famous Temple of Cuzco, which was likewise dedicated to the worship of Pachacamac, who, as the priests pretended, delivered oracular answers to those who came to inquire of Him."—Ibid. p. 388.

The following passage from Sahagun's History, which deserves to be considered in connection with the Peruvian tradition of men having been created by Verachocha, after the images made by himself: " You must make offering of papyrus and copal, and likewise give food to the hungry, who have neither meat nor drink, nor withal to clothe them. Do your best also to clothe the naked ; consider that their flesh is thine[1] and that they are men like thyself, and *especially the suffering*, for they are the image of God."— P. 509, notes.

" Is not this the fast that I have desired, to deal thy bread to the hungry, that thou bring the poor outcast[1] into thy house ; when thou seest the naked that thou clothe him,

---

[1] In this short address there is the essence of the doctrine, as well as the tenor of the language of Scripture. The word translated poor in our version is literally " afflicted," עָנָה involving the idea of adverse circumstances. עָנִי " the children of affliction," necessarily destitute from vicissitudes over which, personally, they had no control.

and that thou *hide not thyself from thine own flesh?*"—
Isaiah lviii. **6, 7.**

This receives much illustration when the following particulars are considered. The king of Israel was not to be a
stranger, (viz. one out of the nations) but a brother—their
flesh and bone; and yet from this *brother-King,* the same
prophet testifies that the remnant of the two tribes, who
returned from the Babylonian captivity, should " *hide their
faces.*" Isaiah liii. Again, there is a prophetic illustration in
the judgment of that brother-King ; for it is to be noted
that although He was born king of the Jews, he acknowledged not the title without the Government and Supremacy
with which at His second coming in *that* character, He
shall be invested. His words as a Prophet, therefore, are,
" When the Son of man cometh in His glory, then shall He
sit upon the Throne of His glory; and before Him shall be
gathered *all nations,* and He shall separate them one from
another, as a shepherd divideth his sheep from the goats.
Then shall He say to them at His right hand, come ye
blessed of My Father, inherit the Kingdom prepared for you
from the foundation of the world; I was an hungered, and
ye gave me meat ; I was athirst, and ye gave me drink ; I
was a stranger, and ye took me in ; I was naked, and ye
clothed me ; for truly I say unto you, inasmuch as you
have done it unto one of the least of *these,* My brethren,
you have done it unto Me."

It is a remarkable fact, that the primitive inhabitants of
the New Continent implicitly obeyed this precept, both in
their reception of the shipwrecked Spaniards, and of the
first handful of feeble and sick Colonists, who settled in
New England, although no ' debtors' of *theirs,* either for
spiritual or temporal benefits.—" Salvation is of the
Jews."

" It is to be regretted that the same writer has to record in the following terms the extensive destruction of ancient monuments and paintings which followed the arrival of Spanish Missionaries in Yutican,[1] which would have thrown light on the colonies of Cozas and his companions. The ecclesiastics of this province, whose care accelerated the conversion of these Indians to our *holy church*—animated with the zeal which they felt for *their interests,* destroyed *all the books* which they possessed, composed after their peculiar style, by which they were enabled to preserve the memory of past events," &c. " This is the reason why some particular facts which I wished to notice in this work cannot be ascertained, but even the knowledge of these historical annals has been denied to posterity, for nearly all their histories were committed to the flames, without any attention being paid to the difference of the matter of which they treated." The writer adds, " Neither do I approve of that suggestion, nor do I condemn it, but it

---

[1] If any thing is calculated to produce astonishment, it is the particular belief which the Indians of Yutican, above all other nations of those extensive king-doms entertained, which renders it at least very difficult to comprehend how that was possible, without the mysteries of the evangelical law having been preached to them, in proof of which I shall cite what Father Remesel relates in his history. He affirms that when the Bishop Don B. Las Casas proceeded to his Bishopric, which was in 1545, he commanded an Ecclesiastic whom he found in Campacha, whose name was Francisco Hernandez, who was well acquainted with the lan-guage of the Indians, to visit them, carrying a sort of Catechism, of what he was about to preach to them, and that nearly at the end of a year, the Ecclesiastic wrote to him, that he had met a principal lord, who, on being questioned respect-ing the ancient religion which they professed, told him that they knew and believed in the God who was in heaven, and that this God was the Father, the Son, and the Holy Spirit, and that the father was named *Yezona,* who had cre-ated men ; and that the Son was Bahab, who was *born of a virgin named Chiri-brias,* and that the mother of *Chiribrias* was *Yxchel,* and that the Holy Spirit was called *Ec-uach.* Of *Bah-ab, Son of the Father, they said that he was put to death, and scourged, and crowned with thorns, and placed with his arms extended on a beam of wood, where he died, and remained dead during three days, and on the third day rose to life, and ascended into heaven where he is with the Father ;* and that immediately afterwards Ec-uach, who is the Holy Spirit, came and filled the earth with whatsoever it stood in need of. Being asked what signification he assigned to these three names, he said that Yez signified the Great Father, and Bah-ab the son of the Great Father, and Ec-uach the merchant—*Chiribrias,* he understood to mean the Mother of the Son of the Great Father. He further added,

appears to me, that secular history[1] might have been preserved in the same manner as in *New Spain* and the *conquered* provinces it has been preserved without being considered to be any obstacle to the progress of Christianity." —
Historia Yutican, lib. iv. c. 6, in Antiq. Mex.

" Besides a certain degree of conformity on these doc-
trinal points, viz. original sin, repentance, vicarial atonement, a future Redeemer, and the Resurrection of the body ;
they likewise seem to have been acquainted with the sacraments, although superstition had lamentably perverted them,
&c. since traces of these may be found in various rites and
ceremonies common alike to the Mexicans and Peruvians.
Having briefly mentioned what particular doctrines these
were which the gravest writers assert were known to the
Indians before the arrival of the Spaniards in the New
World ; we shall proceed separately to adduce proof to
shew that the above-mentioned doctrines *did in reality constitute a portion of Indian faith* ; and although many testimonies from different authors[2] might be cited in confirmation *of each article, it will be sufficient in this place to quote
the single authorities of men like Acosta, Peter Martyr,
Garcia, and Torquemeda, whose writings are highly approved in Spain, and are also known to the rest of Europe.*"

" The doctrine of vicarial atonement, or a sacrifice for sin

that all men would die, &c Being questioned likewise as to the manner in which
they became acquainted with these things, he replied that the lords, (ancients),
instructed their sons in them, and that thus the doctrine was handed down from
generation to generation. They declared that in *ancient times twenty men had
come to that country, the chief of whom was names Cozes, who commanded the
people to use confession, and to fast, for which reason some of them fasted on the
day corresponding to Friday, affirming that Bachab had been put to death on that
day.*" Lib. iv. chap. vi. Cogulludo Historia de Yutican, in Antiq Mex.

[1] " The History of the Hebrews never could be termed *secular* ; their political
economy was strictly religious : not in the manner of *combined* ecclesiastical and
civil, as amongst the gentiles ; but in spirit and constitution : the LAW of the
kingdom being RIGHTEOUS."

[2] " *Lettres Edifiantes des Missions Etrangeres,*" a work published by authority,
and replete with information. Ibid.

whereby the guilt of one party is expiated and atoned for by the guiltless blood of another, was well known to the Indians, and the question is curious, how traces of this doctrine should have been known in America," &c.

The following extract is from the pen of Rosales: " Prosecuting their conquest as far as the country of the powerful lord *Tiunchatipec*, five leagues distant from the city of Conception; they (the Spaniards) found another fortress where were seven stones resembling sculptured pyramids which had been placed there by the Indians of Peru, for the purpose of performing the ceremony of *Chalpainge*. If our surprise was excited by this discovery that the Peruvians were not altogether ignorant of the nature of vicarial sacrifice and atonement, it will be produced in no less degree when we discover that the inhabitants of New Spain generally believed in the *coming of a future Redeemer,* or Saviour, whose advent, as well as the *last destruction of the world,* they seem to have expected at the close of a certain stated period corresponding with the artificial cycles of time which they employed in their calendars," &c. Ibid.[1]

" It was," observes the commentator, " the cupidity of the Spaniards which first introduced to them the belief of the Indians in the *resurrection of the body.* Gomara, after stating that the Peruvians deposited gold and silver vases in

[1] " Mons. de Cheseaux, a Swiss astronomer, had about the middle of last century, submitted to certain leading members of the Royal Academy at Paris, some astronomical remarks on the Book of Daniel, wherein he shewed that the periods of 2300 and 1260 years, and also their difference 1040 years are all astronomical cycles, at the end of which, the sun and moon return to nearly the same positions in the heavens, as they set out from."

W. Cuninghame, Esq. the author of some learned works, observes in his POLITICAL DESTINY OF THE EARTH, " All my endeavours to find the work of Mons. de Cheseaux were, however, ineffectual, till last year, when I procured a MS. copy of his observations on Daniel from the Library of the University of Lausanne. I have since then, in a work published early in the present year, proved the accuracy of the conclusions of Mons de Cheseaux," &c. * *

" At the end of 1040 years, they return to less than two and a half minutes of a degree, and to one hour, eighteen minutes, eight seconds, and nineteen thirds of solar time."

the tombs of the Incas, says, ' When the Spaniards opened those sepulchres, and scattered the bones, the Indians intreated them not to do so, assuring them that they would be raised in the resurrection ; [1] for they fully believed in *the resurrection of the body,* as well as the *immortality* of the *soul.*' Herrera, in several passages asserts that the Indians maintain this belief. In la Historiade de los Indios, he says in his 4th Decade, p. 187, ' In the provinces of Guayacualio and Yutican, they believed that the dead would come to life.' He also says, ' that in the province of Quinabayia, they well knew that there was an immortal principle in man, *although they* thought,' he adds (rather *Sadduceanly*) ' it was a *bodily transfiguration ; believiny that the body would be renewed to life.*' They further explained that its future habitation would be a delightful and pleasant place," &c.

Thus writes Ulloa respecting the contrast between the ancient magnificence and present degradation of the modern Peruvians :—

"The disproportion between what I read and what I am going to relate, is so remarkable, that on a retrospect of past times, I am utterly at a loss how to account for the universal change of things, especially when surrounded with such monuments of the industry, polity, and laws of the Indians of Peru, that it would be madness to question the truth of the accounts that have been given of them ; for the ruins of these works are still amazing. On the other hand, I can hardly credit my own eyes, when I behold

---

[1] Martyr mentions in the ninth chapter of his eighth decade, a singular custom of the Chirubichenses, who, believing the souls of their deceased relatives to be immortal, burned their bones, only preserving the hinder part of the head. " They burne the bones, keepinge the hinder parte of the head, and this the noblest and best of the women bringeth home with her to be kept for a sacred relique." The Jews had an ancient superstitious notion about a small bone which they believed to be the seed of the resurrection, which was situated between the upper vertebrae of the neck and the head." Ibid. p. 226.

that nation involved in Cimmerian darkness, living in barbarism," &c. " But what is still more difficult to conceive, is how these people whose former wisdom is conspicuous in the equity of their laws and the establishment of a government so singular as that under which they live, should at present shew no traces of that genius and capacity which formed so excellent an economy, and so beautiful a system of social duties; though undoubtedly they are the same people and still retain some of the ancient customs and manners."

" Such is the disposition of the present race that if their indifference to temporal things did not extend itself also to the eternal, they might be said to equal the happiness of the golden age," &c.

" They possess a tranquillity undisturbed either by fortunate or unfortunate events. In their mean apparel they are as contented as the monarch clothed with the most splendid inventions of luxury; and so far are they from entertaining a desire for better or more comfortable clothing, that they give themselves no manner of concern about their own, although their bodies continue half-naked. They shew as much disregard for riches; and even that authority and grandeur within their reach is so little the object of their ambition, that to all appearance it is the same thing to an Indian, &c. The same moderation appears in their food. Fear cannot stimulate, respect induce, nor punishment compel them; they are indeed of a singular turn."—See Ulloa in Pinkerton's Collection.

De Mennonville thus writes: " All the Indians on my way were simple, mild, and ingenuous, because at a distance from the Spanish settlements; but from this place to the Guaxa they are sly, subtle, even knavish and idle; and it may truly be said that the neighbourhood of Europeans

has been a pest, a plague equally unfortunate and prompt
of diffusion." [1]

[1] "Justice and peace, tired of mortals by whom they were daily insulted,
these celestial ones withdrew to a corner of North America; yes, to the village
of Dominguello. This little hamlet, simple in appearance, unadorned by any
meritricious works of art, but rich and charming from its site and the confluence of the Rio Grande and that of Las Vueltas, appeared to them worthy
of their abode; and here I enjoyed the mild presence of these estimable but
slighted powers. The circumstance which called forth this remark, I shall
relate. While I was at supper, I sent for a topith, with whom I had entered
into contract for horses. The knave had the address to cheat me of three piastres,
without my noticing the fraud. The keeper of the *cassa reale*, however perceived it, and pointed it out to me: but the topith was out of sight. In the
meantime, after the procession, while walking in the public square, I saw two
Indians carrying each a staff six feet long, on which they rested both their
hands. I paid at first but little attention to this incident, till at length I heard
a cry repeated thrice in the Mexican language. In an instant my rogue of a
guide presents himself out of breath running, and makes a number of bows
to the men with the staffs, the distinctive marks of their office. The one was
the Alcalde, the other his assessor. I saw them advancing towards me; I met
them half way. In my presence, in a very deliberate manner, they interrogated
the topith respecting the number of horses I had ordered, and the price he
had asked. He confessed the sum with the exception of two reals. They next
inquired of me how much I paid. I told them the exact sum. Turning to the
topith, they asked him, if he had shewn me the table of fares, and on his confession that he had never mentioned it to me, the Alcalde very severely, though
without the least symptom of passion, reprimanded him; first, for having
exacted more than the prescribed ordinance; and secondly, for having stated the
sum he had received, two reals less than it really was. While they were speaking, I minutely examined the countenances of these guileless officers. They
exhibited not the least symptom of anger or arrogance. *Immutable as the law;
they judged and decided by its rule;* and never did senator, counsellor, or judge,
with all their sumptuous paraphranalia of office, in silk and ermined robes, in
scarlet, or in black, in coronets, caps, or perriwigs; never, I say, did either
look more august or majestic, than did, on this occasion, these poor tattered
Indians." Mennonville, in Pink. Coll.

HAYTIANS.

ALTHOUGH the following notices of Hayti, whose history is that of all the Western Islands, cannot be said to augment the sum of *historical and internal* proof, which it is the object of this work to point out; it furnishes in that identity of suffering which at the same period marked the race wherever it existed, that kind of *relative* and subordinate evidence which cannot be withheld without impairing the homogenity of the piece. Nor are the *coincidences* which contribute to the unity of the eventful portraiture to be overlooked; for neither was it fortuitous that Columbus should have been not only of *the same* race, but of a royal lineage of that *race*, of whose territorial seclusion he was the discoverer; or that *the same year* had to record (in this discovery of his) an accession to the crown of Spain of one portion of his kindred: and the expulsion of six hundred thousand of another portion from the Spanish dominions. See Appendix.

" It is impossible," writes the late biographer of Columbus, " to refrain from dwelling on the picture given by the first discoverers of the state of manners in this eventful Island before the arrival of the white men. The people of Hayti existed in that state of primitive simplicity which some philosophers have fondly pictured as the most enviable on earth: surrounded by natural blessings without even the knowledge of artificial wants. Hospitality was with them a law of nature universally observed ; there was no need of being known to receive its succour; *every* house was open to the *stranger* as his own." Charlevoix's History of St. Domingo.   *   *   *   *   *

Columbus was neither insensible to the virtue and happiness of the inhabitants of the Western Islands, nor reluctant in eulogising it; the inconsistency, therefore, between his conduct and those benevolent feelings to which he was naturally disposed, is to be attributed to that pernicious system of theology, with which he was blindly identified, and with the inebriating spirit of which he was deeply imbued.

Those who are acquainted with his early determination, stimulated as it was by the promptings of genius and those peculiar studies[1] to which he devoted his attention, may, in some measure be enabled to account for the confidence with which he pledged himself, in an appeal to the avarice of the sovereign, to make rich returns to Spain in the event of the contemplated discovery of the Western Indies.

The position in which he stood :—alive as he was to those impressions of honour which chivalry had[2] borrowed from the slumbering lion of his race ; was that of one at once bound

---

[1] " In his tender years he applied himself to the study of cosmography, astrology, and geometry, because those sciences are linked together ; and because Ptolemy, at the beginning of his Cosmography, says, that no man can be a good cosmographer unless he be a painter too, therefore he learned to draw, in order to describe lands and set down bodies, planes, and rounds," &c.

To their Catholic majesties in the year 1501, he thus writes : " Most serene princes, I went to sea very young and have continued to this day ; and this art inclines those that follow it to be desirous to discover the secrets of the world. It is now forty years since I have been sailing to all those parts at present frequented, and our Lord has been favourable to this my inclination, and I have received from Him the spirit of understanding," &c. " God hath given me a genius, and hands apt to draw this globe," &c. Filled with this desire, I come to your highnesses. All that heard of my undertaking rejected it with contempt and scorn," &c. Life of Chris. Colon, by his son, in Pinkerton's Collection.

[2] " Weep with me o'er the Lion the pride of our sires,
    Who lighted all Spain with his beam—
    While the west was illumin'd by the orient fires,
    Which old chivalry borrowed from him."—Da Costa.

to redeem his pledge to Europe in *that* demonstration of which he had declared his nautical principles capable; and to the allied Sovereigns in realizing those "*profits*" which in their minds were identified with the term "*Indies.*" But together with these motives there was the ambition of adding *his* name to those of an *illustrious* lineage. See Appendix.

These considerations may explain the solicitude with which Columbus sought to effect the objects of his enterprize; but for the methods which he took in the transfer of those fatal profits to the treasury of Spain, involving as these did, the *practical inversion* of the Law of God, a solution must be found in that *sorcery,* which by ecclesiastical "decrees," could convert crimes of the deepest moral turpitude into consecrated auxiliaries in promoting the views and maintaining the interests of the Church; and into meritorious "acts of the faith" in extending and enforcing her authority.

"Thou shalt not covet,"—"rob"—"murder" could have been evaded by ingenuously torturing the words *out* of their integrity, or by stigmatising them as *legal* vestiges of that Law which the infallibility of the Church had superseded; but it was more expedient to grant absolution to these crimes, and constitute them at once commendable and holy, as *means* subserving the all-redeeming *end* of "compelling" the victims of these crimes "to come into that salvation" of which the Church was the administratrix, guardian, monopolist, and "fold."

Thus we find Columbus consoling himself with the available donation which out of this guiltily acquired gain he had devoted towards a pilgrimage to the Holy Land, in order to aid in rescuing the holy sepulchre out of the hands of the *comparatively* God-honouring disciples of the false prophet. At other times we find him in the midst of storms at sea,

vowing[1] to go 'barefoot' to one and another image and
shrine of 'our lady,' under the 'strong delusion' that acts
of *will* worship could supply the *want* of obedience; and
that such 'penances' were not only advantageous as the means
of obtaining pardon and reconciliation; but in procuring an
indemnity for such *meditated* acts of transgression, as expe-
diency might render equally indispensable in future.

In writing to the Castilian sovereigns, the Admiral thus
characterizes the inhabitants of Hayti and Lucaya, &c. " I
swear to your Majesties that there is not a better people in
all the world than these—more affectionate or mild—they
love their neighbour as themselves; their language is the
sweetest and most cheerful, for they always speak smiling,"
 *   *   * Again he writes, " I have before pro-
tested to your Highnesses that the profits of the enterprise
shall be employed in the conquest of Jerusalem, at which
your Highnesses smiled, and said, " You had the same inclination."   *   * " He expressed his belief that a
ton of gold would be collected against his return; and that
the seamen would find the mines, &c. so that before three
years the king and queen might undertake the recovery [2]

---

[1] On occasion of a violent storm in which the Pinta was parted and lost sight
of during the night—on their return in a leaky state to Spain, the biographer
states that " therefore betaking themselves to prayers and *religious acts*, those
a-board cast lots which of them should go in pilgrimage (for the whole crew) to
our *Lady of Guadaloupe*, which fell to the Admiral; afterwards they drew for
another to go to *Loretto*, and the lot fell upon one Petre de Villa. They then cast
lots for a third who was to watch a night at *Saint Olive* of *Meguer*; and the
storm still increasing, they all made a vow to go barefoot, and in their shirts, at
the first land they came to, to some church of *our lady*. On a subsequent storm
on the same homeward passage, the tempest was so great that at midnight it
split their sails; therefore, being in great danger, they made a vow to send one
on pilgrimage to our lady de Cuita a Gueboa, whither he was to go barefoot and
in his shirt. The lot fell again upon the Admiral, God thereby shewing that his
offering was more acceptable than those of others.''
 [2] " The Admiral had vowed that within seven years of his discovery, he would
furnish himself with 50,000 foot, and 5000 horse, for this *pious* object."   *
 *   * " Columbus was fully imbued with the religion of the times, and might
have *sincerely* believed that with the miseries of bondage, he introduced a *panacea*
for all evils, in the faith which he taught." See Gordon's Hist.

of the holy sepulchre—suggesting, moreover, that the Caribean Indians should be exchanged with the merchants of Spain, for domestic animals for the use of the colony."

In a letter to Luis de St. Angel, the Admiral observes, " True it is, that after they felt confidence, and lost their fear of us, they were so liberal with what they possessed, that it would not be believed by those who had not seen it. If any thing was asked of them, they never said no, but rather gave[1] it cheerfully, and showed as much amity, as if they gave their *very hearts.*"

" Columbus exerted himself to send satisfactory proofs of the value of his discovery, and that the royal treasury might the sooner be reimbursed for the expenses of the discovery and colonization, he sent five hundred Indians, *prisoners, to be sold as slaves,* in Seville. Upon the arrival of these unhappy beings, Ferdinand gave orders for their sale in the markets of Andalusia; but the gentler and more consciencious Isabella caused those orders to be suspended, until an ecclesiastical[2] synod should determine whether this disposal

---

[1] One of the most pleasing descriptions of the inhabitants of this Island is given by Peter Martyr, who gathered it, he says, from the Admiral himself. " It is certain that the land among these people is as free as the air and the water—and that *mine* and *thine,* those seeds of all mischief, have no place with them. They are contented with so little, and have so large a country, they have rather superfluity than scarceness, so that they seem to live in a golden world without toil. *They deal truly one with another without laws, without books, and without judges.* They take him for an evil and mischievous man who taketh pleasure in doing hurt to another."

[2] " It would appear from an account given by Peter Martyr and Gomara, (for both of these authors record the *viva voce* evidence given by Friar Ortezius before the council of the Indies) that the Friar, speaking in the name of Pedro de Cordova, and of the Dominicans and Franciscans, and recommending the slavery of the Indians, insinuates that he *omits some charges which might* have been brought against them ; but what charge but one seems wanting to their long catalogue of accusation ? that of *Judaism.* And even if these Indians had been discovered to be all Hebrews, they could not have been more hardly dealt with by the Spaniards, for Gomara says ' *Fray Garcio Loysa dio grandissimo credito a fray Thomas Hortiz y a los ostres frayles de su order. Por lo qual el Emperador con acuerdo del consijo de Indios declaro que fuessem esclavo estando en Madrid,*' &c. This condemnation applied to the Indians of the Continent of America generally." Antiq. Mex.

of human beings was justifiable in the sight of the Creator. The divines on this occasion differed in opinion ; and gave *oppugnant interpretations* of the will of God."   *   *   *

" The queen adopting the theory most consistent with her own disposition, commanded that the Indians should be restored to their native country; and that their countrymen should not be enslaved, but treated in future in the gentlest manner ; but this decree came too late to benefit those who had been torn from their country; the change of condition, grief, and excessive labour, had destroyed the greater part soon after their arrival."   *   *   *

" This act of Columbus," adds the historian, " could not be justified ; no injury comparable to it could be inflicted on the Indian people. The robberies and sensual excesses of the Spaniards might plead extenuation, &c. but for this cruelty—the fruit of cold calculating policy is the justification of one atrocity by another. His contemporaries who have dignified with the name of *conquest, the slaughter and enslavement* of the Aborigines of America, saw in those measures a *wise policy.*"   *   *   " But modern historians have felt that they needed justification." Hist. del Alm. Herrera.

Munoz, in his history of the New World, has treated the subject with a degree of honourable feeling ; he says " ' *the tax* '[1] was heavy and impolitic."

Robertson and Irving have defended them by reasons which set them in a more odious light, and in their closets

---

[1] " According to Columbus, the tribes inhabiting the Greater Antilles were the most unoffending, gentle, and benevolent of the human race—to gratify the Spanish Governor, he imposed a tax in 1494 on all above fourteen years of age. Ovando, the Governor, from 1500 to 1509, nearly exterminated them. This writer describes the original population of Chili as nearly resembling the former. "Those on the plains were of the ordinary stature of men ; those of the Andes surpassed it. Their complexions are of a reddish brown easily changing to white."

have found an apology for deeds, which, if placed naked before Columbus, he would have been ashamed to own.

" It is admitted," says the historian, " that Columbus desired to make wealthy returns to Spain, in order to sustain his credit and influence ; but there was no apology for seeking this avowedly selfish object, by imposing on a free and generous people, the insupportable yoke of slavery ; to convert a terrestrial paradise into a prison, made vocal by the cries and groans of millions of beings to whom he brought the first idea of misery." Navarette Cura de la Placios in Gordon's Hist. vol. i. p. 184.

Columbus repeatedly visited Spain, either to make propositions, or obtain, if not redress, at least a hearing for those misrepresentations which Ovando (a man utterly devoid of principle) had made. It was on his return to Hayti, on the coast of Spain, when himself and crew had suffered shipwreck, that the following illustrations of the character of the islanders was called forth .

" The Admiral finding his men deserting him, and the ship sinking on her side, and the water leaving her; cast overboard such articles as could be most easily saved. He then proceeded with his crew to Nina, and dispatched a messenger to Guacangari, whose residence was half a mile distant, with news of the misfortune."

" The chief showed great sensibility upon the occasion, sending his people with large canoes to assist in unlading and stripping the ship, whilst himself and his train took charge of the effects as they were landed. He used all means in his power to console the Admiral, and tendered to him all he possessed." " The honesty and care of this guileless people were surprising. Every thing before them had at least, the attraction of novelty, and was of a nature to excite their cupidity : but not an article was stolen or lost."

" The Admiral viewed this circumstance as providential, in enabling him to *procure gold* from the Indians, and of making a settlement in their country." " The chief invited the Admiral to an entertainment, at which he displayed whatever his Island contained most agreeable; giving the Spaniards as much reason to admire his delicacy,[1] as his hospitality." " He ate in small quantities with great decorum, washing his hands and rubbing them with odoriferous herbs, and again after the repast, laving them with water. He was served with great deference by his subjects, towards whom his deportment was majestic and graceful."

" The shipwrecked mariners charmed with the delicious abundance which the climate and soil produced, besought the Admiral to permit them to remain on the Island. He readily granted their request, founded on reasons which he had already weighed. He had others quite as cogent, among which the desire to discover the gold mine, was not the least."

" Meanwhile, he continued to cultivate the friendship of Guacangari and his tribe, and received daily from the affectionate prince valuable presents of gold. And so strong had the attachment of the latter become, that he expressed an earnest wish to accompany the Admiral to Castile."

" At one time the present consisted of a large plate of gold; at another, of a great golden mask, for which an earthen bason and ewer were begged. On a certain occasion, the Admiral dining on shore, was received by the Cacique and five subordinate chiefs, each bearing a golden crown; who conducted him to their council-house, and placed him upon the seat of honour, on an elevated place or

[1] " Guacangari invited the Admiral to visit his residence. The generous Cacique did every thing in his power to honour his guest, and cheer him under his misfortune, showing a warmth of sympathy, yet delicacy of attention which could not have been expected, &c. Indeed there was a degree of innate dignity and refinement displayed in his manners that often surprised the Spaniards. His whole deportment in the enthusiastic eyes of Columbus betokened the inborn grace and dignity of lofty lineage." Irving's life of Colum.

dais. Guacangari took the crown from his own head, and put it on that of the Admiral : two of them then presented Columbus with a great plate of gold each." It ought not to be forgotten that in Columbus this people believed that they beheld the predicted friends from another Land, *whom their traditions taught them to expect.*

" He devoted[1] several days in the beautiful and fertile province of Ornofay, to repose and the recreation of his men, where he received new testimonials of that distinguished kindness which had already procured for the inhabitants of Cuba, the character of the most gentle of the race. Whilst there, he erected a *cross,* the symbol of *possession*—and celebrated a solemn mass." Gordon, vol. i. p. 168.

"It was a custom with Columbus," observes his biographer, " to erect, in all remarkable places which he visited, crosses in conspicuous situations, to denote the discovery of the country and its *subjection to the Romish faith.* He ordered a large cross therefore to be elevated on the banks of this river. This was done on Sunday morning with great ceremony and the celebration of mass." " When Columbus disembarked for this purpose, he was met upon the shore by the Cacique and his principle favourite, a venerable Indian of fourscore years of age, of grave and dignified deportment," &c. " The old man brought a calabash of a delicate kind of fruit which he presented to the admiral in token of amity." " Whilst mass was preparing in this natural temple, the Indians looked on with awe and reverence, perceiving from the tones and gesticulations of the priest, the lighted tapers, and smoking incense, that it must be a ceremony of a sacred and mysterious nature." " When the service was ended, the aged

---

[1] Herrera. Muñoz, lib. 5.

man approached to Columbus and made him this oration :
" That which thou hast been doing," said he, " is well, for
it appears to be *thy manner* of giving *thanks.* I am told
that thou hast lately come to these lands with a mighty
force, and hast subdued many countries, spreading great
terror among the people ; but be not therefore vain-glorious.
Know, that according to *our belief* the souls of men have
two journies before them when they are parted from the
body. One to a place, dismal and foul, and covered with
darkness, prepared for those who have been *unjust and
cruel* to their fellow-men ; the other pleasant and full of
delight for *such as have promoted peace on earth.* If thou
art mortal, and dost expect to die, and dost believe that
each shall be rewarded *according to his deeds, beware
that thou wrongfully hurt no one, nor do harm to those
who have done no harm to thee.'*—See Clavegero and Irving's Life of Col.

' Margarite, to whom Columbus intrusted the exploration
of Ciboa, &c. contented himself with sending Ojida to the
fortress of St. Thomas, whilst he took his own position in the
rich plains of La Vega. There he abandoned himself and
followers to the grossest sensualities ; and regardless of justice and decorum, seized upon the provisions, gold, and
female relatives, of the confiding tribe. They robbed the
inhabitants of whatever they deemed valuable, and made
their wives and daughters the victims of their licentious
passions. The son of Columbus remonstrated, but he being a
favourite at court, treated his reproof with contumely and
defiance. Father Boyle too, whose fanaticism and clerical
love of power, were rebuked and controlled by the more
liberal and prudent genius of the Admiral, became an active
member of this faction.

' Gentle as the Indians were, their indignation at the

occupation of their country, and the erection of the fort of St. Thomas, at length became apparent.

' *Caonaba* anxiously watched for an opportunity of avenging the wrongs of his tribe, and of deliverance from a curb which his noble spirit disdained. The prince confiding in his courage, and the fastnesses of his mountains, preserved his warlike attitude, impeding the working of the mines, and menacing the safety of the colony. Whilst Columbus pondered on the means to propitiate or subdue this chief, Ojida undertook to bring him to Isabella as a friend or captive. At the head of ten chosen followers, well armed and mounted, he made his way : he approached the chief with great respect, *assuring him* that he came on a *friendly* visit from the Admiral, who had sent him an invaluable present.

' The Indian prince received Ojida with that frankness and confidence which belong to elevated minds. He endeavoured to prevail on him to repair to Isabella, to treat with Columbus," &c. " *Caonaba* at length consented, but did not place himself at the mercy of his enemies. To the surprise of Ojida he set out with a numerous train, and to a remonstrance from him, replied, that it was unbefitting a great prince to go forth scantily attended."

' The Cavalier had now cause to dread that his wiles would be turned against himself; to prevent which, he had recourse to a singular stratagem. He exhibited a set of manacles, highly polished, which he said had been made in the *Turey* (paradise) that they were worn by Castilian monarchs on rare occasions and were intended as a present for the Cacique. He proposed to decorate him with these ornaments, and, mounted on the same horse with Ojida, that he should return with them to his subjects. Secure against treachery, as he supposed, he readily consented. At length, availing himself of a favorable moment, Ojida dashed into

the forest, went out of sight of the natives, and with the
assistance of his followers bound the Cacique to himself
directing his flight toward Isabella." " In captivity
Caonaba preserved his lofty air and spirit. He met the
Admiral with a haughty glance, vaunted his success at *La
Navidad*, and his intention to subject Isabella to a like
fate. Whilst all others approached Columbus with the
respect due to his station (which he rigorously exacted) the
chief refused him every tribute of superiority." &c.

'He was detained a prisoner till the return of Columbus
from Spain, having accompanied him upon the voyage,
but he died before its termination,' says his biographer,
'the victim of the morbid sensibilities of an unyielding
spirit.'—Herrera, decad. i. lib. ii. c. 16.

'Although one brother of *Caonaba* had fallen into the
hands of the Spaniards, in an attempt at reprisal, another,
called Manicaotax, as warlike as himself, prepared to liberate
or avenge him. By his own influence, and that of *Anacoana* (the widow of *Caonaba*) who possessed great power
over the mind of her brother *Bohechio*; the flame of
war rekindled throughout the Island. The Spanish army
did not exceed two hundred foot and twenty horse, but to
these must be added *twenty blood hounds more terrible* to
the Indians than horse or men. The naked Islanders as-
sailed in every direction by the thunder and lightning of the
fire-arms, borne down and trampled under foot by the horse
and his rider; seized by the blood-hound, who pulled them
to the ground and dashed his fangs instantly into the bowels
of his victims, fled in the utmost confusion and dismay.'

*   *   *   *   *   *   *   *   *

'On his return from Spain, Columbus was greatly
chagrined to find the colony a prey to disease and insub-
ordination. It is to be noted that the criminals of the

Spanish prisons had been disgorged upon the afflicted inhabitants of the New World.

'During the absence of the Admiral, and the administration of his brother, *Anacoana* advised her brother, *Bohechio*, to take warning by the fate of her unfortunate husband, and conciliate a power which they had not the means to resist. This recommendation procured for the *Alentedo*, on his visit to this district, a friendly and courteous reception. Thirty maidens of the royal household came forth to meet him dancing and singing their *traditional areytos*, and waving branches of the *palm tree*, (like those of the olive) emblems of peace, which they gracefully presented to him on their knee.'   *   *   *

'On a visit subsequently made to collect the tribute, he was received by *Anacoana* with hospitality. She, on that occasion, distinguished herself as well by her liberality and complaisance as by her talent and politeness.'

'She entertained him and his retinue at a large house, furnished with abundance of seats, plates, towels, and various vessels, made of hard black wood, highly polished, and curiously carved in *bas relief* with the figures of men, animals, and things of grotesque shape. Her munificence was emulated by her brother, who gave a large quantity of provision beyond the stipulated tribute.'   *   *   *

'Certain " tender mercies " [1] *of the church* were considered perfidious and cruel outrages by *Guarionex* (the Cacique of Vega) and his subjects, which induced him to make another effort to throw off the Spanish yoke. But his designs were betrayed, and he with subordinate leaders, were seized in their villages. Two of the bravest of the latter were put to death, but Guarionex was spared, in consideration of the wrongs he

---

[1] See Appendix.

had received.' 'Several traits of character,' says the historian, 'were developed during this campaign, which, in
justice to *a much calumniated race,* we shall succinctly notice.

'The *Alentedo* sent messengers to *Mayobanax,* promising *friendship* and *protection* on *resigning his guest;*
but extreme vengeance in case of refusal. The magnani-
mous reply of the Cacique was: ' *Tell the Spaniards that
they are bad men ; cruel and tyrannical usurpers of the
territory of others, and shedders of innocent blood. I
desire not their friendship. Guarionex is a good man—
my friend—my guest. He has fled to me for refuge. I
have promised to protect him, and shall keep my promise.'*
' Nor did he change his determination, on a second application ; nor the entreaties of those he tenderly loved, who
amid the smoking ruins of their villages, urged the surrender of the fugitive as the only means of saving their
people.'

' Among the prisoners taken with *Mayobana* was his sister,
the wife of a Cacique, whose territories had not yet been
visited by the Spaniards. She was reputed one of the most
beautiful women of the Island ; devotedly attached to her
brother, she had abandoned the security of her own territory to follow him in his painful wanderings whilst hiding
from his relentless foes. When her husband learned her
captivity, he hastened to the *Alentedo,* and swayed by
an ardent and generous affection, ransomed her by submitting himself and his possessions to the Spanish dominion.'
—Clavegero.

' The civil yoke, intolerably heavy, was not the only
burden imposed on the Indians. The ministers of religion
in that bigotted age would have the *mind* of the Indian a
subject to *their will,* as his *person* and *property* were to the
Spanish magistrates.'

'Father Boyle had left two priests at least, who were zealous of the Church ; Roman Pane, a poor hermit (as he styled himself) of the order of *Saint Geronimus*, and Joan Borognon, a Franciscan. The success of these pious men was not commensurate with their zeal ; and they had frequent occasion to lament that their Catechumens required '*force and punishment*' to keep them in the *prescribed way*. *Guarionex*, listened attentively to their teachings, and complacently repeated the prayers they dictated. But unfortunately their assurances of the purity and excellence of their faith were not sustained by the professors of it ; and the '*savage*' conceived that the seduction or violation of his wife, was evidence of the *falsity* or *insufficiency of their rules* of faith, justice, and self-denial. Indignant at this outrage, and goaded on by the scoffs of his countrymen for *adopting the faith of murderers and oppressors*—he renounced a religion which he supposed tolerated such crimes. The priests, stricken with horror at his *apostacy*, retired from his territory, leaving a chapel with some *pictures, to which* they directed the converts, now reduced to a single family, to offer up their prayers. The *holy figures were removed and buried by order of Guarionex*. A crime so enormous was immediately reported to the *Alentedo*, whose justice accorded to the criminal agents, (six in number,) a formal trial, in which they were convicted of *sacrilege*, and the Lieutenant- of the Viceroy of the most Catholic king *piously burned them at the stake !* This first *auto de fe* was sealed with divine approbation, since we are assured by Father Roman Pane, certain roots which grew where the *pictures* had been buried, assumed the *form of the cross*."[1]
See Gordon.—Escritura de Fr, Roman's Hist. del. Almir.

[1] Father Roman tells the story thus, "We continued with that Cacique Guari-

' Anacoana, who on the death of her brother, governed the province, was no longer the friend of the whites. The *miseries of her people* had converted her love into deep and inextinguishable hatred. Resistance in her dominion to *cruel and rapacious exactions* was magnified into *rebellion,* and she was accused of attempting to *subvert the Spanish power.* Ovando gave ready faith to these accusations, and marched into Zaraqna with three hundred foot and seventy horse, under pretence of paying a *friendly* visit to the queen, and making satisfactory arrangements for paying the tribute.'

' He was received by Anacoana at the head of her tributary caciques and a numerous train of her subjects." * * * ' The Governor advanced, and gave the preconcerted signal, by placing his hand *on the cross* of Alcantara—that pledge of boundless *mercy!* which hung at his breast. Instantly the charge was given. The caciques

---

onex about two years, instructing him in our faith and the manners of Christians; at first he appeared well inclined and gave some hopes of complying and becoming a Christian. He bid us teach him the Lord's Prayer, &c. and he caused all his family to say that prayer twice a-day. Yet he fell off through the fault of some of the principal men who blamed him for embracing Christ, *since Christians were bad men, aud drove them out of their country by force.* We therefore went away to another Cacique, whose name was Maviata. When we set out to go to Maviata, we found Guarionex's people building a house near the house of prayer, where we left some pictures *for the Catechumen's to kneel and pray before them,* &c. It appears that blasphemy had been added to sacrilege by Guarionex, who, having burned the pictures, said, " *Now you will yield much fruit.*" " Some days after," adds Father Pane, " the Catechumen who owned that field, going to dig up his agis and radishes, when in the place where the pictures had been buried, two or three agis were grown in the shape of a cross, as if they had been stuck one through another," &c. *This miracle* has been shewn by God where the *images* were found, God knows to what end ! Father Roman Pane is careful to inform us in conclusion, " With others there *must be force and ingenuity* used to prevent those who have had a good beginning from having a bad ending *in the faith* and therefore there is need of force and punishment of the holy tribunal of the Inquisition." T. F. Roman Pane, Poor Anchorite. Ovale in Pink. Coll.
' *Blood* issuing from those *hosts* which the Jews were at this time accused of *stabbing,* and " *miraculous crosses,*" appearing on the graves of boys whom they had been accused of slaying, to keep the Feast of Passover with their blood— were at this time equally indicative of the same *zeal to do God service* in Europe.' See Appendix.

then assembled in the house of the queen were made prisoners, and *subjected to horrible tortures* in order to compel them to accuse themselves and her of *treason.* Thus convicted, they were bound to the pillars of her house, to which fire was set, and perished miserably in the flames. Meanwhile an undistinguished massacre was committed on the populace, from which no age nor condition was exempted.

' The catastrophe of this act of Spanish *justice* was in accordance with its commencement. The lovely, the high-minded, the generous *Anacoana* was borne *in chains* to San Domingo, tried by a court of *civilized* Spaniards, (the most gallant, chivalrous, people in Europe) condemned on *extorted* evidence, and *hanged in the presence of those on whom she had bestowed a thousand kindnesses.*"[1]   *   *   *   *

" In commemoration of his *triumph* Ovando founded the town of *Santa Maria de la Verdadera Paz!'* (*holy Mary of true peace!*) But his conduct toward the Indians, especially of Zaraqua, filled Isabella with horror and indignation. She received the intelligence whilst languishing on her death bed, and exacted from Ferdinand a promise that he would recall Ovando from the government. But *the rich returns* which that officer made delayed the fulfilment of this promise for more than four years, and then his removal was induced by *other* causes "—Herrera—Oviedo—" The repeated description of cruelties," continues the historian, " is not a pleasant task ; but the *justice* of history should *not* relieve the Spanish nation from the *penalties* of her crimes," &c.   *   *   *   *   *

At this time there was a regular form of ecclesiastical government, the pope having granted authority for erecting

---

[1] " This distinguished princess," adds the historian, " was a favourite subject with the historians of that period. She is painted as eminently beautiful in form and feature, dignified and graceful in her manners; skilled in the *areyto* or traditionary *songs,* tender and susceptible."

archbishopricks, bishopricks, deaneries, parishes, and other spiritual divisions under the patronage of the king of Spain. And with a tact rarely pertaining to a devoted son of the church, Ovando circumscribed the papal power in his new possessions, by reserving to the crown the right to dispose of all benefices in America ; stipulating also, that no papal mandate should be promulgated there, until it had been approved by *his* counsel. Tithes were established for the support of the clergy—and adequate means were given for the erection of churches, and to prevent the inroads of *heresy,* the INQUISITION *extended here too its terrible powers.*[1]   Herrera, Gordon's Hist.

" The distance from Hispaniola to Cuba was only eighteen leagues, many of the distressed natives of the former had escaped thither. Among these was a Cacique Hatuay, who had raised himself to a distinguished rank in his adopted

---

[1] The Hermadad, or brotherhood of the city of Mexico, signified the members of the Inquisition who were styled *the Holy Brotherhood.* That the Inquisition was very active after its establishment in Mexico, we learn from the following passage of the twenty-fourth chapter of the fifth book of Torquemeda's Indian Monarchy. " In the year 1571, the HOLY OFFICE OF THE INQUISITION, *with its familiars,* arrived in New Spain and the city of Mexico. Don Pedro Morode Contreras, who was afterwards archbishop of this metropolis, and a man *skilled in the affairs of government, came as Inquisitor.* This *Holy Tribunal* has," he adds " been of the *greatest utility and advantage* in New Spain, and has *purified the soil which was most contaminated with Jews and heretics,*" &c.—Antiq. Mex. vol. vi. p. 153.

A curious panegyric upon the Inquisition *(Moses being placed first on the list of inquisitors)* is pronounced by Betancourt in his Treatise concerning the City of Mexico, p. 29; it is in the original Spanish, the Commentator adds " When we consider the enormities which the Inquisition has perpetrated *in the name of religion,* and recollect how many victims of all ages have expiated *imaginary* crimes *in the flames,* it is impossible not to rejoice that the dungeons of that horrid tribunal are at last penetrated by the light of the sun—that its portals are thrown open—and its ' bridge of sighs ' is broken : and the pilgrims can now seek repose in those mouldering courts where once blazed the funereal piles."—Antiq. Mex. vol. vi. p. 525.

' There will be no person who will not wonder,' says Montesquieu, ' that *our* ancestors made the fame, fortune, and property of citizens depend on certain things which belonged less to law and reason than to *chance,* and that they should have used constantly those proofs which were neither connected with innocence nor guilt: what we now say of *those proofs,* posterity will say of *the torture,* and will never cease to wonder that *such a kind of proof* was generally in use for so many centuries, in the most enlightened part of the world.'—Clavegero.

country; which he prepared to defend against the invaders. He assembled his people; reminded them of the sufferings which the Spaniards had inflicted upon them, declaring that their *crimes* were the *tribute* which they rendered to the *God* whom *they* worshipped.[1] They come hither *only to seek and to find Him*—let us not keep Him among us, but *cast him into the sea*—for should we hide him in the bowels of the earth where he had his origin, the Spaniards would drag him thence."

At the conclusion of this speech the Indians commenced a *religious song and dance,* which they closed by *casting the piece of gold into the sea."*—Herrera.

" But this mystical devotion to their *invaders' god,* did not avert the approach of the Christians. Hatuey boldly met Valasquez on the shore, and strove in vain to drive him back to the ship." "After maintaining a desultory warfare for some months, he was made prisoner, and Valasquez considering him as a *slave* who had fled from labour, and taken arms against his *master* condemned him to be *burned to death.* When at the stake, a Franciscan friar,

---

[1] Of Vasca Nunez de Bilboa, the following circumstance is related by Father Ovale, in his Historical Relation. " He passed on to the lands of the Cacique Carata, who, not caring to enter into a war, received him peacefully and treated him as a friend. He had a kinsman—a lord that lived in a further country, and his name was Saran, who persuaded a neighbouring prince, called Comagre, to make a friendship with the Castilians; this prince had a very fine palace which astonished them, particularly when they saw in it a kind of oratory, some embalmed bodies lying covered with rich mantles, and many jewels, gold and pearls. The king caressed the Castilians and gave them presents: he had seven sons, and one of them more liberal, gave the Spaniards a present worth four thousand pesos of fine gold, and some pieces of rare workmanship; they weighed the gold, and taking the king's fifths, they began to divide the remainder. In the division two Castilians fell out about their share; the Cacique's son who had made the present, hearing the voice could not bear it, but coming up struck the balance with his foot where the gold was weighing, and threw it all on the ground, saying—' Is it possible you should enrage yourselves against each other about a thing that is unworthy of esteem;—that you leave the repose of your homes, and pass so many seas exposed to such dangers to trouble those who live quietly in their own country? Have some shame, Christians, and do not so value these things.' "—See Ovale in Pink. Coll. vol. xiv. p. 142.

labouring to *convert* him, promised him immediate admission to the joys of Heaven *if* he would *embrace the catholic faith.*"

Hatuay said, "Are there any Spaniards in that happy place of which you speak?" "Yes," replied the monk, "but only such as are worthy and good." "*The best of them,*" returned the indignant chief, "*have neither worth nor goodness; I will not go to the place where I may meet one of the accursed race.*"—Herrera in Clavegero.

"The king created a new office called *Repardidor los Indios.* By a census it appeared that the number of the Indians in Hayti, which in 1508 had amounted to sixty thousand had been reduced to fourteen thousand. These were divided into *lots* and *sold* to the highest bidder, a method of distribution which cruelly broke the ties of affection and vicinage, and added greatly to the sufferings of this devoted race, whilst the heavier burdens and more intolerable labours imposed by new masters, completed its misery and hastened its extinction."

" The Dominicians condemned the *repartiementos,* as contrary to natural justice, the precepts of Christianity, and sound policy; they were most vehement in testifying against them. In the year 1511, Montesino one of the most eminent preachers inveighed against this practice in the great church of St. Domingo. Don Diego Columbus, the principal officers of the colony, and the laymen, who had been his hearers, complained of the monk to his superiors, but they, instead of condemning, applauded his doctrine, *as alike serviceable to God and the king.*"—Herrera.

"The Franciscans took part with the laity to defend the *repartiementos,* but as they could not with decency give their avowed approbation to a system of oppression so repugnant to the spirit of religion, they endeavoured to palliate what they could not justify.[1] This opposition, so far from inducing the Dominicans to relax in their measures, incited them to take a more lofty position. They declared the slavery of the Indians a *grievous sin* and refused to absolve or admit to the sacrament such of their countrymen, as continued to hold the natives in servitude."

" Both parties applied to the king and sent deputies to support their respective opinions. Ferdinand referred this important subject to a committee of his privy council, assisted by the most eminent civilians and divines of Spain. After a long discussion, the *speculative* point in controversy was determined in favour of the Dominicans. The Indians were *declared a free people and entitled to all the natural rights of men.* But notwithstanding this decision, the *repartiementos were not discontinued.* At length Ferdinand issued a decree of his privy council, declaring, that after mature consideration of *the apostolic bull,* and other titles, by which the crown of Castile claimed its possessions in the New World, the *servitude* of the Indians was *warranted by the laws both of God and man.* That unless they were subjected to the dominion of the *Spaniards* and compelled to reside *under their inspection,* it would be *impossible to reclaim them from idolatry!* or to instruct them in the *holy Catholic faith*—that no further scruple should be entertained about the *repartiementos,* as the king and council were willing to take the charge of that upon their own consciences—and that the Dominicans and monks of other religious orders should *abstain* from those invectives which by the *excess of charitable,* but ill-informed zeal, they had uttered *against* the practice.'

' The true reason of this decree will be found in the fact that the bishop of Fonesca, the principal director of

---

[1] Herrera, Oviedo.

American affairs, had *eight hundred Indians as his property.*
The commander, Lope de Conchillos, his chief associate,
had also considerable numbers in the Island of Hispaniola,
Porto Rica, Cuba, and Jamaica."—Herrera, decade i. lib.
ix. chap. 14.

'The inhuman measures of Albuquerque revived the
zeal of the Dominicans, and called forth an advocate for
the afflicted Indians, who possessed the courage, talents,
and activity requisite to support a desperate cause. Bartholomew Las Casas accepted an allotment of Indians, but
surrendered all that fell to his share; declaring that he
should ever bewail his misfortunes and guilt in having
exercised, even for a moment, this impious dominion over
his fellow-creatures. From that time he became the
avowed patron of the Indians, and by his manly interposition in their behalf, and the respect imposed by his
abilities and character, he succeeded in setting some bounds
to the excesses of the Spaniards. He determined to proceed to Spain, having the most sanguine hopes of opening
the eyes and softening the heart of the king by that picture
of the oppression of his subjects which he would exhibit to
his view.'—Herrera, Davilla, Padilla in Claveg.

'He represented to the monarch whom he found in a
declining state, all the fatal effects of the *repartimientos,*
boldly charging him with the guilt of this impious measure,
which had brought *misery and destruction upon a numerous
and innocent race of men,* whom providence had placed under
his *protection.* Ferdinand, whose mind and body were en-
feebled by disease, was alarmed at the charge of impiety—
he listened with deep compunction, and promised seriously to
consider of the means of redressing the evil, but *death prevented* him from executing his resolution.' Herrera, Davilla, Padilla in Clavegero.

' The regent of Castile sent three monks, of the order of
St. Jerome, together with a lawyer of probity, empowered
to regulate all judicial proceedings. Las Casas was appointed to accompany them with the title of ' Protector of
the Indians.' Immediately on their arrival, the superintendants began to exercise their power. The first act was
the liberation of all Indians who had been granted to persons not residing in America.'

' They, fearful of taking any *imprudent* step, deemed it
necessary to *tolerate* the *repartiemientos,* and to suffer the
Indians to remain *under subjection to their Spanish masters:*
they however endeavoured to moderate the evils of *this
policy,* &c. Las Casas was dissatisfied. The enslavement
of the Indians was avowedly *unrighteous,* and a violation
of the soundest, clearest principles of *natural justice and
human right, and productive of a mass of misery which nothing
but the grossest avarice would dare to weigh against the
molten gold,* &c. He therefore justly regarded the sacrifice of
these principles as an unhallowed and timid policy ; and, as
' Protector of the Indians,' he expressed his opinion with
zeal, perhaps with intemperance, and boldly demanded that
the superintendants should *not* bereave the natives of the
common rights of mankind. They received his most im-
passioned remonstrances without emotion, and pertinaciously
adhered to their own system. But the colonists did not
bear with him so patiently, they threatened violence to his
person, and he found it necessary to seek shelter in a convent. Perceiving his efforts in America to be fruitless, he
returned to Europe with a fixed resolution not to abandon
a people so cruelly oppressed. On his return to Spain,
Las Casas applied to the new ministers with assiduity
and address, and in despite of Father Monçanedo, whom
the colonists sent to Spain to resist his appeal, his exertions

to obtain a reconsideration of the measures relating to the
Indians were successful. The fathers of St. Jerome were
called together with their associate Zuago,' &c.   *   *   *

  " Sir Francis Drake, who landed at Hayti in 1585, states
that the Spaniards had *then utterly exterminated the ancient
race*. The means by which this astonishing destruction was
effected are summed up with honest indignation by Doctor
Edwards.   " The Spaniards distributed them into lots, and
compelled them to dig in the mines without rest or inter-
mission, until death, their only refuge, put a period to their
sufferings.   Such as attempted resistance or escape, their
merciless tyrants *hunted down with dogs which were fed on
their flesh*. They disregarded sex and age, and with *impious
and frantic rage and bigotry, even called in religion
to sanction their cruelties*. Some more zealous than the
rest, *forced* their miserable captives into the water,
and after administering the rite of baptism, *cut their
throats*, the next moment, to *prevent their apostacy!*
Others made a *vow*, to *hang or burn thirteen every morning
in honour of the Saviour and his apostles!* Nor were these
excesses only the result of a fanaticism, which exciting our
abhorrence also excites our pity. The Spaniards were
actuated in many instances by such wantonness of *malice* as
is wholly *unexampled in the wide history of human depravity*." Martyr relates that " it was a frequent practice
among them to murder the Indians of Hispaniola *in sport*,
and merely to keep *their hands in use*." " They had an
emulation which of them could most dextrously strike off the
head of a man at a blow, and wagers frequently depended on
this hellish exercise.[1] To fill up the measure of their iniquity,
and *demonstrate to the world that the nation at large par-
ticipated* in the guilt of individuals, the *court of Spain* not

[1] Martyr, Dec. i. lib. 7.

only *neglected* to punish these enormities in its subjects, but when rapacity and avarice had nearly defeated their own purposes by the extirpation of the natives of Hispaniola, *the king gave permission to seize perfidiously on the unsuspecting inhabitants of the neighbouring islands, and transport them to perish in the mines of San Domingo."* Edwards, vol. i, b. 1, c. 3. Gordon's Hist.

*   *   *   *   *   *   *

' Doomed to intolerable labour, *extorted by the lash*, if they fled from the hated toil, they were ' *hunted*' like wild beasts, and when taken, cruelly scourged and laden with chains. Many perished of famine in the forests and mountains—thousands died under their labours, before their stipulated time had expired. The survivors were put forth, to return to their homes without the means of subsistance— exhausted by toil and hunger many sunk by the way." " I have found many," says Las Casas, " dead in the road, others gasping under the trees, and others in the pangs of death, faintly calling for food! Those who reached their homes commonly found them desolate. During their long absence, their wives and children had perished or wandered away, their fields were overgrown with weeds, and their only consolation was, the hope of a speedy death at the threshold of their once happy [1] dwellings. Self-destruction rescued many from insupportable tyranny—and mothers for *very love* of their children, deprived them of the life they had given.'

' Hayti, at the time of its discovery, contained one million of inhabitants, but according to Peter Martyr, who wrote on the authority of Columbus, 1,200,000. Yet twelve years had not elapsed, when this population, so lately endowed with peace, plenty, and ease, was reduced to one-

[1] Las Casas, cap. 14. Irving's col.

sixth of its original number, and that remnant was steeped in the depths of misery.' Martyr, dec. 3, lib. 8. in Gordon's History.

" The inhabitants of the province of Higuey had a peculiarly warlike character, their chief, *Cotubanama*, was remarkable for his size, strength, and courage. Las Casas says he was the tallest and strongest of his tribe, and more perfectly formed than one of a thousand of any nation whatever; that he was a yard in breadth from shoulder to shoulder, and finely proportioned. One of his subordinate chiefs having been torn to pieces by a dog set on him by a Spaniard, his people in requital slew eight whites in the adjacent Island of Saona. To punish this offence, Ovando dispatched Juan de Esquebel at the head of four hundred men. *Cotubanama* prepared for the conflict, and justly distrustful of the sincerity of the Spaniards, refused all overtures of accommodation. The vast superiority of the *armed* Spaniards necessarily prevailed, and the Indians were driven to the mountains and forests, hunted like beasts of prey, and when taken, indiscriminately slaughtered.

The Island of Saona was desolated, the inhabitants made a desperate defence, and when overcome, sought a vain refuge in the caverns. Six hundred prisoners were deliberately massacred, and those who were spared were made slaves. Peace was at length granted at the prayer of *Cotubanama*, on condition that he would pay a large tribute of bread, and permit a fortress to be erected in his dominions. But the exactions of the Spaniards were not to be controlled by any stipulated treaty. When the stipulated grain was delivered, the Indians were required to transport it to San Domingo. The troops of the garrison behaved with their usual licentiousness, violently seizing the wives and daughters of the Indians, and at length were sacrificed to the vengeance of their relatives. *Indian prisoners were compelled by torture,* to tell their retreats. And when these places of refuge were discovered, the fugitives frequently, aged and infirm, women and children, were slaughtered without mercy. Some of the prisoners had their hands cut off, and were sent to *deliver them as letters* demanding their surrender. Numberless were those thus maimed. Others were hung on gibbets with their feet touching the ground, that they might die a *protracted* death. Thirteen were *religiously* hanged in *honour* of Christ and his disciples! Whilst thus suspended and living, their merciless executioners hewed them with their swords, to prove the strength of their arms and the edge of their weapons; and wrapping them in dry straw destroyed them in fiercest agony."

" The cacique *Cotabanama,* sought refuge amid the rocks and forests of Saona, but he was captured after a severe struggle with an athletic soldier. The captors of the chief proposed to *broil* him to death, but abandoned their fiendish design, that his fate might be decided by Ovando himself. The governor who felt not that regard for his captive, which the *brave* feel for the brave, sentenced him to be *hanged.*"

" The religion of that age," adds the historian, " taught to believe that *all means* were lawful to make Christians; and that reducing the heathen to *slavery was a means of conversion as mild as it was profitable.*" Gordon's Hist. vol. i. p. 296.

" The people of Spain were no longer eager to rush to the new world; neither ships nor men could be procured without difficulty. At the instance of Columbus, the sentence of criminals condemned to the galleys, was commuted to transportation to the colonies, to labour there in the public service; and a general pardon was proclaimed to all *malefactors* who should embark for Hispaniola. By these wretched expedients, the Admiral sowed the seeds of many sorrows to the already oppressed natives."

" Ovando had been appointed to succeed Bobadilla, who was recalled for his surpassing cruelties in the new world. He had encouraged the wildest excesses—and enforced the merciless partition of the people among his adherents. *Thus sustained, the convicts from the dungeons of Castile became the most wanton and savage tyrants.* They drove the wretched Indians in crowds to the mountains, to labour in the mines, without mercy or discretion. They reduced the wives and daughters of the princes of the country to the condition of domestic servants, subject to the most horrid indignities. They enforced the attendance of a large train of servants, and were borne on the shoulders of some, whilst others with umbrellas of palm-leaves were obliged to protect them from the scorching beams of the sun—or cooled them with fans of party-coloured feathers. They addressed the Indians in the most degrading terms, and on the slightest pretence, or freak of ill-humour, inflicted blows, and death itself."—Herrera. Clavegero.

The rapid annihilation of the Indian people depriving their colonists of their accustomed instruments of labour, Ovando suggested a remedy, which was to transport the inhabitants of the Lucayan Islands to Hispaniola. The natives of these Islands, it was said, would be *easily civilized and instructed* in religion, if *united* to the Spanish colony, and placed *under the eye of* missionaries. The king could not be deceived as to the *real motive* of the proposal, yet he readily gave his consent. Vessels were accordingly fitted out for the Lucayas, whose commanders, *now* acquainted with the Indian language, informed the natives that they came from *that delightful Land in which their ancestors* [1] dwelt—for the

---

[1] " An early traveller mentions a tribe who burst into tears at the sight of a *stranger*—the reason of this was in consequence of a *tradition* which taught them

purpose of carrying them *thither*, to participate *with them* in scenes of never-ending blessedness." Rejoicing in the prospect of partaking in the happy state of their forefathers, they followed the Spaniards with alacrity. More than 4000 were thus *betrayed* into the miseries which overwhelmed the natives of Hayti, whilst their betrayers glorified themselves in the simplicity of their victims."—Herrera decade i. b. 1. c. I, in Clavegero.

Peter Martyr, of the afflicted Lucayans, observes, "many of them, in the anguish of despair, obstinately refused all manner of subsistence, and retiring to desert caves and unfrequented woods, silently gave up the ghost." * * *

" Others, repairing to the sea coast on the southern side of Hispaniola, cast many longing looks towards that part of the ocean where they supposed their own Islands to be situated ; and as the sea breeze rises, they eagerly inhale it, fondly believing that it has lately visited their own happy shores and vallies, and comes fraught with the breath of those they love—their wives, parents, and children. With this idea they continue for hours on the coast, until nature becomes utterly exhaused ; when, stretching forth their arms towards the ocean, as if to take a last embrace of their distant country and relations, they sink down and expire without a struggle."—Irving's Life of Columbus.

at some future period to expect to be *recalled by their ancients*—these they suppose to have gone on a long journey, and are in constant expectation of their return."—Picart's Ceremonies and Religious Customs.

" *J'ai passé moi même,*" says Chateaubriand in his ' *Souvenir d' Amerique,*' " *chez une peuplade Indienne qui se prenait à pleurer a la vue d'une voyageur parce qu'il lui rappelait des amis partis pour la contrée des âmes, et depuis long tems en voyage.*" The following touching lines, with allusion to this reminiscence of their's, is from the pen of the late lamented Mrs. Hemans.—entitled, ' The Stranger in Lousiana.'

" Where are they ?—thou'rt seeking some distant coast—
Oh, ask of them, stranger !—*send back the lost !*
Tell them we mourn by the dark blue streams
Tell them our lives *but of them* are dreams—
Tell how we *sat* in the gloom to pine
And to *watch for a step*—but the step was thine."

" It was certainly not a work like Dr. Sepulvedas (in the justification of slavery) but a decree of Charles the Fifth, who had taken the advice of *all the learned* in the land, and consulted the Spanish *universities,* whose fame in *theology* was in that age great—that doomed the inhabitants of the islands and continent of America to *slavery.*[1]   This decree was sanctioned by *the council of the Indies;* and a more solemn act could not have emanated from higher constituted authorities.   If it was reversed many years afterwards, this was in consequence of the evils which followed; but was *no condemnation* of a *conceded* point in *divinity and law.*   Those who may wish to learn more of the opinion of the fifteenth and sixteenth centuries on slavery, may consult the writings of Las Casas, and of Dr. Sepulveda, whose work has been termed by later authors a *" bloody-book;"*[2] but Las Casas' pathetic narration entitled *" The Destruction of the Indians,"* by which he endeavours to excite the compassion of the sovereign toward his Indian subjects, deserves still more that appellation, since every page describes some new scene of bloodshed and slaughter; whole provinces are there represented as depopulated; *for the sake of working the mines* thousands are caused to perish; while pearl fisheries,

---

[1] Clavegero thus writes, ' The Europeans never did less credit to their own reason than when they denied rationally to the tribes of America, " and that their state of civilization was sufficient to have corrected that error if it had not been the interest of *the inhuman avarice of some ruffians* to encourage it."   He adds in a note, ' I must refer the reader to the bitter complaints made by the Bishop Garcès, in a letter to Pope Paul III. and by the Bishop of Las Casas, in his Memorials to the Catholic kings Charles V. and Philip II. but especially to the first Bishop of Mexico and Bartholomew Las Casas, first Bishop of Chiapa.'

[2] " Sepulveda, a Spanish divine, wrote a *Justification* of the wars against the Indians.   He requested permission of the Royal Council to print it, but they virtuously refused.   They regarded the subject rather as theological than political, and referred it to the Universities of Alcala and Salamanca ; who both pronounced that it ought not to be committed to the press. The fanatical author being determined to carry his point, sent his book to Rome, where it was printed, but the humane Emperor prohibited its circulation."—See Purchase, book iv. p. 1568. Rees' Cyclo. Casas, Sepulveda.

and the sugar plantations, &c. swept away the scanty remains of the Indian population. Is it then to be imputed to Las Casas as a *crime*, his *pitying* the Indians, whom a long residence among them had taught to consider them as his children, when he beheld them sinking under their burdens? &c. Antiq. of Mex. vol. vi.

Las Casas has by the oppressors of the Indians been called a fanatic, *his* fanaticism was merely an ardent desire to ' *oppose* the dignity of his sacerdotal character and acknowledged talents and learning and the mildness of age, to brutal oppression and injustice.'

" Did they not," says Las Casas, "receive the Spaniards who first came among them with gentleness and humanity? Did they not shew more joy in proportion in lavishing treasures upon them than the Spanards were greedy in receiving them? But our covetousness was not yet satisfied: though *they gave* up to us their riches and their lands, we would *also take from them their wives and children and liberty.* I take God to witness of this, and all the hierarchies and thrones of angels, and the saints of the heavenly court, and all men living ; I also discharge my conscience by declaring that if his majesty should grant the *repartiementos* to the Spaniards, the Indies in a short time will be a desert like Hispaniola."

" Las Casas charged his countrymen, with having massacred above forty millions in less than fifty years ; he enumerates millions slaughtered in Honduras, Venezula, Peru, Mexico, Hispaniola, ; sixty thousand in Jamaica ; while new reinforcements were abducted from the provinces and islands."

" Columbus and his crew were welcomed by the Lucayans with a kindness truly patriarchial, but scarcely had twenty years elapsed before their anti-christian invaders transported them by force or by *artifice* to the mines of Hispaniola. They survived but a few years under the dominion of their oppressors."—Clavegero, Irving's Life of Col.   *   *

The instructions given to Ojida were of the most extraordinary character, and as they contain a *formal exposition of the Spanish right to the possession of the Islands and Continent of America,* certainly merit our attention.

'The commander was required as servant of the kings of Castile and Leon, the conquerors of barbarous nations, to declare to the Indians, that God one and eternal had created the heavens and the earth, and one man and woman from whom they all were descended. But as during the long period of more than five thousand years, the human race had, because one country could not contain them, scattered over the face of the globe, *God had given absolute authority over the whole* to one man named Saint Peter, and to bear the name of *Pope,* which signifies Great Father: and that his power had been continued to *his successors,* and would be continued to the end of the world: and that one of those Popes had *granted* to the catholic king Ferdinand and his queen Isabella, and their successors, *all the Islands and Continents* of the ocean sea ; as was fully expressed in *certain deeds,* which he would exhibit if requested : that most of the Islands where *his title* had been declared, had recognized it ; and had obeyed the religious men sent by the king to instruct the inhabitants in *this holy faith ;* who having become Christians, were received under his most gracious protection, and were treated as his other subjects and vassals. The commissioners were also instructed to proclaim to the nation of *Terra firma,* that they were bound to like obedience, and that if after due reflection they acknowledged the *supremacy of the Church*—the Pope *in his own right,* and his majesty by *his appointment, as the sovereign lord of all these countries ;* and consent to receive *the holy doctrines* of the Church, his majesty would extend to them his love, and would leave their wives and children free from servitude, and themselves in the enjoyment of all they possessed, *in the same manner* as he had done to the inhabitants of the Islands," &c. " But that in case of refusal or *malicious* delay to obey these injunctions, he would enter their country with the horrors of war ; subject the inhabitants to the *yoke of the Church and the crown,* carrying them and their wives and children into *slavery, and do them all possible mischief as rebellious* subjects.[1] And that all the bloodshed and calamities which might follow, should be imputed, *not to his majesty or his agents,* but to their own disobedience." Herrera, dec. 1, lib. 7, c, 14, in Gordon's Hist.

The terms of the Papal bull are " *Out of our mere libe-*

---

[1] ' Some of the first European settlers,' observes Clavegero, ' not less powerful than avaricious, desirous of enriching themselves to the detriment of the Indians, made use of them as slaves; and in order to avoid the reproaches which were made them by the bishops, &c. alleged that the Indians were by nature slaves, and incapable of being instructed; and many other falsehoods, which the chronicler Herrera, mentions against them. Those zealous bishops being unable, either by their authority or preaching, to rescue those unhappy *converts* from the tyranny of such misers, had recourse to the catholic kings. Garcea, bishop of Tlascala, knowing that those Spaniards bore, notwithstanding their perverseness, a great respect to the decisions of the vicar of Jesus Christ, made application in the year 1586 to Pope Paul III. representing to him the evils which the Indians suffered from the *wicked Christians,* and praying him to interpose his authority in their behalf. The Pope moved by such heavy remonstrances, dispatched the original bull, &c. which was *not* made, as is manifest, to declare the Americans *free men ;* for *such a piece of weakness was very distant from that or any other Pope ;* but solely to support the *natural rights* of the native Americans against the attempts of their oppressors, and to condemn the injustice and inhumanity of those who under the *pretence of supposing the people idolatrous, or incapable* of being instructed in the Christian faith, *took from them* their property and liberty, and treated them as slaves and beasts.' See Clavegero, Dissert. 5, b. 546.

" Pope Alex. VI. was the Pontiff who was in the chair of St. Peter : and as in modern times secret articles are sometimes found to have been inserted in treaties, what secret stipulations might not the Court of Rome have made with Spain, when, in the plenitude of long recognized and revered power, she granted to her nearly the whole new world ? And what return could have been too great to have shewed the gratitude of an obedient daughter of the church for such a gift? It would appear that whether she wished or no to conceal from Europe a fact which she feared might shake its institutions, shock and confound the prejudices

rality and certain *science, and from the fulness*[1] *of our apostolic power ;* by the authority of Almighty God, to *us* given *through Saint Peter,*[2] we give, grant, and assign," &c. &c. " Shall we admire most the *justice* of this manifesto, the *strength* of the title which it sets forth, or the grave adherence to municipal form which attended its proclamation? Had they understood the *nature* of the subjection demanded of them, they must have considered the church and prince most gracious and worthy of obedience, who *mercifully* and *disinterestedly* proffered to them—the unburdened denizens of the forest—the enjoyment of *liberty, and full participation in the blessings showered on the inhabitants of Hispaniola!* " Gordon's Hist. vol. ii. p. 64.

of ages, &c. she took all the precautions which she could have done, had she really entertained such a fear."

" But the secret (the consequences of which if openly divulged could not have been calculated) that the Spaniards did discover on their first arrival on the continent of America, Judaism, &c. the policy of the age, and of the Spanish court, (where the highest dignitaries of the church occupied, likewise the chief places of the cabinet) firmly resolved to consign to everlasting oblivion." Antiq. of Mexico, vol. iv. p. 111.

[1] *De nostra merâ liberalitate, et ex certâ sciencâ ae de apostolicæ potestatis plenitudine. Autoritate omnipotentis Dei nobis in beato Petro concessa donamus, concedimus et assignamus, &c. &c.*

[2] See Appendix.

THE MEXICAN EMPIRE.

'The Mexican Empire,'[1] according to Clavegero, 'was comprehended between the 14th and 21st degrees of north latitude; and between 271 and 283 degrees west longitude, from the meridian of Ferro. The vale of Mexico was magnificently crowned with verdant mountains whose circumference at their base exceeded 120 miles,' and environed by about forty eminent cities, while innumerable villages and hamlets were scattered throughout this delightful valley, great part of which was occupied by two lakes; one of sweet and pure water, the other impregnated with salt.

'The Toltics,' observes Clavegero, vol. i. p. 84, ' are the oldest nation of which we have any knowledge ; and that is very imperfect. They affirmed that they had been banished from their mother country, *Hue-hue-Tlapallan* (ancient land of the Red Sea.) The seven lineages who afterwards inhabited that country, and called it Mexico, affirmed that they had originally come from Aztlan or Teo-*Acolhuacan* (land of God) and declared it to be near *Amequemacan.*' Garcia, p. 182, in Antiq. Mex.

'The city of Mexico was at first called *Tenoch-titlan,* after one of the ten chiefs of their lineage.' Gage observes, ' that this name was probably derived from Tenoch, the first chief.'

As the jubilee of the Mexicans occurred every fifty-two

---

[1] For a late statistical notice of the Mexican empire, see Appendix.

years, when the reign of each monarch terminated, and as it
was customary to elect the new king or viceroy, on the
arrival of that period, it is highly probable that the city of
Mexico received that name at the first jubilee after their
settlement, in honour of the Messiah, whom they so devoutly
expected, when *Acampitzen* the first king was *anointed* and
crowned. In the reign of *Itzcoatl,* grandson of this monarch,
academies were instituted for the study of astronomy,[1]
music, painting, history, and poetry.[2]

The city Tescuco, was divided into thirty districts, and
each of these was assigned to the arts of sculpture, jewel-
making, weaving, &c. Temples, edifices, and gardens were
constructed by *Nezahualcozotl.*

" Nezahualcozotl made eighty laws which have been recorded in MS. He ordered that law-suits and trials for
crimes should only last eight days, &c. ; he was very charitable to the destitute, to old people, and to widows. To
prevent bribery, he ordered that the judges should be maintained and clothed, at the expense of government, according

---

[1] See Appendix.

[2] In the cultivation of poetry and dramatic composition, the Mexicans were
not deficient. 'Many of their expressions,' observes Clavegero, 'are so strong,
that they cannot be heightened, especially on the subject of love. In short, all
those who have heard and learned this language, and can judge of its copiousness,
regularity, and beautiful modes of speech, are of opinion that such a language
could not have been spoken by a barbarous nation. A people possessed of so
powerful a language could neither want orators nor poets. Even at present,
(1750) reduced as they aae to a state of *great humiliation,* and retaining not
their ancient institutions, they make orations in their assembles which are so
replete with good sense and propriety, as to excite the admiration of all who
hear them. The number of their orators was exceeded by that of their poets,
in their verses they were attentive to cadence and measure. Their subjects were
various; they composed sacred songs in praise of their God, or to obtain what
they stood in need of, &c. Orazio Carroci, a Milanese Jesuit, published some
eloquent verses of the ancient Mexicans about the middle of the last century;
these were sung in the temples at their sacred dances. It is related that one of
the poets who was imprisoned for some misdemeanour, composed a dirge in
prison, in which he took leave of the world, in so tender and touching a style,
that the musicians of the palace, who were his friends, advised him to sing it to
the king, who was himself a celebrated poet and lover of music, was so much
affected, that (his crime not having been of the first degree) he granted him
pardon.

to their rank. The progress which this king made in the arts and sciences was indeed extraordinary. He was an eminent poet himself, and many of his productions were highly esteemed. He composed sixty hymns in honour of the Creator of Heaven which were very much thought of by the Spaniards ; and his odes or songs, which were translated into Spanish by his descendant, Don Ferdinando Alva Ixtlilxochitl, have been preserved to our days. He had also knowledge of astronomy, and applied himself to the knowledge of plants and animals."—See Bullock's Travels.

Montezuma (archer of Heaven) was the fifth in order, and was celebrated as a conqueror. His first care was to erect a great Temple.

*   *   *   *   *

The governor of Chalco having rebelled, seized the brother of Montezuma, proposing that he should become the king of that city which might then rival that of Mexico. After much solicitation he appeared ready to consent, but proposed first to make an address to the people from a commanding height. A kind of scaffold having been raised on a high tree in the market-place, he addressed those who frequented that place, on the virtue of being faithful, which is preferable to life itself; when he instantly precipitated himself to the ground, and was killed. See Hist. Researches.

Montezuma, in revenge, sacked their city.   *   *   * *   *   The king died feared and beloved ; he was sober, prudent, and just; he made new regulations, and added much splendour to his court.

"The year 1470 was distinguished by the death of Nezahualpilli, king of Acolhuacan, the Solon of Anahuac, and who made Tescuco the Athens of America. He lived eighty years, and reigned forty-four." " During his reign, crimes were infallibly punished. No suit, civil or criminal, could remain undecided more than eighty days. He supported the aged and destitute. He studied the stars, plants, and animals. He deplored to his son the adoration of idols, &c. but felt himself constrained to conform to customs which were established. He erected in honour of the Creator, a tower consisting of nine floors. The upper one was dark, vaulted, and painted blue, and had a cornice of gold. Men resided here to strike plates of fine metal, at certain hours, when the king kneeled and prayed to the Creator of Heaven, to whom he composed sixty hymns; and also two odes or sacred songs which have been translated into Spanish." Hist. Resear. ch. 7, p. 309-10. The people were persuaded that he was *translated*; historians, on the other hand, have concluded that he must have been *secretly burned*.

Ahuitzotl was the eighth king of Mexico. He erected a magnificent Temple, and in four years after the foundation stone was laid, more people assembled to solemnize its dedication than had ever collected on any former festival. Clavegero says, ' some authors affirm that there were six millions.' Vol. i. p. 201. This sovereign was said to have been capricious and tyrannical, but so fond of music, that it was heard in the palace night and day. He raised Mexico to be the first city in the New World. Not having had sons his younger brother Montezuma[1] was elected in preference to the others.

---

[1] He was called Montezumazin for dignity.

ADMINISTRATION OF THE LAW.

" AXAJACATL was elected in preference to his elder brothers *Tizoc* and *Awhitzotl,* and, like] the kings of Israel,
they were inducted by presentation at the Temple, and by
anointing, prayer, sacrifice and incense. When this act
of religion was performed, during which *the king remained
on his knees,* the high-priest sate down and delivered a
discourse to him, in which, after congratulating him on his
advancement, he informed him of the obligation he owed his
subjects, and warmly recommended to him zeal for *religion
and justice—the protection of the poor—and the defence
of his country and kingdom.* The allied princes and nobles
next addressed him *to the same purpose.*"

" After hearing these addresses, the king descended,
with all his attendants, to the lower area or court, where
the rest of the nobility waited to make their obedience, and
pay him homage, in jewels and apparel. He was thence
conducted to an *inner* part of the Temple, called *Tlacatecco,
where he was left alone* four *days, during which time he ate
but once a-day :* he bathed twice a-day, and after bathing
drew blood from his ears (an acknowledgment of having
heard[1] *truly and sincerely) which, with some incense, he
offered to the Most High, making all the while constant and
earnest prayers to obtain that enlightenment of the understanding which was requisite in order to govern his people*

---

[1] This was the " boring of the ear," which was introduced by Quetzalcoatl—
an act emblematic of opening the ear to wisdom, instead of, like the deaf adder,
wilfully closing it against her charming voice.

with discretion. On the fifth day the nobility returned to the Temple, conducting the new king to his palace, where the feudatory lords came to renew the investiture of their fiefs. Then followed the rejoicing of the people—entertainments, dances, and illuminations. It is here worthy of remark, in connection with these renewals of fiefs, that the inauguration of a monarch was always at their *jubilee* period of fifty-two years. No king could reign longer—and if any one died during that period, a regency conducted the government until the new election of a king."

" The power and authority of the kings of Mexico was different at different periods. In the earlier part of their monarchy, their authority was truly paternal, their conduct humane, and their prerogatives extremely moderate; with their conquests and the enlargement of their territory—the increase of their riches—their pomp and the burden on their subjects were multiplied. Notwithstanding the despotism of some of the Mexican kings, their subjects always preserved the respect which was due to their royalty, except that in the case of Montezuma, the ninth king, when no longer able to endure what they justly considered his *dishonourable subjection and subserviency to the Spanish domination,* they treated him with contempt, and wounded him *(as the guest of Cortez)* with arrows."

" The kings of *Acolhuan* rivalled in magnificence those of Mexico ; they had their supreme councils composed of the nobility, in which they deliberated upon the affairs of the government, &c. For the office of ambassador they always chose persons who were both illustrious and eloquent. To entitle them to sacred regard, they wore certain badges by which they were everywhere known,—particularly by a green scapulary, or square cloak, which the religious orders wear, from which hung some *fringes,* or locks of cotton."

" The titles of the Mexicans were chiefly hereditary,—even till the downfall of the empire many families, illustriously descended, preserved their splendour ; and several branches of those most ancient lineages are still existing, though reduced by misfortunes, and obscured and confused among the vulgar. [1]

A custom, evidently of Hebrew derivation, characterized their inheritance of family lands, which were transmitted from father to son without the power to alienate, or sell. These lands were given by the kings, on the condition of their never being alienated. " The daughters were not allowed inheritance, lest the state should fall under the government of a *stranger.*"

" In the kingdom of Acolhuan, the judicial power was divided amongst seven principal cities. The judges remained in their tribunals from sun-rise till sun-set. Their meals were brought to them, *that they might not be taken off from their employment by the concerns of their families, nor have any excuse for being corrupted.* They were assigned possessions, and also labourers to cultivate their fields. Those possessions belonged to *their office,* and could not be inherited by their sons. Every Mexican month (twenty days) an assembly of Judges was held before the king, in order to determine all cases then undecided. If very intricate and perplexed, they were, if not then decided, reserved for the grand solemn general assembly, which was held every eighty days, and was called the conference of the *eighty;* at which all

---

[1] Clavegero observes—' It is impossible to behold without regret the state of *degradation* to which some illustrious families of that kingdom have been reduced. Not very long ago, the Spaniards executed a *locksmith* who was a descendant of the ancient kings of *Michuan :* we knew a poor *tailor* in Mexico who was descended from the very noble house of *Cozcoacan,* but had been *deprived* of the possessions which he inherited from *his* illustrious ancestors. Examples of the same kind occur even among the royal families of Mexico, Alcohuan, and Tacuba.'— Clavegero, vol. vii. p. 347.

causes were finally disposed of, and punishment pronounced on the guilty. The king pronounced sentence by tracing a line with the point of an arrow on the head of the guilty person, which was *painted as an act of History.* In the tribunals, the contending parties made their own allegations. In criminal cases, the accuser was not allowed any other proof than that of his *witnesses;* but the accused person could clear himself from guilt by *his oath.*" This is purely a Hebrew custom, and practised among the Jews. Let any one compare the *morale* of this mode of administration with that of Britain at this day, and thus shall they be able to realize the *sense* of *omniscience* among this primitive people, as contrasted with the want of it among the nations of Christendom, who leave it entirely to the *eloquence* or *ingenuity* of their *advocate* to clear them of the consequence, if not of the *guilt*, which, in the first instance by *their advice*, they augment by denial.

"The punishment of death was inflicted on the seditious—on those who *removed* "*the land-marks*" placed by the laws, or changed the boundaries:—on those Judges also who gave an *unjust* sentence, or one *contrary* to the laws, or made an *unfaithful* report to the king, or superior magistrate, or *allowed themselves to be corrupted by bribes.*"

" He who committed any hostility upon the enemy, *without* the order of his chief; or attacked *before* the signal of battle was given; or *abandoned* the ensign; or *violated* any proclamation published to the army, was invariably beheaded."

" He who at market *altered* the measures established by law, was guilty of *felony*, and was put to death without delay *in the same place.*" Levit. xix. 35. Deut. xxv. 15.

" A murderer forfeited *his own life* for his crime, even although the person murdered was a slave. Levit. xx. 10.

Adultery, Levit. xx. 10, was inevitably punished with *death. Adulterers were stoned to death.* No divorce was lawful without the permission of the Judges. The husband was not permitted to inflict death in Mexico. He who desired a divorce, presented himself before the tribunal and explained his reasons for it. The Judges exhorted him to concord, and endeavoured to dissuade him from a separation ; but if he persisted in his claim, and his reasons appeared just, they *told him to do that which he judged most proper,* without giving *their* authority for a divorce by a *public* sentence. If, after all, he divorced his wife, he *never was permitted to recover her again."* Deut. xxiv. 4.

" Marriages between relations were strictly forbid by the law, except marriage between widows *and their brothers-in-law ;* for,' continues Clavegero, ' it was the custom among the Mexicans, as well as among the *Hebrews,* that the brother of the *deceased husband should marry their widowed sisters-in-law.'* He adds ' in some places which were remote from the capital, the nobles occasionally married their mother-in-law, provided their father had *no children* by her ; but in the capitals of Mexico and Tezcuco, and the neighbouring provincial cities, such marriages were deemed incestuous, and punished with severity." Levit. xviii. 6.

" Vicious men, in order to justify their own excesses, have attempted to defame the natives of America with detestable crimes ; but this calumny, which several European authors have too readily admitted, is proved to be false by the testimony of many other authors who are more impartial and *better informed."*

" According to their law *the man who dressed in the attire of a woman, or the woman who dressed herself in that of a man was hanged."* Deut. xxii. 5.

" The thief[1] of things of *value* was made the *slave of the person whom he robbed;* while he who stole *small* things had to make *restitution.* If the robber had no means of making restitution, and if the stolen goods were *not to be found,* he suffered death. He who stole *more* maize out of the field than satisfied hunger, or *pulled up* bearing fruit trees which were planted by the highway side, was made *slave of the owner of the field:* but every poor traveller was permitted to take of the maize, or the fruit of the trees, to *satisfy immediate hunger.*" Exod. xxii. 3—7, 12.

" He who robbed in the market-place was *there* bastinadoed to death."

" Guardians who *failed to give a good account of the estates of their charges were hanged without pardon.* Exod. xxii. 22. The same punishment was inflicted on sons who *squandered their patrimony in vices;* for they said it was a great *crime* not to set a higher value upon the labours of their fathers."

" He who practised *sorcery,* &c. was sacrified in the temples." Deut. xiii. 9.

" *Drunkenness* in *youth*[2] was a capital offence; young men were *put to death* by the bastinado; and young women were *stoned to death.* In men of advanced years, although not capital, it was punished with severity. If a nobleman, he was stripped of his rank and office, and rendered *infamous;* and if a plebian, they *shaved his head* (a punishment sensibly felt by them) *and demolished his house,* saying, that he who could voluntarily *bereave himself of his senses, was not worthy of a habitation amongst men.* This law

---

[1] Lycurgus permitted theft to the Lacedemonians.

[2] In Europe, drunkenness is frequently urged and admitted as an apology for those excesses to which it necessarily leads ; governments derive revenues from the sale of this instigator to crime—while to these crimes they afterwards award an ignominious death.

did not forbid conviviality at nuptials and other festive occasions." Deut. xxi. 20.

" He who told a *lie* to the prejudice of another, had a *part of his lip cut off.*" Levit. vi. 2.

" He who maliciously contrived to *sow discord* between states was *tied to a tree and burned.*" Prov. vi. 19.

" In the legislature of Acolhuan, if a *nobleman* was intoxicated to the *losing of his senses, he was thrown into a river or lake;* if a *plebian,* for the *first* offence, he lost his *liberty,* for the *second* his *life.* And when the legislator was asked why the law was more severe upon nobles than others, he answered that the crime of drunkenness was *less* pardonable in them, as *they were bound in duty to set a good example.* The same king prescribed the punishment of *death* to those *Historians who should introduce lies into their paintings.*"

" Sons were *stoned to death if declared by their parents to be refractory and rebellious.*" Deut. xxi. 18, &c.

" The senate even prescribed death for such as were *wanting* in duty and respect."

" Incontinence was *rigorously* punished. The punishment of the *tree fork,* or gallows, was the most *ignominious.* That of *banishment* was also deemed *infamous,* as it is supposed the guilty person possessed of *infectious vice.*"

      *   *   *   *   *   *

" Each of the three chief ranks in the army had its distinctive order; one was the chief *man*—another the *eagle*— and the third the *buffalo.* Those belonging to the prince, or chief, or man order, were the highest. To this order, Montezuma the second belonged." Numb. i. 53.

" In first going out to war, even princes of the royal household were required to give some proofs of their courage before they were permitted to change the plain coarse white habit assigned them for another more costly."

" They used shields and breast-plates, and wore on their heads plumes of the most beautiful feathers in battle. The common soldiers were nearly naked, but they coloured their bodies to counterfeit dress. The offensive arms of the Mexicans were arrows, slings, spears, pikes or javelins, swords and darts. Some of their bows required more than five feet of string. They had also standards and musical instruments proper for war. Their standards were staves from eight to ten feet long, on which they bore the *ensigns* of the state, made of gold, feathers and gems. The *armorial ensign* of the Mexican empire was an *eagle* in the act of darting on a *tiger* ; that of Tlascala the republic, was an eagle with expanded wings."

"Those standards were so firmly attached to the person of the bearers, that they could not be seized without cutting him to pieces. The Mexicans placed their standard in the centre of the army. The Tlascalans placed their's in the van, but in times of war in the rear. They made use of various kinds of entrenchments."

*   *   *   *   *   *

" The Spaniards unanimously praise the beauty and extent of the many gardens. Cortez, in his letter to Charles V. of May, 1522, told him that the garden of *Huaxtepec* was the most extensive, and beautiful, and delightful which he had ever beheld. *Bernal Dias*, in chap. 142 of his History, says,—"that the gardens were most wonderful, and worthy of a great prince." Hernandez the naturalist frequently eulogises them in his valuable work. Every kind of medical herb[1] was cultivated in these admirable gardens, some of which were *hanging gardens, and on the lake.*"—

---

[1] See Appendix.

ARTS AND SCIENCES.

In order to convey some idea of the markets, or rather fairs of Mexico, and the other principal cities, so much celebrated by the historians, it will be sufficient to notice that held in the capital. ' Cortez described this as twice as large as that of Salamanca (one of the most famous in Spain) and surrounded by porticos for the convenience of the merchants. Every sort of merchandise had a particular place allotted to it by the judges of commerce; the number of merchants who daily assembled there according to the affirmation of Cortez exceeded fifty thousand. Clavegero says, ' that every five days this number collected, that there were every day assembled from twenty to twenty-five thousand, but at these great markets fifty thousand.' (See b., 7· p. 385.) He adds of the historians who attempt to describe them, that ' after a tedious enumeration, they conclude by saying it is impossible to express them all.' ' All the productions of the empire and adjacent countries were brought to be sold or exchanged in that vast square—all that could serve for the necessaries of life, the conveniences, the luxury, the vanity, the curiosity of man, were there ; innumerable species of animals dead and alive, every sort of eatable, all the metals and gems, medical drugs, simples, gums, oils, minerals, prepared medicines, beverages, ointments, electaries, and every sort of manufacture, embroidery, &c. The potters, goldsmiths, jewellers, painters, stone-cutters, hunters, fishers, the fruiterers of hot countries, mat-weavers, chair-makers, and florests of *Xochimlico*, all assembled there.'

' Certain commissioners were continually traversing the market to observe what happened, and prevent disorder. At the market of Tlascala, *Cortez* states that above three thousand assembled, of merchants and others. *Motolina* mentions that forty years after the conquest, when com-ₐ merce had greatly declined, at the fifth day market, there were not less than eight thousand European hens sold, and that as many were sold at the market of *Acaplayocan.'*

' The gem most esteemed by the Mexicans was the *emerald,*[1] and they were so common that no lord or noble wanted them, and none of them died without having one placed on his body *as his heart.* An immensely large and valuable one, which the pious zeal of the first bishop induced him to reduce to powder, was called ' the HEART of the people.' It will be recollected that the stone of Aaron's breastplate, which represented Judah, was the emerald.

Acosta says, that " when Cortez entered Mexico, it contained 60,000 houses, in each of which there are two, three, and in some ten persons, by reason of which the city is wonderfully replenished with people." " The market-place,

---

[1] *Gomara* affirms "that amongst other inestimable gems which *Cortez* took with him on his first return to Spain, he had five emeralds valued at 100,000 ducats, and for one of them a Genevese merchant offered 40,000, in order to sell it again to the Grand Signor. This was formed into a cup with a foot and four little golden chains, which were united by a large pearl in the form of a button; he had also two emerald vases valued at 300,000 ducats, which vases were lost by shipwreck. At present no such gems are wrought, indeed the mine is now unknown whence they were brought.' After enumerating a list of valuable and exquisitely formed gems, metals, and manufactures, *Gomara* says, " All these were more valuable for the workmanship,* than even the materials. Their works of cast metal are not to be comprehended by our goldsmiths. This which was part of one of the many presents Montezuma made to Cortez, was sent by him to Charles v. in July 1519."

---

* The splendour of the market is to be seen where articles of gold and feathers jointly wrought, are sold. They make butterflies, wild beasts, trees, flowers, roses, herbs in so natural a manner, that it is marvellous to behold; and workmen will turn a feather in the sun to find out its proper shade and position with a wonderful patience, &c. The gold-smiths cast in moulds or engrave with tools made of flint. They will cast a platter with eight corners, some of which are gold without any soldering: also fish, each alternate scale on the back, being of gold or silver. They cast an ape in a mould, with the hands and feet moveable, holding a spindle in his hand, seeming to spin, and an apple as if to eat.' ' The Spaniards were surprised to find their goldsmiths were not to be compared with those of Mexico.' See Clavegero, b. 7, Sect. 80.

Cortez in his letters to 'the king of Spain, greatly extols the Mexican workmanship in gold, numerous specimens of which he transmitted to Spain. " What was sent to Spain, however exquisite the workmanship, *was melted by order of* the government ; for from the earliest period, to the last day of her possessing power in Mexico, *Spain studiously kept from the rest of the world all* information relative to her foreign dominions, and more particularly of New Spain." Antiq. Mex. p. 332.

every fourth day is sometimes attended by 100,000 persons who came to barter their commodities from all parts of the kingdom."

THE LAW OF SLAVES.

The laws of the Indians respecting slaves were patriarchal; ' Of these,' observes Clavegero, ' there were three kinds, the first were *prisoners of war* ; the second those who were *bought* for a valuable consideration ; the third were malefactors who were deprived of liberty in *punishment* of their crimes.' ' Among the Mexicans *a slave was allowed to have cattle, to acquire property, and to have other slaves to serve him ; nor could his owner hinder him, nor have service from such slaves ; for slavery was only an obligation of personal service, and even that was under certain restrictions. Nor was slavery entailed on the descendants of slaves. Owners could not sell their slaves without their consent : unless they were those who had become such for the punishment of their crimes.* Runaway, rebellious, or vicious slaves, had two or three warnings given them by their owners, which they gave for their justification in the presence of some witnesses ; if, *in spite of these admonitions,* the slaves did not mend their conduct, a wooden collar was put about their necks, and *then* it was lawful to sell them at market. If a slave, collared in this manner, happened to escape from his place of confinement, and took refuge in *the royal palace, he remained free ;* and the person who attempted to prevent his gaining this asylum, *forfeited his liberty* for the attempt, *except it were the owner, or one of his children,* who had a right to seize him. Slavery among the Mexicans was not hard to be borne ; their labour was

moderate, and their treatment humane: when their masters
died they generally became free.[1]

Respecting marriage, the Abbe Clavegero observes,
' Although in them, superstition had a share, nothing was
mingled with it which was in the least degree repugnant to
decency and honour.[2] Persons related in the first degrees
of consangunity *were strictly prohibited* to marry with each
other. *The parents settled all the marriages, and none were
ever executed without their consent.'* ' A favourable answer being obtained, and a day appointed for the nuptials,
the parents after exhorting their daughter to *fidelity and
obedience to her husband,* and to such conduct in life as
would do honour to her family, *conducted her with a numerous company and music to the house of her father-in-law;*
if noble she was carried in a litter. The bridegroom, together with his father and mother, received her at *the gate
of the house with four torches*[3] *borne by four women.* The
fire was kept lighted, and they sat down on a new and
curiously embroidered mat; while the priest tied the corner
of the robe of the bride, with the *tilmatli,* or mantle, of the

---

[1] The ancient Silenian law killed all the slaves at the death of their owner. The
Aquilian law made no distinction between a wound given to a slave, and that
given to a beast. But in none of the early periods of the world's history; and by
no heathen nation have slaves been so inhumanly treated as by the representatives of Christendom. The act of *stealing* them from their country, of itself constitutes a new feature of slavery, while the denial to them of human rights—
which is another term for their being the victims of irresponsible and arbitrary
power, is one of the anomalies of what have been erroneously called gospel *times.*

[2] Clavegero writes, " The Mexicans did not obtain their wives but by lawful
and honourable pretensions; and though they presented gifts to the parents,
they were given not as a price for the daughter, but merely as a piece of civility,"
&c. ' If a freeman married a bondwoman, he was not justified on the plea of his
love; for a man derogates from the dignity of human nature when he suffers any
passion to usurp the mastery over his reason.' He adds, ' The manners of the
Mexicans were virtuous and becoming, those of the Romans scandalous and
reprehensible.'

[3] The marriages of the Mexicans, like those of the Jews, were all by torch-
light—in the night: and to this our Lord alludes in his prophetic allusion to
his second coming, as the Bridegroom to His expecting and redeemed people.—
Matthew xxv. 5, 6.

bridegroom, and in this ceremony the matrimonial contract chiefly consisted. *They passed four days in prayer, and fasting, and burning incense.* On the fourth the marriage was consummated, bathing and making presents, and receiving visits followed.'

Clavegero observes, ' At the birth of a child these words were addressed to the infant on bathing it in water. ' *Receive this water*—may this bath cleanse the spots which thou bearest from thy mother's womb—purify thy heart, *and yield thee a good and perfect life.*' Then addressing her prayer to the Deity, she demanded blessings for the child, and taking up the water again with her right hand, she *breathed* upon it ; wetting the mouth, head, and breast of the child, saying, ' May the *invisible* God descend *upon* this water, and *cleanse* thee from every stain of *guilt* and impurity, and *redeem* thee from evil.' Then turning to the child, she addressed it thus : ' Lovely infant, the Gods have created thee in the highest heaven, in order to send thee into this world ; but know that the life to which thou art entering is sad and painful, and replete with trouble and misery ; nor wilt thou be enabled to eat thy bread without labour ; and may God assist thee in the many adversities which await thee.' Clavegero adds, ' the birth of male children are attended with solemnity and *superstition.*'

With respect to the ancient usages in burying the dead, the Abbe goes on to say, ' In the tombs of the rich *they put gold and jewels, &c.* The Spanish knowing of the gold which was buried with the Mexican lords in their tombs, dug up several, and found considerable quantities of that precious metal. *Cortez* says in his letters, that his soldiers at one entry to the capital, found 250 ounces of gold in one sepulchre ; at another sepulchre they found 3000 castellanos, or double the former quantity.'

' The *caves of the mountains* were chosen as sepulchres by the *ancient* Chemechas, but as they came under the Mexican dominion they insensibly adopted their customs. When one of their lords fell sick, *they offered prayers, vows, and sacrifices* for the recovery of his health. If it was restored they made great rejoicings.'—Isaiah xxxviii. 5. James v. 4.

Respecting the government of these tribes, the historian observes, ' In the public, as well as private economy of the Mexicans, the traces of their political discernment—of their zeal for justice, and love of the public good, would meet with little credit, *were they not confirmed by the evidence of their painted records, and the attestation of many faithful and impartial witnesses who have written from their own observation.* Those who are weak enough to imagine they can estimate the ancient Mexicans by their *descendants,* will be apt to consider the account we are to give of their refinement, their laws, and their arts, as fables invented by the Spanish writers. But that we may not violate the laws of History, nor the fidelity due to the public, we shall candidly state that which we have found without apprehension of censure.'

' The education of youth, which is the chief support of a state, and which best unfolds the character of every nation, was amongst the Mexicans of so judicious a nature, as to be of itself sufficient to *retort* the supercilious contempt of certain critics upon themselves, who believe *the empire of reason to be circumscribed by the boundaries of Europe.* In whatever we say, we are guided by *the Historical paintings of the people and their best informed Historians.*'

" Nothing," says *Acosta,* " has surprised me more or appeared more worthy of memorial and praise than the care and method which the Mexicans observed in the tuition of their youth. It would be difficult to find a nation that has bestowed *so much* attention on a point so important[1] to every state. The zeal which they manifested for the education of their youth, upbraids the negligence of our modern fathers of families, and many of the lessons which they taught to their youth, might serve as instruction to ours. All the Mexican children, even those of the royal family, were suckled by their own mothers. If the mother was by sickness prevented from the performance of this duty, she did not employ a nurse till she was well informed of her condition in life, disposition, &c. When they attained their fifth year, they were either consigned to the priests, to be educated and brought up in their seminaries, which was the general practice for the children of the nobles, and even of the kings, or if they were to be brought up at home, their parents began at that period to instruct them *in the existence of God, and to teach them how to pray and implore His protection.* They were led frequently to the Temple that they might become attached to religion. *An abhorrence of vice, a modesty of behaviour, respect to superiors, and love of fatigue, were strongly inculcated.* They were made to sleep upon *a mat,* and were allowed no more food than the *necessities* of life required, nor any other clothing than decency demanded. They were instructed in the agricultural profession, if their parents were husbandmen —if warriors they attended them, after attaining a certain age, to habituate themselves to fatigue and danger. Girls were taught to spin and weave—were obliged to bathe fre-

[1] 'The Greeks endeavoured to form the *minds*, the Mexicans the *hearts* of the youth. The Athenians prostituted their youth to the most execrable vices in those very schools which were destined for their instruction in the arts. The Lacedemonians tutored their children in every *crafty* vice, and whipped them for their want of *dexterity* when they were detected in theft, &c. The Mexicans taught their children together with the arts, religion, modesty, honesty, sobriety, industry love of truth and respect to superiors and elders.'—Clavegero.

quently, that they might be cleanly in their habits and person, and the universal maxim was to *keep the youth constantly employed.*"

" One of the most warmly inculcated precepts was to *cultivate truth* in all *they thought and uttered,*[1] and wherever a lie was detected, *the lip* of the delinquent was pricked with the thorns of the aloe. They tied the *feet* of those girls who were fond of walking abroad without being required to do so."

" In short the instructions and advice which they *received from their parents for whom they had the most profound respect,* were of such a nature that I cannot dispense with transcribing some of the exhortations employed by them ; the knowledge of which was obtained from the Mexicans themselves by the first religious missionaries, particularly *Motolina, D'Olmes, and Sahagun,*[2] who acquired a perfect knowledge of the Mexican language, and made the most diligent inquiry into their manners and customs.'

" My son," said the father, " who art come into the light of this world from the womb of thy mother to endure its travail : we know not how long heaven will grant to us the enjoyment of that precious gem which we possess in thee. But however short the period, endeavour to live in obedience, praying to God continually to assist thee. He created thee, therefore HIS property thou art. He is thy Father, and loves thee still more than I do : repose in Him all thy thoughts, and day and night direct thy sighs to Him.

---

[1] 'Lying, a crime so pernicious to society, has been left unpunished in the nations of Europe. The Mexican legislators perceived that without some disgraceful punishment against lying and drunkenness, truth would be wanting at trials of justice, and good faith become disregarded in contracts. Experience has shewn the fatal effects of the *impunity* of these vices in Christendom.'—Clavegero.

[2] These parental admonitions are referred to page 90 of this work ; the addresses are so replete with the unction as well as the language of Scripture, as to render it unnecessary to multiply references.

Reverence and salute thine elders. Hold no one in contempt. To the poor and distressed *be not dumb,* but use words of comfort. Honour thy parents, to whom thou owest obedience, respect, and service. Guard against imitating the example of those wicked ones, who, like brutes deprived of reason neither reverence their parents, listen to their instruction, nor submit to their correction; whosoever follows their steps will have an unhappy end.

" Scorn not him whom you see fall into some transgression or folly, but beware lest thou fall into the same error which offends thee in another. Go not where thou art not called, nor interfere in that which does not concern thee. Endeavour to manifest thy good breeding in all thy words and actions. In conversation do not lay thy hands upon another, nor speak too much nor interrupt or disturb another's discourse.

" If thou hearest any one talk foolishly, and it is not thy province to correct him, keep silence ; but if it does concern thee, consider first what thou art to say, and do not speak arrogantly ; that thy correction may be well received.

" When any one discourses with thee, hear him attentively, maintaining an easy attitude ; neither playing with thy feet, nor putting thy hand to thy mouth, nor spitting, nor looking here and there ; nor rising up frequently, if thou art sitting, for such actions are indicative of levity and low breeding.

" When thou art at table do not eat as if thou wert hungry ; nor show displeasure if any thing displeases thee. If any one comes unexpectedly to dine with thee, share with him what thou hast: and when any one is entertained by thee do not fix thy looks upon them. Never take precedence of thy elders, unless they require thee to do so.

When thou art at table with them, do not eat or drink, until thou hast attended to them in a becoming manner.

" If thou becomest rich, beware of becoming insolent, and of overlooking the *claims* of the poor; for the God who denies riches to them, offended by thy *abuse* of His gifts, may *make them thy scourge.* Support thyself by thine own exertions that thy food and thy sleep may be the sweeter. I, my son, have supported thee by the sweat of my brow, and have omitted no duty of a father; I have provided thee with everything necessary *without taking it from others.* Do thou likewise.

" When it becomes necessary to relate to another what has been imparted to thee, tell *the simple truth without addition.* Speak ill of no one. Do not *take notice* of the failings which thou observest in others, if thou art *not called upon* to correct them.

" Be not a *news-carrier, nor a sower of discord.* When thou bearest an embassy, and he to whom it is borne is enraged, and speaks contemptuously of those who sent thee, do not report such an answer, but endeavour to soften him, that thou mayest not raise discord and spread calumny of which thou mayst afterwards repent.

" Stay no longer than is necessary in the market-place, for in such resorts there is danger of contracting vices. When the time is come for thee to marry, dare not to enter into any engagement *without the approbation of thy parents otherwise it will have an unhappy issue.* If thou art virtuous *thy example will put the wicked to shame.* No more, my son, enough has been said in discharge of the duties of a father. With these counsels I wish to fortify thy mind. Refuse them not, nor act in contradiction of them; for on them the happiness of thy life depends."

" My daughter," said the Mexican mother, " born of my

substance, brought forth with my pains and nourished with my milk—I have endeavoured to bring thee up with all possible care, and thy father has refined and polished thee like an emerald that thou mayest appear in the sight of men a jewel of *true virtue.*

" Strive always to be *good.* Life is a thorny and laborious path, and it is necessary to exert all our powers to obtain the blessings which the Gods are ready to grant us.

" Be orderly and take pains to manage the economy of thy household. Give water to thy husband for his hands, and make bread for thy family. Wherever thou goest, go with modest composure ; without hurrying thy steps, or laughing with those whom thou mayst meet, or casting thine eyes thoughtlessly first on one side and then on the other. Give a courteous answer to those who salute, and put any question to thee. Employ thyself diligently in spinning, and weaving, in sewing, and embroidering ; for by these arts thou wilt with esteem gain all the necessary articles of food and clothing. Take not much sleep, but be in the open air when thou wouldst repose thyself ; for effeminancy brings with it idleness and other vices.

" *Attend to the Gods in all thy thoughts, and thou wilt give comfort to thy parents.*

" If thy parents call thee, do not stay to be called twice ; but go instantly to know their pleasure, that thou mayest not disoblige them by *slowness.* If another is called and comes not quickly, come thou, hear what is wanted, and *do it well.*

" *Deceive no one, for God beholds your actions. Live in peace with every one.*

" *Love all sincerely* and *honestly,* that thou mayst be beloved by them in return.

" If thou seest any good thing presented to another, give

way to no mean suspicions, for the Gods, to whom every thing belongs, distribute every thing as they will.

" If thou wouldst avoid the displeasure of others, let none meet with it from thee.

" Guard against familiar conversation with men. *Keep not company with those who are dissolute. Attend upon thy household,* and do not upon *slight* occasions, leave thy house; nor be seen wandering in the streets or in the market-place. Remember *that vice like a poisonous weed, brings death to those who taste it; and when it once harbours in the mind it is difficult to root it out.* If, in passing through the street thou meetest with a forward youth who appears agreeable to thee, modestly pass on. If thou enterest into the house of relations, salute them with respect, and do not remain idle, but immediately take up a distaff to spin, or do any thing that occurs. When thou art married *honour thy husband, obey him, and diligently attend to his orders.* If thy husband occasions thee any disgust, let him not know thy displeasure when he commands thee to do any thing, *pass it over at that time,* and afterwards tell him *with gentleness what vexed thee, that he may be won by thy mildness and forbearance and offend thee no farther.*

" *Dishonour him not before others; for thou wouldst share in the dishonour.*

" If any one comes to visit thy husband, *accept the visit kindly, and shew civility.*

" If thy husband is foolish, *be thou discreet.* If he fails in prudent management, admonish him of his failure; but if he is totally incapable of taking care of his estate, take that charge upon thyself; *never omitting to pay workmen punctually.* Embrace, my daughter, the counsel which I give thee. I give thee the result of my own experience.

Fix my precepts in thy heart and *bowels* ; [1] for thus thou
wilt be happy. If by not attending to my counsel, or by
neglecting any of my instructions, any misfortunes befall
thee, *the fault will be thine*, and *the evil also.* Enough,
my child. May God prosper thee."   *   *   *

Well might the poet ask—" Are these savages ? " And
well may the Historian, who repeats the words add, "What
then is civilization? "

   *   *   *   *   *   *   *

Of the famous pyramidal, and other memorials of ancient
Mexican grandeur, Bullock, observes "No one whom I
met knew or cared anything about them ; none of the inhabitants of Mexico have ever been to see them : no person
in that neighbourhood could give me the least information
respecting those wonderful structures. On asking an old
woman we met near the Pyramids, if she could tell me who
made them ; she replied, ' *Si Signor Santo Francisco!* '

" The result of this little excursion of three days, has
thoroughly convinced me of the veracity of the Spanish
writers, whose account of cities, their immense population,
their riches, and the progress of the arts among the Mexicans
are doubted by those who have *never seen* the country. I
firmly believe all the intelligent and indefatigable Abbe
Claverego has related, &c.

" Had Monsieur Du Pauw ; or our better-informed
countryman, Dr. Robertson, *passed one hour in Tezcuco,*
Tescoxingo, or *Huexotlo,* they would never have supposed
for a moment that the palace of Montezuma in Mexico, was
a clay cottage, or that the account of the immense population was a fiction. It is *not in the present* aspect of New
Spain that we are to look for the remains of Mexican greatness, as *every vestage* of its former splendour was *annihi-*

---

[1] A pure Hebraism.

lated by the conquerors." " He (Cortez) was *compelled*
to demolish and level with the ground every house as he
took it, and five thousand Indian workmen followed close
to his soldiers to complete the work of *destruction*. The
foundations of the present city are *razed and stand on the
ruins of the old.*"

" It was the wish of the Spaniards *not to leave a trace of
former greatness,* or a *recollection of the people they had
destroyed,* and they completely succeeded in their object.
Where are the slightest traces of their ancient magnificent
city but in the accounts of early writers? It is well known
that a map of it was made for Cortez by order of Montezuma, &c. and chance brought it to light—it was purchased
and brought to England by his majesty's ship Phaeton, by
myself. It is only a fragment, but the world will learn
from it that ancient Mexico was double the size of the
present city; that it equalled it in the regularity, and excelled it in the number and size of its palaces and temples,
and the account given by Cortez to his sovereign, as well
as that of Bernal Diaz, will no longer be doubted."

' The modern Mexicans,' observes the Abbe Clavegero,
' are as unlike the ancient, as the Greeks of these days are
to those who lived in the days of Plato and Pericles. The
ancient Mexicans had more fire and were more sensible of
impressions of honour.'

' Monsieur Du Paix, speaking of the monuments of antiquity which he discovered, having been sent for that
purpose by his Majesty in the year 1805, describes, among
other valuable remains, his visit to *Teo-pantepec,* which
signifies *the House of God on the hill,* where, upon an eminence, or isolated mount, close to others of greater elevation to the west, there is a pyramid with a quadrangular
base: it consists of four stories, which regularly diminish in

size; of the highest arena, nothing now remains—this oratory, the style of which is Egyptian, is built of lime and stone and is a solid structure, its extreme surface was coated with square stones, when I had the opportunity of observing it some years ago, which at present is quite a ruin,' &c. 'It is to be regretted that when we consider the state of these ancient monuments, that that which neither the lapse of time, nor of revolving ages, nor the branches and roots of large trees growing amongst them, insinuating themselves between the interstices of the stones and in a manner separating them, could effect—indiscreet zeal on the one hand, and on the other the greediness of the occupants of the soil, eager to gain possession of the materials, should have been able to accomplish, which seem to have conspired to dismantle and destroy works certainly worthy of lasting preservation and calculated to throw light on the state of the arts among the Mexicans."—p. 423.

Du Paix continues, " it will readily be conceived that in attempting to describe and explain these interesting monuments of antiquity, I must labour under great difficulty, on account of the originality and peculiarity of the style of the Mexican school, which *superficial* inquirers have spoken of with *ill-placed* contempt. But I shall not on this account be deterred from endeavouring to rescue them from the oblivion in which they have been shrouded by the lapse of ages, and to exhibit them to the intelligent examination of the lovers of antiquity. In connection which this subject, I will here state my opinion of the real cause of the *ignorance* and remarkable diversity of sentiment existing among the Indians, as to the etymology and the signification of the ancient names of their towns, and various remains of antiquity, which for the most part were significatory and illustrative of History. The cause of this confusion is most pro-

bably to be traced to the mixture by marriage and otherwise, of their various tribes, as well as to the establishment
of schools for instruction in the Castilian language. Those
causes are sufficient to account for the corruptions of the
original tongue, and the change of words and family names
peculiar to it." p. 432.

" The monuments of this nation, (which from its antiquity,
language, and its cultivation of the arts, might rank amongst
the most renowned of former times,) will meet the same,
perhaps a more speedy fate. The consuming hand of time
removing even the bases of its pyramids, its temples, its
sepulchres and palaces, threatens their approaching and
total extinction ; the broken statues and sculptured stones
will crumble away, and thus all the monuments of Mexican
grandeur and greatness will be a chaotic heap of ruins."

MONTEZUMA.

Montezuma is peculiarly interesting, as that monarch
with whom the calamitous events of the Spanish invasion
were immediately connected. He is represented by Clavegero and other historians as having been ' grave, religious,
and taciturn. He united the offices of king and priest ;
and when the nobility went to inform him that he was
elected, (a choice which he could not have expected, he
having been the youngest of several brothers) ' they found
him sweeping the pavement of the Temple.'

' After having been conducted to the palace and seated
on the throne, he was addressed by the king of Acolhuacan :
his virtues were eulogized, and the love of the omnipotent
God was declared to be evinced in so happy a choice.
Montezuma heard the address with much attention, and

was so greatly affected, that thrice he essayed in vain to reply, being interrupted by tears. At length checking his emotion, he with great humility expressed his unworthiness of such exaltation, and offering his thanks to the king, he returned to the Temple to pass four days fasting. At the end of that period he was conducted in royal state to the palace.'[1]—Claveg. Histor. Research. pp. 313, 14.

The Mexicans by many unwonted and reiterated signs and prodigies, had been forewarned of some extraordinary event, which from the character of these presages they deemed calamitous. These subjects of direful foreboding continued thoughout the empire during three years before the arrival of the invaders. "These sinister presages continued till 1509, when there was seen, according to the Le Tellier MS. during forty nights and days, a vivid light towards the east which seemed to arise from the ground, and which," adds the narrator, "perhaps was the zodiacal light, the splendour of which is very great."—Antiq. Mex. vol. vi. p. 178.

"The Letters of Cortez to Charles v. fully prove, that about the time when the Spaniards first arrived in America, the expectation was very general of the re-appearance of Quetzalcoatl, and for many years afterwards. So difficult is it," adds the commentator, "to root out ancient prejudices, since the mere report of his having come to redeem them induced the Capotecas to revolt in 1550, a most striking proof of the firmness of their faith."

The expectation in itself was one of great joy; but there could not fail to have been much perplexity in the minds of Montezuma and his councillors as to the identity of the subject of their expectation. On the year of ' one cane' they expected their Messiah, and on the year of that sign

[1] For a description of the state of Montezuma, see Appendix.

Cortez happened to arrive.[1]　On consulting the oracle in the Temple, Montezuma was admonished not to receive these new visitors.　Whether,' adds the Abbe, ' this oracle was the devil, as some authors are persuaded, who delivered it in order to keep every *path shut to the gospel*, or as some others have apprehended, from the priests for the common benefit of themselves and their people, Montezuma resolved from that time to refuse admission to the Spaniards; but that he might appear to act with dignity, and to follow the dictates of his own mind, he sent an embassy to them with a present entirely worthy of his royal munificence.' — Clavegero.

It appears that before the *fatal* arrival a Spanish vessel in which was the brother of Cortez, touched on the Mexican coast, but as the advanced state of the season did not admit of effecting a landing, they intimated to some Indians who were always stationed on the coast that they were proceeding at that time to their own country, but would return speedily to visit their king; whom meanwhile they were to apprise of this intention.　The Indians who had this intelligence came in haste to Mexico, and requested an immediate interview with the Monarch, to whom their arrival

---

[1] "Some viewed the rapid progress of the Spanish arms, as the necessary consequence of the general commotion into which the empire was thrown by the rumour everywhere circulated that the Messiah had come to take possession of His kingdom."—Antiq. Mex. Vol. vi.

Torquemeda, in the Antiq. of Mexico, observes, "On every symptom and demonstration of a change or rumour of any novelty, they immediately thought it was He: and when they received the intelligence which we have mentioned, and further heard that the Spaniards had arrived in the quarter where He had disappeared, and that they had come in large ships through the midst of so vast and dangerous an ocean, they felt convinced that it was He, and could be no one else; and for this reason they were still more vigilant in watching His return; placing sentinels to keep a look-out for him towards the sea—not for three days only during every month in the year, like the sages of the east, but *night and day the entire year round*; at the expiration of which period, Juan de Grizalva, having sailed to Cuba, and the expedition of F. Cortez by the same route being in consequence on his return, it necessarily followed that the Indians saw his ships, and in obedience to the commands of their king, proceeded post to carry him the intelligence, taking with them paintings," &c.

had been announced. The historian observes, "the king was troubled and surprised, as he judged the affair must needs be very urgent, since those whom he had stationed to guard that district, had come without permission to see him: neither was his surprise without just cause, since he had strong reasons to anticipate something untoward from the prodigies which he had beheld, which prognosticated adversity and approaching ruin, so that he was continually pained with the suspicions of the great misfortunes which he foreboded."

When summoned into Montezuma's presence, they prostrated themselves to the ground and kissed it, and, rising, saluted the king saying :—' Lord, we are worthy of death, for having come without your leave into your royal presence, but the nature of the business which has brought us, is so grave and important that it must plead our excuse. It is an undoubted truth that we all of us who have come here, have seen the gods, who have arrived on this coast in large water houses, and we have conversed with them and given them rich mantles, and they have in return given us these precious stones which we have brought with us ;' they then presented the glass beads, and bugles, which they had brought, and said, ' they gave us these,' and added, ' Go to your court, and give them to your Lord Montezuma, and tell him that we are on our return home to our own country, but shall return and pay him a visit.'

' To this speech the Emperor answered not a word: revolving the matter in his breast, he simply observed to the watchers: ' You must feel weary after such a long and speedy journey: go and repose yourselves: and let not a word transpire, lest it should cause a commotion amongst a fickle and easily excited people.'   *   *   *

' Montezuma remained alone pensive and even very appre-

U

hensive of some great revolution in his kingdom; for he was
possessed of much foresight, and reflected on past prodigies
which had happened, and recollected what his soothsayer
had told him, for which cause his house while he was in it,
was ordered to be thrown to the ground, overwhelming
him in the ruins. He also called to mind what his sister
Papan had informed him many years before; and what
Nezuhalpilli had likewise said to him; it appeared to him
that these were not fortuitous coincidences, but that they
portended some great disaster and change in the government;
and since weighty matters of state are wont to be imparted
to confidential friends, and to be debated in counsel, be
caused summonses to be sent to all the persons of whom his
council was composed; who were king Cazama of Tezcuco
his nephew, whom he sent for by express; *Cuitlalmatzin,*
his brother, the lord of *Itzalapalapi,* and ten others of
his ordinary councillors, to whom he declared what had
happened; and a considerable time having been employed
in the interchange of opinions and conjectures, his council terminated their deliberation by persuading themselves,
and being convinced that it was Quetzalcoatl whom in time
past they worshipped as God, and who they likewise expected would return to reign over their kingdoms; since he
himself had long before promised that he would do so when
he departed from them, to the provinces of *Tlapalla,* and disappeared on the coast, going in the direction of the east:
and since they on this account expected him, they thought
that those who had arrived were his train." [1] Antiq. of Mex.

"I do not understand,' observes Torquemeda, ' how
those who drew up that account, of which Herrera availed
himself, could have omitted that which I say in this chapter,

---

[1] Herrera and Gomara make mention of presents having been sent to the
strangers from Montezuma, but they were gone. Ibid.

and many other particulars which shall be observed in the
sequel ; since the circumstances which they mention, and
which I relate, are intimately connected, and those who could
have given an account of the former, could likewsie have done
so of the latter ; although I think that the error lay in their
only seeking information from the Spaniards without verifying
facts, by applying to the Indians who were mainly concerned ;
in most of them, or I may say all, since they were the mark
which all who have written of the affairs of the conquest
strove to hit, and were those who were very well acquainted
with them, and in the beginning recorded them by means of
figures and characters, and afterwards when some of the
more curious among them learned to write, wrote them
down, which histories are in my possession ; and so high is
the estimation in which I hold them on account of their
language, and the style of their composition, that I should
be glad to feel myself competent to the task of translating
them into the Spanish with the same elegance and grace as
the Mexicans penned them in their own language ; and since
these histories are true and authentic, I follow them to the
letter. But lest the accounts which they contain should
appear strange to those who read them ; I affirm, that they
are merely a relation of what *actually* happened ; but that
other authors have not noticed them before me, because the
few who have written on the affairs of the Indians were ignorant of events which then occurred, nor had any one to give
them the requisite information ; neither should I have
mentioned these facts had I not found that they were
verified by Father Bernard Sahagun, a grave and pious
ecclesiastic, who was the first of the investigators of the
most *secret things* of this land, of which he knew all the
secrets, and employed himself for more than sixty years in
composing works in the Mexican language, and in incor-

porating into it all the information which he was able to acquire." Ibid.

*   *   *   *   *   *   *   *   *   *   *

" The Indians who composed the counsel of the king were troubled together with him, and in great perplexity replied, that since it was true that their God Quetzalcoatl had gone to the kingdom of Tlapalla, to visit the supreme God, whose return *all their forefathers* had expected, he likewise who had appeared in the ships might be that God, since it was not, humanly speaking, probable that mortal men could have penetrated so far into the depths of the ocean, without being swallowed up by its waves: and therefore they believed that it was He: and since he had come, it was meet that ambassadors and noblemen should be sent to offer him obedience upon the part of the senate, and receive him, hence we may infer, originated the custom amongst the Mexicans, of the monarchy being elective and hereditary, which we may prove by observing, that if they believed that they had a living king, who at some time or other was to return, it was impossible that they could consent that *another*, should enter upon the perpetual possession, but only that he should hold it like a viceroy, who in the *absence* of a king, exercises all the regal functions with a condition which implies that the exercise of those functions will be for no longer a period than during the absence of the latter, and that he will be *ready* and *prepared to forego* them when, and as soon as the *natural* and *lawful heir* should appear, but," adds Torquemeda, " *This was folly in them,* as was also their folly in believing the magician had gone to visit the Supreme Light, in order afterwards to enjoy the earthly kingdom which he had forsaken ; but I can well imagine that granted that the Devil had invented this piece of fraud, and devised this trick is order to deceive this nation, it was likewise by permission of God, not for the sake of keeping these mistaken men in a state of delusion, but in order that as soon as Christians should arrive with the annunciation and tidings of his holy gospel, they might be already in some measure disposed to receive it from the warning which had been given to them; and the anxiety which they felt at *another's* coming and depriving them of the kingdom. But if the Devil had been able thoroughly to comprehend the matter, he would have known that *Quetzalcoatl,* whom he pretended to be the king and God of that nation, would in reality be the true God and lord of the whole creation ; and that in the same manner as *Cortez came to strip Montezuma of the possession of his kingdom* (whom the Indians *unconscious of the meaning of their message,* sent to welcome as *Quetzalcoatl*) so likewise that this lord and supreme king, would come in the character of the Monarch of the universe, to destroy him and dispossess him of the kingdom, especially as they had already had *forebodings* of the same; it having been predicted to them ten years before by Papan, the Princess of *Tlatelolco,* as we read in the preceding book, in the chapter which treats of the prodigies which portended the destruction of the Mexican empire. Returning to my subject, I say that those Indians having arranged with their king, what, under such peculiar circumstances ought to be done, prepared a great present, with which they sent all the sacerdotal habits which they said had been worn by *Quetzalcoatl* when he was in that country, who, as it would hence appear, was both *priest* and *king*, &c. All the articles of which the present consisted which Montezuma took from his treasury, in order that they might be sent to those strangers, were wrapped up in rich mantles which they put into petataes, which having been done, Montezuma made the following speech to his lords, whom he sent as

ambassadors, ' Go, my friends, and discharge faithfully the
duties of the embassy, which this august senate and myself
intrust to you ; take care that nothing detains you on the
road, but proceed with as much expedition as possible into
the presence of our Lord and King Quetzalcoatl, and say to
him, Your vassal Montezuma, who is at present the regent
of *the kingdom*, sends us to salute your Majesty, and to give
you the present, of which we are the bearers, together with
these sacerdotal ornaments which have always been in the
highest esteem and veneration amongst us.' ' Although the
Spaniards did not understand these words, they knew the
purport of them by signs, and astonished at their demand,
they debated the matter with each other, and said, ' What
can they mean by saying that their King and God is here,
and that they wish to see him ? ' Cortez listened to their conversation, and he and all the rest having considered the
matter well, and deliberated together, they agreed amongst
each other that F. Cortez should dress himself in his richest
apparel, and that they should prepare a throne for him in the
fore part of the vessel, on which he should *counterfeit*
royalty, and that the Indians should be introduced to see and
speak to him. Having accordingly done so, they told the
Indians that they were welcome, and that *He whom they
sought was there*, and that they would be permitted to see
and speak with him. Begging to be permitted to behold
' Him whom they sought,' ' they were accordingly conducted
to the fore part of the vessel, where F. Cortez was already
expecting them, with the mock majesty we have just
mentioned. They were introduced to him carrying the present in their hands; and when they saw him seated majesti-
cally on the throne *believing that he was* their God and
Lord *Quetzalcoatl*, they immediately prostrated themselves
upon the ground, and kissed it.' When rising, he who

was principal of them all, addressed him, ' O God, our Lord, we welcome your arrival, since we who are your vassals and servants, *have long expected you.* Montezuma, your vassal, and the *regent* of your kingdom, has dispatched us to your presence, that we may salute you in his name, and he beseeches you to accept this meagre present, these precious ornaments which you were accustomed to wear when you were amongst us in the character of our King and God.' Having so said, they began to attire him in the ornaments which they had brought; upon his head they placed what seemed like a helmet decorated with gold and gems of great value, and with a rich plume of feathers; they clothed him with a vest of fine texture, named *Xiculli,* which reached from the throat to the waist, and descended to the middle of the arm ; they next threw a chain of precious stones of great value and beauty round his neck; and in this manner they proceeded to load him from head to foot with ornaments and costly *sacerdotal vestments,*" &c. " After they had so done, an interpreter said to them, in the name of F. Cortez, ' What! *is this all that you have brought me to welcome my arrival amongst you ?*' On which the principal ambassador replied, ' Lord, and king, this was what was given to us to carry to your Majesty, and no more.' Cortez then desired some of his men to take them into his cabin, and treat them courteously," &c. " When these Indians came on board the ship, many of the men crowded from the other vessels around the captain's ship to see what was there passing ; and they saw and heard what I have related ; at which they were astonished, and were at a loss for suitable terms by which to express what they thought of such great simplicity and of a scene so new to them."

" They then agreed to terrify those messengers by throwing them into irons, loading them with chains, discharging the artillery and challenging them to wrestle with them—all, with the object of inducing them to report terrible things of them, in order that they might be seized with fear, and dread them as those who were fated to march on to victory, and to become the lords of the country. The Indians slept in the ship that night, and on the next day, as soon as it was morning, the Spaniards put into execution what they had planned the day before: they took the Indians and threw them into irons, and having chained them by the feet, began to fire off the artillery. The Indians who beheld themselves prisoners and in irons, confounded with the noise of the canons and the smell of the powder, fell senseless on the ground, and there remained for a long space of time, as it were dead; the soldiers seeing them in this state, raised them, and seating them, threw water in their faces, and made them drink it, on which they recovered from the terror into which they had been thrown. They then took off their fetters, and the captain said to them, " I am informed that the Mexicans are very valliant, possess great strength, and are good wrestlers, on which account, and to assure myself of the fact, I wish you to contend with my people, that I may see whether you are more valliant than they." He gave them swords, shields, and lances for the contest. The poor unhappy Indians, who, even if they had known how to make use of the arms which had been given to them, were more dead than alive from the chains and the noise of the artillery, did not only not accept the challenge, but declined it by saying, " Lord, this was not the purpose for which we came, nor did Montezuma send us to quarrel with you, or to enter upon a trial of strength with your people, but only to visit you in his name, to kiss your hand as we have done; and if we obeyed your commands, and could be guilty of such great impropriety, we should not only excite his displeasure, but should pay the forfeit of our lives." To this the captain replied, "You need make no manner of excuse, for you *must* do what I order you ; as I have heard of you Mexicans that you are valliant, you must use your utmost endeavours in attacking and defending yourselves from my men." He could not, however, prevail upon them, although, in order to induce them to accept the challenge they loaded them with abusive epithets and dismissed them, saying that they might tell Montezuma that his present had displeased them, and that they would march to Mexico and plunder them of every thing they had, and would take it to themselves. (Whether they knew what they were saying or no, will be known in the sequel ; for they spoke at random, not knowing the future, and without having made any trials of the land.) With this answer and these threats, (worthy certainly of the *folly* of Montezuma and his counsellors) the Indians entered their canoes, and so great was their haste, that every moment's delay appeared to them the herald and harbinger of death ; they immediately, therefore, began rowing—not only the rowers which they had brought for the purpose, but all indiscriminately, each urging and exhorting the other to apply a strong hand to the oar, as well to find themselves at a distance from, and fairly rid of the ships, where they had been treated so *indifferently*, as to hasten their return to give an account to their king of what had passed between them and Quetzalcoatl.

Proceeding in this manner they reached a small Island. The lords of that place entreated them to remain there the following day to rest themselves ; but they replied, " Our haste is urgent ; for the embassy with which we are charged to our Lord Montezuma, is of such a nature that it is unprecedented in these kingdoms, and as it is not

fit that any one should know the nature of it before him,
for this reason it is our duty not to stay to repose
ourselves, but to travel on in haste." They immediately
set off, and proceeded on their journey with such
distressed and harassed feelings, that they reaped no
consolation from food or sleep. Nothing gave them the
slightest satisfaction, but they sighed as they went along
overcome with sorrow, wonder, and dismay. They scarcely
addressed each other, preserving a strange silence; or if at
intervals they spoke, they said:—"We have beheld terrible
and strange things, which portend evils and great tribulation;
but O LORD God! who are they, and from whence shall
they come who shall overcome the Mexicans? *Are not we
the ancient, the powerful, the dreaded of all lands?* Why
do we allow ourselves to be disturbed and pained? Why
do our hearts, heaving within our breasts, forbode to us
future ills? This is the sign of some great impending calamity." "With these and similar reflections, they occupied
their minds on the road, and arrived by rapid stages at the
court of Mexico at an advanced hour of the night, and
proceeded straight to the palace of the king Montezuma,
when they bade the attendants in the ante-room to inform the
king of their arrival, and if he were asleep to awaken him,
for the business upon which they came did not admit of
delay; and to say to their Lord 'the ambassadors have returned whom you sent to the sea to receive our God,
Quetzalcoatl.' The guards went into his chamber and
delivered the message to him, which, when Montezuma had
heard, he answered, "Tell them not to come in here, but to
go to *the hall of judgment* and await me there." "After the
idolatrous ceremony of *sprinkling the ambassadors with the
blood* of the sacrificed victim had been gone through,
Montezuma seated himself upon his throne or seat, in order

to hear, with state and majesty, the tidings which his ambassadors had brought to him, for agreeably to the belief
which he had adopted, he was convinced that it was Quetzalcoatl who had arrived on the sea coast; and he expected
to receive perfect information of the arrangements necessary
to be made preparatory to His visit. The ambassadors prostrated themselves on the ground and in this prostrate state
the principal person among them, who had gone out as
superior of the rest on the embassy, commenced the delivery of the following speech : "

"Potent lord and king! as soon as we arrived at the
sea shore, these, your servants and myself, we beheld some
very large houses of wood upon the water, constructed
very artfully both without and within. We went in
canoes to them and entered the principal ship or water-
house, where was the flag which they carried before them.
The ships were many, and in each were many persons, who
all stood looking at us, until we entered the captain's vessel.
We requested to see the Lord, Quetzalcoatl, (in search of
whom we had come) in order to give the present which we
had brought with us; when they shewed us in a separate
part of the ship, a lord, seated upon a throne, clothed in
very rich apparel, and pointing to him with their finger, they
said to us, *Behold him whom ye seek.*' We prostrated
ourselves at his feet, kissing the ground and adoring him as
a God. We next addressed to him the speech which you
commanded, and proceeded to attire him in the robes and
jewels which you gave to us, and delivered to him the
other articles of which the present consisted ; and having
laid all this at his feet, he gave us to understand that it
was very little. That day they treated us well, and set
provisions before us, and gave us an agreeable liquor to
drink, which they called wine : that night we slept in the

ship; in the morning they wished us to come to a trial of strength, and ordered us to fight with them, which we persisted steadily in declining; they then threw us into chains and discharged artillery, which greatly terrified us with their thunder and lightning, and caused us to fall on the ground as if dead. After we had recovered ourselves, we were shewn their *arms, horses, and dogs, which assist* them in fighting, at which we were still more terrified. *They say that they have come here to conquer and to rob us;* that is all we know. If they should come here, we shall both know what they desire, and how far their power may be commensurate with their will. We can only say we return back greatly alarmed and terrified."

" Montezuma was very much astonished at the words of his ambassadors; his face changed colour, and he displayed extreme sorrow and dismay; the conviction took possession of his mind that he and all the subjects of his empire would have to suffer much and endure many indignities. Under this impression he began to weep bitterly, as did likewise all those by whom he was surrounded; their tears and lamentations spread through all classes of the city, high and low, and they soon began to assemble in groups in the public squares and streets, and to utter lamentations, each one exciting the other's grief by the suggestion of tender and melancholy recollections. They spoke of the great evils which threatened them and of the ruin and destruction which impended over them, as if they had already happened, and their hearts divining what was afterwards to befall them : all were dejected and a prey to grief; fathers sorrowing for their sons, exclaimed, "Alas! my sons, what troubles you must see, and, what is worse, what must you go through and suffer! " Mothers made the same lamentation for their daughters, adding their piteous manifestations of public affliction, and Montezuma, as more interested in preserving the honours and dignity which it might be his lot to lose, felt more acutely than the rest."--Pp. 343--345.

" The above account of Cortez having been supposed by the Mexicans to be the god, Quetzalcoatl, is so curious, that we cannot forbear subjoining in a note, in the original passages in Spanish, remarking at the same time, that if most historians have passed over in silence the events here recorded, it was because they had not access to the same means of information as Torquemeda, or even the opportunity of consulting his history, in consequence of the prosecution which the first edition of his Indian Memoir underwent in the course of the seventeenth century. It furnishes, moreover, an explanation, (affording by so doing, a new proof of its authenticity) of what almost all historians have pronounced the unaccountable conduct of Montezuma, in sending repeated ambassadors with rich presents to the Spaniards, and in still persisting in forbidding them to approach his court, since their threats in the first instance, to burn and plunder his city, and their reception of his ambassadors must have made him very unwilling to receive such visitors in Mexico, and his remaining doubts as to whether Cortez might *not* be Quetzalcoatl, and his cannon some preternatural agency by which to subjugate his enemies, must have suggested to his prudence the precise line of conduct which he adopted, since his last resource, when all other expedients failed, were to resist with arms this invading god."

" Our law," said an aged chief of great authority, " enjoins us to *receive strangers*, but not enemies, who may cause disasters to the state. Those men who demand entrance into our city, appear to be rather *monsters cast up from the sea*, because its waters could no longer endure

them, than descended from heaven, as some have vainly
imagined. Is it possible that gods could so *greedily covet
gold and treasures?*

" He wrongs the honour of his nation who thinks it will be
overcome by a *band of adventurers.* Let their demand,
therefore, be rejected ; and if they dare to try by force, let
our arms repel their temerity."—See Clavegero.

" It is singular, that neither Cortez nor his Chaplain,
Gomara, should say a word of the scene which was acted
on board the Spanish ship in which Cortez, sitting upon a
throne, personated *Quetzalcoatl,* and received the ambassadors of Montezuma. The incident was too extraordinary to escape the memory of either ; and from the
silence of both, it must be inferred either that it never
happened, or that *they must have had some reason* for
consigning so curious a piece of history to oblivion. The
first supposition is altogether improbable, because it directly
contradicts the testimony of authors of *the strictest veracity,*
who had the *best* means of information on the subject, and
likewise indirectly even Gomara himself, since he affirms
that the Mexicans, when they beheld the Spanish fleet
approaching, declared that it was *Quetzalcoatl* who was
coming, bringing his temples along with him *(con sus templos
á cuestas.)* It is necessary therefore to come to the
other conclusion—that Cortez kept the matter a secret,
because there were those who did not wish it to be known
in Europe, that he had been taken for the Messiah[1] in
America."—Antiquities of Mexico.

[1] That the faith of the Mexicans in the second coming of their Messiah,
should have been taken fraudulent advantage of in order to effect the usurpation
and appropriation of their rights, was no fault of theirs. The appearance
of impostors, who repeatedly led the Jews into *unscriptural* errors in doctrine
and life—might justly be considered retributive visitations, authenticating the
declaration that ' those who *reject* GOD's TRUTH, become the *dupes of men's
errors.*' While the acknowledgment of the Messiah in all his offices, whether the
Prophet, like unto Moses—the *atonement*—the risen *Intercessor*—the future

The last dark scenes which closed the reign of the Mexican monarchs are so awfully characteristic of that ' *other* gospel'—that '*other* Spirit' of which the Apostle speaks in the language of warning;—so fearfully illustrative of that zeal to do God service which *acts* in direct opposition to His revealed will; and so impressively admonitory of that illusory *self-deception* which *will*-worship has so often and so fatally *substituted for obedience ;* as to claim a distinct notice in this work.

' TRUTH, which is another term for *moral light*, discovers the shadows, however dark, as well as the lights of that Historical Portraiture which she delineates. It is the very nature of Light to *make manifest* 'good and evil;'—the former (as the fountain of peace and happiness) for acceptance ; and the latter (as the source of misery and remorse) for avoidance.

" History," observes Gordon, " would be philosophy teaching by example ; but she will not attain this character whilst false glory dazzles the historian. Heroes are examples recommended to the human race ; but History owes it to her own dignity to call crimes, however gigantic, by their proper names, and if possible to make their repetition universally odious."—Hist. vol. i. p. 186.

Of Fanaticism it has been well remarked, ' to those who have never experienced or witnessed the effect of delusion in *perverting* the judgment, and *shutting* the eyes of the understanding, its workings are incredible.' ' The mind becomes like a troubled sea, driven and tossed by *every* wind of *impulse*. It is lamentable to see to what depths of *absurdity* we may unconsciously, under delusion, be led.'

Redeemer and King, constituted Montezuma and his subjects, rather the martyrs of Scriptural truth than the victims of fallacious error. The evil power in the one case was over the mind, in the other over the body, which is destined to exist anew.

One of the characteristics of this terribly assured '*enemy
of all righteousness,*' is, that in its idolatry of names, it
'*will not endure sound doctrine.*' "Tyrannizing over men's
minds, he stifles all sentiment and extinguishes the very
light of nature ; he puts to flight all pity—all remorse : no
infamy, no punishment can intimidate him ; every thing is
to him matter of triumph and glory. What is there to
compare to him? *all* the wickedness that ever entered into
the heart of man could never have been achieved without
fanaticism."

"It was on November 8, 1599, on descending the
mountains of Chalco, Cortez first beheld the noble lake, the
palaces, and gilded domes of Mexico;[1] the surrounding
large cities and cultivated fields. Thus the Author of
Historical Researches describes the first interview of Montezuma and the Spanish General :—

"About one thousand persons, adorned with plumes, and
clad in mantles of fine cotton, came and respectfully announced the approach of the king : two hundred more in
an uniform dress, marched barefoot, in deep silence, with
their eyes fixed on the ground. Three nobles, each with a
golden rod, which, when they lifted high, all the people bowed
with their heads, preceded the seat covered with plates
of gold, and carried on the shoulders of four noblemen, in
which was Montezuma, shaded by a rich parasol of *green*
feathers and embroidery. He wore a mantle on his

---

[1] " When Cortez entered Mexico in 1519, it was the pride of the New World,
and the noblest monument of the art and industry of man, while unacquainted
with the use of iron," &c.
" Mexico, when Cortez entered it," says Acosta, " contained sixty thousand
houses, in each of them were two, or three, and in some, ten persons, by reason
of which, the city is wonderfully replenished with people."—Historical Researches, chap. vii. page 337.
' The Spanish writers say, that when Cortez entered Mexico, Montezuma
shut himself up, and continued for the space of eight days in fasting and
prayer.'—Clavegero.

shoulders, adorned with gold and richest jewels; upon his head was a light crown of gold, and upon his feet shoes of gold, tied with leather, embroidered with gems and gold.

"As soon as the king and Cortez saw each other, both alighted; Cortez from his horse, and Montezuma from his litter; when leaning on the arm of the king of Tezcuco and the lord of Tztapalapan, he walked upon cotton cloths with which the ground was covered; and Cortez, making a profound bow, approached and put a cord of gold and glass beads round the king's neck. Cortez was going to embrace him, but was checked by the two lords; when he expressed his respect for so great a monarch.

"The King touched the earth with his hand, and then kissing it, gave to the Spaniard two necklaces of pearl, &c.

"Cortez was conducted to his dwelling, Montezuma accompanying him into the palace hall, where he made him sit on a low stool covered with cotton tapestry of gold and gems; the walls being adorned with the same.

"The King then retired, saying to him, "You are now with brothers in your own house, refresh yourselves after your fatigue, and be happy until I return."

"The palace was so large, that the Spaniards with their allies, servants, &c. in all about seven thousand persons, were accommodated in it.

"Cortez and his officers fared sumptuously, and were served by the nobility. The rest fared abundantly.

"The King, accompanied by some nobles, arrived in the evening with many rich presents and five thousand very fine dresses of cotton.

'The King,' writes Clavegro, 'seated himself and made Cortez sit also, while every other person remained standing. The general began protesting his gratitude, when the em-

peror interrupted him. "Brave general," said he, "and
you, his companions, bear witness to my pleasure at your
happy arrival at this court; if there has appeared any
opposition, it was to humour my subjects. It was reported
that you darted thunder, which made the earth tremble.
Some related that you were monsters, thrown out from the
sea, and such gluttons, that you devoured as much as ten
men could eat. You, in like manner, may have heard that
I am a god; but here, (pinching his arm) you see I am like
all other mortals, although more noble and elevated. You
also perceive that the palace is made of stone and wood,
not of gold. The truth is, that the gold plate, armour,
jewels, and other treasure, I have preserved from my
forefathers, as is the usage of kings, and which you shall
at all times enjoy. Abandoning, therefore all false representations made of either of us, I accept the embassy of
your king, and offer all my kingdom to his obedience, since,
from the *signs* in the heavens, the period seems to have
arrived when *the predictions of our ancestors* are to be
fulfilled—that from the *east* were to come certain men,
differing in habits and customs from us. Our historians
have informed us, that neither my ancestors, nor myself,
nor any of my people who inhabit this Continent, are natives
of it; *we are strangers, and came hither from far distant
parts;* they also tell us, that a Lord, whose subjects we are,
brought our race to this country, and returned to His own
place. You say that you are come from that part where
the sun rises—we believe, and hold to be true, the things
which you tell us of this great lord and king who sent you
hither; that He is our natural lord, as you say that it is now
so many days since He had notice of us. Be therefore sure
we will obey you *for* our Lord, or in the place of the good
Lord who sent you; in this there shall be neither failure nor

deception, therefore command according to your will in all the country."

' In another discourse, Montezuma said to his councillors, whom he had convoked in presence of Cortez: " My brothers and friends—you already know that your grandfathers, fathers, and yourselves, have been, and are, the vassals of my ancestors and myself; by them and by me, you have always been respected and well treated. I believe you also have heard from my predecessors that we are not natives of this country—that they came from a distant Land—that they were brought hither by a Lord who left them here and to whom all were subject. You well know that we have *always expected Him,* and according to the things which the captain has told us of the king who sent him to us, and from *that place* '*from whence he says he comes,* they have been informed about us.

' We have' he added, ' ruled these nations only as viceroys of *Quetzalcoatl,* our God and lawful sovereign; wherefore I think you are the people we looked for.'—Clavegero, vol. ii. page 68. Acosta in Purchase, vol. iii. 1123. Historical Researches, chap. vii. page 327.

" All this," writes Cortez to Charles v. " passed before a notary, who reduced it to the form of a public act; and I required it to be testified as such in the presence of many Spanish. I replied to all he had to say, in the way *most suitable to myself;* especially by making him believe your majesty to be the chief whom they so long expected."

*   *   *   *   *   *   *

*   *   *   *   *   *   *

Clavegero, describing an interview with Cortez, in the chief Temple to which, at the request of Cortez, the king admitted him, continues, ' Cortez thus addressed the king Montezuma, " I wonder, Prince, that a monarch so wise as you are, can adore these abominable figures of the *devil* as gods," &c. Montezuma replied, " If I had known that you would have spoken thus disrespectfully of our religious worship, I should not have yielded to your request ; go in peace," he added, "for I will remain to appease the anger of the Gods whom you have provoked with your blasphemy." " Cortez afterwards," adds the Abbe, "broke the idols which were worshipped there, and placed instead *a crucifix and an image* of the mother of God for having granted him leave to adore him in a place before destined to idolatry,"

" On the same occasion, Cortez ordered his soldiers to destroy the images, when a great massacre of the priests was made. The Commentator on the Antiquities of Mexico, thus describes the conversation which, together with the slaughter of the priests, the Indians had rendered an historical event.

" Montezuma with a pale countenance, replied, " Hearken, O Cortez, the ceremonies of sacrifices, left us by tradition from our ancestors, those we observe, and have hitherto exercised ; but seeing that you say we have so much erred,[1] and that it is displeasing to *our* King, we are greatly pleased to hear this, if so be we may persuade our people thereunto. Neither are you to wonder that we fell into these errors, if they be errors. *Give us a Law*, and we will endeavour to embrace it with all our might." It is added, " Cortez then explained the doctrines *of the church*, exhibiting the *cross*, and an *image* of the virgin to be adored."

[1] " In the letters of Cortez to Charles v." observes the Commentator on the Antiquities of Mexico, " *those passages in italics,* where Montezuma affirms that he and his subjects might have *erred* in matters of religion *from having been aliens for such a length of time from the country of their ancestors,* seem peculiarly worthy of attention. The Lord, to whom he alludes as having conducted the Mexicans to their settlements, and whose " vassals all were " was *Votan* or *Quetzalcoatl.*"—See Antiq Mex.

What a picture of the *blinding* power of delusion is here presented! Cortez having his mental vision engrossed by image representatives, undertaking to remove a splinter of the same beam from that of the Mexican monarch; who devoutly longed for that Law which David in Spirit describes as " a *light* to his feet, a *lamp* to his path," in his walk *with* God. It is in this attitude of mind that Divine prescience has characterized Ephraim as representative of the banished tribes.

The passage referred to is thus touchingly introduced in an address of sympathetic consolation to Rachel, who is represented as bitterly lamenting the banishment of her children—the sons of Joseph.

" Thus saith the LORD: Refrain thy voice from wailing, and thine eyes from tears, because there is a reward for thy labour, saith the LORD, for they shall return again from the land of the enemy; and there is compassion for thy remote [1] posterity, saith the LORD, that thy children shall come again to their own territory.

" I have hearkened, and heard Ephraim thus bewail himself. [2] Thou hast chastised me, and I have been admonished. As a bullock unaccustomed to the yoke, turn thou me, and I shall be turned, for thou art the LORD my God. Surely after I was turned, I repented, and after I was instructed, I smote upon my thigh : I was ashamed, yea, even confounded, because I did bear the reproach of my youth." Jeremiah xxxi. 16.

* * * * " The seige of Mexico, resembling in disasters, and in the slaughters with which it was attended, that of Jerusalem ; lasted seventy-five days, during

---

[1] Poetically, a happy end, or conclusion.
[2] The same term כוד (bewail) also signifies a shaken reed, or wandering outcast.

which time the slain exceeded one hundred thousand. With respect to those who died by famine, Cortez affirms them to have been more than fifty thousand. The city appeared one complete desolation."

Gomara, describing the state of extremity to which the Mexicans had been reduced, and their obstinacy in resisting the Spaniards to the last, says, "Cortez being desirous of seeing how much of the city yet remained to be gained, ascended up a high tower. Looking round him he perceived that there was an eighth part. On the following day, he returned to the attack of the remaining portion. He commanded his troops to kill only those who defended themselves. The Mexicans lamented their unhappy fate, entreating the Spaniards to conclude the work of slaughter; and certain chiefs called to Cortez in a very pressing manner, who hastened to the spot, imagining that it was to treat of surrender. Having placed themselves by the side of a bridge, they addressed him, "Since you are the son of the sun, why do you not finish with his light? kill us at once, and relieve us from such great and protracted sufferings, since we desire death, that we may go and rest *with Quetzalcoatl who is expecting us.*"—La Conquista de Mexico, in Antiq. of Mex. vol. vi. page 841.

*   *   *   *   *   *   *   *   *   *

" Some days afterwards, Cortez visited Montezuma, and demanded reparation for an assault by his people, &c. He required Montezuma to remove to his palace, *promising* that he should be honourably served and attended. The Emperor was confounded and bereaved of speech at this proposal. He at length haughtily replied, that persons of his rank were not accustomed to surrender themselves in that manner, and that his subjects would not permit such an affront. This warm debate continued three hours, when

Valasquez de Leon exclaimed,—"Why waste more time! let us seize him, or stab him to the heart." His fierce voice and gesture terrified Montezuma; and abandoning himself to fate, he complied with their request. The emperor was carried by his astonished and afflicted officers, all bathed in tears, to the Spanish quarters."

" The son of Montezuma was brought to trial for *opposing the Spaniards, condemned by court martial*, and burned alive.

" Cortez, during *this scene*, ordered the emperor to be *fettered*. His attendants, speechless with horror, held up the fetters on his legs to lighten them, while the disconsolate Monarch broke out into loud lamentations and complaints. After *the execution*, the fetters were removed.

" Months were thus passing away, when Montezuma, with groans and tears, in the presence of his chief subjects, acknowledged himself a vassal of the king of Castile; on which there was a sullen murmur among the nobles."

" After various events, the Mexicans attacked the palace. Cortez induced Montezuma to shew himself in hopes of appeasing the tumult; to which he assented, and advanced to the battlements in his royal robes. The Mexicans, at the sight of their revered sovereign, prostrated themselves, and the weapons fell from their hands—every tongue was mute. The Emperor used many arguments to make them cease hostilities. A murmuring was heard, and threats ensued, followed by flights of arrows and vollies of stones. Two arrows wounded the unfortunate Monarch,—a stone struck him on his temple and he fell. The Mexicans fled with horror. Montezuma was carried to his apartment, and *Cortez hastened to console* him. The unhappy Monarch during his confinement, feeling how low he had sunk, in a transport of indignation tore the bandages from his wounds,

obstinately refusing nourishment,[1] and rejecting with disdain the *solicitations of the Spaniards to embrace the
Christian)faith.*"

*　　*　　*　　*　　*　　*

*　　*　　*　　*　　*　　*　　*

*　　*　　*　　*　　*　　*

" Great troubles followed the death of the Emperor.
His brother was raised to the throne, but he very soon died
of the small-pox, which was not known there till the Europeans arrived. Guatimozin, nephew and son-in-law of Montezuma, was elevated to the fatal dignity. The Spaniards,
on their return to Mexico, were enraged at finding so little
treasure; some even suspected that Cortez and his confi-
dants had appropriated a large portion to their own use.
Imagining that Guatimozin might have concealed some of
the treasure, Cortez, without any reverence for the virtues
and misfortunes of the last monarch of the Mexicans, ordered
that he should be *tortured.* The unhappy king bore the
torments with inconceivable fortitude. His principal friend
was also a fellow-sufferer *upon another rack :* overpowered
by anguish, he turned a dejected eye towards his master, as
if to implore permission to reveal what he knew. His
weakness was checked by a look of authority and scorn.
" Am I reposing on a bed of flowers ? " said the Sovereign ;
which awed him into silence, and he expired."

' The cruel heart of Cortez was ashamed of this horrid
scene ; and the Monarch was released from his tortures—and
reserved for new indignities and sufferings. At length in

---

[1] He died about the end of June, 1520, after seven months imprisonment, in
the eighteenth year of his reign, and the fifty-first of his age.

Three of the sons of Montezuma had been cut off in the contest with the
Spaniards. The most distinguished of the survivors was *Johualicahuatzin,* or
Don Pedro Montezuma, from whom descended the Counts Montezuma and Tula:.
From the emperor Montezuma's beautiful daughter, Tecuichpetzin, are descended
the noble houses of Cana Montezuma and Andreda Montezuma in Spain.

1525, on a slight suspicion that Guatamozin had formed a scheme to shake off the Spanish yoke, Cortez, *without a trial*, ordered the unhappy Monarch, together with the kings of Tescuco and Tlacopan—those who were looked up to by the Mexicans with reverence, scarcely inferior to that paid to their Gods—-to be *ignominiously hanged!* Thus did *destruction* crown a conquest which had been achieved by '*fraud and force* ;' and thus ended the Mexican Empire.'— Clavegero, book 13. Hist. Reseaches, chap. vii. p. 336.

APPENDIX.

(Page 50.)

NAMES AND TITLES OF THE CREATOR.

NONE of the names and titles by which the Creator has manifested His character, are without precise signification and special reference; and of this kind of knowledge the sacred writers knew the deep value.

For the information of young readers, it may be useful to remark that the term YEHOVAH, expressive of AM-WAS-SHALL BE, is an exception to the genius of the Hebrew language, which, recognizing only the past and the future, leaves the present tense to be mentally supplied. " And God spake unto Moses and said unto him, I am יהוה (Yehovah). I appeared unto Abraham, unto Isaac, and unto Jacob by my name אל שדי (God Almighty,) but by my name Yehovah was I not known to them; and also I *established* my covenant *with them to give them* the LAND of Canaan, the LAND of *their pilgrimage* wherein they were *strangers:* and I have moreover heard the groaning of the children of Israel whom the Egyptians keep in bondage, and I have remembered My Covenant." Exod. vi. 1—5. It was therefore by the Name Yehovah that the Creator announced Himself as the Saviour and Redeemer of the children of Israel while under the dominion of the posterity of Ham.

Moses was moreover commanded to say to the children of Israel היה (I AM) hath sent me unto you. This was the מלאך יהוה (angel of Yehovah) who appeared as a consuming fire in the midst of an unconsumed bush in Horeb, who would have borne His people as on eagles' wings to the *promised* LAND, but not having, by *regeneration*, become *assimilated* with HIS RIGHTEOUSNESS, they could not enter into HIS REST at *that* time—or in *these* bodies. That *angelic* nature in which the ineffable NAME was enshrined could *neither atone* for transgression, *nor mediate* between the Lawgiver and the transgressors of His holy and righteous Law. Therefore the blood of innocent victims and the mediation of Moses (who was faithful in all his house) served to *prefigure* that future salvation and redemption which the same Yehovah should achieve by His name יה (YAH) when enshrined in the flesh of Abraham's seed, in *whom* the three-fold capacity—to atone—to mediate—and to redeem, should unite; whose name was therefore by the angel Gabriel called יהושע the help of JEHOVAH.

To the Children of Israel it was said, " Behold I send an *angel* before thee to keep thee *in* the WAY, and to bring thee unto the PLACE which I have prepared. Give heed to him and obey his voice—provoke him not; for *he* will not pardon thy transgressions because MY NAME is *in him.* That generation did *err* in their hearts unto whom HE sware in wrath that they should not enter into HIS REST. Again, the ineffable NAME was present to bless in the *tabernacle* at Shiloh *(sent).* But transgression caused the NAME of YEHOVAH to ' forsake' it. Solomon built and dedicated a *sanctuary* in Jerusalem expressly for the enshrinement of the ineffable NAME, and when about to experience the same

fate as the *tent* of Shiloh, the transgressors were thus admonished—' go now unto My place which was in *Shiloh*
where I set my NAME at the first, and see what I did unto it
for the wickedness of my people Israel; therefore will I do
unto this *house* which is called by MY NAME (wherein ye
trust) as I have done unto Shiloh. Whether therefore the
LIFE and LIGHT of the ETERNAL tabernacled in the
angelic form—in a cloud—a tabernacle, or a sanctuary, there
was in all these *inanimate forms* no *will*, and therefore no
power to constitute that astonishing moral glory. Righteousness and Mercy embracing each other in *one* who should
unite in himself the offices of Prophet, Victim, Mediator,
—and eventually of King.

David therefore thus eulogises the future Redeemer—' Our
shield is of Yehovah, and our King is of the Holy One of
Israel. Thou speakest in vision to thy Holy One and said—I
have laid *help* upon a powerful One, I have exalted One
chosen out of the people.' After describing in detail the manner in which the ' Messiah was cut off'—which he characterizes as ' shortening ·the days of his youth, and covering him
with shame,' David thus recognises him as the Advocate
and Intercessor who through death and the grave should, as a
victim without spot or blemish, carry his own peace-speaking
blood before the mercy-seat. " Thou hast ascended on
high—Thou hast led captive captivity—and hast received
gifts for men—even for the rebellious, that the LORD God
might dwell among them." Not only for the transgressors who
had rebelled under the ministration of היה the angel whom
they had provoked to wrath, but those who have " *despised
and rejected*" יה YAH (whether as the Prophet like unto
Moses, or as that Lamb of God) " upon whose head," saith
the prophet, " *thou hast laid the iniquity of us* ALL." The
assurance of this *all-sufficient* Saviour was to David a source

of constant hope and consolation. "Therefore," says he, " my flesh shall repose in hope, because thou wilt not leave my life in hades, neither wilt thou suffer THY Holy One to see corruption." Again, he recognizes Him as the conqueror of death and the grave, and His *resurrection* as the *earnest* and *pledge* of that of His *redeemed inheritance.* " YEHOVAH said to my Adouni, sit thou at MY *right hand* until I bring thine enemies beneath Thy feet." " YEHOVAH hath sworn and will not change. Thou art a Priest for ever after the order Melchisedec. יהוה at *Thy right hand* shall smite down kings in that day of His wrath. YEHOVAH shall send the sceptre of Thy power from Zion. Reign Thou in the midst of thine adversaries. Thy people shall become willing in the day of Thy Power."

In looking forward to *the restitution of all things,* ' which his LORD and Son should accomplish, David thus exults in that prospective reign of righteousness and peace which shall supersede the transgression and misery of the existing kingdoms of this world. O YEHOVAH, *our Adouni,* how excellent is Thy NAME throughout all the earth !'

At once to guard the children of Israel against poly- theism on the one hand, and from the equally atheis- tical error of regarding that oneness which characterizes YEHOVAH rather as an *inert unit* than as an OMNIPO- TENT UNITY ; they were instructed constantly to keep in mind the *Scriptural Truth* in these words,—' Hear, O Israel, YEHOVAH, thy ALOHIEM is *one* YEHOVAH,'—all of which terms, strictly one in essence, implying varied mani- festation and mode of administration. The term *one,* which is the *seal* of this perfect essential unity, is that word which most distinctly warns against volatilizing into a mere uni- versal abstraction the FIRST CAUSE, who has from the beginning *manifested* Himself *by* HIS creating and redeeming WORD. It is therefore to be observed, that אחד (one) is characterized by three alphabetic powers (and these replete with illustration)—while the numeral value of these three letters amounts to a repeated seven, which is an arithmetical infinitude.

In having escaped the Scylla of *polytheism* many make shipwreck on the Charybdis of *atheism,* in refusing to acknowledge that manifestation of the WORD of the MOST HIGH of which creation is the evidence. That universal FIRST CAUSE, say they, whose presence fills all space, in condescension to human imperfection, applies to Himself such attributes, mental emotions, personal transactions, and local circumstances, as cannot be understood literally; and thus *mentally* they blot out creation itself, which is the *effect of that manifestation* of the Father, which by His WORD at the beginning He gave. It is to reduce all things to that void, dark, and chaotic state, *out* of which that WORD called them into existence, light and order. It is even then to volatilize the FIRST CAUSE into a universal abstraction, instead of a glorious self-existent *character,* whose wisdom and goodness delighted in the diffusion of beneficence to innumerable ranks of being, when He designed their creation.

Spinoza was more consistent in following out the whole, than are those who only hold part of the same sentiment. They have taken occasion to infer, that because no man can see His *attribute* of Omnipresence, that therefore no man could see the God of Israel. "Ye heard the voice of His words," says Moses, "but *ye* saw no similitude, only the voice ye heard." But it was otherwise with Moses, whose regenerated heart had nothing to apprehend from that righteousness and holiness with which it was assimilated. For THE LORD thus testifies of His faithful servant, " With him I will speak face to face," even *apparently*, and not in obscure sayings, and the *similitude* of YEHOVAH shall he behold : " Wherefore then were ye not afraid to speak against my servant Moses," Numb. xii. 8. " No man hath seen God at any time, the only " proceeding WORD or SON " which is in the bosom of the Father, he hath *manifested* HIM," John i. 18. The personality, *with* which the WORD or SON of God was continually associated, was cherished by the patriarchs, not only as an object of faith and trust, but of endeared fellowship and communion.

To Abraham, Jacob, Joshua, and many others, He appeared in form as man, and declared Himself, and was addressed by them as Yehovah, the present and future Redeemer. Of the seventy elders who were together with Moses in mount Sinai, (from whence He gave that Law which shall govern His future Kingdom, wherein righteousness shall dwell,) it is declared, " They saw the God of Israel, and under His feet there was as it were a paved work of sapphire stones, and as it were the body of the Heaven in clearness, and upon the nobles of Israel He laid not His hand, also they *saw* God and did eat and drink."

MODE OF ADJURATION.

(Page 166.)

" Their method of adjuring a witness to declare the truth, confirms the former hints, and will serve as a key to open the vowels of the great mysterious four lettered name יהוה On minor affairs the judge, an elderly chieftain, asks the witness, ' *checacohga'-sko?* ' (do you lie?) To which he answers, ' *Ansa kai-e-hoh-ga.*' (I do not lie.)

" But when the judge wishes to search into something of material consequence, and adjures the witness to speak the pure truth, o, e, a-*sko*. ' What you have now said is true by this emblem of the self-existent GOD ? ' To this the witness replies, ' It is true, by the strong pointing symbol of YO-HE-WAH.' When the true knowledge of the affair in dispute is of very great importance, the judge swears the witness thus : ' O, E, A.'—It is true, by the strong pointing symbol of YO-HE-wah-*sko*. ' Have you told me the pure truth by the lively type of the great and awful NAME of GOD, which describes His essential existence without beginning or ending ; and by His self-existent perfect Name, which we are not to profane, and by which I adjure you? The witness answers, ' OEA-YAH, I have told you by the pure truth, which I most solemnly swear by this strong religious figure of the adorable great divine self-existent Name which we are not to profane; and I attest it likewise by His other beloved unspeakable sacred essential Name.' The judge in small controversies asks, ' *Tu-e, u, sko?* ' To which he answers, ' *Tu-e u-hah.*' It is very true, or a certain truth. Such an addition of one or more of the four sacred letters, is proportioned to persons and things—lest otherwise they might in *an unguarded use* of them, *profane* the emblems of the DIVINE NAME."—Adair.

EXPULSION OF 600,000 JEWS FROM SPAIN.

(Page 225.)

Soon after Ferdinand had ended his war with the Moors, he issued an edict, obliging the whole Jewish population to quit Spain in less than four months from that date. Turre

Crematars, who was the soul of that persecution, advised
the king to shorten the term, forbidding the people under
the severest penalties, to afford either victuals or any other
assistance," &c. A new order forbad them to carry away
their goods, except wearables. The Spaniards tell us, that
six hundred thousand, and even some of those who had
been in great esteem at court, among whom was the learned
Abarbanel, was forced to embark for foreign countries ; and
none permitted to stay but those who preferred the faith of
the church to banishment." " The misery of those who
embarked was almost inexpressible. Some of the vessels
took fire, and they either perished in the flames or were
drowned ; others were so loaded, that they bulged or sank
with them to the bottom."

" In some the plague began to rage, and they were set
down at the next shore, where those that outlived it perished
for want ; others reached the city of Fez, where the inhabitants being frightened at their vast number and misery,
shut their gates against them : so that they were left to live
in the fields upon such herbs and roots as they could find on
that arid land. Even this distress might be considered
mercy in comparison of the insults and intolerable hardships
which they were forced to undergo from some barbarians
there, who thought they might, without offence, commit
any inhumanity on these unfortunate fugitives. A seaman
seized a number of Jewish children who were gathering
clams on the shore, and brought them to his ship, where
he gave them some bread—this brought many others, with
whom he sailed away *selling them as slaves*. The captain
of a vessel which was transporting a number of them, took
one day, the resolution to murder them all in *revenge* for
the death of Christ. They represented to him that the
Jews of Spain had been there since the dispersion of the

first Temple, and consequently, never having been at Jerusalem since, could have no share in that guilt; besides which, the blood of Christ was *freely shed as an atonement* for the sins of mankind, and therefore demanded no avenging: and that *He* did not desire the death, but THE SALVATION of a sinner. The brutish seaman, we are told, mitigated his intention to stripping them naked, and setting them down on the next shore, where many perished with hunger, and others became the prey of the wild beasts."

" Ferdinand by this act, done, it was thought, to ingratiate himself with the clergy, ran the risk of a civil war—the resentment and despair of eight hundred thousand peaceable subjects so cruelly used, might have defeated all his measures; and Abarbanel had reason to extol, not only constancy of principle, which chose (as the test of allegiance to their Creator) death in its most terrific forms to what they justly considered *image* worship—but that submission which bowed to the tyrannous decree."

" What induced that monarch, whether pure avarice, or the notion of gaining heaven by the persecution of the enemies of Christ, or the hope of approbation of the ecclesiastics, is to be guessed. However *this zeal* gained him the title of *" most catholic"* from Pope Alexander VI, who received to his jurisdiction those very fugitives whom the other had banished. John II. of Portugal received them on very hard terms, and his successor, Emanuel, banished them in compliment to the Allied Sovereigns, but treacherously retained their children under fourteen years of age. This act drove them to such despair, that some killed themselves, while others, sacrificing natural affection to religion, became their executioners. Every insult and hardship attended those that survived in the ships which transported them. All which outrages were encouraged by Emanuel."

"The proselytes who remained in Spain and Portugal, were in numerous instances treated *as their race.* There scarcely happened a public calamity, but they were looked upon as the cause of it, and made to suffer accordingly. Two thousand," says the historian, "were burnt alive, who acknowledged Christ to be the Messiah. Many others were thrown into dungeons, where they languished a long time ; and those who regained their liberty were declared infamous, and ordered to wear two red crosses on their upper garments, in acknowledgment that they had *deserved the flames.* They did not even spare the dead, but exhumed and burned their bones, confiscated their effects, and declared their children incapable of succession.

"The populace insulted and oppressed without distinction, the recusant and conformist ʾattributing every misfortune to them ; witness the insurrection made against them at Toledo, on a pretended infringement of their privileges, and laying a tax which was made necessary upon the city. They vented all their resentment against the Jews without sparing even the *posterity* of their proselytes. After having plundered their houses and murdered all that came in their way, they passed resolutions and enacted laws for their being deprived of human rights," &c.—Universal History. Basnage.

"It is not surprising that the king and the ecclesiastics of his day, should have been so intolerant of the Jews, when Saint Ambrose declared the prayers of the Jews were so many curses and impious execrations, and that they ought not to be suffered to sing in their houses, nor the ears of the saints to be defiled by them." These remonstrances had their effect, and the Jews were, by the emperor, prohibited from having a synagogue at Constantinople. "Zenoras," adds Basnage, "confirms this."

"*Chilperic,* a wicked king, made it an honour to *force*

the Jews,[1] and present them to the font. But this sacrament was profaned by these new converts, for it was quickly perceived that they observed the Sabbath-day as well as Sunday." Of Dogabert of France, he says, "The king, who set up for bigotry, notwithstanding his scandalous debaucheries, embraced so easy an occasion of pleasing the people and giving public testimonies of his zeal. The clergy approved of the resolution of the prince, which was an argument of his piety, and ordered all the Jews, on pain of death, *to depart his dominions or enter the church*—this was *effected* with *great rigour*. These specimens were before the sixth century. Matters became infinitely worse in the succeeding ones, up to the seventeenth. The crusades kindled a fresh zeal against the Jews passing through Cologne, Mentz, Worms, and Spires in the eleventh century, they massacred twelve thousand, others say, the numbers are incredible. Those of Worms claimed protection from the bishop, but he refused to receive them unless they turned Christians : the people suffered them not to deliberate long ; some embraced Christianity, which they abjured as soon as the form was over ; others killed themselves. The women seeing the crusaders coming, took knives and stabbed their children, saying it were better to send them to " Abraham's bosom " than to abandon them to the Christians." The bishop of Spires had more humanity. This was the first crusade, another was made fifty years after. Rodolphus preached it successfully on the banks of the Rhine. One of the articles of his religion and preachments was that those Jews in the country were first to be cut off

[1] Clavegero describes the number of Catechumens after the slaughter of the Mexican kings, priests, and nobility, as having been very great. He writes thus, ' After the conquest the number of Catechumens was so great that the missionaries were *obliged to omit* the use of their spittle in their baptism, because from doing it so much they dried up and almost excoriated their tongue and their throats.' Clavegero.

the earth, before they went forth to seek them in foreign parts. St. Bernard was not pleased with Rodolphus's doctrine, he wrote to the Archbishop of Mentz, whom this hermit had inflamed by his preaching, to prove that he ought to look upon the persecutions of the Jews as inhuman, that the hermit spoke without vocation, either from God or man, and therefore he advised that he should be sent back to his desert."

"This persecution kindled by the crusaders, was universal. The cry, not only in Germany, but in England, France, Spain, and Italy, was *"Come, let us massacre them in such a manner that the name of Israel shall be no more remembered."* Pope Alexander III. granted his protection prohibiting the seizing of their synagogues and disturbing with insults the celebration of their Sabbath or sacred festivals. The Abbot of Clairvoix also commiserated them, and wrote to intercede with Pope Innocent II. in their favor. The Christian's preparation for Easter-Sunday was breaking the windows of their houses, and stoning whoever came in their way. The bishop having often witnessed the inhuman proceeding, treated with the Jews, and obliged them to *buy off* this insult by *paying him a tribute.* Philip Augustus assuming an air of devotion, banished the Jews out of his kingdom and confiscated their estates, also robbing the fugitives of whatever money they had about them. Those in England suffered much under Richard, the *court* and people being prepossessed with the notion that they were all *conjurors.* A still greater calamity befel them when Richard crusaded. The Jews supposed they had obtained his favor by the great sums they had brought into his treasury; but the people resolved to make a general massacre of them. This was performed in many places, but the storm was terrible in York, where fifteen hundred had fled to the castle for defence. Their offer to redeem their lives having been refused, they cried in despair, "It is better to die courageously for the LORD, than to fall into the hands of the Christians." Every one stabbed his wife and children and at last themselves. These Christians "with satisfaction entered the desolate houses, loaded themselves with plunder, and discharged all their debts by burning the notes they had given to the bankers." So ended the twelfth century in England."—Basnage.

" Of the Church, the idea was " 'Tis a Queen that cannot bear a rival, but ought to assault and destroy her whereever she has the face to appear. The edicts and privileges which necessity extorts from kings *are no bar to her privileges,* nor ought to be any impediment to her pursuits. The erroneous poison and kill the soul, and therefore merit the punishment of murderers and poisoners which is the more justly inflicted because the death which they cause is eternal."

A member of the sanhedrim, held at Paris many years ago, thus concludes his address :—

" It seems as if their doom was *incessantly to suit all the dark and bloody purposes which can be suggested by human malignity supported by prejudice and ignorance and intoxicated by fanaticism."*

" Have they not been weighed down by taxes, and forced to contribute for the support of society, while they are debarred from its rights and privileges? If a destructive scourge happened to spread through a country ; the Jews had poisoned the *springs,* or these men, accursed by heaven, had nevertheless incensed it by their prayers against that nation which they were supposed to hate.

" Did sovereigns want means to carry on their wars ? the Jews were compelled to give up that wealth in which they some consolation against the oppressing sense of their

degraded condition; as a reward for their sacrifices, they
were expelled from the state which they had supported;
and were afterwards recalled to be stript again. Compelled
to wear badges exteriorily as the sign of their abject state,
they were everywhere exposed to the insults of the vilest
populace."

" When from his solitary retreat, a fanatical hermit
preached the crusade to the nations of Christendom; and a
part of its inhabitants left their country to moisten with their
blood, the plains of Palestine, the knell of *promiscuous
massacre* tolled before the tocsin of war. *Millions of Jews
were then murdered to glut the pious rage of the crusaders.*
It was by tearing the entrails of their brethren, that these
zealots sought to merit the protection of heaven. Skulls
of men, and bleeding hearts were presented as holocausts
on the altars of that GOD who has no pleasure in the blood,
even of the lamb—and ministers of peace were thrown into
a *holy* phrenzy by these bloody sacrifices."

" It is thus that Bâsle, Treves, Coblintz, and Cologn,
became human shambles. It is thus that upwards of four
hundred thousand victims of all ages and of both sexes,
lost their lives. And is it *after such* treatment that they
are reproached with *their* vices? Is it after being for
eighteen centuries the sport of *despite,* that they are reproached with being no longer alive to it? Is it after
having *so often* glutted with *their blood* the *thirst of their
persecutors,* that *they* are held out as enemies to the
nations? Is it that when they have been bereft of all
means to mollify the hearts of their oppressors, that indignation is roused, if now and then they cast a mournful look
toward their Temple—their Throne—their Inheritance?"

" By *what crimes* have we then deserved this implacable
intolerance? What is our guilt! is it that generous con-

stancy which we have manifested in defending the Laws of our people ? But this constancy ought to have entitled us to the admiration of the nations ; and it has only whetted their daggers of persecution against us. Braving all kinds of torments[1]—the pangs of death, and the still more terrible pangs of life, *we alone* have *withstood* the impetuous torrent of time sweeping indiscriminately in its career nations, religions, and countries."

COLUMBUS.

(Page 227)

The son of Columbus,—also his biographer, thus writes : " It being a material point in the history of any man of note to make known his country and origin, because they are best looked upon who are born of illustrious parentage ; therefore some would have had me spend my time in shew-ing that the admiral was honourably descended, though his parents, through the peevishness of fortune, were fallen into great poverty and want, and that I should have proved they were the offspring of Junius Colon, of whom Tacitus, in his twelfth book, says, " that he brought king Mithridates pri-soner to Rome, for which service the people assigned him the consular dignity, the eagle, or standard," &c. And they would have me give a large account of those two illustrious Coloni, their predecessors, who, Sabellius tells us "gained a mighty victory over the Venetians," &c.; but I refuse to undertake the task, believing that he was chosen by Al-mighty God for so great an affair, and because he was to be

---

[1] In the time of Ferdinand of Spain, and Pope Sextus IV. two thousand were tortured to death in the Inquisition.

truly his apostle from the Sea to the Rivers, not from courts and palaces, and to imitate himself, *whose progenitors were of the blood royal* of Jerusalem, yet it pleased Him that his parents should not be much known," &c.　In a letter to Prince John of Castile, the Admiral writes, " I am not the only admiral of my family, let them call me what they please, for when all is done, David was chosen to be a king over Jerusalem, and I am servant to the same Lord who raised him to the same dignity."—Life of Christ. Colon. in Pinkerton's Collection, Vol. xii. chap. i. p. 2.

ABUSE OF WORDS.

(Page 237)

" *How strange is the power of accustomed phrases to conceal from the mind the ideas they are intended to convey.*" *Saturday Evening, page* 247.　How still more strange, it may be added, is the sorcery which 'calls *evil* good and good evil,' &c.—Isaiah v. 10.

"They change the common meaning of words," observes Basnage, calling violence " *charity for the erroneous ;* " they call it a *holy severity;* they say the church employs *lenity* in denying all liberty of conscience, *forcing away* their children, *exile confiscations,* are *persuasions* rather than violence or constraints.　In this they say there is no constraint[1] or violence ; *they* are only somewhat *strong* persuasions, and liberty is not forced but *cured ;* the will is not the *less* free ; but it grows the more sound ; there is neither injury nor violence done to mind or body by the *cure* of it, when it is delivered from diseases and healed of mortal

---

[1] Thomassin Traite Histor. des Edites.

wounds though it be *by pain and torture.*" " The council at Paris held that the Church which abhors bloodshed, and delivers up to the *secular* arm all that *it has condemned,* without permitting *its judgment to be raised* is an *indulgent* mother who has *no hand in the murder* of her children. *Those gentle severities,*" adds Basnage, " which oblige a man to banish himself his country, and to seek a sanctuary in forests and caves among unrelenting strangers, where misery and grief eat him up, are *contradictory* things ; if the Church has a mind to punish, and fancies herself authorised to do it, let her speak sincerely, and authorise, if she dare, *cruelty and violence :* but let her not call disgrace, and pain, and misery, an *indulgence :* will it not be acknowledged that exile is one of the severest and most mortifying punishments ? are not the loss of estates confiscated to the church, pecuniary taxes, the depriving of the means of subsistence, the ruin and starving of families caused by *edict,* so many cruel punishments ? "

Shall we say that those thousands of Jews who were banished Spain and perished by famine and misery did not suffer ? or that the necessity of leaving all and exposing themselves to manifest peril of their lives ought to be considered as *persuasion which affected not their liberty !* Let people speak plainly. Father Thomassin authorises himself by the example of Avitas, who said to the Jews of Clermont, " I don't force you by violence to embrace the faith of the Church ; which is so true cried he, that those sorts of menaces or punishments are not violent constraints but *inducements* to remove the impediments to your instruction and conversion. Gregory of Tours related this with applause ; all historians agree that Avitas gave the alternative of entering the Church or banishment ; his injustice was so much the greater, because he not being a a sovereign but an ecclesiastical subject of the kingdom could not banish the inhabitants of Clermont.

In the year 615, a council was held in Paris, of seventy-nine bishops, when canons were instituted against Jews bringing actions against Christians, and on *violating* the *decrees* of the council they were with their families to ' *receive the grace of baptism* at the hand of the bishop! Lastly, can it be said that the Inquisition[1] is a *restoration of the premative penance?* and that the marks it impresses have nothing ignominious in them ; that all ecclesiastical prisons are only places of penitence, where it is wholly in the power of criminals to give themselves by this means an amnesty for all past crimes, as to corporeal punishments."

" Sicebec maintained that men ought to be left at liberty to *reject temporal* goods; but for those of the soul they ought to be forced to receive them as a child is obliged to learn his lesson." The inconsistencies are curious ; in one council it was agreed that men ought to be persuaded and *not* driven ; and anon ' such as have been converted by *violence* are to be *compelled* to keep the faith and continue in the church because they had received the sacraments, &c.' Lesenaud recommends the ecclesiastics to "*force* them to *perseverance.*" The death of the more humane and moderate kings, such as Isadore of Seville, were followed by councils who as the violent are to take the kingdom by force, viz. ' every Jew who shall not be baptized after the publication of the decree, shall receive a hundred stripes—shall be banished, and have all his goods confiscated.' "

---

[1] " A curious publication, showing the number of victims that have been sacrificed by the Inquisition, has just appeared, and according to which 105,285 fell under Torrequemada, 51,167 under Cisneros, and 34,952 under Diego Pesez. Those who suffered under the inquisitors who preceded these three monsters amounted to 3,410,215. It is reckoned that 31,912 have been burnt alive, 15,659 have suffered the punishment of the statue, and 291,450 that of the penitentiaries. 500,000 families have been destroyed by the Inquisition, and it has cost Spain two millions of her children."

THE ORDINATION OF THE APOSTLE PETER.

(Page 258)

The name of the Apostle Peter having during ages of moral darkness been assumed in subservience to foreign and adverse interests, it is due to the character of that Apostle to let in the Light of Scripture testimony, as well to make *manifest* his ordination and ministry as that basis upon which this assumption has been built, together with the nature of those interests which his name has been impiously employed to patronize.

Assumptions having no foundation in Truth, can only retain their place where 'the Law and the Testimony' has been *suppressed* by arbitrary power (as in the time of Antiochus Epiphanes) *withheld* by an exclusive claim to the key of knowledge (as by the Papal domination) or *explained away* by a mental process which volatilizes out of substance, and abstracts from locality (as is too frequently the case in modern times). The power by which ' good and evil' are manifested being *in* and *by* the Light of the Law of God, the most unskilful hand may be as serviceable in letting in that Light as the most efficient.

While the atonement had a universal *intent,* the ministration of the ' Prophet like unto Moses ' had a special commission to the ' Lost sheep of the House of Israel ;' and this is recognized by the Apostle Paul in these words "now I say unto you that Jesus Christ was an *Apostle of the Circumcison* (for the *Truth* of God) to *confirm* the promises made unto the fathers. Before the Good Shepherd laid down his life as a sin-offering, and confirmed by his resurrection the promises made to the fathers, he ordained and commissioned Cephas to fulfil in His stead His own special ministry—and this in an affecting and reiterated appeal to his affection for Himself. "Simon, son of Jonas, lovest thou me *more* than these?" "Yea, Lord," he replied, "thou knowest that I love thee." Jesus said to him—"Feed my lambs."

Again, he said "Simon, son of Jonas, *lovest* thou me?" and still the reply was, "Thou knowest that I love thee."

"Feed my sheep;"—was again urged as the test of that surpassing love.

When his Master the third time said—"Simon, son of Jonas, *lovest* thou *me* more than these?" Peter was grieved, (recurring mentally, as he doubtless did, to a thrice repeated protestation of attachment and fidelity which he had made in his own strength) he therefore said "LORD, thou knowest *all* things—thou knowest that I love thee." Jesus said to him, "Feed MY sheep; truly truly I say unto thee, when thou wast young thou didst gird thyself and didst go whither thou wouldest; but when thou shalt be old, thou shalt *stretch forth thine hands* and another shall gird thee, and carry thee *whither thou wouldst not.*"

Here is an express intimation of the induction of the Apostle Peter into the special ministry of HIM who bare "*the keys of the House of David,*" who opened and no man could shut—and shut and no man could open (Isa. xxii. 22. Rev. xxxvii.) and an equally express allusion to the *manner* of that death by which he should seal his testimony, and of his *unwilling* journey to Rome where he was crucified.

The office of Peter was specified as a messenger in the place or stead of his Master; therefore he never occupied nor claimed the office of bishop or overseer; that office having been assigned to James in the Messiah's witnessing Church in Jerusalem.

Of the specific vocation of Cephas the Apostle Paul thus speaks—

'When they saw the Gospel of the uncircumcision was committed unto me, even as that *of the circumcision was unto Peter* (for he who wrought effectually in Peter to the Apostleship of the circumcision —the same was mighty in me to the Gentiles) and when James, Cephas, and John, who were approved pillars, perceived the grace that was given to me and Barnabas, they gave us the right hand of fellowship, that we should go unto the Gentiles, and they unto the circumcision.' Accordingly, in the spirit of his commission, the Apostle Peter not alone feeds the flock committed to his trust ' with the pure milk of the WORD,' but is earnestly desirous that after his decease—after he should have sealed his testimony with his blood ' they might always have the Truth which he taught in remembrance.' His epistle is accordingly dedicated to his brethren, as the *strangers* scattered throughout those extensive countries which he enumerates. It is to be noted that Asia, which is one of these, joins the New Continent in its extreme eastern coast, where ' the outcasts of Israel' had long been secluded from the tribe of Judah, from whom nearly a thousand years before they had become rent: hence his mention of them in the precise terms by which the prophet Hosea had designated them immediately before their expatriation.

This prophet was to symbolize the impending calamity on the ten tribes, by calling his first-born son *Lo-ammi—(not my people)* and again, (as if an intervening series of ages were a mere parenthesis—' a little moment ') it is added— ' *yet* the number of the Children of Israel shall be as the sand on the shore—which cannot be measured nor numbered —and it shall come to pass that *in the place* where it had been said to them—'*not* my people'—*there* shall it be

said, ye are the sons of the living GOD.   The Apostle
Peter therefore addresses these immeasurably extended ' prisoners of Hope,' whom he describes as strangers spréad
abroad various intermediate places, and in *Asia* (which in
in its most eastern extremity unites with the western hemisphere) precisely in the language which the prophet had
applied to them nearly a thousand years before.   ' Ye
are a chosen generation, a royal priesthood, an holy nation, a
purchased people that ye should show forth the *virtues* of
Him who hath called you out of darkness into his marvellous
Light, which sometime were ' not a people,' but now the
people of God ;' which had not obtained mercy, but now
have obtained mercy.'   This last expression is with reference to the symbolic name of a former child *Lo-ruhamah*—
(for I will *no more have mercy* upon the House of Israel, but
will utterly take them away.)   The Apostle continues—
' Dearly Beloved ! I beseech you, as strangers and pilgrims,
abstain from fleshly desires which war against the soul,
having your conversation honest among the Gentiles, that
whereas they speak against you as of evil-doers, *they may
by your good works glorify God in the day of visitation.*
For this is estimable : if a man for conscience sake toward God, endure grievance, suffering wrongfully.   For
what glory is it, when being smitten for your offences ye
take it patiently ; but if ye do well and suffer for that
taking it patiently, this is acceptable to God ; for even to
this end were *ye* called : because the Messiah also suffered
for us, leaving us an example that we should follow his
steps—who did no transgression, neither was guile found in
his mouth ; who, when he was reviled, reviled not again ;
when he suffered, he threatened not, but committed His
cause to Him who judgeth righteously ; who bare our transgressions in His own body on the tree, that we being dead

to transgression, should live unto righteousness; for all we like sheep had gone astray, but are now returned to the Shepherd and Guardian of our souls.

"Beloved, think not strange *the fiery trial which is to try you*, as though some extraordinary thing happened to you; but rejoice, inasmuch as ye are partakers of the sufferings of the Messiah, that when His glory shall be revealed, ye may rejoice also with exceeding great joy. *If ye be reproached for the name of the Messiah* happy are ye; for the spirit of glory and of God resteth upon you; on their part He is contemned, but on your part He is glorified; but let *none of you* suffer as robbers, or murderers, or as evil doers, or those who intermeddle with the concerns (which belong not to them) or of others."

It was then this very people which had been called for a time *Lo-ami*, which through the Mediator had become the "Sons of the Living God," that the Apostle thus graphically and vividly recognises, admonishes, and comforts, as if every event of their prospective experience were present to his mind; and it was in their more remote seclusion, and at a more mature period of their history, that in the name of this Apostle, and by the authority of that plenary apostolic power conveyed to his assumed successors, that the robbery and slaughter of countless multitudes of this flock (whom he was commanded to *feed for* his Master's *sake*,) was accomplished.

Paul had premonition of this maturity of the "mystery of iniquity" which had, even in his day an incipient existence; he foresaw the *independent* position—the *lawless* power which would, instead of acknowledging the stability of the Root and Stock and the re-engrafting of the *natural* branches (amongst whom the Gentiles were to be received and ministered to as *grafts*) assume an independent standing,

and with it the " strong delusion" that the Root and Stock
and branches of the good Olive served but as the *type* or
shadow of their transcendent experience.

To guard against this unscriptural error and its fatal
results, the apostle entreats the Reigning Domination to keep
in mind that Gentiles, being at the best grafts, bear not the
Stock, but the Stock bears such as are adopted together with those who after a season shall be reclaimed when
the Deliverer shall come forth from Zion to recall them.
Hence with a view to check that growing perversion,' he
adds, " wherefore I take you to witness this day, that I am
pure from the blood of all, for I have not shunned to declare unto you all, *the whole counsel of God.*" Take heed
to yourselves and to the flock over which the Holy Spirit
hath made you overseers, to feed the Church of God, which
He hath purchased with His own blood; for I know this,
that after my departure shall ravening wolves enter in among
you, *not sparing the flock.*" " Therefore watch and remember, for three years long I ceased not to warn every one
night and day with tears."   *   *   *   *   *

*   *   *   *   *   *

*   *   *   *   *   *   *

*   *   *   *   *   *

Where no privilege has been accorded, exculpatory
evidence is admitted for those who have erred; while
severe equity makes no abatement, and accepts of no com-
promise in the case of those who have " *known His
will.*" It was declared that the queen of the south should
rise in the Judgment and condemn the contemporaries of
one greater than Solomon, whose wisdom *they rejected.*

It was also intimated that of *that* generation would be
required the righteous blood which had been shed from the
blood of Abel to that of Zachariah, who was slain at the

altar. The Divine Prophet did not include his own, *that* having been voluntarily shed for the accomplishment of peace and reconciliation, but it will be required where *all* shall be "*found*" which has been shed since the beginning of the world."—Rev. xviii. 24.

" By the sword of Rome, the Messiah's witnessing Church which was composed exclusively of Jews who believed in the *atonement* of the " Seed of the woman " and in His *identity* with the future King of Israel, (was "*cut off.*" By the *same sword,* (for in becoming a nominal Christian, Rome did not relinquish, but *consecrate the sword,*) the Western Hemisphere has been made one vast Aceldama :—a consideration which may yield much reflex light on the prophetic pages, and on none more strongly than on one which were else obscure. " Rejoice over her, ye Heavens, and ye holy *apostles,* and *prophets;* for God hath *avenged you* on her."—Rev. xviii. 20.

STATISTICAL EXPOSITION OF THE PRESENT STATE OF MEXICO.

(Page 259.)

The following sketch of the present aspect of Mexico, is from the pen of a citizen of that place, and appeared in the Philadelphia Evening Post, February 19, 1831:

" The population of the Mexican States is nearly eight millions. It has increased ever since 1794, when it was only five millions ; and even during the civil war of the revolution and independence, since in 1806 it was only 5,500,000.

" The population is divided as follows:

1. The most numerous are the pure Indians,
   which are about -   -   -   -   - 4,000,000
2. The Mertizos, or offspring of Indians and
   Spaniards, are about -   -   -   - 2,000,000
3. The Creoles, or offspring of the Spaniards
   are about -   -   -   -   -   - 1,000,000
4. The Zambos, or offspring of Indians and Negroes, including the Mulatoes of white
   and black blood, and many of mixed origin,
   about -   -   -   -   -   -   - 600,000
5. The Negroes about -   -   -   - 100,000
6. The Guachuppins, or Spaniards born in
   Spain, were 80,000 before the revolution
   and late expulsion, now reduced to -   - 10,000
7. The strangers of various nations, British,
   French, Germans, Italians, Americans,
   &c. about -   -   -   -   -   - 15,000
                                        ─────────
                                        7,725,000

" The relative population shows that the Indians and
Mertizos form the bulk of the nation, and now having
equal rights, are surely to rule at a future time. The
Spaniards were once the rulers: the Creoles have succeeded them, and been compelled to admit the Indians
(whom they *nicknamed* 'unrationals!' calling themselves
' rationals!') to equal rights in order to carry on the struggle
of the revolution, which could not have been accomplished
without their aid; but they foresaw that power cannot last
long in their hands, and wisely try to amalgamate. None
but the most deluded attempt to stem the current of irresistible power and future sway.

" The pure Indians, so much calumniated, are by far the
best in character; they are mild, gentle, good, industrious,
honest, and kind; they love one another; respect their

parents; never cheat, lie, or steal. This applies to nine out of ten, who are all cultivators.

" Those who live in cities, or near them, are more or less tainted by the vices of the Creoles, and exceed them.

" A Question:—How are the feelings of the Mexicans toward the States of North America? (The answer is given by the same citizen of Mexico.) Towards the North Americans, the actual administration bears no good will, but rather distrust and dislike. They complain, 1st. That Poinsett meddled with the politics of the country, and that the conspirators of Pedraza actually met in his house.

2. " That he insulted the Mexican nation by offering to buy ' Texas,' a federal territory, unalienable by constitution, of 160 millions of acres for ten millions of dollars, or six cents (three pence) per acre.

3. " That when he found his offer objectionable, he further insulted the nation by offering a loan of ten millions as *a pawn-broker would,* upon the *pawning* of Texas, until repaid ; which invidious proposal was meant to fill the country of Texas with Americans and their slaves, and to hold it afterwards at any event, the United States never meaning to restore it. This was deemed, even by the patriotic party who were great friends of the Americans and Poinsett, an insult similar to the offer of the Mexicans to buy or pawn Louisiana, or Arkansas, if made to the United States.

4. " The Americans are *secretly encroaching* towards Texas and the frontiers in *the usual manner they employ to dispossess the Indians, by allowing outlaws, squatters, and other miscreants, to intrude and settle unlawfully.*

5. " The citizens of the United States encourage the incursions of the wild incensed predatory tribes against Mexico and the Texas ; furnishing them with arms, buying their spoil, mules, &c. and even Mexican freemen, who are

bought as slaves, and some Mulattoes and Indians, held as such even now in Louisiana.

6. " That American emissaries have suggested several times in Texas, to rebel and declare Texas independent of Mexico, or even to ask a union with *the United States, who will allow the bane of slavery.*

7. " That the United States invading gradually all the Indian lands, and removing the Indians on the borders of Mexico, *commit a great injustice,* and lay a foundation for future quarrels and troubles with Mexico.

8. " That by their *perfidy* against the Indians in the south and west, and *breaking solemn treaties* with them, *the United States evince they will not deem sacred any treaty* with the Mexican nation, the majority of which is Indian population, quite similar to the persecuted Cherokees, Creeks, and Choctaws.

9. " Lastly—That the Spanish invaders under General Barradas, in 1829, were chiefly carried over from Cuba to Tampico, in North American vessels, and some disabled ones were allowed to refit in New Orleans. The Spanish troops were well received, recruited, and actually sailed from New Orleans to invade Mexico."

These subjects of complaint were artfully fomented by the English agents and party; a cry of war was raised against the United States; and a loan of two millions offered to carry it on, invade Louisiana, declare all the Negroes free, expel the Americans from Texas, &c. even the patriotic party and friends of North America were staggered.

" Nothing is more calculated to alienate them than the *bad treatment of the Indians in the United States.*

Formerly the North Americans were welcome any where; now their situation is precarious in Texas, and even in the city of Mexico.

'An American, Mr. M'Clure of Philadelphia, who was highly respected, and wealthy, gave a gift of seven thousand dollars at the Spanish invasion of Barrados, to clothe a regiment of cavalry. This munificent act was ascribed to ostentation. He had offered to educate two hundred select Indian youths at a small expence, in a college on the Wa-bash. The *cautious* Mexican government sent an agent to examine the place and prospects, who has made and printed a Spanish and English report, stating that it was *another deception.*—The college being a mere school under the direction of a vicious and ungodly individual, and the United States are *totally unfit to educate the Indians whom they oppress and defame.*

" In any further contest with North America, the Mexicans think they will be quite a match for their northern neighbours.

" It happens that the nearest States to Mexico have *a large slave population,* which it would be very easy to rouse by an offer of complete freedom. Also the borders of the two countries are filled with Indian remnants, *driven by the United States,* and concentrated in a vulnerable point, which would join the Mexican soldiers who are nearly all Indians.

" The Mexican population will soon equal that of the freemen of North America. They are becoming warlike, and the table-land population has no dread of a colder climate. This does not imply that the Mexicans ever mean to make conquests; but they will retaliate if attacked or deeply aggrieved—and have the means to assail with advantage.

" Against this the Americans have only their numbers— *greedy thirst for lands, slavery, and oppression of the Indians.*

" The Mexican government is taking measures to secure

Texas. Five regiments have been sent to form military colonies, and at the peace with Spain all the disbanded soldiers are to receive grants of lands there, on condition of actual settlement.

"The Mexicans also begin to know the value of unsettled lands; no great grant has been made there since the old one of Austin.

"All late applications and offers have been rejected, even those of **B** * * and **O** * *, both Britons, who offered to bring English settlers as a bulwark against the Americans. But small grants or sales to actual settlers of any nation are made at the rate of forty dollars for one hundred acres, with six years credit, no man is allowed to purchase above 50,000 acres.

"All Indians and Negroes fleeing from oppression and slavery of the United States are received and protected. All slaves become free by entering Texas, when they can reach it (as they do in Canada.) The Indians receive land to settle upon. They are considered as the best bulwarks against the Americans, and a check upon the settlers of North American origin.

"The Choctaus, Creeks, and Cherokees, now driven to despair by the policy of the United States, *refused the privileges of men,* and compelled to leave their homes, would find there an asylum, and be received with open arms. They might be made citizens at once by a special law, or become such in five years: receive grants of lands, either gratis or at a low price, and be deemed the best settlers to form *a barrier of foes* against American encroachments."

On the subject of the religion of the modern Mexicans, the same idividual observes, "The Roman Catholic religion was made *exclusive* in Mexico, for fear that *nearly all the native population would relapse into their ancient religion.*

" The worship of the Spaniards is only a *kind of idolatry.*[1] The Indians call the images or pictures of the canonized saints, *the idols of the Guachupins,* (a contemptuous nickname for the Spaniards) while they call their ancient ones the *memorials* of *their ancestors.*

" In remote villages they keep both kinds, and *crown* their ancient ones with flowers in preference, praying before them in secret. Nay, in some places the prayers at *sun rise* is preserved, and observed privately.

" Many Indians despise their curates, whose lives in remote places, are not without blemish, often indulging in concubines, and even polygamy, which the Indians seldom do. Nay, the curates of Indian blood have a *secret longing to reclaim their ancient worship. When a religious freedom shall be proclaimed, which must happen at some future period*—one half perhaps of the Indians would return to their ancient worship.

The writer of a pamphlet entitled ' On the Ten Tribes of Israel, viz. Aborigines of America,' observes : " For ourselves, the way appears to be preparing by which we are to be chastised by this very people, who will now be concentrated in Mexico, Texas, &c. for the purpose. The present

---

[1] ' Olmeda,' observes Claverego. 'undertook to explain the mysteries of the faith of the holy church from the following incident. Teuititli observed that the Spaniards on hearing the stroke of the bell for Ave Maria, kneeled down before the holy cross, and in wonder asked, *Why they worshipped* that piece of wood ? '

Thus De Menonville, an eye witness, describes the representation of the assumption of the Virgin. " Mary is seen in prostration in a superb chariot with six wheels ; two bishops dressed in copes and mitres hold the naves, mounted behind on the footman's stand ; the trainers are twelve cherubims with blue wings and in *Roman dresses*, a *helmet* on their heads with feathers, and their hair floating in the manner of dancers in the *serious opera* ; they are harnessed to the car with braces, like our cannoneers to the gun. *Elias* on the box with a *lily* in his hand (held like *a whip*) acts as coachman, and his disciple Elisha on horseback as postilion."—Menonville's Travels, in Pinkerton Coll.

(Page 260.)

Like the ancients of the East, the primitive inhabitants of the Western Hemisphere, considered the varied objects and combinations of nature as one vast page of hieroglyphic instruction designed and dictated by unerring WISDOM and replete with lessons of illustration and of analogy ; nor was the emblazoned firmament excluded from the same contemplation and research :—to them it conveyed *more* than that evidence of creative wisdom and sustaining goodness, which it addresses to the *mind* of every intelligent creature under heaven : its language was addressed also to their *heart*, for it was that of " *Hope*."

While Europeans have restricted their attention to astronomy [1] as an abstract branch of science which affords no higher results than such as are subservient to the interests of commerce and of agriculture—and which claimed no other inquiry than that which the most exact calculations and measurement could effect ; the transatlantic Hebrews have characteristically viewed the celestial orbs rather in

---

[1] " Plato called God, the great Geometrician, and Kepler, the worthy successor of such a master, believed that certain perfect numbers and geometrical figures had a hidden analogy to all the operations of nature."

the character of unvarying records, *"for* SIGNS *and for* SEASONS." Genesis i. 14.

However geographically *remote,* or *cut off,* from their promised inheritance, they could not but take comfort in looking up to the constant attestation of these bright chronicles to that treaty of prospective heirship which was made to Abraham and his posterity, and which these words were given to confirm: " Look now to the firmament— count the stars, if thou art able to number them—so shall thy seed be."

Again, in the darkest times of tribulation, when pro- selyting zeal seemed to vie with that of the exterminating sword in " cutting off " the existence of Israel as a People, looking up they could read of the impossibility of the powers of moral darkness to make void the sure cove- nant of national perpetuity, whether in dispersion or in remote banishment. " While sun and moon endure, Israel shall not cease from being a nation before Me for ever ! "

Certain celestial luminaries are also ordained in the cycles which they describe, to act in concert with those SEASONS of which these are indicative, and which were part and parcel of the Law of the promised Land.

These Sabbatical periods were the seventh year and the forty-ninth, or *seven* times seventh year—the Jubilee. Be- yond these are two other cyclical ' *seasons,*' the former con- sisting of " seventy-times seven," Jubilean epochs—the latter so immensely distant as to become rather a subject for faith to receive with awe, than one for season to scan.

These seasons have only been suspended in the Land as regards the non-observance of them by an expatriated people —they are still constituting epochs, until the arrival of that period when they shall be resumed.

" Thus saith the LORD, The LAND also shall be left

of them, and shall enjoy Her Sabbaths while she lieth desolate without them." "And yet for all that, when they are
in the land of their enemies, I will not cast them off, neither
will I destroy them utterly, nor break My covenant with
them; for I am the LORD their God; but I will, for their
sakes' remember the covenant of their ancestors, whom I
brought forth from the land of Egypt in the sight of
the nations—that I might be their God."—Lev. xxvi.
43, &c.

The LORD, to whose mind future is ever present, in
instituting the *Jubilee*, (knowing that it never would be kept
until the Land should have been *redeemed*)—evidently refers
to that future season in these definite words :—" *In the* YEAR
of THIS JUBILEE, *ye shall return every man to his possession.*" Levit. xxv. 25.

The LORD had, as Creator, a supreme claim to the
Land, but inasmuch as it had become alienated or sold to the
adversary, by reason of the transgression of the people; it
is only to be reclaimed by Him, through that power of
redemption which could be exercised by a *near* kinsman, who
should, in paying the arrear, purchase it back to the orignal
occupants.

" The Land shall not for ever be alienated," saith the
LORD, *for the* LAND *is* MINE, and ye are strangers and
sojourners with Me." Levit. xxv. 10.

In the interval the exiled owner might, *if he could*, return
to his possession, by paying the price—but failing in the possibility of being able to meet the demand, the inheritance
must remain in the hand of him who hath purchased it, till
the year of jubilee, and in the year of jubilee it shall expire,
and he shall return to his possession.

" If a dwelling-house be not redeemed within a full year,
then the house that is in a walled city, shall be *established*

for ever to him who *purchased* it, and shall not go out in the Jubilee.

" If a stranger become rich in thy place, and thy brother, who dwelleth by him, become destitute, and sell himself to the stranger, or the stock of the stranger's family, after having been sold, he may be redeemed again, *one of his brothers* may redeem him, and he shall go forth in the year of jubilee and his children with him; for unto ME are the children of Israel servants whom I brought forth out of the land of Egypt."

This Redeeming 'Season' is therefore identical with the Second coming of the Saviour as the Deliverer to those who turn from transgression in Jacob. "The day of vengeance is in mine heart, and the *year of My redeemed* is come."

" Behold the LORD hath proclaimed *to the extremity of the earth*—declare ye to the daughter of Zion—Behold thy salvation cometh; behold His reward is with Him, His recompense before Him. And they shall be called, *The holy people—the redeemed* of the LORD! and thou shalt be called reclaimed, a City unalienated. As the testimony of the Redeemer is the spirit of prophecy which holds to view the *crisis* rather than the continuity of events, it was on His redemption that the prophetic eye of the blessed Mary rested, when her soul magnified the LORD and her spirit rejoiced in God her Redeemer; it was the *result*, not its intermediate steps—(these should pierce her soul,) which Gabriel announced in these words, " He shall be great, and shall be called the Son of the Most High, and the LORD God shall give unto Him the throne of his father David; and He shall reign over the house of *Jacob* for ever; and of His kingdom there shall be no end." It was in the anticipation of this season also that Zacharias uttered these re-animating words, "Blessed be the LORD God of Israel, for He hath visited and *redeemed* His people, and hath raised up a power of salvation in the house of his servant David, as he spake by the mouth of all his holy prophets since the world began. That we should be reclaimed from our enemies, from the hand of those that hate us; to perform the grace promised to our fathers, and to remember His holy covenant—that He would grant unto us, that we being delivered out of the hand of our enemies might serve Him without fear in holiness and righteousness before Him all our lives. It is therefore in sympathy with this season of terrible retribution on the privileged nations, for the neglect or perversion of the means of their salvation, that "the sun shall change into darkness and the moon into blood" at the coming of the great and terrible DAY of the LORD.

But there is not only a relative and chronological affinity recognized between the solar system and the times and seasons which they determine; one of analogy is likewise pointed out to human individuality.

Those who assume *above* the rank of sonship to be "*as gods*," judging *independently* of the Law and the Testimony, (and who consequently are left to the extremes of attraction and repulsion—to conflicting influences, and those arbitrary impulses which drive *on* such as are uncontroled by the WORD); are characterised by the apostle Jude as "wandering stars, to whom is reserved the blackness of darkness for ever."

While the planets are distinguished by those scintillations which indicate their constant adherence to their governing law, the comets (which are also planets) in the erratic deviation of their headlong career, instead of thus being " clothed with light as with a garment," convert that blessing into an ominous train which affords only the warning of that danger which its presence implies.[1]

" Those who bear testimony to Truth, the Divine Prophet characterizes as *stars.* " Ye sent unto John, and he bare witness unto the Truth."—" He was a burning and a shining light, and ye were willing for a time to rejoice in his light ; but I have a greater witness than that of John, for *the works* which the FATHER hath given me to finish— these works that I do, bear witness of me that the FATHER hath *sent* me ; and the FATHER Himself who sent me hath borne witness of me. Ye have never heard His voice *at any time,* neither seen his similitude."

" The Prophet Daniel, in like manner, speaking of the Kingdom to come, says, " they that are *wise* shall shine as the luminous firmament, and they that *turn many to righteousness,* as the stars for ever and ever."

MEDICAL ART.

(Page 270.)

Clavegero observes, "Amongst other arts of the Mexicans, that of medicine has been entirely overlooked by the Spanish historians. They have contented themselves with saying, that the Mexican physicians had a great knowledge of herbs, and that by means of these they performed mi-

---

[1] " Comets are, although planets, distinguished from them chiefly by their fiery tails, which continually issue from the side which is *farthest* from the sun. These vast bodies move in exceeding long intervals, or very eccentric ellipses of such amazing irregularity, that some part of their journey their appear to be so near the sun, as to be almost vitrified by heat, and then go off again into the regions of space, to such immense distances, as must nearly deprive them of the light and heat which the rest of the planets receive from that luminary."

raculous cures; but do not mark the progress which they made in an art so beneficial to the human race." "Those who followed the profession of medicine, instructed their sons in the nature of the various diseases to which the human frame is subject; and of the herbs which the Creator has given for their remedy, the virtues of which had been experienced by their ancestors."

" They taught them the art of discerning the symptoms and progress of different distempers, and to prepare the medicines and apply them. We have ample proof of this in the Natural History of Mexico by Dr. Hernandez, physician to Philip II. of Spain, and much renowned by the works which he published. He was by that Monarch sent to study the natural history of the Empire."

" This learned and laborious inquirer had always the Mexican physicians for his guides, in the study to which he devoted himself in that Empire. They communicated to him the knowledge of twelve hundred plants, with their proper Aboriginal names; and the names of more than two hundred species of birds, and a large number of quadrupeds, reptiles, fishes, insects, and minerals," &c.

" From his valuable, though imperfect history, a system of practical medicine may be formed from that kingdom; and has in part been done by Dr. Farsan in his book of *cures*, by Gregorio Lopez, and other eminent physicians."

" Among the purgatives employed by the native physicians besides pine seed, and the small bean, the *Mecoahan*, so well known in Europe in putrid fevers, was the *Tzticpatli*, much celebrated by Hernandez, and the *Amamartli*, vulgarly called Rhubarb of the brothers. Amongst other emetics made use of by the Mexicans, the *Mexochitl*, and the *Axixtlacotl*, were also highly praised by Hernandez. Amongst their antidotes, the famous *Contraierba* was deservedly valued, commonly called ' serpent tongue,' and *Coapatli*, as remedy against the poison of serpents. Amongst their errhines, was the *Toxojatic*, a plant so efficacious, that it was sufficient to hold the root to the nose, to produce sneezing. For intermittent fevers they generally employed the *Chatlhuic*, and in other kinds of fevers the *Chiautzolli*, the *Tztaczalli*, the *Huehuetzontico-matl*, and above all, the *Tzticpatli*."

" To prevent the illness which frequently followed too much exercise, they used to eat the bark of the *Apzalpatli* soaked in water. We should never finish were we to mention all the plants, gums, minerals, and other medicines, simple and compound, which they employed against all the distempers which were known to them. Whoever desires to be more amply informed on this subject, may consult the above-mentioned work of Hernandez, and the two treatises published by Dr. Monardes, a Sevillian physician, on the medical articles which used to be brought from that region to Europe.

" Among the means employed by the Mexican physicians for the preservation of health, that of the bath was most esteemed. They bathed extremely often, several times in the same day when the weather was hot.

" The Mexicans and other tribes of Anahuac, made little less frequent use of the bath *Temazcalli*, or vapour-bath. This bath is usually formed of bricks. The form of it is similar to that of a baker's oven ; but with this difference, that the pavement of the *Temazcalli*, is a little convex, and lower than the surface of the earth, whereas that of most ovens is plain, and a little elevated for the accommodation of the baker. Its greatest diameter is from eight to nine feet, and its greatest height six. The entrance, like the mouth of an oven, is wide enough to allow a man to creep

easily in. In the place opposite to the entrance, there is a
furnace of stone or raw bricks, with its mouth outwards to
receive the fuel from the outside, and a hole above it to
carry off the smoke."

" The part which unites the furnace to the bath, and
which is about two feet and a half square, is shut with a
dry stone of Tetzontli, or some other porous stone. In the
upper part of the vault is an air-hole like that to the furnace.

" When any one goes to bathe, he first lays a mattrass
within the *Temazcalli*, a pitcher of water, and a bunch of
herbs. He then orders a fire to be made in the furnace,
which is kept burning, until the stones which join the
Temazcalli, and furnace, are *quite hot*. The person who is
to use the bath enters accompanied by a domestic; he is
either naked or slightly covered. As soon as he enters, he
shuts the entrance close, but leaves the air-hole at the top
open for a few minutes to let out the smoke should any have
collected in the vault; when it is all out he stops up the
air hole. He then throws water upon the hot stones, from
which immediately arises a thick vapour, to the top of the
Temazcalli. While the person lies upon the mat, the domestic drives the vapour downwards, and with the bunch of
herbs gently beats the patient on the ailing part. The
herbs are first dipped in the water, which is by that time a
little warm. The sick person falls immediately into a soft
and copious perspiration, which is increased or diminished at
pleasure, according as the case requires. When the evacu-
ation desired is obtained, the vapour is let off, the entrance
is cleared and the sick person clothes himself, or is transported on the mat to his chamber; as the entrance to the
bath is usually within some chamber of his habitation.

" The *Temazcalli* has been regularly used in several
disorders, especially those connected with the digestive

organs. The Indian women use it frequently, and always after child-birth; as also persons who have been stung by some poisonous reptile. It is undoubtedly a powerful remedy for all such as have occasion to carry off gross humours; and certainly it would be very useful in countries where rheumatism is prevalent and afflicting."

" When a very copious perspiration is desired, the sick person is raised up and held in the vapour; as he perspires the more the nearer he is to it."

" The *Temazcalli* is so common, that in every place inhabited by the Indians there are many of them."

" With respect to surgery, the Spanish conquerors attest their expedition and success in dressing and curing wounds: Cortez himself was completely cured of wounds received by the Tlascalan art of surgery. Besides the balsam and *Maripenda*, they employed the milk of the *Tzontpatli* (species of thistle) tobacco, and other herbs. For ulcers, they used the *Nanahuapatli*, the *Zacatlipatli*, and the *Itzcuin-patli*: for abcesses and several swellings, the *Halamatl* and the milk of the *Chelpatli*: and for fractures the *Nacazol* or *Toloazin*, after drying and reducing the seed of this plant to powder, they mixed it with a certain gum, and applied it to the affected part, laid it over with feathers, and over it placed little boards to set the bones."

" It is believed that the vapour baths of the Indians have found a zealous admirer and advocate in the person of the celebrated Mr. Whitlaw, who has introduced them with great success to the notice of the people of Britain. Mr. W. spent several years among the Aborigines of North America, and from them gained much information on the subject of medical plants and roots. It is an interesting consideration that this indefatigable student of nature, in that valuable department of its stores to which he applies his mind, adopts and recommends the Mosaic ritual in the selection of animal food.

In connection with these remarks, it affords a pleasing coincidence to learn that in his researches amongst the Indians, he believed them to be the descendants of the missing ten tribes of Israel. This is stated, however, on the report of some of the friends of Mr. Whitlaw, rather than from personal knowledge of the circumstance.

REGAL STATE OF MONTEZUMA.

(Page 287.)

Peter Martyr gives the following description of Montezuma, and his court, in the fourth chapter of his fifth Decade:

" Let us therefore say something of the palaces[1] of the

---

[1] " Montezuma had many palaces : the one in which he chiefly resided hath three courts ; in one is a fair fountain, many halls, and one hundred chambers from twenty-three to thirty feet long ; and one hundred baths, hot and cold. The walls were of mason's work of marble, jasper, and black stones with veins of red ; the roofs were wrought of timber, cedar, cypress, and pine, without nails ; and were curiously carved. The chambers were painted and hung with cloth of cotton, or else made of feathers and rabbits' hair. For beds they use mantles laid upon mats, or mats alone. There were one thousand ladies ; and including the attending gentlewomen and slaves, about three thousand, many of them were noblemen's daughters. Montezuma took those which he liked best ; and many he gave in marriage to his gentlemen.

" The shield or arms of the king is an eagle, seizing a tiger with his talons.

" There was another palace : which had galleries with pillars of jasper, leading to a goodly garden ; in which are ten or more ponds of fresh and salt water, full of every kind of lake or river bird ; mostly unknown to the Spaniards and ad-mirable to behold. They were carefully attended by three hundred persons. Tapestry, tufts, targets, and rich mantles were made of their feathers, most perfectly worked."

Purchase goes on to state the detail of the Menagerie, and concludes thus :

" The roaring of the lions, the fearful hissings of the snakes and adders, the howling of the wolves, the yelling of the tigers and ounces, when they were to be fed, was a strange sight. It seemed a dungeon of hell and dwelling place of the devil ; and so it was indeed, for near it was a hall one hundred and fifty feet long, and thirty broad, where was a chapel, with a roof covered with plates of silver and gold, store of pearls. agates, emeralds, rubies, and other sorts ; and this was the oratory where Montezuma prayed in the night season ; and where the devil appeared unto him, and gave him answers according to his prayers."

nobility, &c. and of their excellent buildings. Cortez saith that he never saw any palace in Spain, either of kings or any other princes, which the meanest of seventy stone or marble houses doth not match; who saith that they are all built by the curious art of the architect, with pavements of divers sorts, and palaces of jasper stone or white transparent marble, round about the courts and large galleries under the solars. He further addeth, that whatsoever is reported concerning these things ought to be credited, saying, It is no wonder, for Montezuma hath many large kingdoms, in the which a great multitude of noblemen govern many countries, as under the Emperor's crown, many dukes, earls, marquises, and nobles of other titles are shadowed; all these at certain times of the year, by an ancient custom, frequent the court of Montezuma; nor may they do otherwise. It is a thing whereto they are much inclined, that every one should strive in his desires to excel his companions in build-ing of sumptuous houses. I might compare the manner of the Pope's cardinals at Rome to their magnificence, but much otherwise; for the cardinals in the buildings have respect but unto themselves, not regarding succession; but these people being obedient to Montezuma, provide for posterity long to come, for they send their own children to be brought up with Montezuma, especially such as descend from nobility: whereof there is so great multitude, that every day as soon as day-light appeareth, you may see more than five hundred such young noblemen walking in the halls and open solars of Montezuma, with whose familiars, pages, and followers, three great courts and streets before the gates of the palace are filled at that time to the hour of dinner: all these are fed with Montezuma's provision. He saith the cellars are never shut all day long, and that any man may demand drink of the butlers; yet no man seeth the king be-

fore he come forth to dinner or supper, out of the privy
chambers, into the great hall, whose equal in greatness,
Cortez saith, he knows not any. When he is set, four[1]
hundred young men, appareled after the Palatine manner,
come unto him, and every one of them brings several dishes
of divers dainty meats with chafing dishes under them, that
the meats freeze not in the winter time, but they come not
near the table, for it is compassed about with a rail; only
one standeth within the rail who taketh the several dishes
from their hands, and setteth them before the Prince, being
ready to dine.   Montezuma *giveth with his own hands* of the
dishes, to six ancient men of great authority, *standing at his
right hand;* who after the ancient manner, while he dineth,
stand all *barefooted.*   The pavements are covered with
mats.   If it so happen that he call any, he that is called
goeth unto him bowing his body with his *face to the ground,*
and lifteth not up his head at all before he be gone far from
him, going backward; for he may not turn his back towards
him.   No man useth directly to look upon the king; his
familiars and friends, and also the princes, casting down
their eyes, and turning their faces to the left or right hand,
hearken what the king answers, and hereupon they blamed
Cortez, because he suffered the Spanish, whom he called
unto him, to behold him with a direct countenance," &c.

" Every dinner and supper he washeth *his hands on both
sides,* and wipeth them with a very white linen, and the

---

[1] " The emperor," says Gomara, " had a pleasant countenance and good eyes;
gravity and goodness were blended when he spoke: he was neat and fine in his
attire—bathed four times a day—he always ate alone, and with solemnity. his
table was either a pillow, or a couple of coloured skins.   His table-cloth, nap-
kins, and towels were of the whitest cotton, and never used more than once.
Four hundred pages, the sons of nobles, brought in his dinner, and placed it on
the table in the great hall : when Montezuma pointed out the viands he would
eat.   Twenty fair women presented the *basin* and *ewer*—he then seated himself,
and trellis work being drawn before him, the steward serving him alone, barefoot,
and in profound silence, &c.   At a distance were six ancient nobles, to whom the
king gave such dishes as he knew they liked," &c.

towel he once useth he never taketh in hand again. All instruments must never be touched more. The like doth he concerning his apparel. Arising from his bed, he is clothed after one manner as he cometh forth to be seen and returning back to his chamber, after he hath dined he changeth his garments, and when he cometh forth again to supper, he taketh another, and returning back again the fourth, which he weareth until he go to bed ; and once taken into the wardrobe, they are filed up on heaps, and not like to see the face of man any more." " Martyr proceeds to say that Montezuma occasionally made presents of these garments to his friends and distinguished soldiers, and it deserves to be remarked, that frequent change of raiment, and presents of apparel, as a mark of favour from the king's hand, are mentioned in more places than one in scripture. When Montezuma therefore, on his first interview with Cortez, *took from his own neck a chain, and desired that it should be placed on that of the Spanish general,* he treated him in a manner which the Hebrews would have considered *very honourable ;* as is evident from the two following passages out of Genesis and the book of Esther, which describe the marks of royal favour shown to Joseph and to Mordecai, by Pharaoh and Ahasuerus, " And Pharaoh took his ring from his hand, and put it upon Joseph's hand, and arrayed him in vestures of fine linen, *and put a gold chain about his neck,'* " Then the king said to Haman, make haste,"&c. Esther vi. 10. The *eating meat at the king's table,* and receiving dishes of provision sent from him, was also looked upon by the Jews as a *great distinction.* It is therefore recorded in the twenty-fifth chapter of second Kings, that Jehoiachin king of Judah, when in captivity, was treated generously by Evil-Merodach, king of Babylon, who spake kindly to him, and set his throne above the throne of the kings that were with him in Babylon, and changed his prison garments, and he *did eat bread continually before him,* all the days of his life." Antiq. Mex. vol. vi.

LAFITAU'S DESCRIPTION.

(Note page 122.)

"The child destined for a Boyez, or Prophet, was initiated into the mysteries of his profession from infancy, by *abstinence* from several kinds of meats—by *rigorous fasts* and *severe lacerations* of the body after the manner of those who became warriors."—Rochfort. lib. ii. chap. 23.

Lafitau observes, "An ancient boyez or priest, calls the young candidate before him; *after* having sustained years of *trial* under his direction. This is on the eve of the night which is to crown his *invincible patience* and *terminated his long novitiate.* The future is described to him in the most attractive colors—the dignity of his destined office and care dwelt upon to excite him to sustain the frightful wonders of the night without shrinking. Meanwhile women are preparing a lodge in which they suspend three hammocks, &c. An altar composed of baskets, or tables of ozier piled together, is erected, on which are placed *cakes of cassava bread* and a *vessel of onicore. Sacrifice* is *also* offered. Towards the middle of the night, the priest and his disciples enter the cabin alone; the former shouts in a deep and solemn tone the words of a *mystical song,* which are instantly followed, if credit can be given to the narrators, with a terrific distant voice in the air. As soon as this is heard, the priest extinguishes the fire. This being done the *maboyez* enters the cabin with the celerity

of lightning, and a voice like thunder. The trembling occupants fall prostrate and offer their adoration. He inquires
the cause of his invocation, declaring his willingness to
gratify their desire. *I have called upon thee to offer the
youth now present. Cause then to descend, another spirit
like unto thyself, that this youth may be devoted to thy
service.* The affrighted candidate then throws himself out
of the hammock to the earth, cying out in a supplicating
posture, " *O Spirit who deignest to extend to me thy protection, be favourable, I pray thee, to the designs of one
who is nothing without thine aid ; suffer me not miserably
to perish. Be thou propitious to my supplications when I
shall call on thee; and grant me to do whatever shall be
for the welfare of my people.*" " *Take courage,*" replies
the Spirit, " *Be thou faithful, and I will never abandon
thee; at sea and by land I will be ever with thee in the
hour of need. But know that if thou art unfaithful, thou
shalt find none more inexorable than I.*" Immediately the
crowd from the cabins rush in with lights and replace in
their beds, the miserable devotees whom they find *prostrate
on the earth, and almost without life.* The parents and
friends gather round them, and warm them by a great fire
which they kindle, and supply them with food to restore
their exhausted strength. But it is difficult to succeed in
removing from the imagination of the initiated, the horror
with which the older priests have stored it."—Lafitau,
vol. i. p. 44.—Gordon's Hist. vol. ii. p. 162.

ORIGIN OF HUMAN SACRIFICE AMONG THE MEXICANS.

The Abbe Clavegero observes, ' that at a very early
period of their history the Mexicans had been *enslaved* by

a more powerful tribe into whose dominion they had come when journeying at an early period in quest of a settlement.'

'The Colhuas, their masters, had then been unsuccessful in war with a neighbouring nation, and resolved to employ their slaves as allies, without however having provided them with proper weapons for the contest. The Mexicans being persuaded that this was a favourable occasion to win the favour of their lord, resolved to exert every effort of their bravery; they armed themselves with long stout staves, the points of which they hardened in the fire, &c. they also made themselves knives of *itzli,* and targets or shields of reeds interwoven. It was agreed among them that instead of making prisoners they would content themselves with cutting off an ear, leaving the enemy without further hurt. These ears they put in a basket. By the assistance of the Mexicans, the Colhuas obtained a complete victory. The soldiers, as was their custom, presented themselves with their prisoners before their general, as their bravery was not estimated by the number of dead left on the field; but of those who were made prisoners alive, and shown to the general. It cannot be denied that this was a rational sentiment and dictated by humanity. If the prince can vindicate his rights, and repel force without killing his enemies, humanity demands that life should be preserved. The Mexicans were likewise called upon to shew their prisoners, but they having only four which they kept for a particular purpose, they were reproached as cowards by the general and soldiers of Colhuas. Then the Mexicans, holding forth their baskets full of ears, said,—" Behold! and judge from the number of ears, the number of prisoners we might have brought; but we were unwilling to lose time in binding them, that we might accelerate your victiory." '

'At their return, the Mexicans reared an altar to their

God, but being desirous of making an offering of something precious at the dedication of it, they demanded somewhat of their lord for that purpose. He sent them in disdain a rag of coarse cloth, within which was a filthy dead bird ; this was carried by the priests of Colhuas, who, after having laid it on the altar, without any salutation retired.'

' The Mexicans determined on reserving for a future occasion the indignation which this unworthy insult had kindled ; they placed upon the altar a knife of *itzli,* and an odoriferous herb. The day of consecration having arrived, the Lord of Colhua failed not to be present to make a mockery of his slaves.'

' The Mexicans began with a solemn dance in which they appeared in their best garments, and while the bystanders were most fixed in attention, they brought out the four prisoners whom they had kept concealed, and sacrificed them on a stone. This *human sacrifice, the first of the kind* known to have been made in the country, filled the Colhuas with horror, insomuch that they determined instantly to dismiss slaves so cruel ; they were by the king ordered without delay to leave the district and go whithersoever they would.'

' The Mexicans willingly accepted of their discharge from slavery, and proceeded to the present cite of Mexico, which they founded with rejoicing in their deliverance. They reared and consecrated a temple for religious worship ; but again a circumstance occurred which produced a human victim for sacrifice, thus *introducing* the custom. The historian observes,—A daring Mexican having gone in quest of some animal for a sacrifice, he encountered a Colhuan named Xomimitl ; after a few words, the feelings of enmity excited them to blows ; the Mexican was victor, and having bound his enemy carried him to his countrymen who sacrificed him immediately. Of the neighbouring tribes the historian continues to say—they continued long without using them (even animal sacrifices) having neither temples nor idols, but altars on which they offered herbs, fruits, flowers, and copal. Those nations never thought of sacrificing human victims, until the example of the Mexicans banished the impressions of nature from their minds.'— Clavegero.

LINES WRITTEN BY A STUDENT OF THEOLOGY ON PERUSING THE 'HOPE OF ISRAEL.'

*   *   *   *   *   *   *

Judah return'd :—but where was Ephraim still?
  Where the *lost ten* of Jacob's race ?
Roam they through distant deserts, wild and vast,
  Without or home or resting place ?
Is their's the fettered captive's hopeless doom ?
Find they no refuge but the silent tomb?

Again stern war beleaguers Salem's towers;—
  'Tis conquering Rome's remorseless tread ;
The eagle speeding to his gory feast,
  Sweeps o'er the dying and the dead:
'Tis done—the Temple burns—and, Judah, thou
Art crownless, sceptreless, and homeless now !

Thus was the page of prophecy fulfilled ;—
  But was this *all* the light it gave?
Did it reveal Jehovah, strong to smite,
  And not Jehovah, strong to save ?
Beheld the Seer guilt, judgments, woes—to be,
Yet could no future peace, bliss, glories—see?

No! down the vistas of approaching years
Triumphant visions met his gaze;
Lo! Zion's daughter from the dust uprears
Her prostrate form;—around her blaze
The glories of her King, the Mighty One,
The Lord of Hosts, from His eternal throne! (Isa. lx. 1.)

And, lo! from distant east, west, north and south,
Trooping in countless throngs they come;
Rivers, seas, deserts smile around their steps
While haste the God-led pilgrims home:
All, all return—in wond'rous union join
Thy rod, O Judah, and, lost Ephraim, thine! (Ezek. xxxvii. 19.)

Yes, there they come from their long banishment;
In vain the nations rage, the Lord
Hath for His battle-bow strong Judah bent, (Zech. ix. 13.)
His quiver is with Ephraim stored;—
The alien armies perish in his ire,—
For Jacob's God is a consuming fire!

Awake, awake, O Zion, in thy might!
Put on thy strength, thou rescued one!
Lift up thy voice, sing to the Lord thy God,
Who wondrous things for thee hath done!
Who hath redeemed,—sustained thee on thy way.
Thou, Mother of a Nation in one Day! (Isa. xlvi. 8.)

Arise, ye nations! hasten to behold
Salem, the joy of all the earth!
The Holy City of the mighty God!
Whence issue Life's pure waters forth. (Ezek. xlvii.)
Shout, earth! for now o'er all thy wide domains
The Lord our God and His anointed reigns! (Rev. xi. 15.)

W. M. H.

EDINBURGH.

THE TESTIMONY OF MANASSE BEN ISRAEL.

" It was not till Cromwell's time that the Jews received intelligence that the Israelites were settled there; this at first came by a letter to the Rabbi Manasse Ben Israel, from Aaron Levi Montesinos,[1] then travelling through the province of Quif, under the conduct of an *Indian*, as he supposed, but whom he afterwards found to be an *Israelite*; who assured him that vast numbers of them lived concealed behind the long ridge of mountains called *Las Cordelliras*. His curiosity inducing him to pursue his journey toward them, he came at length to the banks of a river, where, upon a signal given by his guide, they perceived a great number of them on the other side, and heard them distinctly pronounce these words in the Hebrew tongue, "HEAR O ISRAEL! JEHOVAH ALOHIEM *is one* JEHOVAH."

The farther account they gave of themselves was, " That they had been brought thither by a kind of *miraculous providence*." They added, " That they were descendants of *Abraham*, *Isaac*, and *Jacob*, and were of the tribe of *Reuben*." Thus far of the letter.[2]

" The Rabbi laid such stress upon this, as to induce him to publish his *Spes Israel*, wherein he not only attempted to

---

[1] The colony of Jews settled near Carthegena, so singular an account of which is given by one of their own race, a Portuguese Jew, named Antonio Montecino :—

" This account was published by Manasseh Ben Israel, a Jew of acknowledged learning and probity, and chief Rabbi of the Jewish synagogue of Amsterdam. He published it under the title of Spes Israel, and dedicated it to the English Parliament in the days of Cromwell, for which he received the thanks of that puritanical assembly. It was replied to by Spezelius, who, arguing in the way in which it was the fashion in Europe in the sixteenth and seventeenth centuries, to discuss all questions connected with the ancient history of America, and the Manners and Customs of the Indians, viz. *by a flat denial of facts, alleged*," &c. See Antiq. of Mexico.

[2] Scriptural Identity by Manasse Ben Israel. Spes Israel, fol. 40, col. 2.

prove this early settlement of the Israelites in America, but hath been at pains to bring them by a new, and *till then*, *unthought-of route*, from Asia into that new part of the globe, by affirming, that these two were anciently joined, and made but one Continent; but were parted asunder by a miraculous providence at the Straits," &c.

" Manasse was not the only person who had attempted to prove the early settlement of the Israelites in America; many others have done the same, though without tacking a miracle to it. And it must be owned that one finds on that spacious Continent *so many* apparent traces of *Hebrew customs*, as might incline one to believe that they might have been the *first* inhabitants of it.

" Manasse affirms that the Roman power sent the most considerable chiefs into Spain as captives, and it is not unlikely that this was done with the same view, which it is said to have had in destroying as many as he could find of the House of David: namely, to prevent their too great distance from Rome's encouraging them to reunite themselves under some enterprising chief of that tribe, or be nearer at hand to suppress it, if any such thing should have been attempted." Universal Hist, p. 501.

" The Rabbi, Manasse, believed the *general* and *final* restoration of *all* the twelve tribes near at hand, and quotes this passage, wherein he says that Isaiah clearly predicts it. " In that day the LORD shall set His hand a second time to *recover* the remnant of his people which shall be left, from Assyria, from Egypt, from Pathros, from Cush, from Elam, from Shinar, from Hameth, and from the Islands of the sea, and He shall set up an ensign for the nations, and shall assemble ' *the outcasts of Israel*,' and gather together *the dispersed of Judah* from the four quarters of the earth,"

" That noble prophecy," he observes, " referred *not*

to the return of the *remnant of Judah* from the Chaldean captivity, because GOD did not call at that time *all* the ' *dispersed*,' much less the *ten tribes*, from *all* places," &c.

To the *East* He has not said *give up*, and to the *West*, " *keep not back*." This promised deliverance is called a ' *second* ' because that from Egypt had preceded it. " The Rabbi affirms that they had been concealed in the land shadowing like wings, which is *beyond* the rivers of Cush ; now called Armenia, and in other parts, where they have been miraculously preserved by divine providence against this *glorious* recall, when they shall come forth from their seclusion, and take their united flight, as doves to their windows to JERUSALEM."

It is in contemplation to add 'to the present work a supplementary volume, to be entitled HISTORICAL ILLUSTRATIONS AND REMINISCENCES, which is intended to describe the northern portion of the wide-spread transatlantic family; these having been but slightly alluded to in the preceding pages.

The declaration of hostilities between the three foreign powers who had obtained possession of their territory, necessarily placed the primitive inhabitants in a position which was at least favourable to the development of national character and genius.

Each rival interest invoking the aid of those chiefs who resided on its frontiers—under the promise of freeing them from the encroachments and injurious influence of the others —constituted themes sufficiently soul-stirring to call forth that oratorial talent for which they have been justly celebrated : although the specimens which have been published in passing through the chilling process of translation, (the interpreters in most cases having been incapable of reaching their mental elevation) retain but little of the eloquence which found utterance in that poetical imagery which vivid thought and impressions supplied.

Another aspect in which the character of this people commends itself, is in the reception which they at first gave to that handful of feeble and helpless colonists which arrived in New England, and the steady ' good will' which they manifested toward them for the space of forty years. And here it is to be noted, that *assumption* with its *train of evils*, is not limited to a particular denomination or period. Those who considered themselves in the days of Cromwell, the victims of intolerance at home, only acquired power and opportunity to become intolerant abroad. *Spiritual pride* is productive of the *same evils* whether under the title of Protestantism, or of Popery. *Assumption* asks itself no questions of right and wrong (having no conscience of either.) And as its arbitrary and despotic supremacy is attained by no process of reasoning (since to the setting aside of reason it owes its existence) ' *Spiritual* Israel' never inquired whether an unjust *usurpation* of the *rights of others*, or *idolatrous* practices furnished in the *character* of the primitive people, a plea or apology for their extermination. The *warrant* was contained *in* an *assumption* which *involved the inference*, that those to whose territory they had come (as martyrs for the faith,) were the *Canaanites*, whom they were required to " root out," of " New Canaan," in order, as they express it, ' that those who are not a people, might make room for those who are a people.'

The historical illustrations having been extracted from the

annals of approved historians of that day, cannot be controverted; neither can they be charged with high-coloured or distorted representation, since the immediate actors in those scenes were those who recorded them.

The lions are fabled to have said: 'We lions have no painters among us.' Even so the Indians might have said. 'We men of the wilderness, have no historians amongst us to do justice to our cause.'

> ' Even that they lived, is for their spoilers tongue,
> By foes alone their death-note must be sung.'—SPRAGUE.

a consideration which forbids the apprehension of undue partiality in those biographical sketches, which are the only memorials of twenty once-powerful nations which animated the extensive territory of New England,—whether in the chase, or under those trees in summer —or that shed in winter, where the council fire was kindled, and the ancient traditionary song recited, and the mystic dance celebrated, or in guiding the light canoe on the noblest of rivers, or in the forest cavalcade, or, as they coursed the praries—' swifter than eagles,—stronger than lions.'

> The chiefs have gone to their early grave,
> Like gleams of a lurid day ;—
> And like the crest of the tossing wave—
> Like the rush of the blast in the mountain cave—
> Like the groans of the murdered with none to save,
> Their people have passed away.

THE END.

SD - #0015 - 130123 - C0 - 229/152/22 - PB - 9780259453130 - Gloss Lamination